The Gallipoli Landing of 25 April 1915 is arguably Australia's best known battle. It is commemorated each year with a national holiday, services, parades and great media attention. 2015, the centenary of the Gallipoli Campaign, was marked by great publicity and the release of many books, articles, films, documentaries and television series. Despite this attention, the Landing is still a poorly understood battle, with the historiography coloured by a century of misinformation, assumption, folklore and legend. *The Landing in the Dawn: Dissecting a Legend – The Landing at Anzac, Gallipoli, 25 April 1915*, re-examines and reconstructs the Anzac Landing by applying a new approach to an old topic – it uses the aggregate experience of a single, first-wave battalion over a single day, primarily through the investigation of veterans' letters and diaries, to create a body of evidence with which to construct a history of the battle. This approach might be expected to shed light on these men's experiences only, but their accounts surprisingly divulge sufficient detail to allow an unprecedented reconstruction and re-examination of the battle. Thus it effectively places much of the battlefield under a microscope. The use of veterans' accounts to retell the story of the Landing is not new. Anecdotes have for many years been layered over the known history, established in C.E.W. Bean, *Official History of Australia in the War: The Story of ANZAC*, Volume I, to cover the existing narrative. Here, detail extracted from an unprecedented range of primary and secondary sources, is used to reconstruct the history of the day, elevating participants' accounts from anecdote to eyewitness testimony. This shift in the way evidence is used to reinterpret the day, rather than simply painting it into the existing canvas, changes the way the battle is perceived. Even though more than 100 years have passed since the Landing, and well over 1,000 books have been written about the campaign, much can be learned by returning to the "primary source, the soldier." The Landing has not been previously studied at this level of detail. This work complements Bean's by providing new evidence and digging deeper than Bean had the opportunity to do. It potentially rewrites the history of the Landing. This is not an exclusive Australian story – for example, one third of the battalion examined were born in the British Isles. This volume, the most current and comprehensive study since Bean's, has been rightly described as a major contribution that will change the way the legendary amphibious landing is viewed.

Dr James Hurst is the author of *Game to the Last: The 11th Australian Infantry Battalion at Gallipoli*, Oxford University Press, Melbourne, May 2005, now in its third printing with Big Sky Publishing. He has written many articles, published in journals and newspapers, and presented papers on the Gallipoli Campaign and other aspects of military history in Australia, Canada and Turkey. James was awarded his PhD from the Australian National University, Canberra for his doctoral thesis 'Dissecting a Legend, Reconstructing the Landing at Anzac, Gallipoli, 25 April 1915' in 2014. He previously earned his Bachelor of Science degree, majoring in Biochemistry and Microbiology, from the University of Western Australia. James was born in Subiaco, Western Australia and graduated from Hale School. In his younger days he spent three years in Britain and one in Washington State, USA, while his father conducted specialist medical research. James has visited Gallipoli eight times for research purposes and is currently researching a book about the 2nd Regiment of Life Guards at the Battle of Waterloo, 18 June 1815. He resides in Adelaide, South Australia with his wife and daughter.

The Landing in the Dawn

Dissecting a Legend – The Landing at Anzac, Gallipoli, 25 April 1915

James Hurst

Helion & Company

Helion & Company Limited
26 Willow Road
Solihull
West Midlands
B91 1UE
England
Tel. 0121 705 3393
Fax 0121 711 4075
Email: info@helion.co.uk
Website: www.helion.co.uk
Twitter: @helionbooks
Visit our blog at http://blog.helion.co.uk/

Published by Helion & Company 2018
Designed and typeset by Serena Jones
Cover designed by Paul Hewitt, Battlefield Design (www.battlefield-design.co.uk)
Printed by Gutenberg Press Limited, Tarxien, Malta

Text © James Hurst 2018
Photographs © as individually credited
Maps drawn by George Anderson © Helion & Company 2018

Front cover: Anzac troops landing at Gallipoli in 1915. Contemporary oil painting by Cyrus Cuneo (1879–1916). Rear cover: 11th Western Australian Battalion aboard HMS *London* (photograph by E. Ashmead-Bartlett, Ashmead-Bartlett Papers, ICS 84 A/11/1-4 and ICS84/D, Senate House Library, University of London).

Every reasonable effort has been made to trace copyright holders and to obtain their permission for the use of copyright material. The author and publisher apologise for any errors or omissions in this work, and would be grateful if notified of any corrections that should be incorporated in future reprints or editions of this book.

ISBN 978-1-911512-46-2

British Library Cataloguing-in-Publication Data.
A catalogue record for this book is available from the British Library.

All rights reserved. No part of this publication may be reproduced, stored in a retrieval system, or transmitted, in any form, or by any means, electronic, mechanical, photocopying, recording or otherwise, without the express written consent of Helion & Company Limited.

For details of other military history titles published by Helion & Company Limited, contact the above address, or visit our website: http://www.helion.co.uk

We always welcome receiving book proposals from prospective authors.

Dedication

I dedicate this book to the generations who made this country what it is, in peace and war, some of whom, of my parents' and grandparents' generations, I was fortunate enough to meet.

And to my father, Dr Peter Edwin Hurst,
8 December 1930–29 January 2017,
who over many decades of commitment and selfless toil,
gave many people years of life they would not otherwise have had.

"At the reaping and the shearing,
At the sawmill and the mine,
In the stockyard and the clearing,
At the pressing of the vine,
By the camp-fire of the drover,
By the fence with slip rail drawn,
Men will tell the story over
Of that Landing in the dawn."

John Sandes, *ANZAC Day, Landing in the Dawn*, 1916

Contents

List of Figures & Maps

Maps

Acronyms and Glossary

AEF Siberia	American Expeditionary Force Siberia
AAMC	Australian Army Medical Corps
ADC	aide-de-camp
AIF	Australian Imperial Force
AWM	Australian War Memorial
AWL	absent without leave
B2455	Service Records of the First AIF. First Australian Imperial Force Personnel Dossiers, 1914–1920. Service Record. 1 Jan 1914–31 Dec1920. Service Records, First Australian Imperial Force 1914-1920. B2455. National Archives of Australia.
CO	Commanding Officer
DCM	Distinguished Conduct Medal
defilade	the protection of forces against enemy observation or gunfire
enfilade fire	Gunfire, usually from a flank, directed along a line from end to end
HMAT	His Majesty's Australian Transport
HMS	His Majesty's Ship
HMT	His Majesty's Transport
HQ	Headquarters
mile	approximately 1.6 kilometres
KIA	Killed in Action
m	metre
NCO	non-commissioned officer
NSW	New South Wales
OC	Officer commanding
ORs	other ranks
POW	prisoner of war
RAP	Regimental Aid Post
RQMS	Regimental Quartermaster Sergeant
QMS	Quartermaster Sergeant
SA	South Australia
WA	Western Australia
Yard	Approximately 0.91 metres
/-	shilling
2IC	second-in-command

2/4/2/27th Regiment	2 Platoon, 4th Company, 2nd Battalion, 27th Regiment
4/2/27th Regiment	4th Company, 2nd Battalion, 27th Regiment
2/27th Regiment	2nd Battalion, 27th Regiment

Acknowledgements

I extend my thanks to many people.

To those whose names are scattered through my notes and spreadsheets, folders and on scraps of paper – the families and others who have for generations kept the records of their forebears. Without such primary sources, this sort of history would not be possible and people and events, great and humble, would be forgotten. These people are too numerous to list, but special mention must be made of Allan and Rae Ellam, formally custodians of the Ellam-Innes Collection in Mount Lawley, Western Australia. Neither is still with us, but their enthusiasm, commitment and unique contribution to our history are fondly remembered. Our history is preserved by many other amateur and professional historians, history enthusiasts, family historians, collectors, reenactors and others who devote their time, money and enthusiasm.

We are fortunate to have institutions such as the National Archives of Australia, the Australian War Memorial, and many museums, libraries and other organisations throughout the country that acquire, preserve and allow access to their collections. Special thanks should go to those institutions, such as the Army Museum of Western Australia, to name one of many, which are maintained largely by volunteer staff, enthusiasts who believe our history and heritage are important and are prepared to dedicate their time to collecting and preserving it for future generations.

Thanks to librarians, curators, historians and archivists, and those who fund them, and the dedicated and highly productive Army History Unit, for both the work they do and for awarding me a research grant under their Army History Research Grants Scheme. The Senate House Library, London, for allowing me to reproduce Ellis Ashmead-Bartlett's photographs, and the Australian War Memorial, for permission and assistance with using some of their photographs. With a little coaxing, these photographs revealed much, and provided an intimacy without which this story would have been much the poorer.

David Cameron loaned me a copy of Şefik Aker's invaluable account of the Landing, and he, historians Wes Olson and Peter Williams, among others, provided comradeship in the many years before the Centenary of Anzac,[1] when Gallipoli seemed a lonely subject. I thank Peter for his support and our discussions on Gallipoli in particular and military history in general. I have fond memories of tramping the Gallipoli scrub with the likes of John and Hedonna Thurgar, David Kirton's family and many others.

Despite this, due to the fact that tramping battlefields for days, unwashed, bleeding, with limited menus and water, is not everyone's idea of a holiday, I spent much of my time at Gallipoli alone. I am grateful for the many hours I spent in those hills and gullies, walking, climbing and bush-bashing miles and miles below Turkey's blue skies, at times parched and footsore, at others frozen by those harsh, unforgiving winds off the sea. Though many, the hours were always too few, and when I regretfully left, some mystery always remained unresolved. I recall having to withdraw before the advances of a particularly aggressive death adder near Third Ridge, and being confronted by a huge, semi-wild dog, no doubt a descendant of George Lambert's 'wolf'[2] – I threw him some bread, but was grateful for the stone rampart and drainage ditch of Shell Green Cemetery that separated us. Once when accompanied by my wife to be, we were joined by a small dog, who padded along faithfully

---

1   There is a great deal of variation in existing sources regarding the use of "ANZAC" and "Anzac." In this book "ANZAC" will be used when referring to the corps as a military unit, "Anzac" in other cases. "Anzac Landing" will be used in accordance with prevalent current use by the Department of Veterans' Affairs.
2   C.E.W. Bean, *Gallipoli Mission* (Canberra: ABC Enterprises in association with the Australian War Memorial, 1990), p.112.

beside us for mile after mile, despite paws worn to bleeding point; the crown of my hat served well as a water bowl. Twice I was followed up Pope's Hill by heavy footsteps, when independent observers at the Nek could confirm I was alone in the valley and on the slopes.

I found a spent cartridge, an anonymous relic, on the forward lip of Plugge's Plateau, and was stunned to discover it was rimless and bore Turkish markings. Its location meant that it had been one of the first bullets fired at the Landing, and from here most of the targets would have been members of the 11th Battalion. We cannot know who fired this shot, but it is staggering to think that we now know which platoon manned this trench on that morning, 100 years ago. Information, detail, facts, research, later distilled the vast anonymity of that distant time, that far off, almost mythical event, into reality and humanity, a personal story. We don't know who fired that bullet, but we can recreate the stories of his platoon, and of his targets.

Wes Olson led us to the site where the 4th Brigade were caught by Turkish machine gun fire in a night advance in August 1915, and the physical evidence on the ground brought the tragedy home to us all; it eventually it became too much for Wes, who had researched these people. Standing there in daylight, looking up at the Turkish machine gun positions, you could almost see the sheets of bullets as they sped towards the bare crest of the ridge, and dropped Queenslanders and West Australians willy-nilly around us. The same happened to me at various places where the 11th Battalion fought, lived, or fell. Being confronted by the reality, the humanity, of such loss leaves you speechless, and years later you find yourself fumbling for words to tell the story.

So in this work I hope to use the words of those who were there, to recreate and tell their story. They are the story, not us. The story is theirs. By recreating it from the fragments we can find, it can perhaps be retold, lest it remain in some lonely grave at Gallipoli, France, Australia or elsewhere. All we can do is tread the ground, walk the corridors of libraries, museums and archives, and visit the suburbs and towns where these people lived or their ancestors live now, and do our best.

Ian Gill shared photographs and support. Professor Mesut Uyar's work on the Ottoman side of the battle was not available when I was working on this work, but he has since taken the time to answer outstanding questions for me.

I would like to thank my supervisors Professors Bill Gammage and Paul Pickering for accepting me as a PhD candidate on faith and Bill's recommendation; and everyone at the Research School of the Humanities and the Arts at the Australian National University. I thank Professor Robin Prior for his support, wit and vast knowledge, and apologise to anyone whose name should be listed here but whom I have missed.

I thank my parents for stimulating a love of many things, including history.

My wife, Margaret Nixon, and sister-in-law, Helen Nixon, for encouragement and support.

I thank my family, Margaret and Lydia, for faith, encouragement and patience.

And, finally, those whose last resting places I have knelt before – thousands of miles from home and loved ones; I hope I have treated your memory with respect, and have done this piece of your lives justice.

Foreword

This book by James Hurst represents a breakthrough in studies of the Gallipoli campaign and perhaps in battles more generally. In recent years there have been a number of studies about the Gallipoli operation as a whole from the Turkish point of view as well as the British and Australian. What has been lacking is a detailed discussion or dissection of the structure and progress of the fighting in particular battles. Because of the limitations of space and the sheer difficulty of the task we have no clear idea of what occurred to a unit in the thick of the fighting.

That gap has now been filled. James Hurst takes a particularly iconic battle, the landing on the Gallipoli Peninsula of the ANZAC forces on 25th April 1915 and deconstructs it. His method is to take a particular battalion (he has chosen the 11th Western Australian Battalion) and investigate what exactly happened to it during the landing and in the twenty four hours beyond. The result will come as a surprise to many, including I think, experts on the Gallipoli Campaign. We are quite used to reading something like the following: 'X Battalion landed on the beach, moved inland to form up and advanced in company with Battalion Y and Z on their objectives. They took them/ failed to take them for three reasons.' After this study that kind of analysis will have to be taken as the barest skeleton which may or may not describe what actually happened. James Hurst dismisses this type of generalisation. He manages, while maintaining a strong narrative thread, to recreate the sheer 'messiness' of battle. He shows that his unit was dispersed over a much wider area than was hitherto thought. He indicates that instead of speaking in terms of a coherent unit such as a battalion, we might be better to speak of much smaller groups of men, sometimes led by an officer, sometimes not; sometimes advancing on a recognised objective, sometimes completely lost. This is micro-history at its very best. Anyone who reads the book will come away with a quite different idea of a battle which many of us thought we knew well.

The Duke of Wellington said that trying to describe a battle was like trying to describe a ball – it was impossible because of the continuous movement of the crowd or couples or individuals. James Hurst, in this study, demonstrates that the Duke was wrong. It is possible and it has been done.

I recommend this book to the general public and experts alike, those interested in the Gallipoli Campaign and those interested in the anatomy of battles, modern and ancient. This book deserves a wide readership and I look forward to future work from James Hurst.

Professor Robin Prior
Visiting Professorial Fellow, University of Adelaide

Preface

This book re-examines and reconstructs the Anzac Landing at Gallipoli on 25 April 1915 by applying a new approach to an old topic – it uses the records of a single battalion over a single day to create a body of evidence with which to construct a history of the battle. This focus on the battle's participants might be expected to shed light only their immediate experience, but their accounts surprisingly divulge sufficient detail to allow reconstruction and re-examination of some of the battle's significant events. This is in part due to the methodology developed to assess and compile evidence, but also to the fact that the chosen battalion, the 11th Battalion, 3rd Infantry Brigade, 1st Division, Australian Imperial Force, landed with the covering force for the Australian and New Zealand Army Corps, and its members fought from Fisherman's Hut to 400 Plateau, on Third Ridge and Battleship Hill. This study therefore places much of the battlefield under a microscope.

The use of veterans' accounts to retell the story of the Landing is not new. Anecdotes are often layered over the known history, established in C.E.W. Bean's *Official History of Australia in the War: The Story of ANZAC*, Volume I, to colour narrative and connect with personal experience. Less frequently are they reliably used as historical evidence. Here, detail extracted from letters, diaries, memoirs, manuscripts, photographs, maps, diagrams and other information, collected from private collections, libraries, museums, archives and period newspapers, the battlefield and many secondary sources, is used to construct events, chronologies and frames of reference in order to reconstruct the history of the day. This shift in the way evidence is collected, collated, analysed and used to redraw the foundation of the day, rather than simply painting it into the existing canvas, changes the way the battle is interpreted; it reveals much that has been hidden for 100 years.

This work will argue that eyewitness testimony can be extremely unreliable when taken in isolation, but when verified, contextualised and validated by a thorough and robust methodology, it can contribute to understanding of some of the outstanding questions of the Anzac Landing. Why did the advance stop? Why was the high ground not taken? Why do the accounts of the adversaries of the best known clash of the day not match? The missing evidence often lies in the smallest of fragments – not in isolation, but when examined in aggregate.

The Landing has not previously been studied at this level of detail. Bean amalgamated the disparate and confused accounts of that day into a narrative. This work complements Bean's, rather than accepting it as gospel or condemning it by criticism. It adds new evidence to Bean's account and digs deeper than he had the opportunity to do, confirming and enriching some aspects of his account, filling gaps, and, in some aspects, resolving questions unanswered by the decades and potentially rewriting the history of the Landing.

There has been much rhetoric over the years and many myths and legends surround this battle. Even though over 100 years have passed since the Landing, and well over 1,000 books written on the campaign, much can be learned by returning to the "primary source, the soldier."[1]

---

1   I.D. Losinger, "Officer–man Relations in the Canadian Expeditionary Force, 1914–1919" (Master of Arts, Carleton University, Ottawa, Ontario, 1990), p.5.

Introduction

"The history of a battle is not unlike the history of a ball … no individual can recollect the order in which, or the exact moment at which … [events] occurred, which makes all the difference as to their value or importance."[1]

"A model, even when flexibly employed, disposes one to look only at certain phenomena, to examine history for conformities, whereas it may be that discarded evidence conceals new significance."[2]

"It was much easier to connect with the human and equine experience up close, much easier to appreciate the physical and mental effort, the connections between horse, rider and the laws of physics. It was the detail that made it make sense, the detail that told the story.

It was the detail that made it all real."[3]

"Memory of the day is a blur, or blank."[4]

Letters, diaries and other primary sources have frequently been used to tell the story of the 1915 Gallipoli campaign. Almost inevitably, anecdotes are extracted to colour narrative, and are interpreted in the context of the established history, primarily the essential Australian work on the campaign, C.E.W. Bean's *Official History of Australia in the War: The Story of ANZAC*, Volume I.[5] A problem with this approach is that new evidence gravitates to the old, consolidating and entrenching the known story, but bypassing the rest and thereby omitting it from the written history. By using eyewitness accounts to provide colour, we may be missing an opportunity to utilise them as evidence.

Many books cover the Gallipoli campaign and its hundreds of thousands of lives and dozens of battles; only recently have a few focussed on the Landing.[6] This book will take a different approach – it will focus on a single battalion on a single day, 25 April 1915. Reconstructing history from such a tight focus enables collection of sources in greater depth than previously, allowing greater cross referencing and verification of detail. This in turn reveals gaps and errors in the existing history; it enables construction of new chronologies, creates a new body of evidence and presents major shifts in the way the battle is studied and the way it can be viewed.

The Landing has not previously been studied in this manner. This approach complements Bean's – Bean began the work by amalgamating the disparate and confused accounts of that day into a

---

1   Arthur Wellesley, First Duke of Wellington, letter to J.W. Croker 8 August 1815, *Wellington Dispatches* VIII, pp.231–232, quoted Jeremy Black, *The Battle of Waterloo, A New History* (London: Icon Books Ltd, 2010), pp.98–99.
2   E.P. Thompson, "The Peculiarities of the English", *The Socialist Register*, Volume 2, 1965, p.350.
3   J.P. Hurst, Royal Adelaide Show, 2011.
4   E.R. Bowler, quoted F. Glen, *Bowler of Gallipoli: Witness to the Anzac Legend* (Canberra, ACT: Australian Military History Publications, 2004), p.47.
5   C.E.W. Bean, *Official History of Australia in the War: The Story of ANZAC*, Volume I (Sydney: Angus and Robertson, 1921 and 1941).
6   Principally P.D. Williams, *The Battle of Anzac Ridge, 25 April 1915* (Loftus, NSW: Australian Military History Publications, 2007), Australian Military History Collection; D. Winter, *25 April 1915: The Inevitable Tragedy* (St. Lucia, Qld: University of Queensland Press, 1994); and D.W. Cameron, *25 April 1915: The Day the Anzac Legend was Born* (Crows Nest, NSW: Allen & Unwin, 2007).

canvas; the work behind this book digs deeper and reconstructs the battle at Z Beach, later known as "Anzac", on 25 April 1915, from a new body of evidence. Chris Roberts' *The Landing at Anzac: 1915*,[7] and Mesut Uyar's *The Ottoman Defence Against the ANZAC Landing, 25 April 1915*,[8] were published many years after the writing of the work presented in this book, but have since been included to contrast with or confirm my arguments. I have not tackled the thorny issue of the presence or otherwise of Ottoman machine guns at the landing of the first troops, but have addressed the question in a separate paper.[9]

Certainly Bean's history and other secondary sources will be used, but as much as possible the story will be created from the "ground up", by extracting evidence from the men's accounts. The intention is to bypass stereotype and myth by returning to whatever source or combination of sources provide the best evidence: eyewitness accounts, official sources, secondary sources, maps, photographs, the battlefield itself, and prosopography, among others. This approach enables two main outcomes. Firstly, to use the resulting detail to carve a more precise picture of the individual experience than previously, and include in the story those who otherwise would be excluded from it. The intention is, generally for the first time, to place these experiences on the battlefield and position them in the history. The second aim is to use the emerging evidence to re-examine some of the key events of the day. As the chosen battalion, the 11th Battalion, Australian Imperial Force (AIF), 3rd Brigade, 1st Division, Australian and New Zealand Army Corps (ANZAC), was scattered over much of the battlefield, this enables examination of a cross-section of much of the battle. Perhaps surprisingly, re-examining significant events from the perspective of the common soldier produces reconstructions that collide with and challenge the existing history and provide a greater understanding of the day as a whole.

The Memories and Manuscript of W.W. Goodlet

One of the majority of those who made the pre-dawn landing and whose story does not appear in the *Official History*, was 19-year-old blacksmith and farrier, Walter William Goodlet, of Mount Barker, Western Australia.[10] Some 20 years after the Landing, Goodlet's breakfast was interrupted by his son's declaration, "It's your birthday, Dad, and it will soon be Anzac Day." Goodlet "drifted into a reverie", which was "rudely" shattered by his son "gloatingly" informing him he had "just put jam in my tea." The boy then outflanked his father by directing a barrage of questions at his mother:

> Mum, why does Dad keep blowing his nose at the Dawn Service when everyone is supposed to keep silent, and when I ask him what's up, why is it he will never look a fellow in the eye, but takes a sudden interest in that old sunken barge that's been in the river for years? And when I ask him what the landing was like, why does he get so absent minded, and keep putting spoonful after spoonful of sugar in his tea? Are you sure he was there?

The veteran's wife sympathetically suggested he should answer their son's questions – "he is old enough to understand now, and I think it will do you both a lot of good." "And so at last," Goodlet committed his memories to paper. He began by pledging his "word of honour as a poor harmless

---

7   C. Roberts, *The Landing at Anzac: 1915* (Newport, NSW: Big Sky Publishing, 2013; second edition, Sydney: Big Sky Publishing, 2015).

8   M. Uyar, *The Ottoman Defence Against the ANZAC Landing, 25 April 1915* (Sydney: Big Sky Publishing, 2015).

9   J.P. Hurst, "'Did anyone see a gun?' The vexed question of Ottoman machine guns at the Gallipoli Landing, Z Beach, 4:30 a.m., 25 April 1915," currently unpublished.

10   909 Private Walter William Goodlet, 19 or 20 at enlistment, blacksmith/farrier, of Mount Barker, born Stawell, Victoria. Goodlet's account had not previously been published or studied at the time of writing.

old digger of 39, that it is true in every detail … Remember it is the Landing as I saw it."[11] Goodlet thereby left us a vivid picture of the fighting on 25 April from the perspective of an individual serving in the ranks.

Goodlet belonged to D Company, 11th Battalion, when he landed at Gallipoli. The Turks opened fire before he left his destroyer, mortally wounding "the best friend a man ever had," "Robbo", who died on the deck alongside him.[12] Later Goodlet saw "three boats which had been on our immediate left … piled high with dead and drifting slowly out to sea," victims of "a machine gun nest firing down one of the gullies which was afterwards called 'Shrapnel Gulley' [sic]."[13] He "pushed inland" for "About two miles," arriving at "a steeply sloping hill … about a mile in length." From the top, his party could see "towards the Dardanelles" and found themselves confronted by:

> the Turkish Army … As our men showed up above the ridge many of them were mowed down with machine guns, almost every one being fatally shot … in the head or upper … body. These rolled down the steep slope to form an army of dead at the bottom … a harassed staff officer, searching for reinforcements … ordered them to follow him … Then he took myself and about a dozen others and we ran for about a mile towards the left. He then pointed to a ridge that was bare and open about 150 yards out in front, and told us to reinforce … it. He explained … that the Turks were making [a] desperate counter-attack on our left flank. Once they broke through, they could prevent our reinforcements from landing, and then surround and massacre us.

The officer told them "it would be better for us to die fighting on the ridge than to be butchered like sheep on the beach."[14]

Goodlet advanced as ordered. He deepened a shallow depression with his entrenching tool, piled his cartridges alongside him "to ensure quick loading" and "settled down to give battle." Lines of Ottoman infantry attacked with rifle and bayonet and such determination "it seemed impossible that the few men on the ridge could ever stop that hoard of savage cut-throats." But with his "fingers … burnt and bleeding" from rapid and desperate loading and the woodwork of his rifle smoking, the young soldier lived to see the attacks fail. Casualties became so severe that Goodlet began to think he "was the only one left alive." Mercifully, a few reinforcements arrived, one of whom was, "wearing my battalion colours, but it was not until he dropped beside me that I recognised a survivor of my platoon, 'Peachy'. Poor old Peachy was in a mess; he was covered from head to foot in blood and mud, his clothes were torn to shreds and his eyes bulged like a frog's." "Peachy" brought news that the battalion had suffered heavily, and that "we were the only survivors." At great risk Peachy crawled through the scrub collecting ammunition bandoliers from the dead in preparation for the next Turkish attacks.[15] He then suggested the pair fire at targets on opposite sides of a small bush to avoid:

> wasting time by shooting the same man. We were just stacking the last of our ammunition … when over they came again, this time in mass … I thought that I was firing fast, but Peachy was like a wizard … he shot two bearded giants about 10 paces in front of us and on my side of the bush … coming at us with their bayonets in spite of all I could do.[16]

11   W.W. Goodlet, manuscript, Ellam-Innes Collection, Perth, pp.1–2.
12   Goodlet, manuscript, p.10.
13   Ibid., pp.11–12.
14   Ibid., pp.12–13.
15   Ibid., pp.13–14.
16   Ibid., pp.14–15.

Just as the Australians thought their line would break, the Turkish attack withered. Soon it seemed the "the air was literally raining lead" from enemy shellfire, "and the position seemed worse than hopeless. Word was … shouted from one survivor to another" that "Turkish cavalry were massing … for a charge." Every man was "to stay firm and sell his life as dearly as possible." Peachy "looked at me and gulped. 'I think this is the last of it, Mulga, we haven't a dog's chance of getting out of here alive'."[17] The two wrote "pitiful little" notes of farewell to their mothers in each other's pay books. Goodlet's "was brief … we were in a desperate position without … hope of living for more than a few minutes … it would be a relief to be dead and with my friend, than alive in that frightful hell of expectancy." This time succour arrived in the form of shells from the Royal Navy, as *Triumph* and *Queen Elizabeth* shattered the attack: "the slaughter," Goodlet later heard, "was frightful."[18]

As the sun began to sink behind the island of Imbros,[19] the Turks waited for darkness before launching their "next attack and … in the meantime" concentrated:

everything they had … on our ridge … a runner came dashing along our line yelling to us to drop back … That man was [a] hero, he earnt a V.C. every step … but I think he perished. Peachy and I started for the rear … The bag of biscuits which I had on the back of my belt … was now dangling on about three feet of cord, and as I ran, the biscuits got between my legs and tripped me up. I went sprawling and so did my hopes … I reached the lip of the hill and received a cheer from the New Zealanders garrisoning it.[20]

Goodlet began "to realise the scheme of things and the part we had played." While he and others had been holding their exposed ridge, a "first class defence" had been established behind. The men then learned that "Turks dressed as Indians" were "placing a deadly little mountain gun" in the allied lines:

to fire directly along our trench. They were speedily despatched. Another message was passed along not to fire on the troops in front as … survivors of the ridge were returning. The answer returned from head quarters that as the Turks were dressing in our uniforms and attempting to get amongst us … it was necessary to shoot all men in front … this was the[ir] reward for the gallant fight … on the ridge.

The withdrawing troops "were now shot in cold blood by the very reinforcement they had prayed for all day … I was like a raving mad man. I ran along the trench screaming and cursing and begging them to let my cobbers in … but the majority were butchered. And so through the hours of darkness continued this hideous nightmare."[21]

Goodlet's account, if followed, in full, chronologically and compared to the ground and the *Official History*, makes very little sense. His location is difficult to establish, his account does not match our understanding of where his battalion fought nor the location of features such as Shrapnel Gully. The army of dead men sounds highly fanciful, the "raving" soldier trying to halt his comrades' fire and men "butchered" by their own side seem at odds with the known picture of the day, and the description of three, body-filled boats drifting out to sea does not fit the 3rd Brigade landing. The reference to "bandoliers" is also curious – bandoliers were worn by mounted troops, the landing was made by infantry. In addition, stories of dispatching Turks disguised as "Indian" artillerymen in the lines and similar events at first glance devalue this narrative as history.

Even some 20 years after the event, Goodlet's sadness and sense of tragedy and loss had not left him. He referred to the Landing, or perhaps the Gallipoli campaign, as "the greatest tragedy of the

---

17   *Ibid.*, p.15.
18   *Ibid.*, p.16.
19   *Ibid.*, p.15.
20   *Ibid.*, pp.15–16.
21   *Ibid.*, pp.16–17.

War." A.S. Thomson wrote of Gallipoli veterans' recollections as "especially risky or troubling if they rub against the publicly acceptable version of events" and that throughout their lives, "Gallipoli veterans engaged in a continuous process of negotiation with competing and changing public perceptions" of their experience.[22] Goodlet was well aware that his recollection contrasted with "Official accounts of the Landing," which he described as "written guardedly and as free from truth as a frog from feathers."[23] Perhaps his reflections were coloured by his later experiences at Gallipoli and the Western Front, the losses of the war or the public's perceptions, his return home, his life during the depression, aging or the passage of time. I, as a later author with historical hindsight, the benefit of the *Official History* and many other secondary sources, and the opportunity to examine the battlefield without being shot at, was consequently tempted to disregard much of Goodlet's account, without questioning its sincerity.

When working through his account, I consequently began deleting anything that seemed too coloured, emotive or far-fetched, hoping to distinguish the obviously flawed recollections and salvage what "evidence" I could. For example, Goodlet's descriptions of stacking his cartridges before battle and bleeding fingers afterwards, give a remarkable, personal and detailed insight into the battle's intensity and the way it was fought by an individual working his rifle and fighting for survival; on the other hand, there are no official records of "Robbo" or "Peachy."

I grew increasingly uncomfortable with my approach. I was ignoring one significant fact – Goodlet was there. I was not. I was using a prism created by people who were not there to filter the account of a participant and witness. Goodlet's viewpoint was limited: he was a private soldier isolated on a crowded battlefield on unnamed foreign ground, shocked by battle and the loss of a good friend. But he was there. He saw what he saw; he recalled and wrote down what he could – coloured, confused, skewed, inaccurate, accurate. When his recollection conflicted with secondary sources, where lay the truth? Goodlet's and other accounts deserved deeper examination.

Goodlet's account is atypical in its length – 19 pages – as letters and diary entries at the time were of necessity very brief.[24] But it is typical in that men rarely told us to what platoon they belonged nor the name of their officer. As features were not yet named, men did not know where they were. In other words, we generally do not know where men fought, with whom nor when the events they described happened. To understand such accounts and use them as historical evidence, we have to begin from scratch. We have to search for clues – in the existing history, in unpublished accounts, on the battlefield – and create or rebuild frames of reference, such as chronologies, structures and the story of the day.

Mortar Ridge

If Goodlet's description of his movements is ignored, his experience and the ground over which he fought have much in common with Bean's account of "One of the fiercest" struggles "of the day,"[25] the fighting on Mortar Ridge. This is rarely described in books on the campaign.[26]

Bean described the Turks advancing "like a flood" to Mortar Ridge's right or right rear, and lapping "around the seaward edge of Battleship Hill," to the ridge's left front.[27] Many Australians were killed, and "fierce fighting" continued on Mortar Ridge "at ever shorter range."[28] Men and ammunition were

---

22 A.S. Thomson, "Anzac stories: using personal testimony in war history", *War & Society*, vol. 25, issue 2, School of Humanities and Social Sciences, University of New South Wales, Canberra, ACT, Australia, p.4.
23 Goodlet, manuscript, p.2.
24 An exception is Mofflin's letter, written from hospital in October 1915, which runs to 38 pages.
25 Bean, *Official History*, Volume I (1921 and 1941), p.432.
26 The *Official History* excluded.
27 Bean, *Official History*, Volume I (1921 and 1941), p.434.
28 *Ibid.*

sent forward to the position as they became available.[29] The line here held until some time after 5:00 p.m., when it withdrew to Second Ridge, leaving behind many dead. Goodlet's account of his fight reflects much of this.

Goodlet's description of his "raving" efforts to stop the shooting of withdrawing men may seem dubious, but Bean confirms that for the troops on Mortar Ridge, the "most dangerous fire came from the rear: Australians on the Second Ridge continually shot at them, regarding their shouts of 'Don't shoot – we're Australians!' as a Turkish ruse."[30] Goodlet's account may well reveal what Bean's doesn't – the distress of a participant in these events, or his later, anguished recollection of it. His reference to Turks disguised as Indian gunners may sound fanciful but stories that Indian troops were arriving on the battlefield are common in 11th Battalion sources and were well known to Bean. During the day an Indian mountain battery fought valiantly for several hours behind the Australian lines, and Goodlet's account may have been the end result of an aggregation of stories and rumour passed from mouth to mouth. Stories of enemy soldiers dressed as officers spreading false orders also circulated – such officers were invariably rumoured to have been "shot," though there appear to be no recorded first-hand accounts of such executions. Some of Goodlet's recollections appear to reflect the intertwining and distortion of rumour and fact as stories passed along the line.

Goodlet's account of his movements on 25 April would not place him on Mortar Ridge. In his case the opposite of the norm is true: rather than his detail providing clues to his whereabouts, it was by standing back and looking at the account differently, once his probable final location had been established, that revealed the significant clues. Some of the anomalies can then be understood. For example, even though Goodlet gives the impression that he saw the boats of dead soon after landing, his anecdote is preceded by "It was now light and looking back to the sea."[31] In other words, he probably saw the boats some time after he had begun moving inland, despite the location of the incident in his chronology. These boats probably therefore belonged not to the 3rd Brigade, but to the 2nd Brigade's 7th Battalion, which were shot up on the left after the 3rd Brigade was ashore.

The most definite information about Goodlet's location and movements on 25 April comes from an unlikely source. On 30 October 1915 the Red Cross interviewed patients at Luna Park Hospital, Egypt, seeking information about the disappearance of Lieutenant Mordaunt Reid.[32] A witness stated that:

> a party was sent out to reinforce the firing line. They met the Turks and had to retire. Witness saw Reid wounded, but not seriously, as he could still walk and cried out that he would … try to get to the beach. He had a pistol and revolver. Later on some bodies were got in but Reid was not found. He would have been recognisable because he had lost a finger. He might well be a prisoner. (Reid's wife is working at the Palace Hospital, Heliopolis).[33]

The witness was Goodlet.

Reid's wounding that Sunday morning on Battleship Hill, at one of the most advanced points reached by Australians on that day, is recorded in many accounts, including the *Official History*, and is virtually undisputed. If Goodlet saw Reid wounded, he too was on Battleship Hill that morning; he does not mention it, though this is presumably the point from which he saw the Dardanelles.[34] The small force fighting on Battleship Hill eventually withdrew, many to the vicinity of Baby 700, a hill

---

29 *Ibid.*
30 Bean, *Gallipoli Mission*, p.91.
31 Goodlet, manuscript, p.11.
32 Mordaunt Leslie Reid, 33 at embarkation, electrical engineer and manager of the Electric Supply Company of Western Australia, Coolgardie. Born Elmore, Victoria.
33 Australian Red Cross Wounded and Missing Enquiry Bureau files. 1DRL/0428, Australian War Memorial.
34 Bean, *Official History*, Volume I (1921 and 1941), p.290.

which adjoined Mortar Ridge. It is entirely possible that Goodlet made his way from Battleship Hill to Mortar Ridge, even though his description of how this happened does not make sense. Goodlet's quoted times contrast with the *Official History*'s, but this is not uncommon – most men had been awake all night and in battle for many hours, and their estimates of time are often unreliable.

That Goodlet's account of his movements appears to make little sense, is not surprising. Twenty years had passed since the battle. In 1915 Goodlet would have had no clear idea of the geography over which he fought, features were as yet officially unnamed, and by 26 April "it seemed as though the whole thing had been some hideous dream."[35] A soldier focussed on going where he is told, working his rifle under fire and shooting to kill in order to live, often had little clear recollection of what was going on around him. Goodlet's account can also be viewed as a jumble of snapshots, not necessarily in chronological order. Some are vivid and detailed memories, others possibly aggregations of memory or rumour. Moving to the "left" may have referred to early movements up Shrapnel Gully and Monash Valley, or to the withdrawal from Battleship Hill, in which case left meant south, or towards Mortar Ridge – such directions are subjective. "Peachy", introduced as "P.G. Brown", appears to be a pseudonym for 907 P.G. ("Peachy") Green,[36] an H Company original, as was 909 Goodlet. A remarkable connection between peace-time Australia and the fighting at the Landing became apparent many years later, when one of "Peachy's" descendants informed me that, even in his later years, Green was known as a rapid and deadly shot when kangaroo shooting.[37] There is also the possibility, though it is less likely, that Goodlet and Green did not fight on Mortar Ridge: Bean could not describe every event of the day, leaving unexplained contradictions between accounts and gaps in our knowledge.

At times working with such accounts felt like trying to make sense of a stopped clock – twice a day the clock accurately displays the correct time, but when? The challenge with accounts of the Landing is to "see" and correctly interpret the evidence; one aim of the work that lies behind this book is to provide the many frames of reference that reveal and validate the grains of evidence in accounts like Goodlet's.

The Gallipoli We Know

The prominence of Anzac Day guaranteed that I was aware of the Landing during my childhood and youth, but the experience was generally invisible. There must have been veterans in our streets and suburbs, but where were they? There must have been Gallipoli casualties listed on the war memorial I passed every day on my way to primary school, but how would I have known? Not until many years later did I discover that the first Australian officer killed in the campaign had lived just beyond the window beside my school desk. Books in my library tended to use the same stock photographs, tread the same paths, repeat the same anecdotes. Poor printing techniques meant that photographs were indistinct, even distorted, sometimes retouched – detail was elusive. For the television mini-series of A.B. Facey's[38] autobiography *A Fortunate Life*,[39] which recreated the Landing, we extras were issued slouch hats, unfamiliar uniforms and equipment, and were filmed storming ashore under shell fire in freezing darkness; the sun rose to find us lying in dozens on the wet, body-littered beach. Yet my

---

35 Goodlet, manuscript, p.18.
36 907 Private Patrick George Green, 23 at the Landing, farmer, of Broomehill.
37 Unrecorded phone contact in about 1998, J.P. Hurst with a member of Green's family, who recalled as a youth kangaroo shooting with the aged Green. Green brought down three moving kangaroos in rapid succession, apparently in fading light and all with shots to the head.
38 1536 Private Albert Barnet Facey, D Company, 20 at enlistment, labourer, born Victoria.
39 A.B. Facey, *A Fortunate Life* (Ringwood, Victoria: Penguin Books, 1985), p.253; *A Fortunate Life*, television mini-series, PBL Productions, 1985.

favourite painting of the Landing (Figure 2) showed a daylight landing,[40] and a photograph in the *Official History*[41] revealed only one corpse on the beach. A painting in a 1968 book about Western Australia,[42] depicted an Australian officer in Sam Browne and tie leading men in what appear to be collarless khaki drill shirts, slouch hats and packs, in an assault on a Turkish machine gun position at the southern end of Anzac Cove. Other portrayals of the Landing present a similarly disorienting range of images – accuracy and inaccuracy, daylight and darkness, old uniforms and new. Around Anzac Day there was much rhetoric about the Gallipoli Landing, but little detail with which to connect. Our nation's highest profile battle was clouded by contradictions and a fog of persistent vagueness.

Anzac Day is our greatest national attempt at remembrance, but sits awkwardly between commemoration of the historical event, the Landing at Gallipoli, and today's "invented tradition,"[43] the institution of Anzac Day. In Pierre Nora's terms, Anzac Day has become a site of national memory, symbolised by "rite and ritual" and "images and representations" that are "revised throughout the ages."[44] Dawn and other services generally share common ingredients – flags, prayers, the Ode of Remembrance, the national anthem and speeches about the Landing. The latter are generally given by prominent office holders who are unlikely to have studied the history of the day. Thus we hear stories of 16,000 Australians and New Zealanders storming ashore under enemy fire at dawn on 25 April, thereby incorporating historical inaccuracy into tradition. This is exacerbated by other levels of miscommunication. One journalist, author of Gallipoli books, articles and a television documentary, announced on national television after a dawn service at Gallipoli, that "All they wanted to be, these Australian kids who died … was remembered … It was pre-machine gun – they didn't realise there were machine guns … the Boer War, was a cavalry war, with horses charging with … swords."[45] It is unlikely that Australians witnessed cavalry charges with swords in the Boer War; other fallacies in this statement will become apparent in coming chapters.

Reporting of the dawn service is hamstrung by deadlines, and often journalists – daunted by the importance of the event – fall back on the templates of previous years. And if, as Maurice Halbwachs advised in a different context, "the past is a social construction … shaped by the concerns of the present," and that "the beliefs, interests, and aspirations of the present shape the various views of the past,"[46] where does this leave our image of the Landing?

No criticism of the artists mentioned above, the commemoration of Anzac Day and those who speak to the public at its various ceremonies is implied; moreover, the day honours the service and sacrifice of all this country's wars, rather than just the Landing. But with all this "remembering," where is the event, and, more importantly, the memory of those who were there? They should be – and are – important. So prominent in our perception is "that Landing in the dawn," that events from other Gallipoli battles have been attributed to it, and men who arrived on the peninsula in later months are sometimes assumed by their descendants to have arrived in a "second landing." Today school children who have been read works of fiction about John Simpson, the "man with the donkey," are surprised to learn he really existed, further blurring the boundaries between fact and fiction, story

---

40 *Landing at Gallipoli, 1915*, By Cyrus Cuneo, originally printed in *The London Times*, n.d., reproduced in *The Silver Jubilee Book, The Story of 25 Eventful Years in Pictures* (London: Odhams Press, 1935), pp.112–113.

41 C.E.W. Bean et al. *Official History*, Volume XII, *Photographic Record of the War*, plate 55, "The Landing at Anzac".

42 Frank Pash, untitled, 1968; Ivan O'Riley, *Giant in the Sun* (Perth: Ian O'Riley, 1968), pp.244–245.

43 "Invented tradition" is taken to mean a set of practices, normally governed by overtly or tacitly accepted rules and of a ritual or symbolic nature, which seek to inculcate certain values and norms of behaviour by repetition, which automatically implies continuity with the past." E.J. Hobsbawm, in E.J. Hobsbawm and T.O. Ranger, *The Invention of Tradition* (Cambridge: Cambridge University Press, 1992), p.1.

44 P. Nora, *Realms of Memory: The Construction of the French Past, Tradition*, Volume II (New York: Columbia University Press, 1997), pp.ix, x.

45 J. King, interviewed by T.J. Grimshaw, Anzac, 25 April 2005.

46 M. Halbwachs, *On Collective Memory*, edited and translated by L.A. Coser (Chicago: University of Chicago Press, 1992), p.25.

and history.[47] Les Carlyon's bestselling *Gallipoli* is promoted as "a work of extraordinary storytelling."[48] Does this mean it is fiction, well-told history, or fact embellished with fiction; how is the reader to know which is which? Albert Facey's autobiography describes his part in the campaign, but there is doubt that Facey participated in some of the events he describes, including the Landing.[49] M. Wallis wrote that at the moment at which the life of W.H. McCarty, famous as "Billy the Kid," became the stuff of media sensationalism and folklore,[50] he became "then and forever after a mirage."[51] Similarly with the 3rd Brigade: at the moment they leapt into the dark water below Plugge's Plateau, the seed of a legend was sown, soon to be celebrated by media and public, and vulnerable to repeated reinterpretation by those who weren't present.

In Australia, the centenary of the Gallipoli Campaign in 2015 was marked by great fanfare and considerable investment of funding and effort. Surely, now was the time to set the record straight, the opportunity to gain an appreciation of the historical event behind the commemoration?

Probably the most significant media undertaking was the television series *Gallipoli*,[52] "Three years in the making" and heralded as revealing the "truth." The Landing is depicted in the first minutes, with incorrectly equipped troops landing virtually unopposed, a distant and barely audible small arms fire suggesting that a battle is going on somewhere, but not here; the voice-over tells us there was "no slaughter on the beach." The accounts of those who were there tell a different story.

Such programs are not intended to be academic histories – scriptwriters have to fill gaps, create dialogue, and are allowed poetic license – but they are the sources from which the public and media commentators acquire their "knowledge" of their history. This is particularly troubling when the public is told this series reveals "the truth."

Similarly, a book published for the Centenary by "Australia's highest-earning non-fiction writer," contained "many passages" which "are actually imagined."[53] "Imagined" non-fiction? Such accounts are guaranteed to perpetuate the misunderstanding of lifetimes. Both the TV series and book referred to received gushing reviews in some of the nation's best newspapers,[54] the latter being described as "a clear and persuasive record of the campaign,"[55] "imagined" passages and all.

So, 100 years after Cyrus Cuneo's tremendously detailed, inspiring and inaccurate illustration, *Landing at Gallipoli*,[56] we have numerous modern formats re-hashing the myths and rewriting the fiction for a new generation. With such dimensions of misinformation, such a drift from the true events and experiences of 25 April 1915, it has been difficult in my lifetime to see through the "patina" of inaccurate "images and representations"[57] to reconnect with the "reality" of the Landing.

47   Anecdotes acquired by author in conversations with the public and schoolchildren.
48   <http://www.panmacmillan.com.au/index.asp>
49   J.P. Hurst, "The Mists of Time and the Fog of War, *A Fortunate Life* and A.B. Facey's Gallipoli Experience", *Melbourne Historical Journal*, 2010, Volume 38, pp.77–92.
50   M. Wallis, *Billy the Kid: The Endless Ride* (New York: W.W. Norton and Company Inc., 2008), p.199.
51   Wallis, *The Endless Ride*, p.199.
52   *Gallipoli*, mini series, Nine Network, Endemol Australia, 2014.
53   P. Stanley, <http://thenewdaily.com.au/entertainment/books/2016/11/14/peter-fitzsimons-war/>, 'Peter Fitzsimons' new battle book spurs war of words', viewed 8 May 2017.
54   S. Loosley, *The Australian*, 13 December 2014, <http://www.theaustralian.com.au/arts/review/gallipoli-by-peter-fitzsimons-takes-us-into-the-cauldron-of-battle/news-story/45d2512d920f118ccfe126df2355512b>, viewed 8 May 2017; 'Gallipoli, by Peter FitzSimons, takes us into the cauldron of battle', accessed 8 May 2017; R. Fitzgerald, *Sydney Morning Herald* <http://www.smh.com.au/entertainment/books/review-gallipoli-20141117-11o9ld.html>, accessed 8 May 2017; G. Blundell, *The Australian*, 7 February 2015.
55   S. Loosley, *The Australian*, 13 December 2014.
56   Cuneo, *Landing at Gallipoli, 1915*, in *The London Times*, n.d.
57   Nora, pp.ix, x.

The Australian *Official History*

Bean's reconstruction of the Landing is an extraordinary achievement, not least because he returned from the war in 1919 and published the first volume, of over 600 pages, in 1921. Bean interviewed the battle's survivors throughout the campaigns in Gallipoli, France and Belgium, and corresponded with them after the war, as he attempted to disentangle confused and conflicting narratives, answer questions, fill gaps, find connections between events, and position them in a backdrop of time and place.

Most Australian works that rely primarily on the *Official History*, retread the paths it established. There is much repetition and anecdotes are drawn and aggregated to the skeleton of history Bean established, leaving the picture beyond these known events vague or blank; events, gaps, inaccuracies and contradictions are, with some notable exceptions, rarely examined. Much is assumed. Put simply, participant's accounts are generally slipped into the existing story, rather than being investigated in their own right. Similarly, writers will often assume that information quoted in a single source, such as the time of an event, is accurate.[58] In this work, I examine such quotes from many angles and sources, and cross reference details of chronology, terrain and experience. This approach might reveal, for example, that an anecdote should not be attached to a known and frequently repeated incident, but be investigated as a separate event, possibly one missing from the existing histories. At other times this approach reveals previously invisible connections between people and events.

One technique Bean adopted to unravel or connect intertwined but often disconnected events was to ask "each officer or man interviewed ... what other officer or prominent man he remembered having seen near him ... the names of these almost always cropped up in other narratives." Given "a few certainties of place and time it was possible to ... reconstruct the story like a jig-saw puzzle."[59] Although this approach enabled a detailed reconstruction of the battle, "rich in detail of individual and group effort,"[60] a close reading of the experience of the 11th Battalion highlights many questions and inconsistencies. It was partly intrigue that I could not answer basic questions of great significance to the battle, such as why the Landing "failed", why the 11th Battalion moved inland after landing instead of to the high ground and why the advance stopped, and more individual ones, such as how the battle was fought "on the ground", that ultimately led me to undertake the research and examinations presented in this book.

Most writers, for example, describe Captain E.W. Tulloch's[61] fight on Battleship Hill; these versions of the story are invariably based on the accounts of the two protagonists, Tulloch and Lieutenant-Colonel Mustapha Kemal. The clash between Tulloch's party and Kemal's 57th Regiment has frequently been portrayed as a crucial turning point in the campaign,[62] but did it happen? Was it a turning point? Why was Tulloch not reinforced, and who accompanied him? Why is Tulloch's the only Australian account of this clash; did no other Australians live to tell? If we knew who accompanied Tulloch, we could tie other accounts to his, confirming or questioning his account, and adding breadth and depth to the history. Was it really Kemal and 57th Regiment who opposed Tulloch's party? If so, why don't the accounts of Kemal and Tulloch appear to match? How reliable is the chronology behind this clash? Where is the evidence, beyond Bean's work, that this confrontation happened as described, or has our image of it been founded on assumptions born of reliance on the existing account and a lack of other

---

58   For example, one writer, relying on the apparently reliable single source of Bert Facey's service record, wrote that Facey reached Gallipoli 12 days after the Landing and therefore his account of the Landing "has to be fabricated." Examination of a range of sources reveals this to be an unsound assumption. C.A.M. Roberts, "Turkish Machine-guns at the Landing", *Wartime*, Issue 50, 2010, p.15; Hurst, "The Mists of Time and the Fog of War", pp.77–92.

59   Bean, *Gallipoli Mission*, p.74.

60   C. Pugsley, "Stories of Anzac", in J. MacLeod, *Gallipoli, Making History* (London and New York: Frank Cass, 2004), p.47.

61   Captain Eric William Tulloch, 11th Battalion, 33, brewer, born Victoria.

62   Lord Kinross, *Ataturk* (New York; William Morrow and Company, 1965; first published Great Britain 1964), p.90; L. Carlyon, *Gallipoli* (Sydney: Pan Macmillan Australia Pty Ltd, 2001), p.157.

evidence? Similarly, we know little of the experience of the 11th Battalion on Baby 700. If failure to take the high ground on 25 April is of such significance to the Landing and the campaign as a whole, why do we know so little about the experience on Baby 700 of the battalion tasked with its capture?

Most of Bean's knowledge of Turkish movements was based on post-war interviews with 57th Regiment's Zeki Bey, a veteran of the Landing. Another Turkish regiment, 27th Regiment, features less prominently, the limited evidence generally coming from the British history of C.F. Aspinall-Oglander.[63] The account of the battle by this regiment's commanding officer, Lieutenant-Colonel Şefik Bey, coincidentally written at about the same time as Goodlet's, has rarely been analysed in Australian accounts.[64] It states that 27th Regiment arrived on the battlefield earlier than realised by most western historians. How might this account alter our perception of the battle? With recorded times varying wildly, can Şefik's chronology and times be verified? If his times are correct, it would mean that the most detailed Turkish source of the crucial early hours, from the first shot until important decisions were made and the covering force was deployed inland, has not been adequately examined. It would also mean that this regiment fought the 11th Battalion early on 25 April, presenting the opportunity to compare 11th Battalion accounts to Şefik's and explore the battle from a new direction. To what extent could Australian battlefield accounts be constructively compared with that of a regimental commander on the other side of the battlefield to reliably reconstruct history?

Methodology

Collective memory is heavily influenced by myth and misinformation, and traditions like Anzac Day by ritual and rhetoric. The *Official History* was put together quickly, a long time ago, and contains anomalies and gaps. Primary sources are replete with contradictions, inaccuracies, subjective observations, assumptions and errors, making their use as building blocks for writing history fraught. How then, nearly a century after the event, are we to connect with the real story and experience of the Landing?

The focus on a single battalion over a single day, enables a much closer examination of the battle and primary sources than Bean was at liberty to do. As E.P. Thompson put it, history "is made up of episodes, and if we cannot get inside these we cannot get inside history at all."[65] Bean's account will be used for guidance, but I will not hammer my sources into his account; rather, these sources will be used to question and complement it.[66]

In order to elevate anecdote to evidence and reveal the experience of the battle's missing participants, the "insiders"[67] of Nora's "tradition," it is necessary to first establish where men may have fought, with whom and when. A four dimensional picture has to be created around them. To do this, letters, diaries, memoirs, manuscripts, photographs, maps, diagrams and other information from private collections, libraries, museums, archives and period newspapers, from throughout Australia and Britain, and battlefield evidence from Gallipoli, was collected. A methodology was then developed to compile, assess and analyse the information.

Utilising a method known as prosopography, or the study of lives in aggregate, I compiled some 300,000 words of detail on the men into a series of biographical matrices. These were then used as a means of cross-referencing to find common ground and contradictions – in some cases, detail as

---

63 C.F. Aspinall-Oglander, *Military Operations, Gallipoli.* Volume I, *Inception of the Campaign to May 1915,* maps and sketches by A.F. Becke (London: Imperial War Museum, Department of Printed Books, 1929).

64 At the time of writing. Since then Şefik account has been extensively quoted, but not to my knowledge as closely examined as in this work.

65 Thompson, "The Peculiarities of the English", p.338.

66 By Thompson's definition, the *Official History* will be treated less as "model" than "framework." Thompson, "The Peculiarities of the English", pp.349, 350.

67 Nora, p.ix. "In order to understand national tradition … one has to combine the insider's view … with the outsider's."

obscure as where men or boys may have worked or attended school, may allow more weight to be ascribed to one battlefield anecdote than others. Bean noted the progress of many officers on 25 April, but we have no way of assigning men's testimony to these groups.

For example, Bean described the 3rd Brigade's second wave landing some time after the first, and this has been repeated by secondary sources for nearly a century. But if this was the case, why could I find no accounts by men who landed peacefully, after the first wave had pushed the enemy back from the beaches? Roughly half of the accounts I had collected should have described landing with the second wave, yet all described landing under fire. The first step was to determine who was in the 2nd wave. And the answer to that would lie in the battalion roll for April 1915, which would tell us who was in which company. There was, in fact, no such roll. I had to start from scratch and create it.[68] This required aggregation of information from all manner of sources, but proved to be the linchpin that enabled disconnected accounts, events, geography and chronology, to be reassembled.

When rolls were made for the unit's embarkation in Western Australia in 1914, the battalions of the AIF consisted of eight rifle companies of about 120 all ranks, designated A to H and organised as two half-companies.[69] On 1 January 1915 the battalions changed to the four company structure of the British army of that time.[70] The manner in which the existing companies were combined varied between battalions. For the 11th Battalion, neither the unit history, *Legs Eleven*[71] nor the unit war diary, describe how this was done. To establish a structure of platoons, companies, officers and men, required cross referencing of letters, diaries, published and unpublished documents, the unit history, *Official History*, embarkation rolls, Red Cross files, Honour Roll entries, photographs and service records, among others, and continued over many years.

The accuracy with which a man's place in the battalion can be determined, and the detail and reliability of whatever written records the ages have left us, vary greatly. Even "primary" sources cannot be assumed to be correct, and in some cases contain errors absorbed from other sources. For example, Roy Thompson's[72] notebook[73] contains a potential treasure trove, a list of names, titled "G Company." Examination of the names shows that this list conforms to the four company battalion structure, in which there was no G Company. It became necessary to source the original document, which, it was discovered, is not headed "G Company"; this was probably added later by a family member copying the original diary. Once this contradiction is resolved, Thompson's notebook reveals a unique list of the men in his platoon, not company, and a valuable insight into their organisation and orders at the Landing. This is the only roll of this type to have come to light.

Secondary sources also contain errors, but the first problem is to identify them. For example, the unit historian, W.C. Belford, quotes "C.S. Maloney," who describes landing practice at Lemnos:

One of "A" Company's boats was trying to get away from the ship's side ... Captain Dicky Annear was in the middle ... Lieut. McDonald [*sic*] was in the stern ... the boat kept bumping into the ship ... a mess-orderly let fly a dixie full of slops and the poor Captain collected the lot ... He gazed aloft, and his language was awful and caused the Colonel ... to retire hastily. After Captain Annear quietened down a bit, he took off his hat and gazed long and sadly at it. Then he ejaculated, "Well! I'm b—!"[74]

---

68   This commenced with the body of work that became *Game to the Last* and this book. J.P. Hurst, *Game to the Last: The 11th Australian Infantry Battalion at Gallipoli* (Melbourne, Victoria: Oxford University Press, 2005).
69   D.A. Wilson, "Morphettville to ANZAC", Part 2, article in *Australian Infantry* magazine, 1980–81, Jan–June 1981, p.21.
70   C.B.L. Lock, *The Fighting 10th: Souvenir of the 10th Battalion AIF* (Adelaide: Webb, Imprint, 1936), p.106. The restructure was in accordance with the 1914 Manual of Infantry Training issued by the War Office on 10 August 1914.
71   W.C. Belford, *Legs Eleven; Being the Story of the 11th Battalion (AIF) in the Great War of 1914–1918* (Perth: Imperial Printing Coy Ltd, 1940).
72   840 Sergeant R. Thompson, 20, stationer, of Geraldton, born Footscray.
73   R. Thompson, papers 1914–1915, private collection.
74   Belford, *Legs Eleven*, p.54. Belford did not join the battalion until after Gallipoli, so would have been relying on information provided by others.

No C.S. Maloney appears to have served in the 11th Battalion, so it is unclear to whom Belford was referring; more significantly, Annear and MacDonald belonged to C Company, not A.[75]

Belford also recorded that Lieutenant J. Newman[76] belonged to C Company,[77] and that Captain A.E.J. Croly[78] was "in one of the leading boats"[79] at the Landing. Detailed research revealed that Newman belonged to B Company and, according to the accepted version of the Landing, he and Croly should have been aboard their destroyers at the time stated. Bean too makes the odd error, such as stating that "Jackson and Buttle" belonged to Tulloch's company.[80] Jackson did belong to Tulloch's company; Buttle did not. Such errors in secondary sources make reconstruction of the battle difficult, lead to erroneous conclusions and reduce the value of primary sources. Even the form of a company or platoon at the time of the Landing was for many years unclear. Bean described a platoon as "normal fighting strength, from 25–40."[81] Other representations have depicted platoons of 30 men organised in three sections of 10, but this is actually a post-Great War structure.[82] The structure at the time of the Landing will be elucidated in the following chapter.

The Australian Red Cross Wounded and Missing Enquiry Bureau[83] files contain notes made by Red Cross personnel or volunteers interviewing sick or wounded men recovering in hospitals in Egypt and elsewhere, but much of the information is unreliable. Examination in the context of the growing body of biographical and other information established for this book, reveals a plethora of errors caused by mistaken identity, mistakes of recollection of interviewees or of transcription by interviewers. Once analysed, and the reliable evidence extracted, the files surrender a wealth of information.

Reconstruction of the battle, connection of disparate events, such as the departure for the battlefield of Turkish forces and simultaneous events at Anzac,[84] required construction of an accurate chronology. Yet quoted times at the Landing are notoriously unreliable, and we cannot assume correlation between them; to do so conceals gaps and errors in the established history. Even the accepted time of the Landing appears to have been a "best guess." Quoted times, particularly in secondary sources, therefore cannot be accepted without verification. Whenever possible, other frames of reference were established to anchor chronologies and connect events.

Battlefield and biographical (or more correctly, prosopographical) information, and visual evidence – maps, diagrams, photographs, video, study of the battlefield and conditions[85] – was then used to determine the reliability of detail in accounts. Terms such as "analysis" and "examination" are consequently often used here in preference to "discussion" as accuracy of sources needed to be determined before discussion could commence. What did "left" mean? Left of a section, platoon, company, feature, or the battlefield? Was it a transcription error? Did observers recall what was there or what they expected to see, a phenomenon Halbwachs had observed in Christian Crusaders'

---

75   Perhaps Maloney was a West Australian serving with another unit, or "C.S. Maloney" was a nom de plume for C.S.M. Such were not uncommon in writings. Les Whiting for example wrote as "Fish Fifty-First."

76   Lieutenant John Newman, 34 at embarkation, agent, of Kalgoorlie, born Port Pirie, South Australia.

77   Belford, *Legs Eleven*, p.68.

78   Captain Arthur England Johnson Croly, 32 at embarkation, agent, of Perth, born Dublin, Ireland. Croly had served with Gough's Mounted Infantry and the Royal Irish Fusiliers, and during the Boer War, on the North West Frontier and in Ireland.

79   Belford, *Legs Eleven*, p.70.

80   Bean, *Official History*, Volume I (1921 and 1941), p.286.

81   *Ibid.*, p.616.

82   *A Fortunate Life*, PBL Productions; *The Anzacs*, Burrowes-Dixon Company, 1985. The Australian Army Centenary Parade in Canberra, 2001, also depicted a section of 10 men.

83   Australian Red Cross Wounded and Missing Enquiry Bureau files, 1DRL/0428.

84   For example, C.A.M. Roberts, "The Landing at ANZAC: an Australian Defensive Action", paper presented at Australian War Memorial History Conference, 9–13 July 1990; H. Broadbent, *Gallipoli – The Fatal Shore* (Camberwell, Victoria: Viking, Penguin Books, 2005).

85   Such as study of the darkness and other conditions on several anniversaries of the Landing.

accounts of the Holy Land,[86] or were they describing events recounted by others? After assessment, evidence could be woven into the emerging fabric, making it tighter and broader, in a two-way process that allowed new evidence to shed light on the old, and vice versa.

This approach reveals that one reason we don't know the answers to large and small questions of the day, is because the evidence lies in pieces. In this book the work of assessing and aggregating the fragments into a narrative or argument is largely invisible behind the text. Verifying evidence was at times like pouring sand into gaps in the history, enabling a glimpse into the reality of the experience beyond the fogs of war, time and myth,[87] or exposing missing facts that cast a faint light onto anomalies that have existed for decades.

This book is presented as a narrative, an accretion of detail and experiences built on the foundation produced by the method outlined above, but a great many conundrums had to be thrashed out and argued before the narrative could be constructed. In some cases a piece of possible evidence casts its light on a number of issues, a parachute flare above a jungle canopy, fleetingly illuminating fragments of images, which then had to be interpreted and examined.

Much of the information on 25 April 1915 is long gone, as the majority of those who participated in the Landing are invisible: some men left memoirs of many pages, for some only portions of a letter may remain, for most there is next to nothing.[88] This book began as a project to trace as many members as possible of the 11th Battalion on 25 April 1915. Many of their surviving accounts consist of little more than a letter to family, a letter that was brief, censored, and coloured by many influences, including the desire to put a happy spin on things; the writers were probably aware that they might be dead before distant families received their letter. Whenever possible, peoples' accounts are logically or chronologically grounded, but in some cases may appear for no other reason than to include the man in the story, to give him a voice, a place and time on the battlefield and in history. Men will consequently appear and disappear throughout.

I will repeatedly contrast my findings with Bean's, but to build on his foundation is not to criticise. Bean did what he could with what he had, and his histories cover the campaigns at Gallipoli and on the Western Front. His achievement is not questioned and I have little doubt that I would not have the privilege of undertaking this work if not for Bean's efforts at collecting, recording and writing the history of the AIF and establishing the Australian War Memorial, which, as much as his published works, is his legacy. My findings are offered as a contribution to the historical record of a day in which so much significance is invested in Australia; the methodology utilised to undertake it is offered as a guide for "getting inside" other episodes in other times and places.

For those who landed at or before dawn on 25 April 1915, Anzac Day dawn services bore a special significance and carried a hidden burden. Goodlet closed his reminiscence with a hint at the loneliness that follows loss, in his case of "the truest friend I ever have known," a man whose name is today lost, one of many to lie "unshrouded, and forgotten by the country for which he gave his life."[89] This book aims to pay the people of those times the respect of reconstructing and telling their story as accurately as possible, and perhaps bring forward into the history those whose lives and experiences are otherwise invisible. By telling the stories that we can, we can shed light on the experience of the invisible majority who sat in the boats, lay in the scrub or charged or fell alongside those about whom the ages have allowed us to write.

---

86   Halbwachs, determined that Christian Crusaders, "on their visits to the Holy Land, imposed what was in their eyes on the land they thought they were describing", *On Collective Memory*, p.27.

87   The issue of whether or not the Landing was made in the right or wrong place will not be examined in this book, other than to quote men's opinions if given; that issue has been dealt with many times, notably by T.R. Frame in *The Shores of Gallipoli: Naval Aspects of the ANZAC Campaign* (Sydney: Hale & Iremonger, 2000), pp.183–210.

88   Beyond official sources, such as service records.

89   Goodlet, manuscript, p.19.

Figure 1. Cyrus Cuneo, *Landing at Gallipoli, 1915*. Chisel-chinned and determined, Australians in a variety of 1915 uniforms assault Plugge's Plateau. (Originally printed in *The London Times*, n.d., reproduced in *The Silver Jubilee Book, The Story of 25 Eventful Years in Pictures* (London: Odhams Press, 1935), pp.112–113)

1

Towards the Greatest Tragedy of the War

"In order to understand national tradition …
one has to combine the insider's view … with the outsider's."[1]

In the waist of the troop transport HMT A4 *Suffolk*, Lieutenant-Colonel James Lyon Johnston[2] assembled his battalion for the last time before committing them to their first battle. The ship was one of a mighty fleet anchored in Mudros Bay on the Greek island of Lemnos, 60 miles west of the entrance to the Dardanelles. Troops crowded decks, rigging and other vantage points as the colonel began his address.

"Boys, we have been instructed … to form a covering party for the Australian landing on the Gallipoli Peninsula … The position of honour … vanguard for one of the most daring enterprises in history." The men listened intently and in silence. The "General informs me that it will take several battleships and destroyers to carry our brigade to Gallipoli; a barge will be sufficient to take us home again!"[3] Private J.F. Fox[4] recalled "Thunderous cheering"[5] greeting the colonel's grim news, despite the fact that, as Rob Lowson wrote, all realised they "were practically a sacrifice, that our landing place was practically unknown and that once landed there could be no retreat."[6] "We were not only ready," wrote Fox, "we rejoiced that our chance had come."[7] Despite tears rolling down the colonel's cheeks, Private S. Newham[8] noted he was still "smiling and went on with his speech with a good heart."[9]

Most of the men had enlisted a little over eight months before. They had travelled thousands of miles to be here, lived and trained for months in the sands of the Egyptian desert and been cooped up aboard ship at Lemnos for seven weeks. This, their first battle, was to be the most difficult of operations, a seaborne assault on a fortified enemy coast and, apart from a few veterans of colonial wars, most had not experienced enemy fire. With the "climax of their lives" at hand, predictions of heavy casualties and the finality of knowing evacuation was not possible, there was perhaps little else to do but cheer, as "the 11th Battalion determined to do or die."[10] "We … saw to it that the points of our bayonets were sharp."[11]

---

1 Nora, p.ix.
2 Lieutenant-Colonel James Lyon Johnston, sharebroker and secretary, of Boulder, born Aberdeen, Scotland. Johnston is alternately referred to as "Lyon Johnston ", "Lyon-Johnston", and "Johnston." As official sources, such as the Nominal Roll, refer to "Johnston", this will be used throughout the text, unless appearing otherwise in quoted passages.
3 Belford, *Legs Eleven*, pp.63–64. Accounts vary as to who said this. Some say MacLagan, Eastcott thought Walker, Goodlet thought Hamilton. Johnston is the most likely.
4 166 Private (at embarkation) Joseph Frederick Fox, 35 at enlistment, commercial traveller, of Perth.
5 J.F. Fox, "I Was There", personal account of the Landing, Ellam-Innes Collection, Perth, p.6.
6 70 Private (at embarkation) Robert James Lowson, A Company, 21 at enlistment, clerk/lithographer, born Dundee, Scotland; R.J. Lowson, "Under Fire, My Impressions", 1 July 1915, Ellam-Innes Collection, Perth, n.p.
7 Fox, "I Was There", p.6.
8 579 Private Sydney Newham, 25 at enlistment, labourer, of Bunbury, born Windsor, Victoria.
9 S. Newham, "Recollections of a Returned Soldier", manuscript, n.d., private collection, n.p.
10 F.G. Medcalf, manuscript, J.S. Battye Library, Perth, MN 1265, pp.60–61; Belford, *Legs Eleven*, p.64.
11 Fox, "I Was There", p.6.

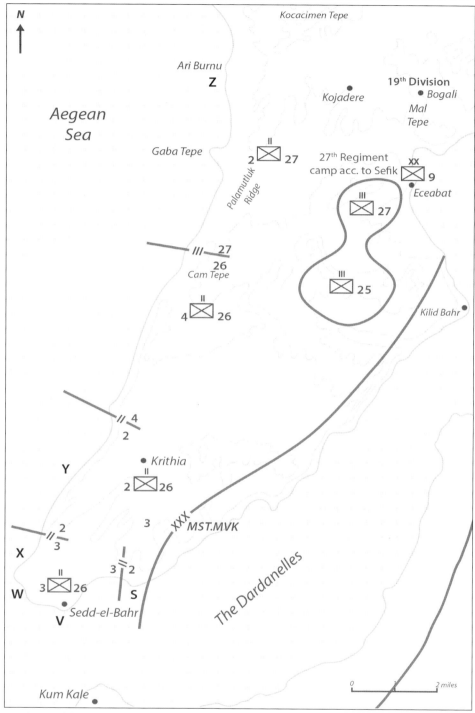

Map 1. The peninsula, showing the approximate positions of the landing beaches of 25
April and camps of 19th and 27th Regiments. The Australians and New Zealanders
landed at Z Beach. Şefik's map placed his regiment's camp further north (to the
north west of Eceabat/Maidos) and closer to Z Beach than indicated here.

It was the afternoon of 23 April 1915. The battalion would land on the Gallipoli peninsula before dawn on Sunday, 25 April. When they assembled less than a week later, only 350 of the thousand-odd, fighting-fit men addressed by Johnston would answer their names.

Personnel

The 11th Battalion officially came into being at Black Boy Hill camp, near Perth, Western Australia, on 17 August 1914.[12] The 1st Division's 1st Brigade was being raised in New South Wales, the 2nd in Victoria, and the 3rd from the less populated or "outer" states: Queensland (9th Battalion), South Australia (10th Battalion), Western Australia (11th Battalion), and a combination of men from Tasmania, South Australia, and Western Australia (12th Battalion).[13] A battalion at the time numbered a few over 1,000 all ranks.

An examination of the attestation papers of 500 of the original 11th Battalion's recruits[14] established the average age to be 25.8 years – not the "kids" sometimes described.[15] It also revealed that:

89% were single;
33% were born in Britain and 1% in Ireland;
17% were born in Western Australia;
31% were born in Victoria;
23% enlisted in Perth, 23% in the goldfields;
27% were from rural areas;
20% were labourers, 12% industrial workers, 7% professionals, 16% transport workers;
12% were in primary production, 8% in mining, 8% clerical work;
58% were Anglican.[16]

Johnston, 51, the battalion's first commanding officer (CO), of Boulder in the West Australian goldfields, was a Scottish-born sharebroker. Captain Ray Leane,[17] 36, from Prospect, South Australia, was a merchant in Kalgoorlie. Major Edmund Brockman,[18] 30, of Mount Lawley, Perth, was a barrister and Captain Dixon Hearder,[19] 35, who joined the battalion shortly before the Landing, was a solicitor. London-born Captain Charles Barnes,[20] 34, of Guildford, Chief Clerk of WA Trustee Executors, had been the youngest officer to serve in the Boer War, receiving the Queen's Medal with four clasps for meritorious conduct in the field. Captain W.R. "Dick" Annear,[21] 39, of Kalgoorlie and Perth, born Ballarat, was a commercial traveller, master printer and area officer for the army. Lieutenant "Dave" MacDonald,[22] 24, was on the Permanent Military Staff. Captain E.T. "Doc"

---

12 Belford, *Legs Eleven*, p.2.
13 The 12th Battalion was considered to be a Tasmanian unit. Fifty percent of the original battalion were Tasmanian, 25 percent South Australian, and 25 percent West Australian.
14 By Suzanne Welborn, published in S. Welborn, *Lords of Death, A People, A Place, a Legend* (Fremantle: Fremantle Arts Centre Press, 1982).
15 J. King, interview, 25 April 2005; *Gallipoli's Deep Secrets*, Prospero Productions (2010).
16 Welborn, *Lords of Death*, pp.53–54; Tables, Appendix A, pp.188–193.
17 Captain Raymond Lionel Leane, 36, merchant, of Boulder, born South Australia.
18 Major Edmund Alfred Drake Brockman, 30, barrister, of Mt. Lawley.
19 Captain Dixon Hearder, 35, solicitor/barrister, of Fremantle, probably born Wales.
20 Captain Charles Albert Barnes, 34, chief clerk, of Guildford, born London.
21 Captain William Richard Annear, 39, commercial traveller, master printer, area officer of Kalgoorlie and Subiaco, born Victoria.
22 Lieutenant David Henderson MacDonald, 24, military officer, of Cottesloe, born New South Wales.

Brennan,[23] 27, and Lieutenant A.P.H. Corley,[24] 37, were medical practitioners. With Brennan filling the role of battalion medical officer, Corley chose to serve as an infantry officer.

Of the enlisted men, "Bernie" Walther,[25] 19, born in Australia of German extraction, was a clerk in the Colonial Secretary's Office; due to pre-war machine gun experience with the militia, he became a member of the 11th Battalion's Machine Gun Section. The section's first sergeant, "Wally" Hallahan,[26] 25, had been training to be a chemist. "Jack" McCleery,[27] bedding manufacturer, was aghast to learn that Hallahan intended to follow his citizen's forces training as a machine gunner – a role considered suicidal in time of war.[28] David Simcock,[29] 31, was a fruit seller whose wit, hard work and personality had made him a Perth identity, known as "Pink Top." When he embarked for service overseas he left a successful business, wife and two children and corresponded with the state premier. George Medcalf,[30] 25, was a surveyor from Cottesloe, and Tom Louch,[31] 20, having recently returned from school in England, was serving his articles as a law clerk in Albany. Frank Goundrey,[32] 23, and brothers Edward Gee,[33] 24, and Arthur Gee,[34] 23, all from England, Roy Retchford,[35] 20, of Kalgoorlie, and nine others were constructing the Transcontinental Railway Line when they heard the news and decided to enlist. They downed tools and caught the first train west, travelling all night and waking the next morning in the Kalgoorlie rail yards.[36] In Geraldton, Arthur Browne,[37] 19, brothers Roy and Claude Thompson,[38] 20 and 21 respectively, Walter Fathers,[39] 20, and others were on their way to play football when they noticed a crowd outside the Drill Hall – "That was the end of the football match."[40] The next morning they were included in the area's first contingent of 23 for the 11th Battalion. "It was jubilation for some, and heartbreak for those who had been rejected. Everyone thought the war would only last for a few months and wanted to get cracking."[41] Fred Ashton,[42] 21, a clerk with the WA Bank, had also planned to play football in Geraldton that day. He was a member of the Geraldton brass band, and would become a bugler in the 11th Battalion. Ivo Joy,[43] 19, a bank teller at the Union Bank in the town of Katanning, near his family's farm, commanded the first party of recruits to leave Katanning for the camp at Black Boy Hill.[44] H.J.V. Priestley,[45] 27, of Perth, wrote to his sister that he "had to volunteer" as

23   Captain Edward Thomas Brennan, 27, medical practitioner, of Fremantle, born Stawell, Victoria.
24   Lieutenant Anthony Purdon Hagarty Corley, 37, medical practitioner of Pingelly, British subject, educated Ireland.
25   505 Private Bernhardt Hermann Walther, Machine Gun Section, 19 at embarkation, civil servant, of Perth, born Victoria.
26   503 Sergeant Walter Rewi Hallahan, Machine Gun Section, 25 at embarkation, amalgamator, of Kalgoorlie, born New Zealand.
27   697 Sergeant John Malcolm McCleery, C Company at Landing, 37 at embarkation, bedmaker, of Kalgoorlie, born Sydney, New South Wales.
28   J.M. McCleery, taped interview by S. Welborn, Perth, 1976, for *Lords of Death*, Reid Library, University of Western Australia.
29   951 Private David John Simcock, D Company at Landing, 31 at enlistment, dealer, of Perth, born South Australia.
30   1048 Private Ferdinand George Medcalf, A Company at Landing, 25, surveyor, of Albany, Kondinin and Cottesloe, born Sydney, New South Wales.
31   923 Corporal Thomas Steane Louch, 20 at embarkation, law clerk, of Albany, born Geraldton.
32   660 Private Frank Shelton Goundrey, C Company at Landing, 23 at embarkation, labourer, born Oxford, England.
33   661 Private (at embarkation) Edward Gee, C Company at Landing, 24 at embarkation, farmer and "navvy", born Oxford, England.
34   662 Private (at embarkation) Arthur Gee, C Company at Landing, 23 at embarkation, labourer, born Cardiff, Wales.
35   388 Private (at embarkation) Albert Roy Retchford, Signaller, 20 at embarkation, fireman, of Kalgoorlie, born Victoria.
36   Belford, *Legs Eleven*, p.2.
37   751 Private (at embarkation) Arthur James Sturgeon Browne, D Company at Landing, 19 at enlistment, clerk, of Geraldton, born Britain.
38   840 Sergeant Roy Thompson, D Company at Landing, 20 at embarkation, stationer, of Geraldton. 841 Private (at embarkation) Claude Thompson, D Company at Landing, 21 at embarkation, machinist/woodworker, of Geraldton.
39   782 Private (at embarkation) Walter Lamont Fathers, D Company at Landing, 20 at enlistment, printer, of Geraldton, born Gippsland, Victoria.
40   A.J. Browne to Geraldton Sub-Branch, RSL, the *Geraldton Guardian*, Tuesday 4 May (year unknown).
41   Browne to Geraldton Sub-Branch, RSL.
42   743 Bugler Fred Ashton, D Company at Landing, 21 at enlistment, clerk, of Geraldton, born Sydney, New South Wales.
43   919 Lance Sergeant Ivo Brian Joy, D Company at Landing, 19 at enlistment, bank clerk, of Katanning, born Melbourne, Victoria.
44   D. James, family history notes on I.B. Joy, private collection, Sydney. The party numbered six, including Joy.
45   335 Private Henry James Vivian Priestley, B Company at Landing, 27 at enlistment, computer and draughtsman, of Perth, formerly of Victoria, born Westbury, Tasmania.

the "fighting blood … got too strong," adding that times "are going to be mighty bad so a fellow may as well be earning 6/- a day as probably earning nothing in a few months time." The thing that most upset him was leaving his young wife, who "is about broken-hearted … we have been very happy during our short married life"; for her benefit, he put his "things in order in case of accidents."[46] Priestley's sister would later tend wounded aboard ships at the Dardanelles. Hedley Howe,[47] 22, seaman, fisherman, pearler, and well sinker, travelled south from Broome to serve. He would contribute to the history of the Gallipoli campaign by returning to the battlefields with the official historian after the war.

The Battalion

In 1915 an infantry battalion notionally consisted of 30 officers and 977 other ranks (ORs). Each rifle company had six officers and 221 ORs, divided into four platoons of four sections.[48] The 11th Battalion achieved this new formation by combining the pre-existing A and B Companies to form the new A Company – mostly from Perth; C and D to become B – mostly from Fremantle and districts; E and F to become C – the goldfields and the south-west; and G and H to become D – country districts.[49] Each new company was commanded by a major or senior captain, with a captain as second-in-command and a subaltern and sergeant commanding each of its four platoons.[50] Officers did not necessarily stay with the formations they had previously commanded.[51] In some instances, enough information has come to light to establish which company or half company of the original structure became which platoon or pair of platoons of the later structure, enabling a man to be assigned to a single or pair of platoons; for example, the original A Company became 3 and 4 Platoons. I believe the following to represent the battalion structure for January 1915:

Headquarters (HQ)

Lieutenant-Colonel J.L. Johnston	Officer Commanding (OC)
Major S.R.H. Roberts[52]	Second-in-Command (2IC)
Captain J.H. Peck	Adjutant
Captain E.T. Brennan	Medical Officer
Lieutenant J. Peat[53]	Machine Gun Officer

A Company

Major E.A.D. Brockman	Officer Commanding
Captain R.W. Everett[54]	Second-in-Command
Lieutenant A.R. Selby[55]	1 Platoon

---

46   H.J.V. Priestley, letters, private collection.

47   188 Lance Corporal Hedley Vicars Howe, A Company at Landing, 22 at embarkation, seaman, born Singleton, New South Wales.

48   *An Officer's Manual of the Western Front 1914–1918* (Army Printing and Stationery Service, London, 2008 edition by Conway, an imprint of Anova Books Ltd, London), p.158.

49   Determined by cross-referencing available primary sources, including a document on the history of the 11th Battalion, unidentified author, Defence Library, Perth, Western Australia.

50   E.J. Richards, manuscript, Australian War Memorial, 2DRL 301.

51   C.A. Barnes, diary, 1 January 1915, 1DRL/0091, Australian War Memorial, provides some examples.

52   Stephen Richard Harricks Roberts, 40 at embarkation, civil servant, of Subiaco, born Ararat, Victoria.

53   Lieutenant James Peat, 27 at embarkation, surveyor, of Boulder.

54   Captain Reginald William Everett, 42 at embarkation, business manager of Subiaco, born Goulburn, New South Wales.

55   Lieutenant Arthur Roland Selby, 21, soldier, of Perth, born New South Wales. Selby attended Scotch College, Perth, Adelaide University and graduated from the Royal Military College, Duntroon.

Lieutenant J.H. Morgan[56]	2 Platoon
Second Lieutenant A.H. MacFarlane[57]	3 Platoon
Lieutenant W.H. Rockliff[58]	4 Platoon

B Company

Captain C.A. Barnes	Officer Commanding
Captain R.R. Reilly[59]	Second-in-Command
Second Lieutenant S.H. Jackson[60]	5 Platoon
Second Lieutenant F.P.D. Strickland[61]	6 Platoon
Lieutenant A.H. Darnell[62]	7 Platoon
Lieutenant J. Newman	8 Platoon

C Company

Captain R.L. Leane	Officer Commanding
Captain W.R. Annear	Second-in-Command
Lieutenant D.H. MacDonald	9 Platoon
Lieutenant A.P.H. Corley	10 Platoon
Lieutenant C.A. La Nauze[63]	11 Platoon
Second Lieutenant J.H. Cooke[64]	12 Platoon

D Company

Major J.S. Denton[65]	Officer Commanding
Captain A.E.J. Croly	Second-in-Command
Lieutenant J. Williams[66]	13 Platoon
Second Lieutenant H.H. Walker[67]	14 Platoon
Lieutenant M.L. Reid	15 Platoon
Second Lieutenant C.F. Buttle[68]	16 Platoon[69]

The battalion also had quartermaster, signals, medical, machine gun and transport sections.

---

56 Lieutenant James Harold Morgan, 22, civil servant, of West Leederville, born Victoria.
57 Second Lieutenant (Lieutenant by 25 April 1915) Archibald Henry MacFarlane, 27, metallurgist and analytical chemist, of Perth and Subiaco, born Victoria.
58 Lieutenant William Hudson Rockliff, 29 at embarkation, schoolteacher, of West Perth, born New South Wales.
59 Lieutenant Reginal Ronald Reilly, 36 at embarkation, civil servant, of Perth. Assumed command of the battalion signallers shortly before the Landing.
60 Second Lieutenant (Lieutenant by 25 April 1915) Samuel Henry Jackson, 24 at embarkation, civil servant, of Mount Lawley, born Bundaberg, Queensland.
61 Second Lieutenant (Lieutenant by 25 April 1915) Frederick Phillip David Strickland, 39 at embarkation, civil servant, of South Perth, born Melbourne. Strickland had served with the West Australian forces in the Boer War.
62 Second Lieutenant (Lieutenant by 25 April 1915) Aubrey Hugh Darnell, 28, civil servant, of Claremont, born Ireland.
63 Lieutenant Charles Andrew La Nauze, 32 at embarkation, bank officer/accountant, of Boulder, born Mauritius.
64 Second Lieutenant Joseph Henry Cooke, 32 at enlistment, accountant, of Wickepin, born India. Cooke had served 12 years with the 1st Battalion, Lancashire Fusiliers, finishing as colour sergeant.
65 Major James Samuel Denton, 38 at embarkation, civil servant, of Pazely, Great Southern Railway, born Port Adelaide.
66 Lieutenant John Williams, 41 at embarkation, clerk, c/o Military HQ Perth.
67 Second Lieutenant Harold Holmes Walker, D Company at Landing, 23 at enlistment, clerk, of East Perth, born South Melbourne. Walker was promoted lieutenant on 25 April 1915.
68 Second Lieutenant Clement Francis Buttle, 20 at enlistment, engineering cadet/mechanical engineer, of Perth. Buttle was promoted to lieutenant in February 1915.
69 Due to the complexities of following the battalion's many officers and men during the battle, this list is repeated in Appendix IV.

Figure 2. The 11th Battalion, Cairo, January 1915. Photographer unknown, 10 January 1915. (Author's collection)

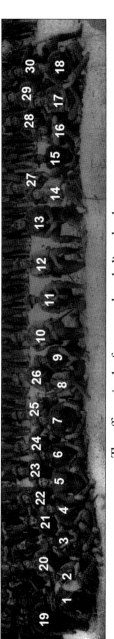

The officers in the foreground are believed to be:

Front row:

1. Lieutenant J. Newman; 2. Major S.R.H. Roberts; 3. Major J.S. Denton; 4. Captain C.A. Barnes; 5. Chaplain J. Fahey; 6. Lieutenant A.P.H. Corley; 7. Captain J.H. Peck; 8. Captain R.R. Reilly; 9. Lieutenant D.H. MacDonald; 10. Lieutenant-Colonel J.L. Johnston; 11. Captain R.W. Everett; 12. Major E.A.D. Brockman; 13. Captain E.T. Brennan; 14. Captain R.L. Leane; 15. Lieutenant A.H. Priestley; 16. Lieutenant A.R. Selby;* 17. Lieutenant H. James; 18. Second Lieutenant H.H. Walker

Second row:

19. Lieutenant F.P.D. Strickland; 20. Second Lieutenant S.H. Jackson;[†] 21. Captain A.E.J. Croly; 22. Lieutenant K. Mclennan; 23. Second Lieutenant A.H. MacFarlane; 24. Lieutenant C.A. La Nauze; 25. Captain W.R. Annear; 26. Lieutenant M.L. Reid; 27. Lieutenant W.H. Rockliff;[‡] 28. Second Lieutenant J.H. Cooke; 29. Second Lieutenant C.F. Buttle; 30. Lieutenant J. Peat[§]

There is still conflict between sources as to the identity of several of these officers. The above list is compiled from a range of sources, with as much cross referencing and comparison of photographs, many of them from the Ellam-Innes Collection, as possible. A valuable source was an anonymous, handwritten list I discovered in a filing cabinet many years ago, its origin now forgotten. Although untitled, the names corresponded with the position of officers in the Cheops photograph, with a sufficient number of undisputed identities to establish its credibility. Discussion with Allan and Raye Ellam led us to believe the list was created by a battalion member in the 1960s. As far as I can recall, there was only one name on this list that I disputed. In recent years the Western Australian Genealogical Society (WAGS) has committed many dedicated hours to identifying as many men in the photograph as possible; where my list differs from theirs, the variations are noted in the footnotes.

* The WAGS website has this man labelled as Lieutenant W.H. Rockliff (January 2016)
† The WAGS website has this man labelled as Lieutenant J.H. Morgan (January 2016)
‡ The WAGS website has this man labelled as Lieutenant A.H. Darnell (January 2016)
§ The WAGS website has this man labelled as Lieutenant J. Williams (January 2016)

Shortly before the Landing, reinforcement Tulloch became 2 IC B Company; Lieutenant C.A.P. Gostelow[70] assumed command of 13 Platoon; and Hearder "owing to previous experience in Field Batteries," replaced the seriously ill Peat as OC Machine Gun Section.[71] The "drill, tactics etc. of Machine and Field Guns have nothing in common," wrote Hearder, "but the average infantry officer knows nothing of either." He began studying the books Peat "had luckily left."[72]

Accurately determining to which sections the enlisted men belonged can only be done in a minority of cases. Some men, notably Louch (16 Section, 16 Platoon, D Company), Medcalf (1 Section, 1 Platoon, A Company), Roy Thompson (13 Platoon, D Company), "Ted" Mofflin[73] and Ed Inman[74] (7 Platoon, B Company) have left records naming some or all of the members of their sections or platoons.[75] Although it is not always known whether these lists are complete, they often provide clues that can be substantiated by cross-referencing against other sources. It is unwise to assume too much – men knew others from school, employment, sport, social groups or family connections, and knowledge of each other does not imply membership of the same section, platoon, company or battalion. To complicate matters, the 1st and an undisclosed number of the 2nd and 3rd Reinforcements joined the battalion before 25 April, the latter to bring the battalion to war strength before the battle. Assigning these men to companies and platoons is more difficult and often not possible.

An infantry battalion also contained a range of specialists. These are generally named on the 1914 embarkation roll, but this does not account for movements – Simcock, for example, initially belonged to the HQ, but landed with D Company. In April 1915 the machine gun section consisted of one officer and 17 other ranks, most or all of whom had pre-war machine gun experience, two water-cooled Maxim machine guns with accessories and one limber. Many men embraced any opportunity to improve their skills. At sea, H.J. "Bull" Eastcott[76] and the medical section assisted in the "ship's hospital" where "four nursing sisters … gave us quite a good grounding in nursing." He and the rest of the section had been selected for their role as "we all had some experience of ambulance work, and our sergeant," Lance Sergeant William Wright,[77] was a Royal Army Medical Corps veteran of the Boer War.[78]

From Fremantle to the Aegean Sea

The 11th Battalion embarked at Fremantle on 31 October 1914, believing that they were en route to England, but learning during the voyage that they were being diverted to Egypt to continue training.[79] On 28 February 1915, the battalion left Cairo for Alexandria, arriving at the island of Lemnos a few days later. There they lived aboard ship, "went ashore for exercise whenever storms … permitted,"[80] route marched, indulged "in sham fighting, or hill climbing, anything to keep fit,"[81] and "coughed the dust of Egypt from their chests."[82] Despite this activity, Brockman was concerned there was insufficient "exercise to keep in condition."[83] By 17 March, veteran Barnes felt that the men

70   Lieutenant Charles Arthur Pearson Gostelow, 23 at enlistment, clerk, of Perth.
71   D. Hearder, manuscript, Private Records, Australian War Memorial, 3DRL 3959, p.7.
72   Hearder, manuscript 3DRL 3959, p.7.
73   464 Corporal Edward Walter Mofflin, 26 at embarkation, lumper, of North Fremantle, born North Adelaide.
74   448 Edwin Stanley Inman, 20 at embarkation, grocer, of South Fremantle, born Emerald, Victoria.
75   In some cases these records are little more than references to shared experiences over a period of months; further investigation establishes the people named to be members of the same platoon or section.
76   395 Herbert John Eastcott, 21, locomotive cleaner, of Wagerup.
77   398 Lance Sergeant William Wright, 34, dispenser, of Perth, born England.
78   H.J. Eastcott, manuscript, Ellam-Innes Collection, p.2.
79   Belford, *Legs Eleven*, p.31.
80   Brockman, letter to wife, 25 May 1915, West Australian, 28 July 1915.
81   Hearder, manuscript 3DRL 3959, p.8.
82   J.H. Peck, letter to wife, n.d., printed unidentified newspaper, 13 July 1915, Army Museum of Western Australia.
83   Brockman, letter, 25 May 1915.

could mostly "handle a boat well," but wondered "how well they will do it … under fire."[84] The troops were reminded of the proximity of the war by the occasionally audible naval "bombardment of the Dardanelle forts"[85] and the return of damaged ships to port. One day, Walther and friends swam "to one of the minesweepers" where they "were smilingly received and treated like lords. The galley gives evidence of one of the Turks' 15 pounders and is a little draughtier on that account."[86]

On 9 April the battalion received maps "of the objectives"[87] for the forthcoming operations, though George Blay[88] had recorded being advised as early as 23 March that "the 3rd Brigade have been picked … a great honour and expect only a few would come out of it."[89] If any doubt remained in the minds of the enlisted men, it must have been dispelled by their next pay, which was made in notes "superscribed in Turkish."[90]

The routine work of mounting guards, loading and unloading stores, maintaining discipline and other requisite duties continued. In March, "Paddy" Reid,[91] "a huge and fractious"[92] Irishman, was awarded one month's Field Punishment No. 1 for, not for the first time, being absent without leave and other misconduct. The charge may refer to an incident in which "Read" fell foul of the local "very poisonous 'gargle'". Unable to ascend the ship's side by rope ladder, he was hoisted aboard "in a pig net," calling amiably to Colonel Johnston, nicknamed "Tipperary", "Good day! Tip, old boy!"[93] Early in April, Reid was charged with drunkenness, resisting arrest and violence, possibly while still serving his earlier punishment, and was sentenced to 12 months hard labour and to be discharged with ignominy from His Majesty's Service.[94]

The youthful Goodlet was amazed by the "true comradeship" of members of his platoon.[95] "I was recovering from an illness … and the way in which the older men … cared for me and shouldered my share of fatigue work left me dumb with gratitude and wonder." One of these was "a burly veteran … we called Robbo. He had been like a mother to me and had often told me stories of his adventures in other wars."[96] Goodlet describes a bond usually concealed behind such terms as "mateship", or the silence or tears of veterans: "we came to understand and love each other during those few months … with a love that you, who have not been to War, can never understand."[97]

Colonel Johnston appears rarely in the *Official History*, but appears to have been respected and well liked by the other ranks. Walther described a route march at Lemnos when "Tipperary … put up a splendid show. He set a rattling good pace … He's a goer and a sport if ever there was one. We 'fought our way' back to the ship."[98] On such marches, the West Australians, possibly with only weeks or months to live, found themselves passing though a peaceful, ageless annual cycle of birth and growth. Norman Pittersen[99] noticed local crops "up about a foot when we were there and everything

84   Barnes, diary, 17 March 1915.
85   Newham, "Recollections of a Returned Soldier", n.p.
86   B.H. Walther, diary, 17 April 1915, private collection, Perth.
87   Belford, *Legs Eleven*, p.55.
88   411 Lance Corporal George Harry Blay, 24 at enlistment, storeman, of South Fremantle, born Deal, Kent.
89   G.H. Blay, diary, 23 March 1915, Ellam-Innes Collection, Perth. This might be presumed to be an error, 23 April being meant, but this entry is in the correct context in the diary.
90   Belford, *Legs Eleven*, p.55.
91   708 Private Patrick Reid, A Company, 26 at embarkation, butcher, born Belfast, Ireland. Reid had served two years with the Royal Irish Fusiliers.
92   H. Howe, "The Senior Private of the AIF; Celebrities of the AIF", *Reveille*, 1934, p.30.
93   Belford, *Legs Eleven*, p.53.
94   First Australian Imperial Force Personnel Dossiers, 1914–1920, 1 Jan 1914–31 Dec 1920, Service Records, B2455, National Archives of Australia. Subsequently "B2455".
95   Goodlet, manuscript, p.3.
96   *Ibid.*, p.5.
97   *Ibid.*, p.4.
98   Walther, diary, 1 April 1915.
99   822 Norman Pittersen, 27 at embarkation, grocer, of Perth, born Victoria.

looked pretty."[100] The local Greeks, whom he described as "very clean … different to … Egypt,"[101] found the troops "profitable clients … plenty of money and no sense of value."[102]

On 12 April, the battalion commanders of the 3rd Brigade were "taken by warship" to study the Gallipoli coast.[103] Boer War veteran Barnes thought the operation would require:

> a tremendous effort … will need every man English, French and Australian … the Peninsula is very strongly held … I expect … a very warm reception … it looks … a damned tough proposition. I hope it is not going to be a very long job as I would personally like to be sent along to the French and Belgian Front.[104]

The Corps "Staff, brigadiers, and battalion commanders" conducted their own reconnaissance on 14 April. Bean described Colonel E.G. Sinclair-MacLagan, commander of the 3rd Brigade, thinking that if "that place is strongly held with guns … it will be almost impregnable for my fellows." The divisional commander, Major-General W.T. Bridges, "thought him pessimistic."[105]

The covering force was to land from ships' boats in two waves, the first from battleships, the second from destroyers, and practised this when the weather allowed. On 17 April they practised disembarking from the battleship HMS *London* and the following evening conducted a "night landing practice."[106] Fall "in and over the side … towed ashore, land, form up on the beach, then on board again, and back to the *Suffolk* … *London*'s Commander" timing "everything … noting where improvements could be made."[107] Correspondent Ellis Ashmead-Bartlett watched troops, presumably 11th Battalion, disembarking from *London*:

> This is the first time I had seen anything of the Australian troops and they certainly create an excellent impression with their fine physique and general bearing. But their ideas of discipline are very different … The men seem to discipline themselves, and their officers have very little authority over them … personality plays a much bigger role … many of the officers … little better trained than their men … lack the experience and authority which comes from years of service.
>
> Nevertheless, they appear a body of men who can be relied on in any emergency; whatever they lack in discipline I feel will be compensated for by their native intelligence and initiative.[108]

W.W. Scott[109] wrote that once the troops heard "of the task in front of us we did train, I can tell you."[110] Meanwhile, they watched the invasion force gathering in the harbour, "transport after transport … a glorious sight," and a rousing display of "England's powers."[111] A "warm friendship" rapidly developed between the "blue jackets from the North," and the soldiers from "under the Southern Cross."[112] Walther noted making "quite a happy family with the sailors and marines" and the "fourteen and fifteen year old 'middies' who practically hold the same authority as our sub-

100 N. Pittersen, letter to mother, 4 May 1915, printed *Swan Express*, Friday 4 June 1915.
101 *Ibid*.
102 Goodlet, manuscript, p.3.
103 Belford, *Legs Eleven*, p.58.
104 Barnes, diary, 13 April 1915.
105 Bean, *Official History* (1921 and 1941), Volume I, p.222.
106 3rd Brigade War Diary, August 1914–June 1915, AWM4 Australian Imperial Force Unit War Diaries, Australian War Memorial, Canberra.
107 Hearder, manuscript 3DRL 3959, p.8.
108 F. and E. Brenchley, *Myth Maker, Ellis Ashmead-Bartlett, The Englishman Who Sparked Australia's Gallipoli Legend* (Milton, Queensland: John Wiley & Sons Australia, 2005), p.62.
109 716 Corporal Walter William Scott, C Company, 36 at embarkation, salesman, of Kalgoorlie, born South Australia.
110 W.W. Scott, to unidentified friend, n.d., letter, printed Kalgoorlie Miner, 6 September 1915.
111 Newham, "Recollections of a Returned Soldier", n.p.
112 Brenchley, p.62.

lieutenant."[113] These youthful midshipmen would command the boats delivering the 11th Battalion to the enemy shore.

"At last the 'heads' seemed to get suddenly busy – after Sir Ian Hamilton," General Officer Commanding Mediterranean Expeditionary Force, arrived "and there were daily confabs."[114] Activity in the harbour increased. "Tip" gave the troops "quite an interesting lecture on the campaign" and "gave us just a little idea what we are going to do."[115] Briefings continued daily – "we were shown the map and the three landing places pointed out ... By now the lads were getting worked up."[116] The troops were also briefed about the culture and sensitivities of the Turkish civilians they expected to meet and were ordered to treat them with respect.[117] Walther recorded an "imaginary night attack," "trench digging" and a "bonzer swim."[118] On Wednesday it was "Raining and blowing for all it's worth ... Tucker getting pretty crook – especially noticeable as the canteen is dreadfully dry ... trial disembarkation ... another little lecture by the Colonel. (Cut Murph's[119] hair.)."[120]

With the uncertainty of a baptism of fire and an opposed landing before them, each man confronted his fears and concerns. Foremost for many was that they not "be found wanting" – that they not let their comrades, their country nor themselves down during the ordeal ahead. Simcock's concern was submerged barbed wire. He put his mind to work and, "sedulously encouraged by his mates,"[121] paraded before the colonel with his solution – "a pair of leggings fashioned from a biscuit tin worn under the puttees. The colonel," it would seem, "was not impressed."[122] Walther's corporal had also been using his initiative and had made a "periscope which ... was most useful" for "throwing spuds ... into the Ionian's portholes."[123] One wonders whether this invention made its way ashore, a forebear of the improvised periscopes later used by the "Anzacs" in the trenches.

The landing was scheduled for 23 April, but on 20 April strong winds led to a 24 hour postponement; this was repeated the following evening. Late on the "22nd ... cross-movements of troops between various transports"[124] became possible once more. By now, "you could see several men around the grindstone" every day, "grinding their bayonets"; Mofflin got his "pretty sharp but I never used it."[125]

Uniforms and Equipment

The Landing at Anzac has been depicted many times in paintings, films, documentaries and other dramatisations, but the great variation in these representations creates a vagueness and confusion in the eyes of anyone who grew up with such images. Examining 11th Battalion primary sources and photographs allows a more precise picture to be drawn.

In 1914 the troops had been issued the standard uniform worn by the AIF throughout the war – slouch hat, tunic, breeches, puttees and brown boots (Figure 3). The infantry were equipped with British Pattern 1908 web equipment, which was designed to sustain a man for 24 hours of battle by carrying ammunition, bayonet, entrenching tool, a quart of water and one day's rations. For marching

---

113 Walther, diary, 16 April 1915. Why Walther, who would land from a destroyer, was aboard *London*, is not known.
114 E.T. Brennan, letter, 1915, unidentified recipient and newspaper, Army Museum of Western Australia.
115 J.R.T. Keast, diary, 17 April 1915, ANZAC (Aust), Liddle Collection, Brotherton Library, University of Leeds.
116 E.W. Mofflin, letter to Nesta and family, 20 October 1915, Army Museum of Western Australia, Fremantle, p.9.
117 Eastcott, manuscript, p.3.
118 Walther, diary, 18, 19 April 1915.
119 504 Corporal Fred Unwin Murphy, Machine Gun Section, 19 at embarkation, clerk, of Perth.
120 Walther, diary, 21, 22 April 1915.
121 Bean, *Official History* (1921 and 1941), Volume I, p.472.
122 E.W. Bush, *Gallipoli* (London: Allen & Unwin, 1975), p.177.
123 Walther, diary, 17 April 1915.
124 Bean, *Official History* (1921 and 1941), Volume I, pp.242–3.
125 Mofflin, letter, 20 October 1915, p.9.

order, a pack containing anything not required in action, such as blanket, spare clothing and personal effects, was worn on the back, attached to the webbing shoulder braces by a pair of buckles and secured to the waist belt; a smaller haversack was worn on the left hip (Figure 3).

Towards the end of their stay at Lemnos the troops were issued with colour patches, to be sewn onto the tunic sleeve below the shoulder; the shape and combination of colours enabled a man's arm of service, division, brigade and unit to be identified at a glance. The 11th Battalion patch was a rectangle of two colours, chocolate over saxe-blue. The rectangle identified the 1st Division,[126] the blue colour in the lower half represented the 3rd Brigade, and chocolate in the upper half identified the third battalion in the brigade. Many men posted a colour patch home, and they would come to be worn "with pride and affection," "the most revered symbol of the battalion."[127] Louch adds that the metal "Australia" badges were removed from tunic shoulder straps, "to trick the Turks; we were then issued with … colour patches."[128] It is difficult to confirm this, and pre-landing photographs appear to show "Australia" badges in place.[129] Perhaps Louch meant that the metal "11 INF" badges were removed from shoulder straps – these appear to be absent from photographs and this would explain their replacement with colour patches. Flat-topped British Field Service caps were issued to prevent the Australians' distinctive slouch hats revealing their nationality.[130] There is evidence that some units were ordered to remove the wire from the caps' rim[131] to break up the highly visible flat crown, though photographs suggest this was not done in the 11th Battalion. These attempts at denying the enemy intelligence about the units opposing them were initially effective – most contemporary Turkish sources referred to the "English" landing at Ari Burnu.

11th Battalion sources and photographs (Figures 6–9) reveal different uniforms and equipment to those generally depicted (Figures 2–3). Unlike later specialists such as marines or commandoes, the covering force was not equipped with specialist equipment and official and ad hoc additions and variations were made to standard equipment. As it was unclear when supplies would reach the troops, as much as possible would be carried ashore. For the Landing, Bean notes that each enlisted man's ammunition pouches carried 200 rounds of ammunition.[132] Ammunition pouches only held 150 rounds and 11th Battalion sources record the additional 50 or 100 rounds being carried in one or two cloth bandoliers, each holding 50 rounds. Photographic corroboration of bandoliers in 11th Battalion photos is difficult to find, but they were certainly issued, there is evidence of them being collected and used on the battlefield[133] and they may have been carried in haversacks.[134] The men carried "the current day's rations and two iron rations." The latter, "a tin of bully beef, a small tin of tea and sugar, and a number of very hard coarse biscuits",[135] issued in two white bags, were for the "second and third days."[136]

For the Landing, packs were disconnected from the braces and the narrow webbing straps that usually secured the pack to the waist belt were instead looped over the shoulders. Bean notes that this was to enable the pack to "be thrown off immediately if a boat were sunk,"[137] but there was another reason. Packs were usually removed before battle, but on this occasion were to be carried ashore and removed immediately after landing. Tunic shoulder straps were to be unbuttoned to enable a more

---

126 Primarily, although the Fourth Brigade, of the New Zealand and Australian Divison, also wore a horizontal rectangle.
127 Belford, *Legs Eleven*, p.57.
128 T.S. Louch, manuscript, Ellam-Innes Collection, Perth, p.13.
129 For example, photographs P02934_016 and J03299, Australian War Memorial.
130 L.M. Newton, *The Story of the Twelfth: A Record of the 12th Battalion, A.I.F. during the Great War of 1914–1918* (Hobart: J. Walch & Sons, 1925), p.56.
131 For example, Newton, *The Story of the Twelfth*, p.56.
132 Bean, *Official History*, Volume I (1921 and 1941), p.245.
133 Goodlet, manuscript, p.14.
134 AWM RC00058 and C00578 show men of other units wearing cloth bandoliers on 25 April.
135 Bean, *Official History*, Volume I (1921 and 1941), p.245.
136 1st Division War Diary, Appendix 1, 18–19 April 1915, 7.(ii), AWM4 Australian Imperial Force Unit War Diaries.
137 Bean, *Official History*, Volume I (1921 and 1941), p.245.

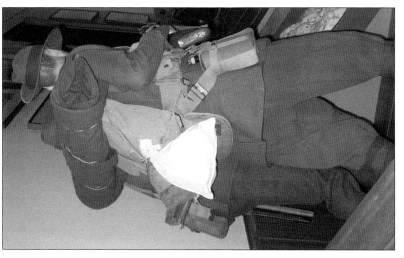

Figure 3. 11th Battalion figures, Australian War Memorial, old (left) and new (centre and right). The figures are intended to represent a battalion member at the Landing, but in fact show marching order with a few additions, rather than what was worn on 25 April 1915. 11th Battalion accounts do not mention the carrying of firewood. Packs were not attached to the webbing straps (as shown left), but looped over the shoulders (as shown centre and right). As the pack was to be dropped on the beach, there was no point attaching to it anything that might be needed, such as mess tins and rations (as shown left, centre and right). Even within the battalion there is variation as to the manner of carrying of equipment, but many men carried haversacks as per battle order, rather than marching, but perched atop packs. Water proof sheets were more likely to be folded beneath the flap of the pack, sandbags rolled, two ration sbags carried rather than one, and a cloth bandolier added. (Photographs by J.P. Hurst, n.d., author's collection)

rapid jettisoning of equipment if necessary.[138] Photographs and men's accounts reveal that everything to be carried into battle – mess tins, sandbags, ration bags, haversacks – was attached to the belt equipment, not the pack, as generally incorrectly depicted.[139] The men were expected to recover their packs later, "if we lived,"[140] but few saw them again.

Pre-landing 11th Battalion photographs reveal other variations. In the 11th Battalion, most of the haversacks were attached to the braces, as normally done for battle, but in this case were balanced atop packs. This would have proved less hindrance than marching order in the crowded boats[141] and enabled an instant transition to battle order once the pack was dropped. Pockets and packs were full and bulging, the latter with a waterproof (oil) sheet folded under the flap. Two to three sand bags appear to be rolled and attached to the belt below the pack, as described in letters and diaries, so that they too could be carried forward. The 11th Battalion do not appear to have carried firewood as often popularly depicted (Figure 3), though Mofflin noted that when the "WA company of the 12th came aboard," they did.[142] Roy Thompson notes that his platoon of the second wave also carried boxed small arms ammunition (SAA), two water bags, wire cutters, bundles of entrenching tools, and bill hooks,[143] for chopping "away barbed wire."[144]

The men of the covering force, who were expected to jump ashore under fire and thrust up the ranges for their objectives, were so heavily laden that Louch recalled "we looked more like camels than soldiers and were only just mobile."[145] Mofflin "could hardly lift the gear … with one hand."[146] Even the battalion's command would later record that "It was a mistake to land with packs."[147] The reason for taking all this gear ashore, seems to have been simply to save the division the inconvenience of landing it later. The weight of this load was increased when it and uniform "became soaked in the sea."[148]

Less information is available on the kit worn by officers. By order, swords were not carried, those belonging to the Commonwealth being returned to stores before the landing.[149] Fox wrote that officers "were equipped exactly the same as ourselves, but only carried a switch."[150] This is confirmed by photographs which appear to show the officers wearing the same tunics as the enlisted men. Some carried a pistol, others appear to have taken a rifle. Bert Facey, who had recently joined the battalion from the 3rd reinforcements, added that "stripes and rank markings" were "removed from uniforms."[151] This is difficult to confirm – photographs taken on 24 April clearly show rank markings (Figures 6, 9),[152] though these may have been removed before morning.

---

138 1st Division War Diary, Appendix 1, 18–19 April 1915.
139 See, for example, Figure 3 and the film *Gallipoli/Gelibolu*, Tolga Örnek, 2005.
140 Goodlet, manuscript, p.7.
141 Than wearing them on the hip, which was usually done when the pack was worn.
142 Mofflin, letter, 20 October 1915, p.10.
143 R. Thompson, notebook, Papers 1914–1915, private collection, Geraldton.
144 Goodlet, manuscript, pp.6–7.
145 Louch, manuscript, p.14.
146 Mofflin, letter, 20 October 1915, p.10.
147 Johnston or Peck, Official History, 1914–18 War: Records of C.E.W. Bean, Official Historian, Australian War Memorial, AWM38 3DRL 606 item 25, pp.7–10.
148 Anon. MS account of the landing by Leane's observer, an unidentified member of C Company, Ellam-Innes Collection, Perth.
149 D.A. Wilson, "Morphettville to ANZAC", Australian Infantry, Jan–June 1981 p.24; Bean, *Official History*, Volume I (1921 and 1941), p.291.
150 Fox, "I Was There", p.8.
151 Facey, *A Fortunate Life*, p.253.
152 J03299, Australian War Memorial and Ashmead-Bartlett's photographs.

Orders

On 22 April Hearder was "At last … given war maps of Gallipoli … We … gathered with maps, and note books" for an officers' meeting at 8:00 p.m. and were "given the localities of Battery after Battery, Redoubt [after] Redoubt, miles of trenches, emplacements, entanglements, machine guns … told for the first time where we were landing … the Brigade had been chosen for the great HONOR of being the first to land … It looked impossible."[153] This briefing was probably held in response to MacLagan's Operation Order No. 1, issued on 21 April.[154]

The covering force consisted of "fighting troops" of the 9th, 10th, 11th and 12th Battalions; the "Bearer subdivision of 3rd Field Ambulance" and the 1st Brigade's 1st Field Company, all "less … horses and vehicles."[155] Their role was to "cover the landing of the Army Corps" at Z beach (Map 1) "by seizing the ridge extending from square 212 l to square 238 V" on "Reference Map: Gallipoli Peninsula 1/40000" (Map 2). Curiously, the 1st Division's instructions to MacLagan stipulate "212 i" rather than "212 l"[156] – possibly a mistake in the landing orders. The 11th Battalion "plus Engineer Demolition Party" were to take the "South Western edge of spur 400 in Sq 224 M and N" as its first objective and, by advancing along Second Ridge from Brighton Beach,[157] the "feature extending from Sq 224 F 9 – to Sq 225 A 1 thence to Sq 237 Z 8" as its second.[158] The second objective was the upper junction of Third Ridge with the main range between Chunuk Bair and Battleship Hill,[159] and the inland slope of Battleship Hill. It is curious that this objective is not continuous, being split by the upper reaches of Legge Valley; nor does it include brigade objective "238 V", the inland slope of Chunuk Bair.

Bean recorded MacLagan's concern about the length of the front his brigade was expected to hold,[160] and Belford added that as MacLagan and Bridges parted "before the attack," MacLagan quipped "if we find the Turks holding those ridges in any strength, I honestly don't think you'll see the 3rd Brigade again."[161] Bean described the plan thus: "The formal operation orders … of which the wording was perfect, informed" Lieutenant-General W.R. Birdwood[162] that the covering force was to land "between Gaba Tepe and … Fisherman's Hut … to seize and hold … the lower crests and southern spurs of Hill 971." From here this force would guard the northern flank, while the "main body of the corps" seized "the inland spur of Hill 971" and "Mal Tepe." "Subject to these … instructions, the planning … was left entirely" to Birdwood, Rear-Admiral C.F. Thursby and their Staffs.[163] These plans have "a curiously vague quality,"[164] though they were supported by numerous briefings and we cannot know all that those on the ships were told.

Bean continues that Hamilton "suggested" Birdwood "at least" occupy the "arrowhead of ridges" around Chunuk Bair, Battleship Hill "and their spurs running to the sea on either flank," creating "a strong covering position, and Hamilton left it to Birdwood's discretion whether" or not to seize "the actual summit of 971." Birdwood thought "storming Mal Tepe" may be "difficult" and decided "that his first task" was to seize "971 and its seaward spurs," presumably to establish a covering position which

153 Hearder, manuscript 3DRL 3959, p.9.
154 Operation Order No 1, Colonel E.G. Sinclair-MacLagan, 21 April 1915, 3rd Brigade War Diary.
155 1st Division Unit War Diary, Appendix 1, 18, 19 April 1915.
156 *Ibid.*
157 Bean, *Official History*, Volume I (1921 and 1941), opposite p.226.
158 MacLagan, Operation Order No. 1.
159 Bean describes the 11th Battalion's objectives as "Scrubby Knoll" and Battleship Hill. Bean, *Official History*, Volume I (1921 and 1941), p.228.
160 Bean, 3DRL 606, item 25.
161 Belford, *Legs Eleven*, p.63.
162 Lieutenant-General Willian Riddell Birdwood, General Officer Commanding (GOC), Australian and New Zealand Army Corps.
163 Bean, *Official History*, Volume I (1921 and 1941), pp.220–221.
164 T. Travers, *Gallipoli 1915* (Stroud: Tempus Publishing, 2001), p.66.

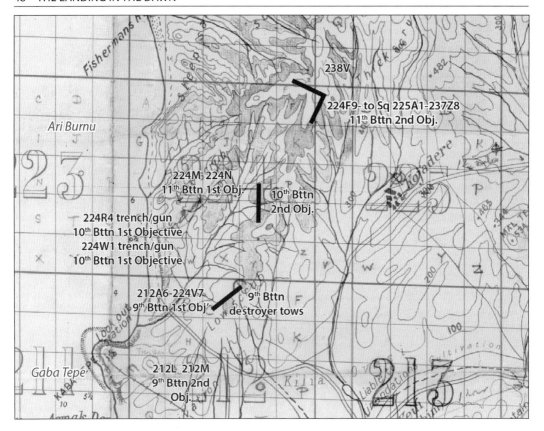

Map 2. 3rd Brigade objectives overlaid onto photograph of map 'Gallipoli 1:40,000 Sheet 2', which was the map issued to officers for the Landing. Each lettered square (a b c d e, etc.) could be subdivided into nine, numbered: 1, 2, 3 (top row); 4, 5, 6 (middle row); 7, 8, 9 (bottom row). (RC02298, Australian War Memorial)

held the crest of the main range. This would create a good foothold for the division. Concerned by the perceived presence of three Turkish field batteries, two inland and one "said to be behind the neck of land connecting Gaba Tepe with the main ridge," Birdwood felt that the first troops ashore should rush them and "instructed General Bridges that the covering brigade should seize and occupy the ridge from Gaba Tepe towards Chunuk Bair. The rest of the Australian Division … would secure the main ridge to the north … and attend to the left flank." Bridges then issued orders for the "main part" of the 3rd Brigade "to push inland, rushing the batteries … to the long spur which was its objective … The northern parties of the 3rd Brigade were to reach and hold Battleship Hill," while the remainder were to seize "knolls on the ridge from Scrubby Knoll to Gaba Tepe."[165] Two companies of the 9th Battalion were to rush the battery behind Gaba Tepe.[166] To add to this confused picture, Birdwood added that, should Turkish artillery fire too heavily on the beach, "I shall move the whole landing" towards Fisherman's Hut, "but the country there is so very difficult and broken that it is impossible to attempt a landing there while it is dark."[167]

Bean's overview reveals, though does not state, that the plans were being altered at each level of command until the 3rd Brigade's role became vaguely split into two mutually exclusive parts. Where

165 *Ibid.*, pp.225–226.
166 *Ibid.*, p.226.
167 *Ibid.*, pp.229–230.

now lay the force's priority – Battleship Hill on the left or the ridge in the vicinity of Scrubby Knoll on the right?

Robin Prior has recently elaborated on significant detail missing from Bean's account. He adds that Birdwood, concerned about being attacked from "both north and south," changed the plan, ordering that Gun (Third) Ridge "be taken as a first priority for the covering force. Only when Gun Ridge was secure should his force turn its attention to the heights of Sari Bair to the north."[168] This interpretation is based on Birdwood's instructions of 18 April, the day after his Operation Order No. 1,[169] in which the preceding paragraph reiterates the importance of the original objectives. Birdwood's concerns about the right had "extended" the length of the "objective by some 1,500 yards." Prior continues that "there is no evidence to suggest that Birdwood discussed the changes with" Hamilton and Braithwaite (Hamilton's Chief of Staff) nor any "evidence that they grasped the implications if he did."[170] Williams also noted a deterioration of orders at successive levels of command, interpreting it as a progression in aim from attack to defence.[171] Bean may have thought the wording of Birdwood's orders was "perfect," but the "objectives were lamentably unclear."[172] This confusion about priorities goes a long way to understanding MacLagan's unexplained decisions and the fate of various 11th Battalion, and other, parties on 25 April.

Johnston relayed his orders to his battalion, adding that the "first line" would be commanded by Roberts with "A Company on the right … C Company on the left." The "MG Section, B and D Companies and the engineer demolition party will form the second line," though some of the 1st Field Company actually landed with the first line.[173] The 9th Battalion were "to attack on the right; the 10th Battalion in the centre" and the 11th Battalion on the left. The "7th Indian Mountain Artillery Brigade" would support the attack from "spur 400 square 224 m."[174]

The first wave of 1,500 infantry, with some HQ and Engineer details, landed from 36 boats:

A and C Companies, 11th Battalion, from HMS *London*
B and C Companies, 10th Battalion, from HMS *Prince of Wales*
A and B Companies, 9th Battalion, from HMS *Queen*[175]

The boats were to be towed inshore by steam-powered pinnaces, after which they would row themselves to the beaches.

The second "line", of about 2,500 men, "included the remaining halves of the 9th, 10th, and 11th Battalions, the 12th Battalion (the brigade reserve)," 3rd Field Ambulance[176] and some of the 1st Field Company.[177] Their transports would "rendezvous off the peninsula" and transfer the troops to seven destroyers which, with decks crowded and empty boats alongside, would "follow the first wave until they were as close to the shore as safety allowed." The troops would then row themselves ashore

---

168 R. Prior, Gallipoli, *The End of the Myth* (Sydney, NSW: University of New South Wales Press, 2009), pp.110–111. Based on "General Birdwood's Instructions to G.O.C. 1st Australian Division" 18/4/15, and Aspinall-Oglander, *Gallipoli Maps and Appendices VI*, Appendix 15, pp.42, 43.

169 Birdwood, "Operation Order No 1", 17 April 1915, *Gallipoli Maps and Appendices VI*, Appendix 14, pp.37–41.

170 Prior, *Gallipoli, The End of the Myth*, pp.110–111. Based on Birdwood, "Operation Order No 1" 17/4/15, *Gallipoli Maps and Appendices VI*, Appendix 14, pp.37–41.

171 Williams, *The Battle of Anzac Ridge*, p.38.

172 Prior, *Gallipoli, The End of the Myth*, p.86.

173 1st Field Company Unit War Diary, AWM4-14-20-8, 24 April 1915.

174 3rd Brigade War Diary, Appendix 3, copy number two, Operation Order No. 1 by Lieutenant-Colonel J. Lyon Johnston, probably 24 April 1915.

175 Hurst, *Game to the Last*, p.38.

176 Bean, *Official History*, Volume I (1921 and 1941), p.228.

177 R.R. McNicholl, *The Royal Australian Engineers, 1902–1919*, pp.26–27.

or be picked up by pinnaces returning from the first wave. The "remainder of the 1st Division, and in turn the New Zealand and Australian Division"[178] would follow.

At battalion level, the 11th Battalion's surviving written orders are largely administrative, detailing where packs were to be dropped and who was to guard them. Each company was to carry two boxes of ammunition inland and leave four on the beach. "All ranks" were "reminded of the importance of conserving ammunition." Reserve ammunition "for MGS [machine gun section] will be carried by" pioneers, presumably of the 1st Field Company, who would also act as their escort. The Medical Officer was to establish a dressing station and report its position. In addition to the ordinary semaphore flags, "Indicating flags for artillery" were to be carried to signal "ships to cease fire" if they shelled their own. Tools would be "carried forward by B and D Companies."[179]

Special Instructions from 3rd Brigade added that rifles were not to be loaded, nor magazines charged, until ashore; entrenching tools were to be carried as far forward as possible; water bottles and water bags were to be filled; no rifle fire "until broad daylight. The bayonet only is to be used"; the "strictest maintenance of discipline as for night operations is essential"; the "inshore advance towards the main objective is to be conducted as rapidly as possible"; and "no bugle calls" were to be sounded.[180]

At platoon level, this was relayed to Thompson's 13 Platoon of the second wave as:

1.   2 men to be detailed to carry 1 box of SAA…
2.   2 water bags per platoon…
3.   Snipers [sic] names wanted.
4.   Names of men carrying wire cutters. One reserve man. Bill hooks to be carried by buglers.
5.   No. 14 and 15 platoons take 7 bundles of entrenching tools
6.   Boat crews to be detailed, 7 men.[181]

In the boats, rifles were to be "carried in the hand and not slung," "no one is to stand up," equipment was to be loosened. "On arrival at the beach all troops are to remain seated" until ordered to land.[182] Sergeants were to ensure "every man has his pay book and identity disc. On landing, officers or NCO in charge of boats, report to OC beach party … On reaching beach, men lay down and fix bayonets."[183] Thompson recorded a platoon roll, allocation of tasks and loads to men and of men to boats. His lists are liberally sprinkled with the names of those with whom he had left Geraldton more than eight months before.

Mofflin recounted the relayed orders:

No 1 boat would go on the right and no 6 on the left … hop out quietly, wade ashore … on the left form section and that would bring us into one straight line … lie down. Then wait for the whispered orders … to charge magazines, fix bayonets, drop packs and advance … everything in silence, take a machine gun and the first trenches with the bayonet … be in a certain position six miles inland by 9 a.m.[184]

S.M. Wood[185] added that "we must stay there and hang on to whatever we found."[186]

178 Hurst, *Game to the Last*, p.38.
179 3rd Brigade War Diary, Operation Order No. 1 by Lieutenant-Colonel J. Lyon Johnston, probably 24 April 1915.
180 Captain A.M. Ross, Special Instructions, Appendix A of 3rd Brigade War Diary, Operation Order No. 1, Colonel E.G. Sinclair-MacLagan, 21 April 1915.
181 Thompson, notebook.
182 1st Division War Diary, Appendix 1, 18–19 April 1915.
183 Thompson, notebook.
184 Mofflin, letter, 20 October 1915, p.12.
185 248 Private (at embarkation) Sim McGregor Wood, A Company, 30, civil servant, born Scotland. Wood had previously served in the military forces in Scotland and in the Calcutta Rifles.
186 S.M. Wood to J.S. Seddon, letter, 3 May 1915, collection of E. Rose, Toodyay.

Since that morning over a 100 years ago, sources have been sprinkled with contradictions about whether rifles were supposed to be unloaded and whether men who fired during the assault were disobeying orders. Some of the confusion originated with the orders themselves. The 1st Division orders state that "in the boats … rifles are not to be loaded; magazines will be charged and cut offs closed."[187] This meant that rifle magazines were loaded, but closed cut offs ensured no round could be chambered. In 3rd Brigade orders this appears as "Rifles are not to be loaded, nor are magazines to be charged until troops have landed … No rifle fire … until broad daylight."[188] This suggests that the 3rd Brigade, whose landing and survival relied on surprise, was determined to ensure silence by keeping rifles and ammunition separate. The closed cut-offs and empty chambers of later waves may have been more for reasons of safety than surprise.

MacLagan added that "Landing on an enemy coast in the face of opposition" was a "most difficult operation." Selection "by the Divisional Commander as the covering force" was "a high honour … We must be successful at any cost … the covering position" must be gained "as rapidly as possible" and "held … even to the last man … there is no going back … 'Forward' is the word … 'Hang on' is what we have to do." He urged his men to reorganise whenever possible, preferably "under cover."

> Once ashore don't be caught without a charger in the magazine. Look after each cartridge as if it were a ten pound note … Good fire orders, direction, control and discipline will make the enemy respect your powers and give us all an easier task in the long run … Don't show yourselves over the skyline …We must expect to be shelled … we must "stick it."

Ominously, he added that they were "only a very small piece on the board," and:

> [some] pieces have often to be sacrificed to win the game … You have a very good reputation … and now we have a chance of making history for Australia and a name for the 3rd Brigade that will live in history. I have absolute faith in you and believe few, if any, finer brigades have ever been put to the test.[189]

Messages from Hamilton[190] and Birdwood were also read to the troops, the latter stressing: "Concealment … Covering fire … Control of fire and … your men … Communications."[191]

The 11th Battalion were in little doubt of the dangers involved in the operation and that heavy casualties would probably accompany success, "but if we made a mess of it?", wrote W.B. Murray[192] to his parents. The "Navy … couldn't guarantee to take us off again … you know what that means."[193] Peck wrote of a "simmering excitement … raised to boiling pitch." When the colonel broke the news to his battalion that the time had come, "How they yelled. The Britishers on neighbouring boats lined the rails, attracted by the cooees, kookaburra calls and kindred noises."[194]

The battalion historian wrote, with hindsight, that the plan was "simply asking the impossible of any troops."[195] Certainly the troops appreciated the enormity of their task, but it seems to have hardened their resolve more than dishearten them. W.G. Hastings[196] wrote that "All hearts … beat

---

187 1st Division War Diary, Appendix 1, 18–19 April 1915.
188 Ross, Special instructions, Appendix A, Operation Order No 1, 3rd Brigade War Diary.
189 Belford, *Legs Eleven*, pp.59–60.
190 *Ibid.*, pp.63–64.
191 Newton, *The Story of the Twelfth*, p.59.
192 77 Private (at embarkation) William Brinley Murray, A Company, 26 at enlistment, steward, of Cannington, born Cumberland, England. Murray had served in the 1st Royal Scots and the Border Regiment.
193 W.B. Murray, letter to parents, 16 May 1915, Ellam-Innes Collection, Perth.
194 Peck, letter to wife, n.d.
195 Belford, *Legs Eleven*, p.62.
196 182 Lance Corporal William George Hastings, A Company, 37 at enlistment, bank official, born "at sea" near Hong Kong, of New South Wales.

high with pride." The "danger" of the task "was the measure of honour, its perils but added to our zest."[197] Facey later confessed to being "scared stiff," but "eager to be on our way."[198]

Les Whiting[199] recalled that after Johnston's address there was "some banter about cold feet, stomach aches, etc." "Tweedie", possibly G.H. Read,[200] one of three men with whom Whiting enlisted from the gold mining town of Day Dawn, declared that:

"lords, dukes, and other high-bred people would fight better … than the common folks." He quoted Julius Caesar, Richard the Lion Heart, and other noted stoushers … My old mate, "Nick," championed the cause of the commoner, and settled the argument to his satisfaction by landing "Tweedie" a solid punch on the jaw, which laid him out on the deck … they stripped for action … Nick won, so I suppose the cause of the commoner was upheld.[201]

As a company Roll Book survives for this company, and states that Read was in hospital at the time of the Landing, it may be that he missed the battle as a consequence of this fight.[202] The other two men who enlisted with Whiting were W.H. Pain[203] and C.H. "Nick" Carter.[204]

Glad That The Time Had Finally Come

Finally, on Saturday 24 April, came the order: "Parade on the boat deck in full marching order!" "'Medcalf!', said Harvey",[205] as heavy web equipment was hauled on and "the mess decks left for the last time", "the business at last!"[206] The men were paraded and ammunition issued. Despite the ominous significance of being issued with live, ball ammunition before battle, no-one noted being downhearted. Belford recorded that as "Croly was giving his company a look over" before the trans-shipping, "he spied" "Paddy Reid with a golf cap on his head."[207] "After looking Reid up and down, Croly said: 'Everything seems all right, Reid. But where's your golf bag?'"[208] Reid's golf cap may have been a parody of the British service caps as he may not have been issued one – he had been released from prison by OC 3rd Brigade the previous day, to allow him to fight with his battalion.[209]

They "were happy and enthusiastic fellows who … streamed down the sides" of the transport onto the destroyers,[210] with a "lot of good natured chaffing, goodbyes, and promises to meet in Constantinople, or in Hell."[211] The destroyers delivered A and C companies to HMS *London* (Figures 4–10).[212] The men were "allotted our deck space," allowed "the run of the ship"[213] (Figure 10) and given a midday

197 W.G. Hastings, letter, 10 June 1915, unidentified newspaper, private collection.
198 Facey, *A Fortunate Life*, p.254.
199 1432 Private Leslie Whiting, B Company, 26 at enlistment, miner, born Victoria.
200 1402 Private (at embarkation) George Henry "Harry" Read, B Company, 23 at enlistment, labourer/team driver, born New South Wales.
201 L. Whiting, "'Fish Fifty-First' to 'Non-Com', 'Blood Will Tell!'", unidentified newspaper, private collection.
202 Unit roll books, 1914–1918 War, AWM 9.
203 1398 Private William Henry Pain, 25 (at enlistment), miner, of Day Dawn, born Essex England. Pain had previously served with the Territorials in England.
204 1324 Private (at embarkation) Charles Henry "Nick" Carter, B Company, 24 at enlistment, labourer/teamster, born Hobart.
205 196 Private (at embarkation) Cecil Leonard Harvey, 24 at enlistment, commercial traveller, born Kent, England.
206 Medcalf, manuscript, p.61.
207 Belford, *Legs Eleven*, p.64.
208 *Ibid*. Anomalies with this story are that Croly's D Company was not trans-shipping at the time, and Reid belonged to A Company.
209 B2455, Reid.
210 Hastings, letter, 10 June 1915.
211 Goodlet, manuscript, p.6.
212 Fox, "I Was There", p.6; J.M. Aitken, letter to mother/diary, 1DRL item 13, Folder 1, Australian War Memorial, p.17.
213 G.F.S. Combs, manuscript, Ellam-Innes Collection, Perth.

Figure 4

Figure 5

Figure 6

Figure 7

Figure 8

Figure 9

Figure 10

Figure 4. 11th Battalion troops aboard River class destroyer HMS *Chelmer*. This probably shows the transfer of A Company to HMS *London* on 24 April. (Photographer unknown, P02934.021, Australian War Memorial)

Figure 5. 11th Battalion troops aboard the destroyer HMS *Usk*. This was probably taken during transshipping to London on 24 April. These two photographs provide an insight into the cramped and uncomfortable journey to the peninsula of B and D companies the following morning, although by then they had been joined by two platoons of the 12th Battalion, increasing their numbers by roughly 50%. (Photographer unknown, P02934.022, Australian War Memorial)

Figure 6. Ladder being lowered from HMS *London* to enable heavily laden 11th Battalion troops to come aboard from HMS *Usk*. (Photographer unknown, P02934.020, Australian War Memorial)

Figure 7. 11th Battalion troops, probably C Company, aboard HMS *London* after embarking from the destroyer in the background. The different equipment of the officer and man in slouch hat on the left may indicate that they are members of the 1st Field Company, Engineers. (Photographer unknown, P02934_019, Australian War Memorial)

Figure 8. 11th Battalion troops, probably of A Company aboard HMS *London*. Naval officers and the ship's chaplain are observing. (Photograph by E. Ashmead-Bartlett, Ashmead-Bartlett Papers, ICS 84 A/11/1-4 and ICS84/D, Senate House Library, University of London)

Figure 9. 11th Battalion aboard HMS *London*. The troops on the left are probably of C Company, those on the right of A Company. The single gun is an improvised anti-aircraft gun, attached to a capstan. The narrow, diagonal strip across the chest of the man second from right may represent one of the elusive cloth bandoliers. Most men either have their webbing braces over their shoulder straps or the latter are unbuttoned, in case of a boat being sunk. Many appear to anticipate a cold night, wearing their issue cardigans beneath tunics. (Photograph by E. Ashmead-Bartlett, Ashmead-Bartlett Papers, ICS 84 A/11/1-4 and ICS84/D, Senate House Library, University of London)

Figure 10. HMS *London*, afternoon of 24 April 1915, soon after leaving Mudros en route for the Dardanelles. (Photograph by Clive De Mole, J03301, Australian War Memorial)

meal, recalled by G.F.S. Combs[214] as "the best … since I left home … soup, roast meat or meat pie and vegetables … pudding, tin fruit with tea, coffee or cocoa."[215] Officers and men were soon overwhelmed by the hospitality of the Navy – "by Jove they did us well. The Tars fed us like fighting cocks and treated us like lords."[216] Eastcott wrote that "We were not allowed to pay for anything"[217] and W.A.C. Guy[218] that the sailors' "fellowship and kindness" would remain among his "pleasantest recollections until the end of my life."[219] Murray described the "Blue jackets" as "a jolly lot of fellows" who "did every thing in their power to make us comfortable"[220] and Medical Officer "Doc" Brennan added: "If you ever hear anyone say anything derogatory about the Navy … just plug him, and explain it's from me … the finest lot of men I have ever met."[221]

The 1st and 2nd Brigades had earlier left Mudros harbour and anchored on the other side of the island.[222] That afternoon, in brilliant sunshine and "amid a storm of cheering,"[223] the covering force, the Australian and New Zealand Army Corps' spearhead, left harbour and sailed for the enemy coast.[224] Fifteen-year-old Midshipman Eric Bush, aboard *Bacchante*, described "Our flagship … *Queen*," leading "us out," her band playing "Fall in and Follow Me." *Triumph*, *Prince of Wales*, *Bacchante* and *London* followed. The "picked troops who will be the first to land … are all on deck cheering and shouting slogans."[225] "What a glorious sight! …the cheering was deafening and to the plaudits of all the other troops – Australian, French and British – the 3rd Brigade set forth on its … entry into the Great War."[226]

Ships lining the route, some with hammocks lashed to bridges for "protection from shell splinters and bullets,"[227] dipped their flags in salute, their sailors standing at attention. Then they cheered until Goodlet "began to think we really must be heroes."[228] The soldiers replied, cheering themselves hoarse.[229] Ashmead-Bartlett, aboard *London*, later described it as "the most majestic and inspiring spectacle I have ever seen, but withal there was an atmosphere of tragedy. Many, now full of life and hope and joy, will never see another sun sink to rest. The weather", he continued, "was beautifully fine."[230]

Barnes wrote of the "beautiful sight and one I'll never forget … will be fighting before too long." In case he didn't live to post his diary home he added, "Please forward to Mrs W Barnes Johnson St Guildford WA" and signed, "Your affectionate son Charlie. Am in fine form and absolutely well so don't worry."[231]

At sea at 4:00 p.m. a "short but impressive"[232] church service was held aboard *London*. Ashmead-Bartlett recalled that this was begun by "Captain Armstrong" reading "Admiral de Robeck's proclamation wishing success to all ranks. His place was then taken by the ship's chaplain."[233] Robert Brodribb[234] felt he would "never forget" that service. "We marched out to … the naval band."[235]

214 525 Corporal George Fred Sutton Combs, C Company, 21 at enlistment, railway employee, of Northam, born Mildura.
215 Combs, manuscript.
216 Wood, letter, 3 May 1915.
217 Eastcott, manuscript, p.4.
218 41 Lance Corporal William Alexander Charles Guy, A Company, 28 at embarkation, civil servant and teacher, born Isle of Wight.
219 W.A.C. Guy to A.A. ("Gus") Tanner, 10 May 1915, MsC 254 Library, University of Calgary.
220 Murray, letter, 16 May 1915.
221 Brennan, letter, 1915, Army Museum of Western Australia.
222 Bean, *Official History*, Volume I (1921 and 1941), p.243.
223 Fox, "I Was There", p.7.
224 Fox, cited Hurst, *Game to the Last*, p.36.
225 E.W. Bush, "Anzac Remembered", *The Gallipolean, the Journal of the Gallipoli Association*, Number 7, Christmas 1971, p.26.
226 Belford, *Legs Eleven*, pp.64–65.
227 Bush, "Anzac Remembered", p.26.
228 Goodlet, manuscript, p.7.
229 Mofflin, letter, 20 October 1915, p.11.
230 E. Ashmead-Bartlett, *The Uncensored Dardanelles* (London: Hutchinson and Co., 1928), p.44.
231 Barnes, diary, 22–23 April 1915.
232 Aitken, letter/diary, p.17.
233 Ashmead-Bartlett, *The Uncensored Dardanelles*, pp.44, 45.
234 636 Private Robert Hebden Brodribb, 30, of Fimiston, born Ararat.
235 R.H. Brodribb to Mr T.J. Callery. 17 July 1915, *Kalgoorlie Miner*, 23 August 1915.

Hastings described that "dramatic scene and hour … Those serried ranks of fighting men" drawn up on the quarterdeck, sailors on one side, soldiers the other, "standing bareheaded in worship, and joining in prayers so eloquent of the grim task before us" (Figure 11).[236] *London* Midshipman C.H. Drage also found it "an impressive scene. After nearly nine months of active service one can realise that this show is going to be no picnic."[237] The ship's chaplain "commended the adventure and the participants to the care of heaven."[238] "We are going on a tough job," he continued, as the sea slipped astern and the convoy cruised towards the enemy coast. "Some will not return. With God's help we'll win. If we pass in, it's a good, clean man's death … God bless you."[239] Peck recalled that at about five minutes it was "the shortest" but "most impressive" service he had attended.[240]

The men were dismissed. They continued to explore the ship and enjoy the Navy's hospitality. Despite the approaching battle, the chroniclers of shipboard life, the wide-eyed tourists of Egypt, were yet nourishing themselves on the details and magnitude of the world. Or perhaps the imminence of the fight and possible death added an urgency to these hours – Medcalf thought that day "one of the most interesting in the lives of the boys,"[241] and J.R.T. Keast[242] that they "thoroughly enjoyed ourselves … none of us seemed to realise that in a few hours we would be under fire."[243] Either way, the men's observations and engagement in the moment suggest an absence of anxiety. They "were living in the eleventh hour of an adventure, rivalling … all the history books."[244] The "bright, sunny hours of the afternoon were spent in what almost appeared to be a pleasure cruise on the blue Mediterranean"[245] (Figure 10). Time was killed playing cards, and "there was … a good impromptu concert."[246]

Aboard *Suffolk*, a concert was also suggested. It "was going well until some crack-brain sang 'Just before the battle, Mother'. That was the end of the concert."[247] Goodlet described nerves "strained to breaking point" and Robbo's efforts at ensuring "a keen edge on his bayonet" causing "quite a laugh, but he was not satisfied until he had finished it off with an oil stone." Sergeants were issued with "dull black" to reduce the shine of cold steel. Waiting in the "blood thirsty queue" at the grindstone, Goodlet felt "sick and scared … afraid I would be a coward" when tested:

> I marvelled [*sic*] at the way the diggers chaffed each other and joked about their prospects … Robbo noticed I was not looking too good, so he took me away … for a quiet talk. I told him I was scared, but he only laughed. "You're not scared, son, that's only stage fright. They are all the same … but when the curtain goes up, you will wonder why you were nervous at all. Stick with me, 'Mulga' … and into them!" I felt a lot better … went about packing my gear and filling my pouches with bullets.[248]

Many wrote a last letter home. Private Thomas Davis[249] wrote on his birthday, 24 April: "Just a line to … assure the people of the west that their boys are splendid … happy and light-hearted as schoolboys … They are all 'fair dinkum' … I can't write to all my pals. Say I wish to be remembered kindly to them all."[250] Scott found the sailors "at a loss to understand our fellows' free and easy spirit

236 Hastings, letter, 10 June 1915.
237 C.H. Drage, diary, 24 April 1915, Vol. I CHD/1, Imperial War Museum, p.143.
238 Medcalf, manuscript, p.62.
239 Peck, letter to wife, n.d.
240 *Ibid.*
241 Medcalf, manuscript, p.61.
242 967 Private (at embarkation) John Richard Trelawney Keast, A Company, 23 at embarkation, carpenter, born Sydney.
243 Keast, diary, 24/25 April 1915.
244 Medcalf, manuscript, p.62.
245 Hastings, letter, 10 June 1915.
246 Fox, "I Was There", p.7.
247 Goodlet, manuscript, p.8.
248 *Ibid.*, pp.5–6.
249 648 Private (at embarkation) Thomas Davis, HQ Company and 20 at embarkation, miner, of Kalgoorlie.
250 T. Davis, 24 April 1915, letter *Sunday Times*, 25 July 1915.

Figure 11. Bareheaded in worship: Divine service aboard HMS *London*, 24 April 1915, navy on the left, army the right. Roberts, facing camera, and Johnston both appear to be visible. (Photographer unknown, author's collection)

… prepared for anything. We were all fit, brown and trained to the hour, and it would have done WA people good to see the improvement."[251]

Storeman J. E. Carrington[252] should have remained behind, but had "worked it" to land with his company, "as a base job was no good to me … if I did not go on and have a bit of a scrap I would never be satisfied." On 24 April, with the landing now imminent, he wrote home, "I guess that a good many of the 11th Battalion have seen the sun rise for the last time."[253] Somewhere aboard *Suffolk*, Louch "made a last-minute will" for his friend Charlie Puckle,[254] then wrote to his mother. Landing first was:

> Very honourable – but … I have no doubt that … Constantinople [will] fall again, and it will be rather fine to be there. It is splendid to see how quietly everyone is taking things. In a few hours we shall be right in the thick of things, yet everybody is cheerful … playing cards … singing ragtime … writing – you would think there was no war within miles … but now there seems little to say.[255]

Bartlett recorded the men aboard *London* being provided a hot evening meal on the mess deck and enjoying a "smoke" before turning in for the night.[256] At "At seven o'clock" the Australian officers were "entertained as our guests" in *London's* wardroom. "Everyone feigned an unnatural cheerfulness, the wine passed round, not a word was said of what the morrow might bring forth, yet over the party there seemed to hover the dread angel of death."[257] Commander C.C. Dix recalled dinner that night as "a rather quiet feast", as the Navy's "guests had a good deal to think about – but was enlivened at the end by an excellent speech from the paymaster, who voiced our good wishes and complete confidence in the Army."[258]

As night settled over the blacked-out ships, the troops "made ourselves as comfortable as possible and composed ourselves to sleep."[259] *London* was "crowded but the officers and crew all insisted we

---

251 Scott, letter, n.d.
252 412 Private James Edward Carrington, B Company, 33, fitter and blacksmith, of Fremantle, born Bendigo.
253 Belford, *Legs Eleven*, p.66.
254 818 Charles Edward Murray Puckle, 27 at enlistment, farmer of Morawa, WA, formerly of Victoria. Puckle's B2455 records his promotion to corporal on 5 May 1915; Thompson's notes show him to have been a corporal at the Landing.
255 Louch, manuscript, p.14.
256 Bartlett, *Uncensored Dardanelles*, p.45.
257 *Ibid.*
258 C.C. Dix, Private Papers, 6440, Imperial War Museum, p.7.
259 Fox, "I Was There", p.7.

have … their quarters."[260] Ashmead-Bartlett gave his bed to Peck,[261] then retired to snatch "some sleep in the wardroom chairs,"[262] as did naval officers who had surrendered their cabins to the Australians. The "wise sought what sleep they could snare," but Hastings found that the "brilliant moonlight, and the fatefulness of the hour conspired to keep us wakeful."[263] "Things will be bloody tomorrow!" whimsied Harvey to Medcalf.[264]

Aboard *Suffolk* "Brothers and pals drifted off to different parts of the darkened ship to have perhaps their last talk together. Horny hands were clapped and hearts lain bare as the ship, in total darkness, ploughed her way towards the greatest tragedy of the War."[265] Goodlet and Robbo "talked of many things and made plans of what we should do after the war … We decided to go to New Guinea. Robbo had been there … and was sure we could find gold." Eventually Goodlet asked the veteran what he thought of their chances. "Robbo peered at me in the darkness as if he were trying to read my very soul." If surprise was achieved, he surmised, they "may do all right" [*sic*], otherwise, perhaps referring to being caught in their boats on open water, "'we haven't a chance'. Then, as if regretting what he had said, he laughed and shook me roughly."[266]

Facey managed some sleep that night.[267] A.J. "Darkie" (or "Darky") Williams,[268] rope quoits champion of the AIF in Egypt, had sailed to war once before – on that occasion his boat arrived in Cape Town Harbour just as peace was declared. Now, with the 3rd Brigade's landing imminent, he confided to some of his mates that "I have a presentiment I will not see any more of this war than I did of the South African War."[269]

Rifles had been cleaned and oiled, bayonets sharpened, ammunition, water and rations issued. Drill had been learned, field training carried out and disembarkation practised. Decks had been marked in white to help sections and platoons to form up; equipment was left where it could be found in the dark, wills and last letters written. The waiting – to sail from Australia's shores, to leave Egypt, to end their ship-bound weeks in Mudros Harbour, to join the war – was almost over. It is not surprising that many, aware that, should they sleep, it might well be the "last before" their "everlasting,"[270] found such release difficult.

The troops had not been equipped with weapons that would prove so useful later in the war – Lewis guns, hand bombs or Stokes mortars. Louch would write with hindsight that their training – skirmishing and charging with rifle and bayonet – "was no sort of preparation" for Gallipoli.[271] But hindsight was for the future. The men had worked hard; they believed they were ready. Facey "thought we would tear right through the Turks and keep going to Constantinople."[272] Carrington closed his letter with "If this should happen to be the last, which I hope not, you can take it as a good-bye letter. We are under steam! Hoo roo!"[273] Scott described the trip through "a beautiful moonlight night" as "magnificent."[274]

260 Eastcott, manuscript, p.3.
261 Peck, letter to wife, n.d.
262 Bartlett, *Uncensored Dardanelles*, p.45.
263 Hastings, letter, 10 June 1915.
264 Medcalf, manuscript, p.62.
265 Goodlet, manuscript, p.8.
266 *Ibid.*
267 Facey, *A Fortunate Life*, p.253.
268 496 Private Arthur James Williams, 37, timber hewer, of Kirup, born Victoria. Served with the Australian Commonwealth Horse during the Boer War.
269 Blay, diary, 25 April 1915.
270 Combs, manuscript.
271 Louch, manuscript, p.11.
272 Facey, *A Fortunate Life*, p.254.
273 Belford, *Legs Eleven*, p.66.
274 Scott, letter, n.d.

2

The Last Awakening On This Earth

___

The Other Side of the Divide

In the darkness on the hills and ridges opposite the 3rd Brigade, outposts of the Ottoman 27th Regiment stood waiting. Most of the 27th Regiment's soldiers had been recruited in the local area and were combat veterans defending their villages and towns. Their commander, Lieutenant-Colonel Mehmed Şefik Aker, was a "respected," "uncompromising" officer, a "serious commander with little tolerance for inefficiency."[1] Şefik believed the area where the Australians would land to be "critical terrain,"[2] a belief ultimately "verging on obsession."[3] He believed the enemy would be at their most vulnerable when in their boats and had worked his troops hard to dig platoon, machine gun and reserve positions along the coast; they had built roads to hasten deployment to the beach areas and had rehearsed their response plans. Şefik had ordered that there was to be no retreat from their coastal positions, and if necessary they were to fight to the death to buy time for the reserves to counter-attack.[4]

27th Regiment belonged to the 9th Division of the Fifth Army, the army formed to defend the Dardanelles. In March, Field Marshal Otto Liman von Sanders took command of Fifth Army and overturned the existing defence strategy, deciding to man the coast lightly with "observation and screening posts" and keeping his reserves inland.[5] The logic behind this approach was that spreading forces along the coast would mean that the defence was strong nowhere, and the spear point of a strong attacker might break through anywhere. The alternative was to keep strong reserves in positions from which they could deploy rapidly to deal with any landing once the enemy showed their hand. The other reason for keeping guns and reserves inland was to keep them safe from naval gunfire. Von Sanders believed the landings would most likely take place at Bolayir.

Like Şefik, Lieutenant-Colonel Mustafa Kemal had seen active service and believed the two most likely landing areas were Helles and Gaba Tepe; he too had been working hard to get the units of his 19th Division properly equipped, trained and ready to defend the peninsula. On 19 April Kemal had conducted a training exercise designed to test his division's response to landings at certain points along the coast, and as a result moved his headquarters to the town of Boghali (Bigali), "exactly four miles directly east of Anzac Cove."[6] At the time of the landings the 57th Regiment was camped near Boghali and the 72nd and 77th Regiments near Mal Tepe (Maps 1, 8, 9).

While the troops aboard the invasion fleet bided their time and whiled away the hours of darkness before battle, their opponents ashore were on the march: the two battalions of the 27th Regiment not already on outpost duty on the Gaba Tepe – Fisherman's Hut coast were undertaking a forced march and tactical exercises at Gaba Tepe, in rehearsal for an enemy landing in the area.[7] They returned to their camp near Maidos "exhausted" soon after midnight.[8]

___

1   Uyar, *The Ottoman Defence*, p.62.
2   *Ibid.*, p.66.
3   *Ibid.*, p.68.
4   *Ibid.*, pp.66, 67.
5   *Ibid.*, p.88.
6   Bean, *Gallipoli Mission*, p.131.
7   Şefik, para. 52.
8   *Ibid.*

Standing at the Threshold

The troops aboard *Suffolk* were roused at about 11:00 p.m. Conversations were "cut short by a whispered command to fall in … the engines stopped … the ship began to slow." Goodlet and Robbo "hurriedly assisted each other into our equipment, and then fell in … a destroyer had come up on each side … Ours, the *Usk*, was on the port side."[9] They "climbed down that rope ladder in pitch darkness" and assembled on the destroyer's deck "packed as tightly as we could stand."[10] On the opposite side, Mofflin's platoon boarded *Chelmer*,[11] as did the machine gun section[12] and, by his own account, Tom Louch. The "steel deck was hot and the air very cold, but we sank down under our loads and some managed to sleep."[13]

There are discrepancies between sources as to which company landed from which destroyer. Belford's statement that B Company landed from *Usk* and D from *Chelmer*[14] is confirmed by Bean's Map 11[15] (here Map 6), but 11th Battalion letters and diaries contradict this. B Company's Mofflin, Blay and Clohessy stated they landed from *Chelmer* and D Company's Goodlet from *Usk*. Goodlet thought *Usk* was to *Chelmer*'s left, which is supported by Bean's Maps 10[16] (here Map 4) and 11[17] (here Map 6), but not Map 9[18] (here Map 3). In summary, in contradiction to Belford and Bean, primary sources suggest that B Company landed from *Chelmer* and D from *Usk*. This is confirmed by the location of men after landing and, Louch aside, is not contradicted by primary sources. It appears Louch, who at times quoted the *Official History* in his memoir, transcribed the error from there, as possibly did Belford. If so, it would appear that an error in a secondary source was transferred not only to other secondary sources but to at least one "primary" source – Louch's memoir.

To *Suffolk*'s right, two 10th Battalion companies boarded *Scourge* and *Foxhound* and two from the 9th Battalion *Beagle* and *Colne*.[19] To her left, one company of the 12th Battalion and members of the 3rd Field Ambulance boarded *Ribble* from *Devanha*; the night was so still the latter lowered her gangway to ease the disembarkation.[20] Ashton wrote that *Suffolk* did the same.[21] Soldiers and sailors wished each other "good luck"[22] and a little before midnight the destroyers carrying the 2,500 men of the second wave of the covering force departed, steaming "into the unknown under the pale light of the sinking moon."[23] Initially the men were "allowed to smoke and … talk quietly"[24] as, in line abreast, their destroyers slowly proceeded, "hardly moving,"[25] towards the invisible enemy coast, about 15 miles distant.

Aboard *London*, Newham was rudely awakened by a sailor rolling out of his hammock for duty, so he "had a good wash" before being "collared" to round up his section for "something to eat."[26] The troops crowding *London*'s decks, messes and cabins were roused at about 12:30 a.m., "the second

9   Goodlet, manuscript, p.9.
10   *Ibid.*
11   Mofflin, letter, 20 October 1915, p.11.
12   Hearder, manuscript 3DRL 3959, p.9.
13   Louch, manuscript, p.14.
14   Belford, *Legs Eleven*, p.64.
15   Bean, *Official History*, Volume I (1921 and 1941), follows p.256.
16   *Ibid.*, precedes p.252.
17   *Ibid.*, follows p.256.
18   *Ibid.*, p.251, opposite p.256 and p.246.
19   *Ibid.*, p.247.
20   *Ibid.*
21   F. Ashton, manuscript, ACC 973A, J.S. Battye Library, Perth, p.13.
22   J. Clohessy, diary, Ellam-Innes Collection, Perth.
23   Ashton, manuscript, p.13.
24   *Ibid.*
25   Blay, diary, 25 April 1915.
26   Newham, "Recollections of a Returned Soldier", n.p.

great awakening for me," wrote Peck. "The first was at Blackboy Hill on the morning of our departure from Australia. For many alas! it was the last awakening on this earth."[27] Few others had slept. All attempted to make the best of the "glorious meal" served by the Navy, not knowing when they might get another and aware that it "would be probably the last for a number of us."[28] Newham thought it the best meal since leaving "home … beef steak and kidney pie, potatoes … tinned peas and cabbage" and "a beautiful cup of cocoa", after which he "did not feel much like fighting."[29] McCleery had reason to celebrate – 25 April was his birthday. Before disembarking he was entertained in the "sergeants" – presumably the senior sailors' – mess.[30]

Then the command, "Fall-in," was quietly passed around the ship. The significance of this, the order which signified the commencement of the operation, was not lost on the men, though Newham noticed that "everyone" was "cool and collected … ready for what was coming"[31] and Medcalf that "All were intensely interested but not unduly excited."[32] Midnight to dawn "was a most anxious time," wrote Brigade Major C.H. Brand. "Never was the discipline of any brigade put to so severe a test. It faced the unknown with confidence."[33] Ashmead-Bartlett witnessed these moments aboard *London*. The untried "Australians … were cheerful, quiet, and confident, showing no sign of nerves or excitement … Men who six months ago were living peaceful civilian lives" found rifles and equipment, struggled into heavy webbing,[34] and quietly assembled in the darkness. "Very quietly" the sailors also began their preparations for what was to come.[35]

Formed up on deck, metal-heeled rifle butts resting by their right boots, webbing heavy on their shoulders, the night fresh, dark and silent around them, the soldiers waited silently, alone with their thoughts, powerless to influence the future. To many the previous months would have been the richest and most diverse experience of their lives, yet they had not undertaken their prime task – to fight. The dark water separating them from their enemy, was a divide between their old world and the one to which some might one day return, between those who have experienced battle and those who have not. They could only ponder the realities of the far side of that divide, of death and wounding, of never returning home, of their imminent ordeal by fire. Few recorded giving much thought to this confrontation with mortality. Perhaps they had made their peace with themselves earlier, possibly when writing their wills in their pay books. Most seem to have been more concerned with the responsibilities of the task before them. In sight of "towering hills," soon to become "the scene of Death or Glory to our lads," Rob Lowson pondered the test that "would either make or mar the name of Australia's sons … on us rested the terrible responsibility … if we failed everything would fail … we were untried" yet "determined … we could only fight to the death as we could not retire … one ray of hope to which we all clung … surprise."[36] Regardless of their thoughts and feelings, outwardly they appeared as "calm as if about to take part in a route march."[37]

The *London* lay motionless on a flat sea, all as "still as the grave."[38] Brennan thought the night "glorious," but the moonlight was "so bright we had to keep well away from the land," now discernible through the darkness.[39] "Every nerve" was strained waiting for the orders that would send the men

27   Peck, letter to wife, n.d.
28   Combs, manuscript.
29   Newham, "Recollections of a Returned Soldier", n.p.
30   McCleery, interview, Welborn.
31   Newham, "Recollections of a Returned Soldier", n.p.
32   Medcalf, manuscript, p.62.
33   C.H. Brand, "Memories of ANZAC Day – 20 years Ago", *Reveille*, 1 April 1935, p.4.
34   Brenchley, p.65.
35   Newham, "Recollections of a Returned Soldier", n.p.
36   Lowson, "Under Fire", n.p.
37   Bartlett, *Uncensored Dardanelles*, p.45.
38   Lowson, "Under Fire", n.p.
39   Brennan, letter, 1915, Army Museum of Western Australia.

shoreward.[40] "One could hear the sound of a subdued chatter and an occasional giggle, but at times you [would] see a moist eye or a 'faraway' look and the owner would draw himself up as if ashamed of his weakness and would continue a light conversation with his neighbour."[41] Officers flitted from group to group,[42] issuing final instructions, or perhaps final farewells and "good lucks" before the units were split up. Committed to battle, the men could do little but "trust in God and await the issue."[43]

Dix "suggested that the men" be "given a 'tot' each to keep the cockles warm during their cramped and tedious passage in the boats."[44] Others confirm this,[45] Keast adding it was "very nice too,"[46] but not everyone accepted it. Newham defiantly recorded being offered "some Dutch courage … and the boys did not like that, and a lot of them would not accept … they did not want any of their Dutch courage."[47]

At about 1:30 a.m., the "final order from" *London*'s bridge was at last given, "spoken softly, every word pronounced distinctly and in the same monotonous voice." The "Bluejackets" quietly stole "out of the shadows" and prepared the boats for landing.[48] "Boats were lowered,"[49] orders passed, and the heavily laden men began to move. The quiet clank of equipment, the grounding of a rifle butt on the wooden deck, and "the slightest shuffling sound" being "the only indication"[50] that the men had "started the great march."[51] Bean wrote that "Many a naval officer noticed how silent and orderly, now that it had come to business, were these troops whose name had terrified Cairo."[52] Awaiting them in the boats were the crews who would take them shoreward, "Lieutenants in khaki, midshipmen – not yet out of their 'teens – in old white duck suits dyed khaki … carrying revolvers, water-bottles, and kits almost as big as themselves," and "sturdy bluejackets"[53] to row the empty boats back to the fleet.

As the troops struggled in twos and threes down the rope ladders, the men of the Navy watched and bade them adieu. Friendships had been forged in recent hours and small gifts – clasp knives from soldiers, cap bands from sailors – were exchanged.[54] Goodbyes and "God bless yous" were murmured the length of the decks, and "answered from several of our boats … reckon we'll see you at Constanti."[55] Bean would later append his notes of these hours, describing the "old service" launching "this fine new force."[56]

By 2:35 a.m. the last of the troops from *London* had settled onto their hard wooden seats. Packs, webbing, pockets and boats were full and heavy, smoking forbidden, the future uncertain. Packed "like sardines,"[57] with dawn yet two hours away, they faced a long, uncomfortable, cold and anxious wait.[58] At 2:53 a.m.[59] *London*, *Prince of Wales* and *Queen* began moving slowly eastward, strings of heavily-laden boats trailing behind. "All eyes" watched the "silver moon" slowly sinking into:

40   Lowson, "Under Fire", n.p.
41   *Ibid.*
42   Bartlett, *Uncensored Dardanelles*, p.45.
43   Lowson, "Under Fire", n.p.
44   Dix, private papers, p.7.
45   A.H. Darnell, letter to F.A. Darnell, 27 May 1915, 1DRL 233; Hastings, letter, 10 June 1915; A.F. Marshall, letter, 9 May 1915, *Sunday Times*, 25 July 1915.
46   Keast, diary, 24/25 April 1915.
47   Newham, "Recollections of a Returned Soldier", n.p.
48   Lowson, "Under Fire", n.p.
49   Hastings, letter, 10 June 1915.
50   R.W. Everett, talk on the Landing, St. George's House, Perth, at the request of United Services Institute, unidentified newspaper, author's collection.
51   Lowson, "Under Fire", n.p.
52   Bean, *Official History*, Volume I (1921 and 1941), p.248, and pp.128–130.
53   Bartlett, *Uncensored Dardanelles*, p.45.
54   Belford, *Legs Eleven*, p.66.; mementoes in the Ellam-Innes Collection, Perth.
55   Lowson, "Under Fire", n.p.
56   Bean, 3DRL 606 item 25, pp.7–10.
57   Combs, manuscript.
58   S.T. Forbes, letter, 29 May 1915, *Sunday Times*, 11 July 1915.
59   Bean, *Official History*, Volume I, p.248.

a blaze of rippling waves … the air grew cooler, the shadows longer, the still night more eerie, more mystic and more deep. Who can tell the tale of that waiting time … of waning moonlight and deepening shadows? It was a trysting place of life and death, of love and duty, of pause and action – a panorama of mind and memory. Inspiring scenes from British history, martial deeds of immortal fame, passed in quick review. Faces of dear ones came to soften and to strengthen; we greeted again pals and heard their "Good luck, old fellow." Snatches of songs, soft love ballads, stirring war chants, rang in our ears.[60]

Some distance astern, sailors with "hot cocoa, biscuits and cheese" had moved quietly among the troops crowding the destroyers' decks[61] before the whispered order "for cigarettes out and silence."[62] Decks throbbed to powerful engines,[63] and the dark shapes of the transports began to slip into the darkness behind. Two to three miles later, the destroyers halted to await the sinking of the moon. It was an uncomfortable time. "We were packed all ranks on the decks,"[64] "could hardly move"[65] and "got mighty cold … weren't allowed to smoke or talk."[66] Mofflin found his way to *Chelmer's* engine room, where he could talk and chain-smoke, "my heart was beating like a sledge hammer. I shall never forget that trip … we didn't know what to expect."[67]

When the moon set at about 3:00 a.m., the night became "intensely dark."[68] At 3:30 a.m. the battleships stopped. Land was dimly visible through the darkness,[69] but estimates of the time and distance from land vary greatly. Thursby[70] and Bush[71] estimated two miles; Callwell, Kitchener's Director of Operations, thought one and a half miles, Birdwood believed about four miles and the 1st Division War Diary recorded one mile.[72] Ashmead-Bartlett thought the distance 3,000 yards and the time 4:30 a.m.[73]

Orders were received "to carry on under our own steam."[74] The pinnaces cast off, the hawsers took up the strain and "without a whisper,"[75] the tows began to move under their own power. Ashmead-Bartlett and the officers aboard *London's* bridge watched them go, their "gunwales almost flush with the water, so crowded were they … To our anxious eyes it appeared as if the loads were too heavy for the pinnaces, that some mysterious power was holding them back, that they would never reach the shore before daybreak."[76] Behind them the destroyers had also begun to move, "getting along the water like mice until we came to four big dark things … Battleships."[77] As the distance closed Mofflin could "just make out the boats crowded with men leaving their sides."[78] The silent, densely packed infantry, "glided quietly into the night."[79]

The tows attempted to manoeuvre the heavily laden boats into line, 12 abreast, the southernmost tow providing the direction, but the night was so dark there was difficulty in achieving this. Despite some

60   Hastings, letter, 10 June 1915.
61   Blay, diary, 25 April 1915.
62   Ashton, manuscript, p.13.
63   *Ibid.*, p.14.
64   Hearder, manuscript 3DRL 3959, p.10.
65   Mofflin, letter, 20 October 1915, p.11.
66   *Ibid.*, p.11.
67   *Ibid.*, pp.11–12.
68   Bean, *Official History*, Volume I (1921 and 1941), p.248.
69   Newham, manuscript; Hastings, letter, 10 June 1915.
70   Winter, *The Inevitable Tragedy*, p.92.
71   Bush, *Gallipoli*, p.99.
72   Winter, *The Inevitable Tragedy*, p.92.
73   Brenchley, p.66.
74   Newham, "Recollections of a Returned Soldier", n.p.
75   Combs, manuscript.
76   Bartlett, *Uncensored Dardanelles*, p.46.
77   Clohessy, diary.
78   Mofflin, letter, 20 October 1915, pp.12–13.
79   Lowson, "Under Fire", n.p.

sandwiching "themselves into a wrong place,"[80] pinnaces, tows, and war vessels managed to form "one continuous line" and begin moving once more "towards the Gallipoli coast."[81] "Now was the time that every man felt very lonely … we hardly dared breathe. I shall never forget that sight," wrote Newham.[82]

A plan of the distribution of the platoons in the tows would provide a starting point for determining where men fought, but is not documented in Australian sources. Some men wrote that each platoon occupied a boat, but with boats varying in capacity, this cannot be presumed. Drage's midshipman's notes contain a detailed diagram of the tows that carried A Company's 224 men and six officers, and 40 officers and men of HQ.[83]

No. 9 tow carried 1 and 2 Platoons in:

a launch	96 men
lifeboat	21 men
cutter	35 men

No. 10 tow carried 3 and 4 Platoons in:

a lifeboat	21 men
cutter	35 men
pinnace	56 men[84]

Some platoons were clearly spread over more than one boat. HQ was also "distributed over various boats, so that a lucky … shot would not deprive the battalion of its leadership."[85]

Bush wrote that each tow was under command of a midshipman,[86] and five also had a commissioned naval officer aboard. Lieutenant-Commander J.B. Waterlow, on the extreme right of the line (No. 1 tow) was in charge of putting the tows down in the correct place and Dix, extreme left tow (No. 12), was Senior Naval Officer.[87] 11th Battalion men wrote of "our admiration for the calmness and bravery" of the "amazing"[88] "youngsters"[89] or "midshipmites"[90] who commanded the boats carrying the heavily laden infantry into battle that morning; they made Eastcott "proud I am British."[91] Decades later Howe could recall details of Midshipman C.F.H. Churchill: "I was sitting at the after oar in the cutter about 3 or 4 feet in front of you. Major Brockman and the coxswain were in the stern. You appear to have been standing by the tiller or sitting on the gunwhale … you seemed to tower over us … red hair … plainly visible."[92]

The boats continued to "the soft exhaust of the pinnace" and the sound of "water swirling alongside."[93] One man recalled that it "took all" his "strength" to keep his "wretched … oar" upright, "they are about 10 feet long and extremely weighty."[94] As CO 7 Platoon, Darnell should have landed

80   Bean, *Official History*, Volume I (1921 and 1941), p.249.
81   Everett, talk, St. George's House, n.d.
82   Newham, "Recollections of a Returned Soldier", n.p.
83   Drage, diary.
84   *Ibid.* The arithmetic is out by 6, but where the error lies is not known.
85   Peck, letter to wife, n.d. It would appear from the totals in each tow that HQ landed predominantly with No. 9 Tow or with C Company. Perhaps some of the 1st Field Company also landed with Tows 9 and 10.
86   Bush, *Gallipoli*, p.98.
87   *Ibid.*
88   Eastcott, manuscript, p.5.
89   Anonymous, Leane's observer, manuscript.
90   Brockman, 3DRL 606, item 27.
91   Eastcott, manuscript, p.5.
92   Howe, letter to Churchill, 30 November 1962, 3DRL 6673/477.
93   Eastcott, manuscript, p.5.
94   Anonymous, Leane's observer, manuscript.

from a destroyer, but as OC Scouts he "was in the bows of the 1st boat" of a battleship tow – "There was some excitement I can tell you."[95]

Lowson cast a last "look back and could see the dark outline of the ship and the tars getting the huge guns ready for action, then my eyes were fixed on the silent hills."[96] The troops were committed and alone. "There is something very consoling when one can see a battleship … we set our teeth, and wriggled to get into anything approaching a comfortable position."[97] Everett found it "difficult to believe that the men seated in the boats like stone images were the same Australians who had come in for such severe criticism … in Cairo."[98] Darnell found that voyage "hard to describe … it seemed to go on forever. Except for the low throb of the engines the dead silence got on one's nerves."[99] Eastcott was "beginning to feel somewhat jittery … I had not got a clue what it was like to be under fire … How they all kept position" in the darkness "has ever been a mystery to me."[100]

The tows were in fact having great difficulty maintaining position. Bean described a change of direction as the boats approached shore,[101] but 11th Battalion accounts describe so much movement before this that one man likened the tows to "snakes" weaving "through long grass,"[102] Fox referred to "zig-zagging" and Keast described going "first this way, then that and circling around."[103] "A naval commander in the next tow" several times asked Fox's "steering officer," "sotto voce, 'to be more careful'. He appeared to take no notice; and his superior roared 'for heaven's sake, steer straight, or you will spoil the whole show!'"[104] "Some of the boys started laughing," Newham recalled, "but were soon shut up by Lieutenant Macdonald."[105]

The tows were also having trouble staying in touch. They were supposed to be 150 yards apart to allow the troops the required frontage to form up ashore, but darkness made this "impossible" and Bush closed "in fear of losing touch."[106] The tows "concertina'd" in and out of sight, watching the phosphorescent bow waves of the nearest boat,[107] and eventually "reducing the frontage by one third."[108] How much this may have contributed to a drift from course is not known.

Eventually the "intense darkness" began to fade and the land loomed closer,[109] "very high and rough, but that did not dishearten us."[110] With no sight or sound of the enemy, soldiers and sailors peered into the darkness, nerves taut as bowstrings, wondering whether they would achieve the surprise for which they hoped. The water was "smooth as satin" and the night "gloriously cool, peaceful."[111]

The invisible enemy had in fact been watching them for hours. At what Şefik recorded as 2:00 a.m., two sentries, apparently on German Officer's Spur,[112] reported seeing "many enemy ships." The men belonged to 3 Platoon, the reserve platoon of No. 4 Company, 2nd Battalion, 27th Regiment (henceforth designated 3 Platoon, 4/2/27th Regiment), whose company CO, Captain Faik, was apparently with the remainder of the platoon near Courtney's Post, or Boyun Mevkii.

95 Darnell, AD82/175.
96 Lowson, "Under Fire", n.p.
97 Fox, "I Was There", p.7.
98 Everett, talk, St. George's House, n.d.
99 Darnell, 1DRL 233.
100 Eastcott, manuscript, p.5.
101 Bean, *Official History*, Volume I (1921 and 1941), p.250.
102 Anonymous, Leane's observer, manuscript.
103 Keast, diary, 24/25 April 1915.
104 Fox, "I Was There", p.7.
105 Newham, "Recollections of a Returned Soldier", n.p.
106 Bush, *Gallipoli*, p.100.
107 Steel, N. and P. Hart, *Defeat at Gallipoli*, Papermac, London, 1995, p.54.
108 Bush, *Gallipoli*, p.100.
109 Eastcott, manuscript, p.5.
110 Newham, "Recollections of a Returned Soldier", n.p.
111 Bean, *Official History*, Volume I (1921 and 1941), p.250.
112 Uyar, p.99.

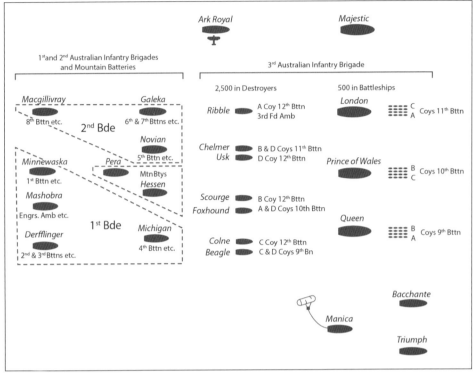

Map 3. Adapted from Bean's Map 9, showing *Chelmer* to port of *Usk*. (Bean, Map 9, *Official History*, Volume I (1921 and 1941), p.246)

Through binoculars Faik saw "straight in front … a long way off, a large number of ships." He could judge neither their size nor whether they were moving,[113] but telephoned a report to his "battalion CO, Major Izmet"[114] at battalion HQ at Gaba Tepe.[115] Izmet replied "There is no cause for alarm. At worst the landing will be at Gaba Tepe," and told Faik "to continue watching." Uyar adds that Izmet's lack of concern was because the naval activity was little different to previous nights.[116] Faik changed observation points. "This time I saw them as a great mass, which … seemed to be moving straight towards us." At "about 0230 hours" he telephoned divisional headquarters. How many were "transports and how many warships?" he was asked, but it was too dark to tell. Soon after "the moon sank below the horizon" and the ships disappeared into the blackness of the night. The "reserve platoon was alerted"; Faik "watched and waited."[117] Uyar suggests that Faik committed a "serious error" by not alerting the two platoons defending the beaches.[118]

In general, it is not possible to assume correlation between quoted Turkish and allied times, but in this case, using moonset as a reference point, Faik's times appear to correlate well with Bean's. In other words, as the first wave had assembled on *London*'s decks, staring into the darkness, pondering their fate and the chances of surprise, the Turks were staring straight back. They had already been seen.

---

113 Lieutenant-Colonel (Ret.) Şefik Aker, "The Dardanelles: The Ari Burnu Battles and 27th Regiment", manuscript, 1935, para. 36. Subsequently "Şefik."
114 Şefik, para. 36. Major Mehmed Ismet, according to Uyar, p.99.
115 Şefik, para. 34.
116 Uyar, p.99.
117 Şefik, para. 36.
118 Uyar, p.99.

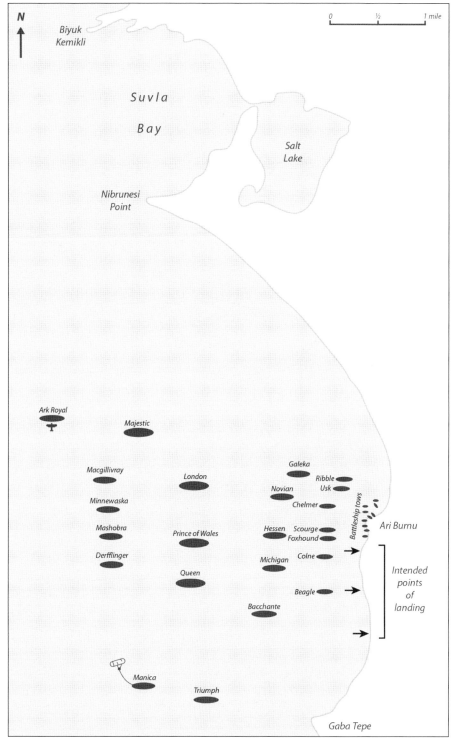

Map 4. Adapted from Bean's Map 10, showing *Usk* to port of *Chelmer*.
(Bean, Map 10, *Official History*, Volume I (1921 and 1941), p.251)

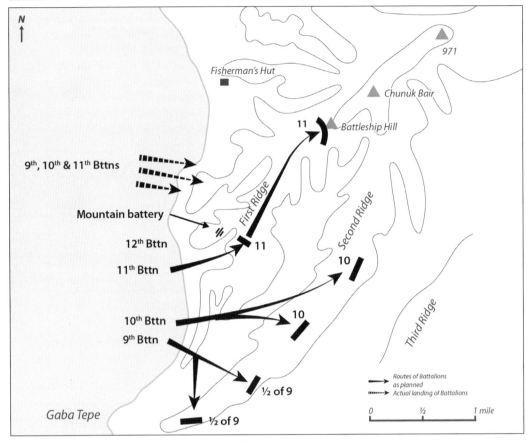

Map 5. Adapted from Bean's diagram of the 3rd Brigade's proposed and actual landing sites and routes to objectives. (Bean, *Official History*, Volume I (1921 and 1941), p.255)

As the boats neared shore, things began to happen. Bean distilled the confusion of those moments into a narrative accepted ever since. With the night still too dark to see any but the nearest tows, Peck and others recalled Dix calling "More to starboard" (south)[119] in response to tows on his right looming out of the darkness towards him. Howe recalled an officer to his right calling "more to the north," as the officer at the southern end of the line noticed the tows on his left drifting north.[120] The naval officer in the southernmost tow steered north across the bows of the others, who in turn swung several hundred yards northward, before turning due east once more. One of the central tows, carrying members of the 10th Battalion, was now about 40 or 50 yards from shore; it cast off its boats and they began to row. There was still no sign of the enemy.[121]

Part of the change of direction was due to Waterlow, who, having spent the previous weeks minesweeping in the Dardanelles, was unfamiliar with the coastline.[122] He believed they were too far south and tried to take the boats further north, but Dix, on the left, thought the opposite and tried to drag the line to the right.[123] Dix thought it a "mistake" and a "naval failure" to place him aboard

119 Johnston or Peck, 3DRL 606 item 25.
120 Bean, *Official History*, Volume I (1921 and 1941), p.250.
121 *Ibid.*
122 Steel and Hart, *Defeat at Gallipoli*, p.56.
123 C.C. Dix, 6440 private papers, Imperial War Museum, p.7.

London and Waterlow aboard *Queen*. Presumably he meant that placing Waterlow aboard *Queen*, the southernmost of the battleships, gave the responsibility for landing the tows in the correct place to an officer unfamiliar with the coast – a "ludicrous muddle" indeed.[124] This comment in Dix's papers, nestled in the collection of the Imperial War Museum, appears to represent a significant, missing part of the answer to the long standing question of the "misplaced landing".

Bean continues that "from the funnel of one of the northern most steamboats there flared out a trail of flame."[125] Many refer to the flaring funnel,[126] though it may not have been a unique occurrence – Bush found it difficult to prevent "tell-tale sparks coming out of the funnels."[127] It is easily assumed that the flaring funnel alerted the enemy, but Şefik's account does not mention it.[128]

Dix shouted "Tell the colonel … that the dam' fools have taken us a mile too far north."[129] Who Dix meant by "the colonel" is not stated. Perhaps MacLagan, when he later came ashore from *Colne*, or, if someone in the tows, probably Johnston. That Roberts was placed in command of the battleship tows suggests Johnston was not with them, though this is contradicted by a scout who appears to have landed from *London* and states that "Tip" "was in our boat."[130] The photograph of the church service aboard *London* appears to show both Johnston and Roberts (Figure 11).

11th Battalion accounts of this period in general support Bean's, which was partly compiled from interviews with Leane, Brockman, Johnston, Peck and others. Peck or Johnston noted some of the boats looking "as if they were going to collide" during one of the more dramatic changes of direction and at some time during the journey "some other tows got between us."[131]

At "4.29 a.m." continues Bean, "a thousand yards south there flashed a bright yellow light," which "glowed for half a minute and then went out. There was deathlike silence."[132] Recollections of lights ashore vary,[133] but their significance was not lost on the men – "we had been seen … we were right in for it now, from the very soles of our boots to the last hair in our heads."[134] Brennan uneasily noticed the coast looking "distinctly different from what it should have been … But it was too late to mend the error."[135] Others were also observing the skyline. Howe stated to Brockman, "with whom I had been at school, 'I don't believe it. They couldn't mistake that cliff [the Sphinx] in front of us for anywhere else.'"[136]

Bush noted a tenseness gripping the men as they prepared for their collision with their enemy, "adjusting their equipment, tightening their chin stays," but what stirred his "imagination most" was "the look on the men's faces."[137] Newham's boat let "go the tow lines" and the rowers "got to work."[138] Further south, Midshipman J. Savill Metcalf saw "Turkish troops running along the top of the cliffs from the south" – presumably racing to their fire positions, or withdrawing from the most exposed, forward posts. Feet crunching on the shingle told of the first Australians ashore.[139] Peck "heard

---

124 Dix, 6440 private papers, p.6.
125 Bean, *Official History*, Volume I (1921 and 1941), p.252.
126 Everett, interview, probably by C.E.W. Bean, Ellam-Innes Collection, p.239.
127 Bush, *Gallipoli*, pp.99–100.
128 In a 1967 interview, for example, Howe described the sparks, followed by a Turkish signal light and the first shot. Transcripts of Recorded Interviews (and Tapes), G–J, copy of ABC Historical Library Record, WRP15 3 July 1967, Tape 584, Peter Liddle Collection, The Brotherton Library, University of Leeds.
129 Bean, *Official History*, Volume I (1921 and 1941), p.252.
130 Anonymous scout, letter, 15 May 1915, apparently A Company, *Sunday Times*, 11 July 1915.
131 Johnston or Peck, 3DRL 606 item 25, pp.7–10.
132 Bean, *Official History*, Volume I (1921 and 1941), p.252.
133 Leane, 3DRL 606 item 28; Johnston or Peck, 3DRL 606 item 25 pp.7–10.
134 Newham, "Recollections of a Returned Soldier", n.p.
135 Brennan, letter, 1915, Army Museum of Western Australia.
136 Howe to Churchill, 30 November 1962.
137 Bush, *Gallipoli*, p.100.
138 Newham, "Recollections of a Returned Soldier", n.p.
139 Steel & Hart, *Defeat at Gallipoli*, p.59.

voices" from the darkness ahead. With senses straining for sight or sound of their enemy, the men in the boats then heard "one loud voice," "carried distinctly" on the clear night air, of "what appeared to be a sentry giving a warning." Peck "whispered to … Leane that they had seen us."[140] The tows "turned in again. The order to cast off" was given.[141] "Look at that chap!" exclaimed Leane – a Turkish soldier could be seen moving on the skyline of MacLagan's Ridge above.[142]

Dawn was "beginning to break."[143] Leane's observer thought it was Dix who then yelled "Down with our oars lads, get to shore."[144] Other tows were also casting off their boats. Newham's and Combs' crews were rowing for shore,[145] Aitken's keel was grating on the shingle. Medcalf's pinnace released its tows[146] and Retchford's began to do so.[147] B Company's "Bandy" Turner[148] was rowing ashore, George Blay[149] had just disembarked from *Chelmer* and Mofflin[150] and Ed Inman[151] had just received orders to do so. "The destroyer next to" Chaplain Fahey's[152] began to offload "her men" into the boats[153] and Ashton's boat from *Usk* had begun rowing ashore.[154] Brennan's crew "were lowering the oars to pull in the last 40 or 50 yards."[155]

Then "bang!"[156]

A "single rifle" thumped "in the stillness, and everyone jumped about a foot off his seat."[157] There was a pause; then within "about five seconds the fire opened from the whole hill in front of us."[158] That "started them properly" wrote Redmond,[159] "bullets were flying about in all directions. They had machine guns and shrapnel onto us as well."[160] To Fahey "it seemed as if the heavens opened …[a] hail of bullets from machine guns and rifles" riddled the destroyer's funnels "just above my head."[161] The firing soon resembled the "crackling of a huge Australian bushfire."[162] "My word," wrote Forbes,[163] "they did pour the lead into us."[164]

Everyone remembered that first shot. It is a reference point that transcends the errors of watches and recalled times. Estimates of distance from shore at this first shot vary greatly, though some of the variation is due to difficulties of judging distance in the dark – Darnell quotes "200 yards" in one account and "about … 400 yards" in another.[165] Everett estimates his tow was "half a mile from shore,"[166] after which it turned north, nearly dragging "the last boat in the tow over" before turning

140 Johnston or Peck, 3DRL 606 item 25, pp.7–10.
141 *Ibid.*
142 Leane, 3DRL 606 item 28.
143 Darnell, PR82/175.
144 Anonymous, Leane's observer, manuscript.
145 Newham, manuscript; Combs, manuscript.
146 Medcalf, manuscript, p.62.
147 A.R. Retchford, letter to mother and brother, 14 and 15 May 1915, Kalgoorlie Miner, 7 July 1915.
148 365 Private Benjamin Turner, 23, labourer, of Bellevue, born South Australia. Bandy was a Perth identity, a state amateur heavyweight boxing champion with "a great big punch and a great big heart." Hurst, *Game to the Last*, p.101.
149 Blay, diary, 25 April 1915.
150 Mofflin, letter, 20 October 1915, p.13.
151 E.S. Inman, diary, 25 April 1915, Army Museum of Western Australia.
152 Chaplain John Fahey, 31 at embarkation, clergyman, of Kalgoorlie, born Ireland.
153 M. McKernan, *Padre: Australian Chaplains in Gallipoli and France* (Sydney: Allen and Unwin, 1986), p.48.
154 Ashton, manuscript, p.14.
155 Brennan, letter, 1915, Army Museum of Western Australia.
156 Aitken, letter/diary, p.18.
157 Brennan, letter, 1915, Army Museum of Western Australia.
158 *Ibid.*
159 259 Signaller Daniel Alexander Redmond, 24 at embarkation, clerk, of West Perth, born West Melbourne, Victoria.
160 Redmond, letter, 1915.
161 McKernan, *Padre*, p.48.
162 Medcalf, manuscript, p.62.
163 205 Orderly Room Corporal Sydney Trovorrow Forbes, 20 at embarkation, teacher, of Claremont, born Victoria.
164 Forbes, letter, 29 May 1915.
165 Darnell, AD82/175 and 1DRL 233.
166 Everett, talk, St. George's House, n.d.

once more and racing towards the beach.[167] Eastcott, apparently in the same tow, recalled a "wall of black water" rising "on each side … as we raced on,"[168] "a red exhaust" flaming "high over the funnels" of his pinnace as the throttles were opened "full power."[169] The machine gun section's Murphy[170] thought *Chelmer* had approached to "about 50 yards from the shore"[171] when the "furious rifle and machine gun fire" opened from "a range of about 100 yards."[172]

Darnell's tow raced at "full steam"[173] into bullets that "came like hail, sighing and whining over our heads."[174] "I shall never forget 'Tip'," wrote one of the scouts.[175] "He was an old man but he set us all an example."[176] At the sudden outburst of fire Howe's crew "stopped pulling" possibly "to avoid fouling the boat ahead."[177] Their midshipman later commented drily that he "must have said something to persuade them to continue."[178] Howe's sergeant, W.A. Ayling,[179] a veteran of the South African War and the North West Frontier, had told his platoon during training that incoming bullets sang "just like little birds." Howe recalled Ayling's "reputation in the battalion was not tremendous,"[180] and most of the platoon believed "his experience under fire was limited to marking at the rifle range."[181] The bullets were coming over "pretty thick,"[182] and one of the infantrymen said "If that ginger-haired kid," referring to Midshipman Churchill, "doesn't sit down he'll be hit."[183] A bullet shattered W.R. "Combo" Smith's[184] oar. Smith, also a South African War veteran, an "old soldier" always ready to get a laugh at the expense of any figure of authority who had not earned his respect,[185] nudged Howe and "queried in a most interested tone, 'Just like little birds, aren't they, Snow?' The whole boat laughed."[186] A previously wounded veteran so trivialising the situation must have provided great reassurance and a welcome release of tension to men helplessly under fire for the first time.

Another veteran, J.F. Kite,[187] asked Medcalf how he felt: "What a … fool I am to be here!"[188] thought the latter. Fox wondered "how they missed any of us,"[189] R.C. Cockburn[190] thought "It made us feel shaky all right"[191] and Redmond could not "explain exactly the sensation that went

167 Everett, interview, Ellam-Innes Collection, p.239.
168 Eastcott, manuscript, p.6.
169 *Ibid*. This was after the "alarm" – the firing of the first enemy shot.
170 504 Frederick Unwin Murphy, machine gun section, 19 at embarkation, clerk, of Perth.
171 F.U. Murphy, letter to father, printed *Sunday Times*, 6 June 1915.
172 Murphy, letter, *Sunday Times*, 6 June 1915.
173 Darnell, 1DRL 233.
174 *Ibid*.
175 Anonymous scout, letter, 15 May 1915.
176 *Ibid*.
177 Howe to Churchill, 30 November 1962.
178 C.F.H. Churchill to E.W. Bush, undated, written Ponterwyd, Cardiganshire, 3DRL 6673/477.
179 189 Sergeant Walter Anthony Ayling, A Company, 28 at embarkation, carpenter and bridge builder, of Yuba, via Northampton, born near Melbourne. Ayling had served 8 years with the West Yorks. His age and marital status vary between records, and he may have been farming with his brother at Yuba when he enlisted. He had served in South Africa on the North West Frontier, 1908.
180 H.V. Howe, Official History, 1914–18 War: Records of C.E.W. Bean, AWM38 3DRL 8042 Item 7.
181 Howe, "The Senior Private of the AIF", *Reveille*, No. 42.
182 H. Howe, "The Senior Private of the AIF", *Reveille*, No. 42.
183 Howe to Churchill. 30 November 1962.
184 232 Private William Raymond Smith, A Company, 33 at enlistment, stockman and horsebreaker, born Victoria. Smith had served in South Africa with the 3rd Australian Bushmen and then with the Imperial Light Horse until the end of hostilities.
185 See Hurst, *Game to the Last*; J.P. Hurst, 'Damn little to Laugh At', *Wartime: the Official Magazine of the Australian War Memorial*, Issue 26, April 2004, pp.8–11. By contrast, Smith was "fiercely" loyal to good leaders and good soldiers.
186 Howe, "The Senior Private of the AIF", *Reveille*, No. 42.
187 1079 Private James Francis Kite, A Company, 40 at enlistment, engineer, born Middlesex, England. Kite had served with the South African Mounted Police and also apparently on active service with the British Army. He appears to have understated his true age to enlist.
188 Medcalf, manuscript, pp.62–63.
189 Fox, "I Was There", p.7.
190 15 Private Robert Cecil Cockburn, A Company, 22 at enlistment, mill hand of Nannup, born Scotland.
191 Cockburn, diary, 28 April 1915.

through a fellow in that boat."[192] Lowson was hoping landfall would "save us from a watery grave," as "the Maxims" showered them with a "perfect hail of lead."[193] The "strain was terrible … no shelter … simply had to sit still and wait. … rowing for dear life. I stole one look at my companions, some were staring straight in front while others had their heads bowed, but on every face was the same set expression. There was no panic whatever."[194]

The men around Everett "were steady as rocks"[195] and Retchford's party "were in great spirits … laughing and joking all the way."[196] Years later Howe would also assert there was no sign of fear amongst his comrades at this stage: "everyone was quite unconcerned."[197] John Turner[198] was studying the ground ahead and pondering the fight that was in store for them: "terribly precipitous … scrub so dense that one imagined all sorts of … ambush."[199] Lance Sergeant A.F. Marshall,[200] who had minutes earlier been "thinking there was to be no opposition,"[201] now felt and heard "bullets glancing off the wood work"[202] beside him. The "*London*'s Jacks" urged the rowers to "Pull up, lads," "They'll never hit us."[203]

"A searching machine gun" drummed against *Usk*'s sides, then lifted. The "dull smack of bullets striking flesh and the groans of the wounded, froze the blood" in Goodlet's veins:

> Smack behind me, a gurgling cry, and poor Robbo fell forward … spewing blood all over me. He grabbed at me … slid sideways onto the deck. I dropped beside him … His right arm was shattered, and the bullet had entered his side high up … he opened his eyes and tried to speak … but no sound came. He squeezed my hand with his left and then I had lost the best friend a man ever had … the Sergeant … ordered me to my boat.[204]

Goodlet carried his friend's rifle and bayonet ashore in place of his own.

A search of men of the former G and H Companies killed at the Landing and with "Rob" anywhere in their name does not produce any likely candidates for the identity of "Robbo." Broadening the search to include all fatalities of those companies produces two older men.

Crispin Kenworthy Battye,[205] aged 39 when he enlisted in Perth, was missing from the day of the Landing. He had served in the 5th West Australian Mounted Infantry in the South African War. Frederick William Johnston's[206] B2455 records service with the Capetown Highlanders in South Africa, an age of 33, and that he was wounded and missing at the Landing until, in April 1916, being pronounced killed in action (KIA).[207]

Johnston's age appears to make him less likely to be the burly veteran described by Goodlet, except that his wife stated his age to be 44 – not 34 – when he died.[208] To the best of her knowledge, Johnston

192 Redmond, *Sunday Times*, 25 July 1915.
193 Lowson, "Under Fire", n.p.
194 *Ibid.*
195 R.W. Everett, interview, *Sunday Times*, 12 September 1915.
196 Retchford, letter, 14 and 15 May 1915.
197 Howe, Tape 584, Peter Liddle Collection.
198 108 Private John Wesley Gladstone Turner, A Company, 31 at embarkation, sleeper hewer, of Beenup, born South Hampshire, England.
199 J.W.G. Turner, letter to mother, 25 June 1915, Ellam-Innes Collection, Perth.
200 567 Lance Sergeant Alexander Fraser Marshall, C Company, 36 at embarkation, civil servant, of Kalgoorile, born Chiltern, Victoria.
201 A.F. Marshall, letter, 9 May 1915 and 15 May 1915, *Sunday Times*, 25 July 1915.
202 Marshall, letter, 9 May 1915.
203 *Ibid.*
204 Goodlet, manuscript, p.10.
205 864 Private Crispin Kenworthy Battye, D Company, porter, of Bunbury, 39 at embarkation, born Hindmarsh, South Australia.
206 920 Private Frederick William Johnston, D Company, 33 according to emabarkation roll, rural worker, of Wagin, born Carlisle, England.
207 B2455, Johnston.
208 On Johnston's Roll of Honour Circular.

had no previous military experience, but added that "I know very little of his life in Australia. He left England in 1902 for South Africa and went from there to Australia … I do not think he would wish his life recorded. He as [*sic*] made good by dieding [*sic*] for his country."[209] The easiest assumption is that Johnston reduced his age by a decade on enlistment and may well have experienced the life described by Goodlet. Perhaps "Robbo" was a pseudonym for "Johnno." Medcalf's account also uses pseudonyms.[210]

Clearly the experiences of the 11th Battalion boats varied. At the first shot, some were still attached to their pinnaces, others were rowing, at least one had reached shore while others were some hundreds of yards from it. One reason for the variety of experience is that the curved North Beach gave the northernmost tows a greater distance to travel, another may be variations of perception or memory. Although Bean mentions the change of direction of the tows, accounts by those in the boats provide a greater sense of its significance, dramatic nature and unexpectedness. They also suggest minor changes during the earlier part of the voyage – one gets a sense of things beginning to go awry much earlier than Bean implied. Officers and other ranks made different observations – the latter refer to zig-zagging, the officers, better briefed and knowing that they would have to assume command on land, noticed specifics, such as direction and distance, course changes and intermixing of the tows.

This was the first time most of the men in the boats had been under enemy fire; for all it broke the almost unbearable suspense.[211] For those aboard the battleships and transports, that first rifle crack provided the first insight into the fate of the tows. Peering into the darkness from *London*, Ashmead-Bartlett saw the "enemy … alarm light" at 4:50 a.m., and heard the first shot at 4:53 a.m.[212] Bean gave 4:29 a.m. as the time of the first shot, but in 1915 had recorded firing commencing at 4:18 a.m.,[213] and when he briefed Lambert in 1919 for the painting now hanging in the Australian War Memorial, told him 4:53 a.m.[214] 1st Division HQ recorded 4:32 a.m.,[215] Vice Admiral De Robeck and Major Brockman 4:20 a.m., the 3rd Brigade War Diary and *London* 4:15 a.m. and the 12th Battalion diary 4:10 a.m.[216] Leane wrote on his map "Landed Gaba Tepe April 25th 1915 4.55 a.m." Other 11th Battalion accounts record a similar range.[217] It appears that Bean, when writing the *Official History*, examined the information available to him and made a "best guess" estimate of 4:29 a.m. This has been cited repeatedly as the time of the Australian Landing.

The problem of assigning times to events continues throughout the day. Not all men possessed watches and those that existed weren't synchronised. In the coming hours men were generally too busy to record the time, and with the stresses of the day were unlikely (with some exceptions) to remember it reliably. If they did, their testimony suffered the problems of faulty memory and disorientation caused by stress and having been awake all or part of the night. With such problems inherent in recorded times, other frames of reference are required. The problem is that, with such disjointed fighting over unnamed or unidentified topography and with troops often out of sight of each other, few such references are available. That first Turkish shot provides perhaps the most definite anchor to pinpoint men in place and time. Hastings wrote, "No pen can convey, no time

209 Johnston's wife believed "he worked on a farm and on the railway" in Australia. E.L. Johnston, B2455, Johnston.

210 In Medcalf's manuscript, Selby becomes "Selwyn", Drake Brockman becomes "Dockson", Medcalf becomes Blobbs. Many others are represented by their true names.

211 Fox, "I Was There", p.7.

212 E. Ashmead-Bartlett, "Cabled report of Mr Ashmead Bartlett's account of the Landing of the Australian Troops at the Dardanelles", published in the daily papers on 8 May 1915, Department of Public Instruction, New South Wales, 18 May 1915, Australian Defence Force Academy Library.

213 C.E.W. Bean, "How the Heights Were Stormed", report, 13 May 1915; printed *Commonwealth of Australia Gazette* 39, Monday 27 May 1915.

214 Winter, *The Inevitable Tragedy*, p.97.

215 Australian War Memorial (AWM), Sub-class 1/42, AWM4, Australian Imperial Force Unit War Diaries, 1914–18 War: 1st Division War Diary, April 1915, Part 1, 25 April 1915.

216 Winter, *The Inevitable Tragedy*, p.97; E.A.D. Brockman, AWM38 3DRL 606 item 27.

217 W.P. Luttrell, letter to father, 16 May 1915, *Kalgoorlie Miner*, 7 July 1915; Darnell, 1DRL 233 and AD82/175.

can efface the emotions, the incident fact of the thrilling, momentous, tremendous moments that followed that fateful initial report."[218]

No-one was hit in Cockburn's or Forbes' boats despite a "a murderous fire."[219] A.J. Webb[220] felt "we must have been in God's good books"[221] and Combs that it was like going "through a hail storm without one piece hitting you. The rowers were pulling hard" when Combs' boat "struck a bank" and the midshipman called, "You are aground boys, out you jump." Combs leapt into "icy cold" water "up to our necks ... the majority went right under ... swallowing quantities of salt water." They stumbled ashore, lay down and removed their packs.[222] 11 Platoon's La Nauze, with Sergeant E.A. Hardey[223] behind, jumped into "water ... past my waist ... machine guns and rifles on us ... water was absolutely foaming."[224] Aitken landed in water up to his armpits and, spurred on by "the pitiful cries of those who'd been hit,"[225] fixed his bayonet while struggling ashore. Doug Gallaher[226] jumped out and went for his "life like a madman ... up to our necks in water ... some of the poor lads ... were drowned without ... seeing a Turk or getting in a shot."[227]

Others also refer to men being drowned – as sterns were further out than bows and the heavier boats grounded in deeper water, this is possible.[228] Leane's observer scrambled:

over the side ... four chaps ... killed in my boat ... hanging onto the side of the cutter with my left hand holding my rifle ... in my right ... when ... should I reach the bottom ... up to my armpits ... could not move for the weight of all my gear ... I ... slipped and down I went ... lost my hat ... my rifle ... I had to go and grope about for it ... "Pings" as each bullet passed by your head ... at last I reached the shore ... exhausted ... could hardly stand ... could only stroll ... down I dropped gasping for breath. I thought of my heavy smoking which had made me so short winded.[229]

Others agreed that "It was a mistake to land with packs" which slowed and "upset" the men.[230] Even today the underwater stones along that beach are treacherously slippery, and on 25 April 1915 many a top-heavy man took a ducking, perhaps giving rise to the rumour of barbed wire beneath the water.[231]

Leane's observer "heard a little groan" behind and looking back, saw Annear "fall backwards into the sea, stone dead ... shot in the head"[232] just as he reached shore. Brodribb was "alongside ... Annear and we had not advanced 20 yards up the beach before he fell shot through the mouth, dying instantly. Lt MacDonald ... fell slightly wounded at the same time."[233] Both these accounts contradict the *Official History*, which states that Annear was killed atop Plugge's Plateau[234] (Figure 13).

218 Hastings, letter, 10 June 1915.
219 Cockburn, diary, 28 April 1915; Forbes, letter, 29 May 1915.
220 849 Private Albert James Webb, 23 at embarkation, labourer, of Geraldton and Kalgoorlie, born Moonta, South Australia.
221 A.J. Webb, letter to mother, *Kalgoorlie Miner*, 7 July 1915.
222 Combs, manuscript.
223 667 Sergeant Edward Alex Hardey, C Company, 35 at enlistment, comission agent, of Kalgoorlie, born Christchurch, New Zealand.
224 C.A. La Nauze, letter to wife, n.d., *Kalgoorlie Miner*, June 1915.
225 Aitken, letter/diary, p.19.
226 654 Corporal Douglas Wallace Gallaher, C Company, 31 at embarkation, labourer, of Boulder and East Perth, born Auckland New Zealand. Gallaher had served with the 4th Battalion, Australian Commonwealth Horse in the South African War.
227 Gallaher, letter to wife, *Kalgoorlie Miner*, illegible date, June 1915.
228 Goodlet, manuscript, p.11; Siefken, letter, 3 September 1915, private collection; Leane's observer, manuscript.
229 Anonymous, Leane's observer, manuscript.
230 Peck, Johnston, 3DRL 606 item 25 pp.7–10.
231 Fox, for example, believed "Under the water was a network of wires ... tripping and slipping about frightfully." Fox, "I Was There", p.7.
232 Anonymous, Leane's observer, manuscript.
233 Brodribb, interview, *Kalgoorlie Miner*, 24 August 1915.
234 Bean, *Official History*, Volume I (1921 and 1941), p.260.

Orders to "fix bayonets!" were shouted for those who hadn't already. Fixing bayonets for the first time in action must be a chilling event, but in this case there was another reason for its significance. With rifles unloaded, the 3rd Brigade had essentially landed unarmed on an enemy coast; fixing bayonets at least provided them a stabbing weapon. "The Captain," presumably Leane, called out "the success of the enterprise depends on your taking this hill with a rush."[235] Without waiting to charge magazines those nearby stormed forward into the scrub.[236] Others scrambled ashore as their boats grounded. "No orders were given – or wanted," wrote Fox. "I handed my rifle to a sailor … a shrapnel shell burst overhead and killed him … the noise was beyond imagination."[237] Bullets "were flying in all directions" as Forbes dropped, removed his pack and tried to "collect the boys together."[238] Peck thought a Turkish machine gun crew ceased firing to load a new belt as he landed[239] and Brennan that his boat suffered "only a few casualties … the machine gun didn't get into it." No time was wasted "getting out of the boats" and "to the shelter of the bank." Even here they were enfiladed "from a bit of cape about 200 yards to the south".[240]

The majority of the battalion were still offshore, rowing "like men possessed."[241] Casualties were immediately replaced without a word uttered.[242] Newham's boat "began to sink."[243] Behind Eastcott's, "a calm voice hailed the pinnace in the slow navy drawl … 'No 3 boat sinking, Sir'. Back came the answer 'Cut her adrift'. Followed immediately by 'Aye Aye Sir' and the sound of a couple of blows."[244] The sinking boat may have been Newham's or Everett's, the latter also having been holed by bullets and taking water.[245]

Ashton thought his comrades behaved "splendidly … one … quietly announcing that he had been wounded in the leg. The noise of the bullet striking him and going through the woodwork of the boat could be distinctly heard. It gave us a most peculiar feeling of unreality."[246]

Those still aboard the destroyers could hear "a terrible row" ashore. In front of Mofflin, "Darkie Williams was killed … the news flew round and that sent us mad."[247] This first B Company casualty was recalled by many.[248] Blay and A. Sampford[249] also believed Williams was killed at the time, though he actually lingered until death claimed him on 28 April. *Chelmer* moved suddenly astern as the men were disembarking, shooting her boats forward.[250] "We were mad to get at them" wrote Mofflin, to "help our mates," and even though his boat was "only half full … away we went," charging magazines in the boats.[251] Signaller H.V. Hitch[252] was heading for his boat when Tulloch spotted and called to him: "Hitch you stay with me." Tulloch wanted Hitch "at hand to interpret any messages we got."[253]

Facey wrote of "all hell" breaking loose, "heavy shelling and shrapnel fire commenced. The ships that were protecting our troops returned fire. Bullets were thumping into us in the rowing-boat.

235 Johnston and Peck, 3DRL 606 item 25.
236 Leane, AWM 38 3DRL 606 item 28(2).
237 Fox, "I Was There", p.7.
238 Forbes, letter, 29 May 1915.
239 Peck, letter to wife, n.d.
240 Brennan, letter, 1915, Army Museum of Western Australia.
241 Darnell, AD82/175.
242 Darnell, 1DRL 233.
243 Newham, "Recollections of a Returned Soldier", n.p.
244 Eastcott, manuscript, p.6.
245 Everett, interview, Ellam-Innes Collection, p.239.
246 Ashton, manuscript, p.14.
247 Mofflin, letter, 20 October 1915, p.13.
248 Blay, diary, 25 April 1915.
249 487 Private (at embarkation) Arthur Sampford, B Company, 26 at enlistment, labourer, of Collie and Subiaco, born Victoria.
250 Inman, diary, 25 April 1915.
251 Mofflin, letter, 20 October 1915, pp.13–14.
252 443 Lance Sergeant (at embarkation) Herbert Vesper Hitch, B Company, 27 at embarkation, clerk, of Victoria Park East, born London, England.
253 Hitch, interview, May 1974, p.7.

Men were being hit and killed all around me."[254] Facey's book contributes to the perception of carnage getting ashore, yet his service record reveals that he did not join the battalion until after the Landing. The implication is that his account was gained second hand from its veterans, or even "fabricated".[255] These are not safe assumptions. 2nd Reinforcement Whiting wrote of joining the battalion at Lemnos before the Landing, yet his service record states that he did not join until 7 May – the same date as Facey. A 3rd Reinforcement, W.A. Telford,[256] wrote in late May 1915 that he "didn't come ashore until the Wednesday (28th April),"[257] yet according to his service record, he joined the battalion on 2 May. Facey's service record once contained a letter, not visible today,[258] written by him in 1978, enquiring about a campaign medallion, presumably his Gallipoli medallion: "As far as I can remember we joined the battalion the day before the landing." Facey did not need to claim this to have been eligible for the medallion and clearly believed he had taken part in the Landing. It is likely the fault lies with these men's service records, though Facey's account may have been written too long after the event to be reliable.[259]

Hearder was second in command of the troops aboard *Chelmer*. "Within a minute" of the first shot, Hearder thought "At least two maxim guns" and "a field gun … firing shrapnel" had opened fire.[260] Many accounts support this – the men believed there was one machine gun on the left, probably at Fisherman's Hut, and another atop Ari Burnu. The presence of these guns and the firing of shrapnel at this early stage are today disputed.[261] Of note is the fact that Hearder commanded the machine gun section, and his corporal, Murphy, also thought they were exposed to machine gun fire.[262] It might be expected that these two would have been able to differentiate between rifle and machine gun fire.

A "most cheery" voice from *Chelmer*'s bridge called out "Go on lads … these fellows can't shoot for tawfee," prompting a laugh from the troops. Lieutenant-Commander H.T. England was on the bridge, "arms folded … smiling, his pipe in his hand, as if he was looking on at a sports meeting … It was the right note to strike."[263] Blay also was impressed – "from the highest to the lowest", the Royal Navy "did a man's job."[264] Hearder noticed "a boy standing … appalled at the noise, so I … said 'Come on lad, no one is being hit'." As the two made their way to their boat, the boy "just said 'Oh' and pitched face downwards on the deck."[265] The machine gun section "very calmly" loaded their heavy guns and equipment into the boats[266] and the "Tars cast off."[267]

Near shore, Louch watched "two Turks in the machine gun nest" on Ari Burnu bring their gun into action. "They fired one or two short bursts, but fortunately not at us, and then the picket boat came in and silenced them. The two men were knocked over backwards, taking their gun with them."[268]

There was conjecture for many years about the veracity of such accounts as it was believed the naval crews were under orders not to open fire, and there was confusion about whether the pinnaces

---

254 Facey, *A Fortunate Life*, p.254.

255 Roberts, *The Landing at Anzac*, first edition, p.169.

256 1648 Sergeant William Alfred Telford, 3rd Reinforcements, A Company, 22 at enlistment, pearler, of Broome, born Perth.

257 W.A. Telford, letter to wife, 21 May 1915, quoted in I. Gill, *Fremantle to France, 11th Battalion AIF 1914–1919* (Perth: Ian Gill, 2003), p.420.

258 Not visible in the scanned version at <www.naa.gov.au> at the time of writing.

259 For an examination of Facey's account, see J.P. Hurst, 'The Mists of Time and the Fog of War, A Fortunate Life and A.B. Facey's Gallipoli Experience', *Melbourne Historical Journal*, Volume 38 (2010), pp.77–92.

260 Hearder, manuscript 3DRL 3959, p.10.

261 J.P. Hurst, 'Ottoman Machine Guns at the ANZAC Landing, 25 April 1915', unpublished at the time of writing.

262 Murphy, letter, *Sunday Times*, 6 June 1915.

263 Hearder, manuscript 3DRL 3959, p.10.

264 Blay, diary, 25 April 1915.

265 Hearder, manuscript 3DRL 3959, pp.10–11.

266 Murphy, letter, *Sunday Times*, 6 June 1915.

267 Hearder, manuscript, p.11.

268 Steel & Hart, *Defeat at Gallipoli*, p.61. Darnell also noted "There was" a machine gun "right in front of us." Darnell, PR82/175.

were armed with machine guns or three pounder Hotchkiss guns.[269] Louch's version is supported by many others. Darnell believed it was his pinnace that opened fire[270] and W.P. Luttrell[271] suggests the same.[272] Howe recalled "the picket on the right cast off its tow, ran in … and began to sweep the beach with machine gun fire."[273] Marshall watched the "machine gun on the hill" pumping "lead into the boats on our right" when "the launch next to ours … silenced" it – "it would have done you good to hear the Australian yell."[274] 3rd Brigade orders corroborate that steamboats had "orders not to open fire" with their Maxims, but were permitted to do so on orders from "the Senior Military Officer of the tow … Such a fire is not to be opened unless … imperative to effect a landing."[275]

Turkish sources confirm the incident. When the Plugge's Plateau garrison opened fire the enemy replied with "fire from the sea" wounding the platoon commander, Second Lieutenant Muharrem,[276] "in both shoulders"; the Gaba Tepe post also reported "fire with machine guns from the landing craft."[277] Some of the shots passed over Faik who was inland, probably on Second Ridge near Courtney's Post. According to Uyar, Muharrem had been slow to work out what was going on, and when he realised that the boats were about to land under his nose, suffered "command paralysis." Instead "of ordering his platoon to occupy the main trenches position on Ariburnu Knoll … (as they had often practised), he remained in the support trenches with his men."[278]

By this account, the troops on Ari Burnu had withdrawn there from a squad position near the beach. Remarkably, an otherwise unexplainable account by a 10th Battalion scout appears to corroborate this. Lance Corporal W.A. Bradshaw[279] was sitting in his boat next to a scout he knew to have uncanny eyesight. The other man said "there is somebody on the beach." Bradshaw couldn't see anyone and replied "No, there is nobody there," whereupon the other man continued "he is going up the cliff" and "almost immediately after a shot rung out."[280]

In Brockman's boat the men bent "their heads and backs" as the enemy fire grew "fiercer."[281] When the bow grated, the red-headed midshipman "clambered over the backs of the men revolver in hand, jumped onto the beach and ran up … yelling in his squeaky voice 'Come on my lads, come on my lads!' … Then … realised he had to go back to his boat and his face dropped."[282] Howe confirms the story,[283] which appeared in the *Official History*,[284] but many decades later the midshipman, Churchill, refuted it. Churchill described leaving "the tiller to the coxswain" and clambering "over the backs of the men" to "go forward … in case of … rocks." "Most certainly" he "never left the boat," absenting himself "from my place of duty in the face of the enemy." He added that "I did load my service revolver after the firing started and I realised the enemy were close to the beach. I had never handled a loaded service revolver before" and "was nearly as frightened of it as I was of the enemy. So I'm sure

269 Louch, T.S., letter, unlabelled correspondence, Louch file, Ellam-Innes Collection, Perth. Louch almost definitely the author.
270 Darnell, 1DRL 233, PR82/175.
271 685 Private William Patrick Luttrell, C Company, 19 at embarkation, blacksmith, of Boulder, born Ballarat.
272 Luttrell, letter, 16 May 1915.
273 Howe, 3DRL 8042 item 7.
274 Marshall, letter, 9 May 1915.
275 E.G. Sinclair MacLagan, Appendix A, Special instructions, Operation Order No 1, 21 April 1915, 3rd Brigade War Diary, AWM4, Australian War Memorial.
276 "Deputy Officer" according to Uyar. Uyar, p.100.
277 Şefik, para. 37.
278 Uyar, p.100.
279 787 William Arthur Bradshaw, 25, 10th Battalion scouts, carpenter, of Broken Hill, born Manchester, England.
280 W.A. Bradshaw,, interview, P. Liddle, May 1974, ANZAC (AUST) Recollections, AIF, Liddle Collection.
281 Brockman, 3DRL 606, item 27.
282 *Ibid.*
283 Howe to Churchill, 30 November 1962.
284 Bean, *Official History*, Volume I (1921 and 1941), p.255.

I did not brandish it."[285] The image of a "kid"[286] being sent into battle with a weapon he had never before used, provides a tempting metaphor for the undertaking of the landings as a whole.

This is one of many cases in which apparently reliable primary sources contradict each other. Perhaps Churchill's recollections were clouded by his youth at a time of such excitement, or the conservatism of his age in 1965 after many decades' service as a professional naval officer. Or a compromise may reconcile some of the differences. Perhaps Churchill's clambering to the bows was misinterpreted by the troops as a charge for the shore, and loading his revolver as "brandishing" it. His call to the men to land may have been in response to the boat grounding, rather than his attempt at leading them into battle. Perhaps Brockman even saw Churchill on the beach – he may have been getting out of the infantrymen's way or steadying the boat, rather than leaving it. Thus can perceptions enter the written record as history.

Despite the bullets, Howe could see no muzzle flashes[287] ashore. One man who had landed in deep water was hung onto and towed along by someone in the boat, another "got his kit caught on a rowlock." "Combo" Smith shouted "Come on Snow" and he and Howe leapt over the side.[288] "Half a dozen" men were caught by a machine gun burst, "right under the bow of the cutter."[289] Darnell thought it seemed to take a "year" to reach shore, "but at last we arrived with a huge bump … boat healing over to starboard,"[290] the "Turks all the time giving us hell," wrote another scout.[291]

Further north, the tow carrying 3 and 4 Platoons landed later, crossing the distance under fire. On the beach packs were lain in front as protection "while the others came up."[292] Lowson was in water "up to our necks … no-one hit as yet."[293] Everett's sinking boat "grounded about twenty yards" out; he ordered "every man ashore" and they leapt into deep water.[294] He later heard of a naval officer's impression that "the Australians dived into the water and came up with fixed bayonets."[295] Eastcott:

> went under … battled for a foothold … deadly fear of drowning … got my head above water … scrambled frantically after other dim shapes I could see splashing wildly ahead of me. And through it all the cracking of bullets and the sobbing wail of men as they were hit.[296]

"All that could be seen of the enemy" ahead, recounted Everett, "were the tiny blue spurts from the rifles."[297] Bullets from the "machine guns" at Fisherman's Hut were striking sparks from the stones.[298] Everett's boat suffered its first casualties as it reached the beach,[299] possibly as it entered the "beaten zone" of fire from Fisherman's Hut.

Those landing from the destroyers had similar experiences. Blay attributes his survival to the poor light, though "many" others were hit. He too was inspired by the "pure cool courage" of the "lad" of the Navy, who "did not turn a hair all through that slow pull to shore under a terrible fire … Hats off to him." Blay struggled ashore and "up the steep" slope, the fire heavy, men "falling everywhere … I got a bullet through the right leg of my pants just below the groin which left a red burn on

285 Churchill to Bush.
286 Brockman, 3DRL 606 item 27.
287 Howe, 3DRL 8042 Item 7.
288 *Ibid.*
289 Howe to Churchill, 30 November 1962.
290 Darnell, PR82/175.
291 Anonymous scout, letter, 15 May 1915.
292 Murray, letter, 16 May 1915.
293 Lowson, "Under Fire", n.p.
294 Everett, interview, Ellam-Innes Collection.
295 Everett, *Sunday Times*, 12 September 1915.
296 Eastcott, manuscript, pp.6–7.
297 R.W. Everett, account of talk, St. George's House, unidentified newspaper, private collection.
298 Everett, interview, Ellam-Innes Collection.
299 *Ibid.*

my thigh."[300] Bill Bellamy[301] was shot through the neck as the boat carrying 7 Platoon grounded 30 yards from shore, but survived to rejoin the unit and fight on until returning to Australia in 1918.[302] A sailor handed Mofflin his rifle, "shook hands" and wished him luck.[303] Sergeant Frank Seccombe[304] was shot dead soon after.[305] As Darnell was commanding the scouts, this would have left Sergeant Arnold[306] in command of 7 Platoon.

Hitch described "distant bullets" making a "ping," closer ones a "pop" and "closer still they made a crack."[307] An order was given to change course "half right" to avoid Fisherman's Hut, whose "machine gun" – it "was all machine gun fire at first" – indicated a strong point, but the "young midshipman who had the tiller … was shot through the shoulder. So one of our men took over."[308] When rowers were hit their oars trailed in the water, recalled Hitch, slowing the boat, "and we had to get them out of the way and other men to take their place and ship the oars again."[309] Further north, Otto Siefken's 6 Platoon boat was hit many times but suffered no casualties before grounding. There "was a rush to … get busy … It was some cold … tried to run ashore … could only walk, as my stuff was all soaked."[310] His and another boat landed "about 200 yards away to the left from the main body."[311]

Hearder, like others before him, was horrified to discover "we were being towed" towards "almost inaccessible cliffs" instead of "a shelving shore … and an orchard running almost on to the beach." Their pinnace ran aground and "It took no end of time to get the oars out, as they were 18 feet" long and the densely packed men "were sitting on them."[312] Perhaps this was a consequence of the haste in which some of the destroyers' boats were filled after coming under fire.

Buttle's 16 Platoon boat grounded north of Ari Burnu. The muzzle flashes of the Turkish rifles could be seen from, as Louch thought, the direction of the Sphinx[313] or "the foothills of Walker's Ridge – 500 yards away."[314] "Dick" Crerar[315] was "killed as he reached the shore."[316] Louch made it across the beach and "shed our packs, lay down and awaited orders."[317] Despite being a corporal, Louch told Bean that he landed "not knowing where he was to go, or what he was to do or anything," and believed it was the same for most men.[318] Johnston appeared beside him, and a bullet from the left "hit the ground between them … Louch asked the Colonel 'What are we to do Sir?' … Old Johnston said 'Oh, I don't know I'm sure – everything is in a terrible muddle'."[319] Johnston had taken a dunking while landing.[320] C Company's Stan Williams[321] had been removing his pack when "a fellow dropped down … in great distress" saying "'I nearly got drowned' … I recognised him then." It

---

300 Blay, diary, 25 April 1915.
301 406 Private William Samuel Bellamy, B Company, 25 at embarkation, customs officer, of Cottesloe.
302 Inman, diary, 25 April 1915 and B2455, Bellamy.
303 Mofflin, letter, 20 October 1915, p.14.
304 497 Sergeant Frank William Seccombe, B Company, 34 at death, piano tuner, of Perth, born South Australia. Served in the South African War.
305 Inman, diary, 25 April 1915.
306 397 Sergeant John Neil Arnold, B Company, 38 at embarkation, labourer, of Fremantle, born Ballarat.
307 Hitch, interview, May 1974, p.8.
308 *Ibid.*
309 *Ibid.*
310 Siefken, letter, 3 September 1915.
311 *Ibid.*
312 Hearder, manuscript 3DRL 3959, p.11.
313 Louch, manuscript, p.14.
314 T.S. Louch, AWM38 3DRL 606 item 27 – 206–215, Australian War Memorial.
315 873 Private David Knox Crerar, 27, electrical engineer, of East Wagin and Canada, born England.
316 Louch, manuscript, p.14.
317 *Ibid.*
318 Louch, 3DRL 606 item 27.
319 Louch, 3DRL 606 item 27.
320 Lock, *The Fighting 10th*, p.149.
321 733 Lance Corporal Stanley Maunder Williams.

was Johnston. Johnston "then said, come on boys, off your packs and up the hill."[322] A bullet hitting "the sand just clear" of Louch's and Johnston's noses convinced Louch this "was no place for dallying; so lugging our box of ammunition," he and his "mate"[323] began climbing. Facey, probably of the same platoon as Louch, remembered: "machine-guns sweeping the … beach … We all ran for our lives" across the open, men "falling all around me … stumbling over bodies … I would think for days, 'I should have helped that poor beggar'."[324] Reid's 15 Platoon landed near Buttle's.[325]

Hearder[326] recalled five men being hit in his boat, but apparently none belonged to his section.[327] Getting ashore under fire with the added burden of machine guns, tripods, tools and ammunition,[328] in addition to their infantry kit, was "no easy game but the chaps took it like heroes."[329] Fahey, either oblivious of the order that no chaplains were to land on the first day, or choosing to be so,[330] also landed with the destroyer tows. As he landed "a bullet passed between my knees."[331]

The "aim of the Turks became more true" as "the distance decreased," wrote E.J. Richards[332] of 13 Platoon:

> rifle and shrapnel bullets ziffed overhead or splashed the water … machine guns on our left flank opened … A bang on the side of the boat announced the first hit and a second later the seaman let go the tiller with an ejaculation of disgust – a bullet had passed thru his forearm. As the keel grounded on the beach another bullet struck a soldier in the groin.[333]

Norman Pittersen was in the same platoon but possibly not the same boat. "I will never forget it … the Turks were sending the lead into us like hell with machine guns, rifles and shrapnel. Talk about two or three hives of bees around you." The first wave had woken "the Turks up, they did pepper us as soon as we landed."[334] Private E.P. Stables probably also landed with this platoon, which Gostelow described landing under a "perfect hail of rifle and machine gun fire" beneath Walker's Ridge.[335] Stables had scored well against the rest of the division in a shooting competition in Egypt,[336] but would not live to use his rifle against the enemy. Crossing the beach A.J. Stevens, probably 14 Platoon, saw the "badly wounded" Stables lying on his stomach, "shot through the back".[337] This probably describes the exit wound of a bullet hitting Stables from the front; such wounds could be so severe that many men believed the Turks were using explosive bullets. Stables has no known grave. A "Lieutenant Palmer" lay nearby. This may in fact have been 14 Platoon's Second Lieutenant H.H. Walker, as no 3rd Brigade officer named Palmer appears to have become a casualty this day. Walker had run across the beach and "lay subjected to a very heavy fire from the Turks."[338] A bullet hit him in the right shoulder, severing an artery. His promotion to lieutenant is dated 25 April 1915, but he

322 S.M. Williams, interview, P. Liddle, May 1974, ANZAC (AUST) Recollections, AIF, Liddle Collection.
323 Louch, manuscript, p.14.
324 Facey, *A Fortunate Life*, p.254.
325 C.F. Buttle, 3DRL 8042 item 7, Australian War Memorial.
326 Hearder, manuscript 3DRL 3959, p.11.
327 C.F. Forrest, letter to father of G.H.H. Smith, 3DRL 7247, Australian War Memorial.
328 Murphy, letter, *Sunday Times*, 6 June 1915.
329 C.F. Forrest, letter to mother, 3DRL 7247, Australian War Memorial.
330 McKernan, *Padre*, p.50.
331 *Ibid.*, p.48.
332 826 Private Edward John Richards, 29 at enlistment, journalist, of Northam, born Victoria.
333 Richards, manuscript, 2DRL 301, pp.33–34.
334 Pittersen, letter, 4 May 1915.
335 C. Gostelow, diary, 25 April 1915, private collection, Perth.
336 Richards, manuscript, 2DRL 301.
337 Australian Red Cross Wounded and Missing Enquiry Bureau files, 1DRL/0428.
338 H.H. Walker, letter to mother, Mrs E.M. Walker, East Perth, *The West Australian*, 2 June 1915.

would not fight again. In 1917 the hapless Walker was dismissed from the service by court martial for an apparent minor fraud, losing pay, medals and return passage from England to Australia.

Gostelow's discovery that he was "away to the left … separated from the rest of the battalion,"[339] provides further evidence of the intermixing of troops. Gostelow's D Company landed from *Usk*, which was to the left (north) of *Chelmer*, yet a large part of B Company (from *Chelmer*) and several hundred yards separated Gostelow from Louch and others of D Company (from *Usk*). In addition, the second wave came in behind the first, intermixing B and D Companies with A and C.

Gostelow consequently decided "to lie still and wait for daylight."[340] Facey did the same, using, our "trenching tools to dig mounds of earth … the Turks never let up … The slaughter was terrible … there wouldn't have been one of us left if we had obeyed that damn fool order to line up on the beach.[341] This "fool order" may not be as ridiculous as it sounds. Facey's reference in the context of a bullet-swept beach creates an impression of an incompetent staff out of touch with the realities of the battle. Mofflin's earlier description[342] suggests the order was based on an unopposed landing, with men forming up in silence on the beach.

Then Gostelow "decided to locate the beggars who were firing on us."[343]

---

339 Gostelow, diary, 25 April 1915.
340 *Ibid.*
341 Facey, *A Fortunate Life*, p.254.
342 Mofflin, letter, 20 October 1915, p.12.
343 Gostelow, diary, 25 April 1915.

3

Assault from the Beach

The scramble from the boats and up the cliffs is arguably the most written about event of Australia's best known campaign, yet many contradictions remain and, beyond 57th Regiment's counter-attack, the Turkish experience has until recently been all but invisible. This chapter will use the foundation and methodology established in previous chapters to reconstruct and re-examine the 11th Battalion's experience and reveal the Turkish side of this part of the battle. It will argue that even after nearly a century, details buried in primary sources can be used to sculpt a clearer picture of such a confused event, incidents can be "fleshed out" and explained and questions answered.

The area from Plugge's Plateau to Hell Spit was occupied by up to 80 men of 2 Platoon, 4/2/27th Regiment. Sections of nine men had been detached to a position north of Ari Burnu, Hell Spit and the area between, later known as Anzac Cove, but the bulk of the platoon, possibly 50–60 rifles, fired on the landing from Plugge's Plateau.

3 Platoon were in company reserve at or near Courtney's Post. On the outbreak of firing, Faik had "ordered the platoon to … occupy the trenches on the high ridge which dominates North Ari Burnu" and sent "two sections under the command of Sergeant Ahmed[1] to the trenches on the central hill overlooking the beach." Faik wrote a report to his battalion CO "that the enemy was about to begin landing at Ari Burnu … I ordered the withdrawal by telephone and set off immediately with the platoon. On the way, we came under fire from the ships."[2] The meaning of some of this is unclear, but Uyar wrote that the two sections under "Ahmet" were on German Officer's Hill.[3] Faik took the remaining seven squads of No. 3 Platoon to a position on Russell's Top dominating Ari Burnu, Plugge's Plateau and the beaches to their north. Şefik's map shows this position being to the south of the Sphinx, and in 2005 there was still a deep trench here. When the Turks reached Russell's Top they "occupied the trenches opposite the northern beach of Ari Burnu" and opened fire at "1300 m,"[4] initially firing on the boats.[5] Faik also sent a runner to the mountain battery near the Cup on 400 Plateau, requesting that they open fire on the landing. He also wished them to move, if possible, to a position on the high ground of, he intended, Chunuk Bair, but named Hill 971 instead as he apparently, and surprisingly, did not know the name of Chunuk Bair.[6]

It is unclear when the trenches on Russell's Top were occupied, though Şefik's comment that before "the landing and defence forces came face to face … 3 Platoon … had already entered the struggle"[7] implies that they opened fire early.[8]

The company's 1 Platoon occupied trenches in the region of Fisherman's Hut, from where they enfiladed the troops landing north of Ari Burnu. Australian sources claim that there was a machine gun at Fisherman's Hut and another at Ari Burnu – Şefik does not mention these.[9] The number of

---

1   'Ahmet' according to Uyar, p101, 'Ahmed' on p.95. Uyar, pp.95, 101.
2   Şefik, para. 36.
3   Uyar, p.101.
4   Şefik, para. 36.
5   Uyar, p.101.
6   *Ibid.*
7   Şefik, para. 38.
8   Uyar wrote that these troops were in place at 4:40 a.m., but I have not cross referenced this time with other sources.
9   Şefik, paras. 34–38. Australian sources suggest anything up to four machine guns being present.

Turks was not great, but at this early stage, before 3 Platoon joined the battle, if their 100–140 riflemen fired 10 rounds per minute, they could have subjected the 3rd Brigade's first wave to up to 1,000–1,400 rounds per minute (16–23 per second). Uyar states that because of "their precarious and exposed position," the fire from the troops on Plugge's was not "organised and coordinated … and certainly not a fierce fusillade as commonly described in modern literature." As has been seen, those on the receiving end of this fire disagreed. Uyar adds that a strip of dead ground provided "effective cover immediately beyond the beach."[10] None of the beach was "dead" to the garrison of Ari Burnu, and, as will be seen, a curious trench on the forward face of Plugge's may have been positioned specifically to cover the dead ground referred to.

Some men landed on an empty beach, some behind or alongside others. All were exposed to enemy fire, from the skylines above or in enfilade, and as they had orders not to fire at this stage of the landing, the only covering fire they had was from the single picket boat that fired briefly at Ari Burnu. Officers and NCOs yelled to assemble their sections, platoons and companies, to be joined by whatever fragments were able and within hearing. Some men were pinned down or out of contact in the darkness and scrub; others had headed inland with the nearest officer, NCO or other men. Some platoons, spread over two boats, may have been separated by the intermixing of the tows. The fragmentation of the force had commenced before the charge inland began.

Leane recalled men not stopping "to charge mags" but fixing bayonets as they ran across the beach and throwing off their packs.[11] His observer made it across the beach where he dropped into cover, "gasping for breath." In "the morning dew" the scrub "gave forth a perfume" he learned "to loath and shall always." Bullets zipped so close past his ears they made his "eyes blink" as he "crawled up and up … mud on my wet garments … fixed my bayonet … charged … not an officer was to be seen, there was not two men of the same battalion together, the men did all on their own initiative."[12]

MacDonald threw himself down alongside Newham. "My word Mac that bullet was close." "Yes yes Newham," MacDonald replied. They rushed forward to better cover. A "shell sounded overhead … some of our unfortunate comrades caught it solid. Well Mac said it is no good staying here, I said … 'they can only kill us once', and so he turned round and said 'now there boys, up and into it', and we did."[13]

Brennan "heard an officer sing out 'Fix bayonets lads, and up we go'"[14] and bayonets clattered onto rifle muzzles "as fast as cold fingers and wet clothes would allow."[15] Someone, possibly Walter Stagles, called "Right lads, into the bastards, as quick as you can get."[16] Men who "went down at the start," recalled Luttrell, "begged us to leave them and devote our attention"[17] to the enemy. With a "Coo-ee" the men "rushed up the hill," opposed by, Luttrell thought, "500 Turks."[18] He doubted they would have managed the climb if this were not "the real thing," and wondered "how we would stand once the excitement of the first few moments had worn off."[19] It "would have done your heart good to see the Kal[goorlie] boys … charging," Hilliard[20] wrote, "the Turks clearing for dear life."[21]

---

10   Uyar, p.100.
11   Leane, AWM 38, 3DRL 8042 item 15.
12   Anonymous, Leane's observer, manuscript.
13   Newham, "Recollections of a Returned Soldier", n.p.
14   Brennan, letter, 1915, Army Museum of Western Australia.
15   Luttrell, letter, 16 May 1915.
16   1176 Private Walter Stagles, 1st Reinforcement, C Company. In one account, Stagles stated that "it was me who said come on lads, into the bastards." In another, he words it differently. W. Stagles, interview, ANZAC (Aust) Recollections, Liddle Collection, Brotherton Library, University of Leeds; and Sound recording, reference 4240, Imperial War Museum.
17   Luttrell, letter, 16 May 1915.
18   *Ibid.*
19   *Ibid.*
20   670 Lance Corporal James Clifford Hilliard, 22 at embarkation, bank officer, of Kalgoorlie, born Brunswick, Victoria.
21   J.C. Hilliard to Mr G.H. Watson, 20 May 1915, *Kalgoorlie Miner*, 21 June 1915.

Men continued to arrive and join the climb as their boats grounded, crawling "on hands and knees" if necessary,[22] pausing "to regain breath; but with dreadful yells" rushing on.[23] Darnell's scouts, after "cleaning the sand off our rifles ... went for the Turks ... we had to take that hill ... previous orders were set aside."[24] Howe met T.H. Porter[25] and "Drafty" Batt,[26] Morgan's batman, on the beach and headed inland.[27] Selby yelled orders to Medcalf and others sprinting towards the scrub through the enfilading "machine gun fire," the bullets raining "harder than ever" as they charged up the hillside. The guns at "Gaba Tepe ... had opened fire" and "machine guns on a hill also enfiladed"[28] the attack.

La Nauze found himself confronted by a slope as "high and straight as a wall. How we did it I don't know."[29] Aitken:

> quite forgot to be frightened. Then ... got quite annoyed and reckoned to have my money's worth if I were to be shot. So ... did my bit with the rest ... The boys behaved steadier than many veterans would have ... drove the Turks from seemingly impregnable positions ... with the exception of a few isolated examples we were not led by our officers. The men acted on their own initiative and ... saved a very critical situation.[30]

Most men "never fired a shot until we reached the crest of the first cliff,"[31] though Luttrell noted "The lads ... kept potting away at heads that occasionally showed themselves."[32] Darnell recalled "No firing – all bayonet work ... men dropped all round me, it was mad, wild, thrilling."[33] The men yelled the "familiar cries of the Egyptian" – "Egzacock," "Two for arf," "Orringas," "Shockerlate," "Nestlesses," "Imshy," "Yalla," "Talla Hina Abdul" and others, as they charged. "What a din!" wrote Keast, "shouting and hurraying and some of them were calling the Turks (none of whom we could see) nasty names. I shall never forget it."[34] With the "noise and the cracks of the Turks' rifles, it was just a terrible nightmare,"[35] and "must have been terrifying to the enemy."[36]

Men scattering as they found a route inland from beaches sweeping away from Ari Burnu point, and imprecision in perception and recollection, make it difficult to determine precisely men's routes to the crest, though Bean's comment that the "boats of the 11th Battalion hit the shore 200 or 300 yards north of the point of Ari Burnu"[37] is an over-simplification. Leane noted "three boats," presumably a single tow, "to the left of us containing 9th Battalion men ... the 10th Battalion and one of the 11th were on the right of my boat."[38] Hastings believed "Not a shot" was fired "by the rising wave ... the only sound British hurrahs from Australian throats" and "the rustle and break of the brush and scrub. One hundred and fifty feet brought us to the summit," presumably of Ari Burnu, "only to find another frowning above, with a steep descent between. Down the incline ...

---

22   Brennan, letter, 1915, Army Museum of Western Australia.
23   Marshall, letter, 9 May 1915.
24   Anonymous scout, letter, 15 May 1915.
25   204 Private Thomas Hedley Porter, A Company, 38 at enlistment, miner, born Yorke Peninsula, South Australia. Served in South Africa with the 4th Contingent of the West Australian Imperial Bushmen.
26   149 Private Thomas Silas Batt, A Company, 31 at enlistment, labourer, born South Wales. Served in the South African War and 12 years with the Gloucester Regiment.
27   Howe, 3DRL 8042 item 7.
28   Medcalf, manuscript, p.63.
29   La Nauze, letter to wife, n.d.
30   Aitken, letter/diary, p.18.
31   Gallaher, letter, *Kalgoorlie Miner*, June 1915.
32   Luttrell, letter, 16 May 1915.
33   Darnell, 1DRL 233.
34   Keast, diary, 24/25 April 1915.
35   Combs, manuscript, Ellam-Innes Collection.
36   Taylor, letter, *Kalgoorlie Miner*, 7 July 1915.
37   Bean, *Official History*, Volume I (1921 and 1941), p.255.
38   Winter, *The Inevitable Tragedy*, p.98. Brockman, for example, told Bean he had landed "on the point of Ari Burnu – exactly on the point." 3DRL.606 item 27.

then up and on again … hanging on by tufts of shrubs." Puffing "panting, cheering and resting" they crawled and climbed, "rifles with white, pointed, relentless bayonets fixed" in the "grey dawn." The skyline above spat:

> fire and whirring bullets … a halt before the last determined rush … an officer, swaying and balancing himself on the hillside. "You are not wounded, sir?" I anxiously asked. "No, no. It's tough climbing though," was the smiling reply, as he wiped the sweat from his streaming brow. He was Captain Annear … and must have been shot within two minutes time. With a grand hurrah again, we all pressed on.[39]

The troops climbing Ari Burnu and Plugge's Plateau scrambled "round bushes and dead Australians" and Turks[40] (Figure 12). Shots "were fired at us from the rear. Men shouted back – 'Don't fire on your own men' – but they were snipers who were missed."[41] Whether this fire came from Turks or Australians is not known. That there were Turks scattered through the bushes is well documented,[42] but Bean also refers to casualties caused by "friendly fire."[43]

On "we went" wrote Newham, "routing them out of the trenches and pushing them along for our dear lives."[44] "Straight over the knocked out maxim" went Darnell, "cheering, swearing, I never heard such awful language."[45] Many men refer to this gun, but few to actually seeing it during the ascent. Bean described its position as a "small square machine-gun post … The Turks … were bolting from the top … In the trench lay a wounded Turk."[46] This post enfilades the beaches to its south and north.

Men were "moving everywhere" as Howe climbed. He believed the Turkish machine guns "could not suppress their muzzles sufficiently to fire on the troops climbing the steep slope,"[47] and "About half way up" he came across a Turkish trench.[48] This is not the Ari Burnu post but a small trench, traces of which still remain, on the north-west side of Plugge's Plateau. The role of this isolated trench, established on a cliff face and apparently out of touch with the main position on the crest, is difficult to fathom, unless it was to cover the dead ground referred to earlier:[49] Sections of Faik's 2 Platoon had been despatched to cover the southern side of Ari Burnu and those in this trench may have been there to cover its north.

Some "half a dozen" of the trench's garrison threw their hands up, others ran.[50] A Turk near Howe "jumped up like a rabbit"; Howe's rifle was "full of sand," but he managed to bayonet the man "through a haversack – and stopped him – 9th Battalion man hit him on the head with the butt of his rifle and knocked him down."[51] That a 9th Battalion man was with Howe supports Leane's comments that boats of that battalion were to his left. "They ratted him but all he had were some

39   Hastings, letter, 10 June 1915.
40   Newham, "Recollections of a Returned Soldier", n.p.
41   Peck or Johnston, 3DRL 606 item 25, pp.7–10.
42   For example, Major M.F. Beevor, 10th Battalion, "My Landing at Gallipoli," manuscript, 940.481MYL, Defence Regional Library, Adelaide, p.14; A.R. Perry, 10th Battalion, *The Anzac Book, written and illustrated in Gallipoli by the men of Anzac* (London, New York, Toronto, Melbourne: Cassell, 1916), p.2; Lieutenant T. Miles, 12th Battalion, 2DRL 554, Australian War Memorial; Newton, *The Story of the 12th*, p.89.
43   Bean, *Official History*, Volume I (1921 and 1941), p.261.
44   Newham, "Recollections of a Returned Soldier", n.p.
45   Darnell, PR82/175.
46   Bean, *Official History*, Volume I (1921 and 1941), p.258.
47   H.V. Howe, "Sparks From an Old Controversy", *Australian Army Journal: Periodical Review of Military Literature*, Number 191, April 1965, p.6.
48   Howe, 3DRL 8042 item 7.
49   That 11th Battalion accounts do not refer to heavy casualties being sustained during this part of the climb suggest this slope may have been dead ground. Before the troops crested Plugge's Plateau, most of the fire seems to have been directed at the boats and the beach.
50   Bush, *Gallipoli*, p.102.
51   Howe, 3DRL 8042 item 7.

raisins and cigarettes in a bit of newspaper."[52] In another account, Howe describes jumping into this trench "on top of one" of the surrendering Turks "and cut the waist band off his pants, taking his belt away. I took some raisins and dried apricots out of his pockets."[53] The call went up "Prisoner here!" and received the reply "Bayonet the bastard."[54] Bean thought this reaction was a consequence of warnings, based on "experience of the Kurds and less disciplined Turkish troops, that the Turks mutilated men whom they captured or found wounded."[55] The prisoner, minus his buttons, was instead handed to a wounded man to take back to the beach.[56] As other men also went through the Turk's pockets, this may be one of the first documented instances of the AIF "ratting" prisoners.[57]

Mofflin recalled:

> yelling and shouting like mad men ... somebody sang out "Wait for the Officers!" "Oh! D____ the Officers, come on, they can't hit us." Wild Australians bluffed Jacko that morning ... It was a charge, just a mob climbing the hills as best we could, pulling and shoving each other up ... I was shouting to try and keep my little section together and about half way up ... I prodded Major Brockman in the seat with my bayonet.[58]

Ed Inman joined his brother Jack,[59] Mofflin[60] and Jack Nelson.[61] Mofflin paused for "a blow," probably at "the top" of Ari Burnu, when he was joined by "the sailor I had shook hands with on leaving the boat," who related that "The man just behind you was killed ... so I grabbed his rifle and equipment and came too." Seconds later he "gave a sort of half groan and fell down ... quite dead ... I went on again, with a great chum of mine Percy Andrews,[62] nicknamed 'the Rajah' because he was so dark ... we help each other up ... 'Hot work eh?' 'Could be worse' ... and away we'd go again."[63]

Lugging an ammunition box, Louch and his mate:

> stopped for breath ... and saw the first shell to be fired by the Turkish battery near Gaba Tepe. First there was the report of the gun, then the whine of the shell, then the flash and a puff of smoke ... finally the patter of the shrapnel pellets in the sea. It was quite pretty to watch.[64]

Two thirds of the way up, Combs saw "in the faint, dim light ... two great fat chaps clamber over the top,"[65] possibly withdrawing from the isolated trench attacked by Howe. Nearer the crest Combs was confronted by "a Jacko's head" appearing "out of a trench a few feet away: the chap alongside – who had disobeyed orders by loading his rifle – gave him a bullet point blank ... I searched him ... then smashed his rifle."[66] Retchford shot "a Turk point blank before getting halfway to the top ... I just got in before he did."[67]

---

52   *Ibid.*

53   Bush, *Gallipoli*, p.102.

54   Howe, 3DRL 8042 item 7.

55   Bean, *Official History*, Volume I (1921 and 1941), p.258.

56   Howe, 3DRL 8042 item 7.

57   Bush, *Gallipoli*, p.102.

58   Mofflin, letter, 20 October 1915, p.14.

59   1202 Private John William Inman, B Company, 25 at enlistment, postal assistant of Fremantle, born Emerald, Victoria.

60   Inman, diary, 25 April 1915.

61   469 Lance Corporal John Alfred Nelson, B Company, 29 at embarkation, labourer, of South Fremantle, born Collingwood, Victoria.

62   392 Lance Corporal Percy Andrews, B Company, 22 at enlistment, ironmonger, of Fremantle, born Gympy, Queensland.

63   Mofflin, letter, 20 October 1915, p.15.

64   Louch, manuscript, pp.14–15.

65   Combs, manuscript.

66   *Ibid.*

67   A.R. Retchford, letter to mother and brother, 14 and 15 May 1915, *Kalgoorlie Miner*, 7 July 1915.

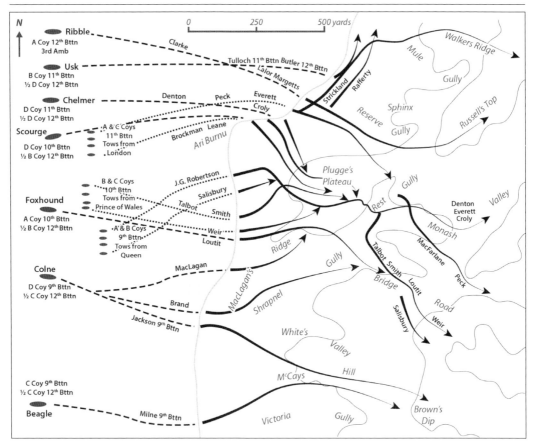

Map 6. Adapted from Bean's Map 11, depicting routes taken by elements of 11th Battalion and 3rd Brigade officers. (Bean, Map 11, *Official History*, Volume I (1921 and 1941), opposite p.256)

Those to the north had landed slightly later. Eastcott found the beach "dotted … with the bodies of poor fellows who hadn't made it." He threw himself down to "the incessant crackle of the bullets … the cries of the wounded, and the peculiar wail of those who were mortally wounded. I had never heard it before but knew what it was without any doubt."[68]

On the beach, bullets were kicking up "spurts of sand" around Murray, then one hit him.[69] His sandbags, rolled and tied "to the small of my back… got wet through and … to that … I owe my life." He later found "a bullet hole in my rolled up sandbags about half an inch from my spine." The wet material turned the bullet "and it ran round and round … cutting the bags as though with a knife … I offered up a prayer as I took it out."[70] A captain, presumably Everett, called:

"Is that you Murray." "Yes Sir." "You stay here and guard the packs." "But I am a sharp shooter" … "Doesn't matter … You stay here" … I didn't relish … staying on the beach in full view … I would rather have gone in with the boys … we got as many packs as were within reach and made a barricade … they stopped a good many bullets.[71]

---

68   Eastcott, manuscript, p.7.
69   Murray, letter, 16 May 1915.
70   *Ibid.*
71   Murray, letter, 16 May 1915.

Everett told the others to "crawl … into the scrub,"[72] but Eastcott felt:

[A] terrific blow on the head, an intense white flash and utter darkness. I screamed out "I am hit!" … convinced … I had been shot through the eyes … the blindness passed off … discovered a gash under my left eye. The bone seemed … OK and as the shock was wearing off I decided I would probably live a little longer.[73]

He began tending the wounded around him.

Six men were hit in Jackson's 5 Platoon boat.[74] "A machine gun was firing from Walker's Ridge" and the 12th Battalion "landing further north … came under deadly fire from Walker's, men falling as they reached the beach."[75] Bean recorded the "fire from the left" being "very heavy"[76] and, possibly unclear about how to interpret the many eyewitness accounts, described "A machine-gun on some height beyond Walker's Ridge … playing on"[77] this section of beach, suggesting the Fisherman's Hut gun, but leaving his options open. Perhaps this fire came from Faik's 3 Platoon, 4 Company, on Russell's Top, as Faik describes his men's fire hitting men in the boats.[78] Two trenches on the seaward crest of Russell's Top, one north of the Sphinx and one south, have good fields of fire onto North Beach and the north side of Ari Burnu. In addition to the troops of the 11th Battalion, the 12th Battalion's HQ, A and D Companies, possibly 5 and 8 Platoons, and members of the 3rd Field Ambulance landed in this area.

Otto Siefken,[79] 6 Platoon, found cover under "a little bank next to Ben and Sergeant Wilson."[80] Wilson "dropped with a bullet through both legs"; he survived to be wounded in the thigh again at Leane's Trench in August. "A minute later Ben dropped." Ben Bailey[81] "did not speak, just gave a groan and was dead,"[82] "shot right through the centre of the head."[83] "Bill" Bruton[84] and "Bandy" Turner also landed here – Bandy saw Bailey's body and Bruton wrote to Bailey's parents of an instantaneous death.

Ashton was on the beach sheltering from "a fairly heavy fire" from above and the left. Paradoxically, the rifle flashes and sound of bullets "striking close by, or singing away over our heads … drove out any feeling of fear. It was a shock … to find that the man lying immediately in front of me had been struck by a bullet and wounded, not two feet from my own head." With their officer, presumably Walker, "lying on the beach with a gaping wound in his chest, covered with blood," the men were "at a loss to know what" to do, so fired "at the rifle flashes away to our left," tended the wounded and waited for orders.[85]

Peck had somehow moved to the north after landing. He later wrote that he was looking for HQ; if so, he must have missed it. He instead reported to Colonel L.F. Clarke, 12th Battalion, but as the 12th was brigade reserve, Peck "yelled for officers and was answered by Lieutenants Rockliff and MacFarlane," who "had about 100 men between them." He ordered MacFarlane's platoon to join those visible "charging up the precipitous slopes"[86] to the right, presumably Plugge's Plateau. Peck

72 Everett, interview, Ellam-Innes Collection, p.239.
73 Eastcott, manuscript, p.7.
74 Belford, *Legs Eleven*, p.71.
75 S.H. Jackson, Ellam-Innes Collection, Perth.
76 Bean, *Official History*, Volume I (1921 and 1941), p.269.
77 *Ibid.*, p.271.
78 Şefik, para. 36.
79 354 Bugler Otto John Siefken, B Company, 20 at enlistment, butcher, of Maylands, born Brighton, Victoria.
80 373 Sergeant Claude Manly Wilson, B Company, 20 at embarkation, vigneron, of Caversham, born Broken Hill.
81 272 Private Ben Harold Bailey, B Company, 21, blacksmith, of West Guildford, born Bunbury.
82 O.J. Siefken, letter to mother, 3 September 1915, quoted Gill, Fremantle to France, pp.406–409.
83 W. Olson, Gallipoli, The Western Australian Story, University of Western Australia Press, Crawley, 2006, p.48.
84 968 Private (at embarkation) William Charles Bruton, 24 at embarkation, cook, of Geelong.
85 Ashton, manuscript, p.15.
86 Peck, letter to wife, n.d.

was joined by Everett and Jackson, and the 10th Battalion's Lieutenant C. Rumball. "Come on boys, by God I'm frightened!"[87] Peck yelled as he led his party towards the ridge later known as "Razor Edge"[88] (Figure 15). Croly was reputedly seen dashing up an unnamed slope "waving a Turkish sword or bayonet and crying, 'Come on, the bloody 11th!'"[89] (Map 6).

On Plugge's Plateau, Mofflin:

> [S]aw 3 Turks firing down onto the beach. There was nobody between them and me, it was a trifle dark for shooting, but I thought I'd risk it, so I dropped on one knee and let him have it ... hit him fair between the eyes. Killed my first Turk with my first shot. I was that pleased I could have danced on his body.

Selby "took his rifle and bayonet" and Mofflin a tobacco pouch – "a curio from my first Turk."[90] Selby, who landed near Leane, MacDonald and Annear, had reached the crest with Lieutenant E.W. Talbot-Smith of the 10th, to be greeted by a "heavy" fire.[91] A trench lay a few feet in from the crest, overlooking North Beach. Bean describes Selby, Leane, MacDonald and Annear flinging themselves down behind its heaped-soil parapet,[92] as they believed the trench could have been mined.[93] The fire was "very hot,"[94] coming mostly from a trench on the inland side of the plateau, and even the far side of the gully behind it. Three Turks in a trench "on top of MacLagan's Ridge stood up and fired – Annear was killed by two shots[95] and MacDonald hit through the shoulder."[96] Corporal A.J.E. Wallish,[97] 1 Platoon, was immediately behind Annear, who fell into his arms. Wallish checked his pulse and moved on – Annear had been shot "pretty much" between the eyes.[98] 11 Platoon's James Palmer was nearby and confirmed Annear had been "shot clean through the head."[99] Palmer would be wounded five times, the first being when he "caught a bayonet on the upper lip in the first quarter of an hour ashore."[100]

The location of Annear's death is uncertain. A trench still exists on the crest of Plugge's Plateau where Bean places it,[101] but, as previously noted, two witnesses[102] recalled Annear being killed on the beach. In one account Brockman told Bean that Leane, "Annear and MacDonald were lying together in the scrub at the foot of the hill when Annear was shot through the head."[103] He was at the time describing the Turks in their trench on Ari Burnu, which is beneath Plugge's but above the beach. Selby's account is probably the most reliable, as it provides an unbroken chronology of his climb with Annear, their arrival at the crest, a description of the terrain and of Annear's death. This account matches Bean's. The balance of evidence places Annear's death on either Plugge's Plateau or

87   Bean, *Official History*, Volume I (1921 and 1941), p.270.
88   Jackson, Ellam-Innes Collection.
89   Belford, *Legs Eleven*, p.73. It would seem that this anecdote could not have happened as stated, and was possibly transposed from a later incident, when Croly is more likely to have been able to aquire an enemy sword or bayonet; except for the fact that, as Bradshaw's accounit shows, recent evidence has revealed that a Turkish squad was deployed near the beach north of Ari Burnu. Perhaps Croly had landed near here, and had indeed picked up a Turkish bayonet.
90   Mofflin, letter, 20 October 1915, p.15.
91   A.R. Selby, 3DRL 8042 item 7.
92   Bean, *Official History*, Volume I (1921 and 1941), p.260.
93   *Ibid.*; Selby, 3DRL 8042 item 7.
94   Selby, 3DRL 8042 item 7.
95   Richard Annear was unmarried, and left behind a brother, living in Kalgoorlie, and a sister in Subiaco. His father had died before the war; his mother was to pass away in 1917. He had left his will with his sister; it began with the words "If I should get blown out ..." Most of his possessions he left to his family, with a few carefully chosen ones to be sent to a female friend in Tasmania.
96   R.L. Leane, AWM38 3DRL 606 item 28(2).
97   1186 Corporal Albert Joseph Wallish, A Company, 24 at enlistment, miner, born Apsley, Victoria.
98   Ned Wallish, quoting A.J.E. Wallish, interview with J.P. Hurst, 25 Nov 2004.
99   J. Palmer, letter, n.d., quoted in unidentified newspaper, Ellam-Innes Collection, Perth.
100 Palmer, letter.
101 Bean, *Official History*, Volume I (1921 and 1941), p.260.
102 Anonymous, Leane's observer, manuscript, and Brodribb.
103 Brockman, 3DRL 606 item 27.

Figure 12. Seaward slope of Plugge's Plateau climbed by many of the 11th
Battalion. (Photograph by J.P. Hurst, n.d., author's collection)

Ari Burnu. Either of these possibilities would refute the death on the beach, and are supported by a
number of other accounts, such as Hastings'.[104]

Passing to the right of the trench "on … Ari Burnu," Brockman glimpsed "a quick fight" as the
men killed the Turks who shot Annear. Minutes later he reached the plateau – to be charged by
three Turks with bayonets fixed. Brockman "thought he was done for."[105] Bean's description of what
happened next is surprisingly brief: "An Irishman, an old soldier of the Dragoon Guards, killed all
three."[106] In fact, it was "Paddy" Reid who had reached the crest behind Brockman and went straight
for the three Turks. He clubbed the first: over the head with his rifle butt:

[the] second Turk … went for him. Paddy bayoneted him and apparently could not get the bayonet out –
so he dropped it. The third Turk came at him but he brushed his rifle aside and caught hold of the Turk,
threw him onto the ground and kicked him on the head and killed him.[107]

Reid was wounded in the right forearm on 25 April, possibly in this fight. Reid's character and
past suggest a plausible explanation for this extraordinary feat. He had served two years in the

---

104 Hastings, letter, 10 June 1915. Buttle describes seeing Annear's body "towards the top of the first heights." Buttle, letter to
Bean, 1 June 1920. Curiously, Ashton describes coming across "one of our officers, shot through the head, the blue hole in his
forehead" still clearly recalled many years later. This matches descriptions of Annear's fatal wound, but Ashton places this well
inland; either he was referring to a non-11th Battalion officer, or his chronology was awry. Ashton, manuscript, p.17.

105 Brockman, 3DRL 606 item 27.

106 Bean, *Official History*, Volume I (1921 and 1941), p.260–61. One account, apparently inspired by this incident, described a
sergeant driving his bayonet "through one man, then through two together", before clubbing two more to death. Olson, p.358,
quoting Frank McAdam.

107 Brockman, 3DRL 606 item 27.

Figure 13. Plugge's Plateau and Ari Burnu. According to Bean, Annear and MacDonald
were shot while lining the lip of the crest of Plugge's, in about the centre of this photograph,
below the cemetery marker. (Photograph by J.P. Hurst, n.d., author's collection)

Royal Irish Fusiliers, where he probably learned rifle and bayonet drill long before enlisting in the
AIF. Bayonet training at the time taught a number of movements. A thrust at the left side of a
right-handed man's body could be parried left and followed through with a blow from the butt of
the rifle. A thrust at a man's right could be parried to the right and followed with a bayonet thrust.
This training appears to be reflected in Reid's fight with the first two Turks, but perhaps his size and
history of violence served him and Brockman well that morning: Reid had a habit of fighting, often
under the influence of alcohol. It will be recalled that he was supposed to be in prison for assault
at the time of the Landing, and in coming years he would frequently be charged with drunkenness
and violence. In May 1918 he was discharged from the AIF as "undesirable," his services no longer
required, after serving a year's imprisonment with hard labour and forfeiting more than a year's pay.
He had been described in various reports as "incorrigible," a "bad example," and "worthless" and
was denied his war medals. Brockman was to rise to the rank of brigadier-general. Clearly, for a few
seconds on the morning of 25 April, the "worthless" Reid was of great value to the AIF.

When Ed Inman reached the crest the Turks were "leaving for their lives ... on the right, they
captured two machine guns and a 3 pounder."[108] Any Turk remaining near the forward lip of the
plateau had to contend not only with the enemy troops to his front, but to his flanks and possibly
rear. Some fought, others withdrew to a trench on the inland side of the plateau and continued
to shoot at the advancing Australians, "a number" of whom "went down, but it did not stop the
advance which went straight across."[109] With bullets "zipping around us" Hastings found "doubled
up in the shrubbery ... my first dead foeman ... This first contact with a yet warm victim, and

---

108 Inman, diary, 25 April 1915.
109 Bush, *Gallipoli*, p.102.

the swift realisation that we were there to kill, gave one a curious and ghastly thrill."[110] Two Turks jumped up and fired.[111] They hit Batt, who fell alongside Howe and "Almost in front of" Hastings.[112] "The poor fellow was shot in the side, and in terrible pain, but, brave heart that he was ... through grinding teeth, called out, 'Well done, lads; go it boys'."[113] Howe's party rushed the Turks, who ran. An Australian stepping from behind a bush drove his bayonet through one, just below the arm. The other was shot as he reached the far crest and slid, dead, part way down the gravel slope.[114] "With levelled rifles, on we rushed."[115]

In "the excitement," Darnell had forgotten to draw his revolver, so he "secured the rifle and bayonet of the first dead man."[116] Newham found himself confronted by a "row of trenches, thick with Turks, but it did not take us long to shift them with the bayonets. As we walked through them we were inclined to stop, but one of the Officers sang out go on men, I have no orders to take prisoners yet, and of course we went on."[117]

When the "sprinters" reached the Turks in the far trench and bayoneted or evicted them, resistance on the plateau ended.[118] The only Turks remaining when Hastings reached this trench were those "who had learnt the Australian could shoot."[119] Brodribb encountered "little opposition" on the top, believing "our war cry frightened hell out of them."[120] Confronting the Australians on the inland crest was a valley, 280 feet deep.[121] The left of the slope was sheer; towards the right, a zig-zag path descended into the valley; three Turkish tents stood on a relatively level patch of ground about half way down.[122] Beyond, Turks could be seen in the valley, "hundreds of feet below, dashing from shelter to shelter ... Occasionally a rifle would ring out," and one would fall.[123] Most accounts refer to the enemy doubling or running,[124] though Howe described them retiring "in good order," to vanish "in the thick scrub of the valley below."[125] Goodlet's account was more brutal – "the diggers pursued them and murdered them as they ran."[126]

Some of the 3rd Brigade were still climbing Plugge's or the ridges to its north and others were landing or organising on the beach. Fisherman's Hut, as yet undisturbed by attack, continued to enfilade the landing. Twenty minutes earlier, most of the men assembling on the plateau had not heard a shot fired in anger. In the space of a few minutes they had survived their first enemy bullets, seen leaders and friends killed and wounded, confronted and fought their foe and undertaken what they believed to be the hardest part of the operation – getting ashore. They looked through the enemy trenches, tended or comforted their wounded, examined the dead littering the scrub, studied the few prisoners; one apparently took some clandestine photographs (Figure 14). "Drafty" Batt stifled the pain of the wound that would kill him. Dongara farm labourer T.G. Carroll[127] may also have lain dead or dying in the scrub, one month short of his 24th birthday. His brother would

---

110 Hastings, letter, 10 June 1915.
111 Howe, 3DRL 8042 item 7.
112 Hastings, letter, 10 June 1915.
113 *Ibid.*
114 Howe, 3DRL 8042 item 7; Bean, Volume I (1921 and 1941), p.260.
115 Hastings, letter, 10 June 1915.
116 Darnell, 1DRL 233.
117 Newham, "Recollections of a Returned Soldier", n.p.
118 Peck or Johnston, 3DRL 606 item 25 pp.7–10.
119 Hastings, letter, 10 June 1915.
120 Brodribb, letter to T.J. Callery, 17 July 1915, *Kalgoorlie Miner*, 23 August 1915.
121 Bean, *Gallipoli Mission*, p.78.
122 Bean, *Official History*, Volume I (1921 and 1941), p.261. In *Gallipoli Mission*, p.79, Bean states that there were two tents.
123 Hastings, letter, 10 June 1915.
124 Brockman, 3DRL 606, item 27.
125 Howe, "Sparks From an Old Controversy", p.6.
126 Goodlet, manuscript, p.11.
127 1015 Private Thomas George Carroll, C Company, 23, farm labourer, of Dongara.

be killed four months later. W.M. Edgar,[128] C Company, probably died on the plateau.[129] Scottish labourer S.G. Bell[130] was recorded as missing until 1916; his burial on Plugge's Plateau may support Mofflin's evidence that some B Company men participated in its capture.

Mofflin's and other evidence reveals that Bean's statement that the "northernmost of the destroyers, carrying … 11th and 12th Battalions and the 3rd Field Ambulance landed their men … a few hundred yards further north than any of the battleship tows"[131] to be a simplification. In Gostelow's case it is correct,[132] but Mofflin, 7 Platoon, climbed Plugge's Plateau neck and neck with members of A Company, and the battleship tows' Everett and Eastcott landed beneath Russell's Top. Buttle told Bean that 15 and 16 Platoons landed beneath the Sphinx but climbed MacLagan's Ridge, some 800 yards to its south, and Tom Louch, who landed with Buttle,[133] thought he was about 500 yards south of Walker's Ridge.[134] So it can be assumed that "beneath the Sphinx" suggests anywhere between Ari Burnu point and Walker's Ridge. Given such difficulties in interpreting accounts, the best that can be deduced is that B and D Companies landed between the northern foot of Plugge's Plateau and the beach beneath Walker's Ridge.

Şefik noted that the Ari Burnu garrison was not, as believed by the Australians, taken by surprise. The ships had been seen before moonset and the trenches on Plugge's and Ari Burnu had consequently been manned.[135] Şefik adds that "the platoon at Ari Burnu … did not open fire until" the tows were about to land their troops and that this "was a mistake"; here he may be criticising the "command paralysis" noted by Uyar, without saying as much. He believed if fire had been opened at "100 metres … getting the Australians ashore would have been … very costly." Casualties were also reduced by machine gun fire from the pinnace and dispersal of the Ottoman's firepower "among twelve craft,"[136] presumably meaning 12 tows. This phase of the operation may have seemed a dramatic and costly episode to the Australians, but Şefik believed it could have been a lot worse.

Şefik also evidences that the single pinnace that fired briefly at Ari Burnu, if indeed only one opened fire, had a greater impact than realised, and raises the question of how the Landing may have fared had it been covered by co-ordinated fire from all pinnaces. Could they, for example, have silenced the deadly fire from Fisherman's Hut? Şefik also thought that boats left on the beaches north of Ari Burnu evidenced the effectiveness of the fire from Fisherman's Hut and Russell's Top, which caused "the British" to refrain from landing "on that side."[137] This confirms that the 11th and 12th Battalions' landing here were exposed to heavier fire than those south of the point, and provides one probable reason later brigades landed in Anzac Cove, thereby launching it into the Australian psyche. It also suggests that Russell's Top was occupied early.

In Volume XII of the *Official History*, first published in 1923, there appeared a photograph that showed only a single body lying on the beach of what would become named Anzac Cove or Anzac Beach. This photograph has recently been used to claim that this "belies the myth of the Australians suffering heavy casualties as they came ashore."[138] This evidence is further used to argue that "If the

128 535 Private Wolverton Mason Edgar, C Company, 35, labourer, of Bunbury, born Yorkshire. Edgar had moved to Australia in 1910 after working as a "gentleman's servant", serving in the 2nd East Surrey Regiment and aboard HMS *Terrible*.
129 He was killed in action 25 April 1915 and buried on Plugge's Plateau.
130 275 Private Scot George Bell, B Company, 28, labourer, of Coorow, born Scotland. Bell was missing until declared killed in action in 1916. One report stated that he was lost well inland.
131 Bean, *Official History*, Volume I, p.267.
132 Gostelow, diary, 25 April 1915 and Figure 16.
133 Louch, manuscript, p.14.
134 Louch, 3DRL 606 item 27, 206–215.
135 Şefik, para. 37.
136 *Ibid.*, para. 38a.
137 Şefik, paras. 38b and c.
138 Roberts, *Landing at Anzac*, p.97.

Australians did land under machine-gun fire one would expect considerable casualties."[139] Certainly believing myths is unwise, but as has been seen, most of the 11th Battalion's casualties occurred on a different beach, beyond Ari Burnu, and others on the scrub-covered slopes. Perhaps also there had been some attempt to remove dead and wounded from the beach: the photograph was taken some three hours after the first members of the 3rd Brigade had crossed it, and might it not be demoralising for troops landing later to have to step over the bodies of their comrades?

Şefik's account suggests there were no Turkish machine guns firing on the 3rd Brigade landing. If so, Australian perceptions of their fire were probably due to the effectiveness of the rifle fire, perhaps exaggerated by echoes from the cliffs and the "crack" of passing bullets. Inexperience, expectation, rumour and the sound of the pinnace's machine gun may have reinforced belief in the presence of machine guns. Accounts by men who saw Turkish machine guns are more difficult to explain.[140] A brief, jumbled but intriguing statement by A. Ozgen, then a 27th Regiment Second Lieutenant "in the machine guns," states that Ozgen's position was "In front of" MacLagan's Ridge, and, in response to a question about the Australians landing at 4:30 a.m., said that he "remembers the first landing." His "position was well placed. We had a little forest in which we had our guns."[141] This is too vague to be accepted as concrete evidence and it is possible Ozgen accompanied Şefik to the battlefield, meaning that he arrived later. Broadbent quotes from the 27th Regiment's Major Halis Bey's memoir that before the landing "half a machine gun company" was assigned to positions "on the ridge behind Ari Burnu," with orders to "establish itself behind the position in such a way as to bring the northern shore of the Ariburnu[sic]–Kaba Tepe sector under fire."[142] Where this machine gun company came from is not stated. Williams, citing Turkish sources, also notes deployment of a Turkish machine gun company to the area.[143] Recent research has produced more concrete evidence of Australians overrunning a machine gun on Ari Burnu, and circumstantial evidence that the coastal defences were reinforced by guns stripped from battleships.[144] Perhaps the Australians who believed they were fired on by machine guns were correct after all.[145]

It is not known how many Turks died in the defence of Plugge's Plateau. Uyar thought "about half" the garrison of Plugge's "were wounded or killed during the initial exchanges of fire," as their "upper bodies were exposed."[146] Here appears to lie another paradox between Australian and Ottoman sources. There was not supposed to be any initial exchange of fire, as the Australians were supposed to be using the bayonet only, and only a few men had loaded their rifles. Witnesses recorded a short burst of machine gun fire from the pinnace, a little close range shooting, and that some Turks were clubbed or bayoneted. Australian accounts describe most of the Turkish casualties occurring during fighting on the plateau and the garrisons' withdrawal; others may have died during subsequent fighting. Faik learned on "rejoining the regiment that … only three or four men" of the Hain Tepe platoon "escaped"[147] and Şefik described the losses of 2 and 3 platoons as "a splendid example of self-sacrifice to the point of annihilation."[148] The number of Australians killed taking the plateau is

---

139 Roberts, *Wartime*, p.18.
140 Cockburn wrote that "when we got on top of the hill", i.e. Plugge's Plateau, they "found two machine guns that had been left behind." Cockburn, diary, 28 April 1915.
141 A. Ozgen, typed transcript of interview with Peter Liddle, July 1972, Tape 69, TU01, Liddle Collection, Brotherton Library, University of Leeds. Ozgen continues that success was in part due to "good orders from our high command," which were "To fight the enemy and kill them. That was our order."
142 Major Halis Bey, *Canakkale Raporu* (Istanbul: Arma Publications, 1975), p.91, quoted Broadbent, *Gallipoli – The Fatal Shore*, p.43. Halis was actually a captain at the time according to Şefik.
143 Williams, *The Battle of Anzac Ridge*, pp.64–65, citing Genelkurmay Baskanligi, *Birinci Dunya Harbinde inci Cilt Canakkale Cephesi*, 2nci Kitap (Ankara: Genelkurmay Basimevi, 1973), vol. 2, pp.90–94, and Maps 14, 16, 28.
144 M. Ewen, "The Gallipoli Maxims", *The Gallipolian*, Autumn 2014, pp.17–28.
145 Hurst, "Ottoman Machine Guns at the ANZAC Landing, 25 April 1915", currently unpublished, examines this issue in depth.
146 Uyar, p.101.
147 Şefik, para. 37.
148 *Ibid.*, para. 37e.

also unknown. Howe later estimated "40–50 casualties to either side" on "the plateau itself."[149] 11th Battalion accounts, which mention very few Australian casualties, suggest this figure to be too high.

Despite Bean's attempts at interpreting the details he had collected, the events of that morning are still confused and eyewitness accounts confusing. Helpless exposure to fire for the first time from an enemy hidden by scrub, trenches and darkness, combined with excitement and pre-landing briefings, led to assumptions of a much greater Turkish force than was present. The first Australian wave alone outnumbered the Turks on Ari Burnu and Plugge's Plateau by roughly 10 to one. Other myths arose because men believed them to be true and indeed, from their perspective, they may well have been. Those who began the assault without seeing an officer or receiving orders from one, proudly recalled the

Figure 14. De Mole's photograph of Ari Burnu from the crest of Plugge's Plateau. This appears to be the earliest known photograph of the Anzac Landing (Clive De Mole, J03307, Australian War Memorial).

men undertaking the attack on their own. Recollections of noise and silence, quiet determination and spontaneous charges, are no doubt all true, at different places and times. The 10th Battalion's Major M. Beevor was instructed by MacLagan to get his men "to give a cheer" as they climbed.[150] The resulting "roar" may have been the "faint British cheer" that Ashmead-Bartlett, aboard *London*, reasonably assumed told "that the first position had been won."[151] By such assumptions has the history of 25 April been written.

A dark photograph lying inconspicuously in a private collection at the Australian War Memorial has been overlooked for many decades. Titled "Reinforcements arriving 25/4/15," it appears to have been taken from Plugge's Plateau by Howe's mate, Clive de Mole.[152] Recent research[153] has uncovered a letter by de Mole which describes these first moments on Plugge's Plateau:

[W]e hit the top and had a blow, occupying the Turkish trenches above the first little hill I spoke of, and which we could look down on and see the machine gun which did the most damage to us when we were in the boats and on the beach. By this time more troops were landing … Here I leaned over the trench so nobody could see me and took a couple of snaps of them landing.[154]

This confirms de Mole's photograph to be the earliest to have yet surfaced of the Landing at Anzac.

149 Howe, "Sparks From an Old Controversy", p.6.
150 Beevor, "My Landing at Gallipoli", p.14.
151 Ashmead-Bartlett, Department of Public Instruction, New South Wales, 18 May 1915.
152 216 Clive Moulden de Mole, 28 at enlistment, clerk, of Adelaide, born South Melbourne.
153 Hurst, *Game to the Last*, between pp.56, 57; Hurst, 'Gallipoli, The First Photo?', *Wartime: the Official Magazine of the Australian War Memorial*, Issue 58, Autumn 2012, pp.32–35, 'Mail call', *Wartime*, Issue 73, Summer 2016, p.3.
154 C.M. de Mole, letter to mother, 21 May 1915, family collection.

4

Fisherman's Hut, Changing Orders and Moving Inland

Bean describes the attack towards Fisherman's Hut and departure of the 11th Battalion's parties from Plugge's Plateau for destinations inland, but much about this period is poorly understood. Battlefield movements imply that important strategic decisions were being made, but these are not discussed in the *Official History*. The most nagging unanswered question from this phase of the battle is – why did the bulk of the 11th Battalion move inland from Plugge's Plateau, to Second Ridge, rather than to their ultimate objective, the high ground on the left? This chapter reconstructs this early hour or so, adds to the existing history, highlights and examines some of the unanswered questions and lays the groundwork for some later analyses.

Not everyone assaulted Plugge's Plateau. "With a yell, much language and coo-eeing," Peck and others "charged up" the "slippery clay"[1] slopes leading to the southern end of Russell's Top and Razor Edge. The permanent army officer thought the "conduct of the lads was splendid ... cool, brave, and wonderfully intelligent considering their short period of training."[2] Today it is difficult to understand how they climbed those slopes, and Peck thought that if not "for the few bushes growing on the side we could never have done it."[3]

Everett's party also moved off "as quick[ly] as they could"[4] and found it hard going, climbing "with sopping clothes, but a yell from the south showed that another party had landed, and an answering yell returned the encouragement."[5] The climb then continued in silence.[6] Murray watched them climbing "on hands and knees." He was on the beach, exposed to enemy fire, but "couldn't shoot back as we might hit our own men."[7]

Enemy fire could have been coming from Fisherman's Hut, Walker's Ridge, Russell's Top or nearer. Everett's party located and cleaned up[8] snipers as they went, while other Turks fired from "up at the Cathedral."[9] This presumably refers to Faik's 3 Platoon near the Sphinx. "A couple of men tried to climb up and get around to these" and Everett heard "that they had killed them."[10] He later spoke of Turks "with the boughs of trees tied about them" or "with their faces painted green," who "would fire until the Australians were within ten yards ... then they would throw up their hands, but no prisoners were taken along the way."[11] Other sources confirm the presence of snipers: Lalor pulled one out of a bush "by the leg."[12] Şefik does not refer to snipers, but given the length of time between the defenders first seeing the invasion fleet in the darkness and the first troops splashing ashore, there was ample time for them to deploy. Perhaps the "snipers" were in fact riflemen from

---

1   J.H. Peck, interview, AWM38 3DRL 606 item 25.
2   Peck, letter to wife, n.d.
3   J.H. Peck, interview, AWM38 3DRL 606 item 25.
4   Everett, interview, Ellam-Innes Collection, p.239.
5   Everett, talk, St. George's House, Perth.
6   *Ibid.*
7   Murray, letter, 16 May 1915.
8   Everett, interview, Ellam-Innes Collection, p.239.
9   *Ibid.*
10   *Ibid.*
11   Everett, talk, St. George's House, n.d.
12   Captain Joseph Peter Lalor, 30 years old at the Landing, 12th Battalion. Newton, *The Story of the Twelfth*, p.89.

Figure 15. Razor Edge connecting Plugge's Plateau to Russell's Top. The Sphinx
is on the left, the Turkish monument at the Chessboard visible upper right. This
photograph was taken after fire had cleared the scrub, and was not as it would have
been at the Landing. (Photograph by J.P. Hurst, n.d., author's collection)

two "observation sections," each of nine men,[13] despatched from Fisherman's Hut by No 1 Platoon;
perhaps they had been cut off and prevented from returning to their platoon by the landing of some
of the northernmost boats and were lying low or withdrawing inland.

Tulloch landed just south of the foot of Walker's Ridge.[14] His description of enemy fire, including
that of a machine gun, "coming from a sheer position high up on the left where the Turks had a
semicircular trench apparently round the edge of the end of the knuckle,"[15] probably refers to the
Fisherman's Hut/ No. 1 Outpost area, as it was "apparently the same" as had "knocked out the boats on
the left."[16] He took the troops with him into a "thickly timbered" creek "about 8 feet deep and pretty
narrow" and "heavily enfiladed from the north."[17] In single file the party began climbing Walker's Ridge.

The fire from the left became more accurate with the growing light. The Bearer Division of the
3rd Field Ambulance lost three killed and 14 wounded as they landed[18] and Bean noted the 12th
Battalion "getting a hell of a time of it."[19] 13 Platoon's Gostelow,[20] Richards[21] and Pittersen[22] landed

13   Şefik, para. 34.
14   E.W. Tulloch, account of the Landing, Records of C.E.W. Bean, AWM38 3DRL 606 item 206 – diaries nos. 192–205.
15   Tulloch, 3DRL 606 item 206 – diaries nos 192–205.
16   *Ibid.*
17   Tulloch, 3DRL 606 item 206 – diaries nos 192–205.
18   T. Curran, *Across the Bar: the Story of "Simpson", The man with the donkey: Australia and Tyneside's great military hero* (Yeronga, Queensland: Ogmios Publications, 1994), p.209.
19   Bean, *Official History*, Volume I (1921 and 1941), p.323.
20   Gostelow, diary, 25 April 1915.
21   Richards, manuscript, 2DRL 301, pp.33–34.
22   Pittersen, letter, 4 May 1915.

on this stretch of beach (Figure 16), as had Eastcott who, sight restored, turned his attention to two wounded alongside him. "One had been shot in the head and seemed hopeless"; the other believed he had been shot through the chest and weakly told Eastcott that "I am done." Eastcott eventually discovered a spent "bullet sticking in his armpit ... I pulled it out ... didn't even ... bleed, so I sterilized it ... secured the dressing ... told him to get up. He said he couldn't, he was going to die." Eastcott gave the survivor the bullet as a souvenir, but had a hard time convincing him he would live; eventually he "went off after the others."[23]

Colonel Clarke assembled his men on a "scrubby knoll," still visible, "below the Sphinx."[24] He ordered Lieutenant R.A. Rafferty, 12th Battalion, to deal with what were thought to be "two machine-guns and many rifles" at or near Fisherman's Hut.[25] Strickland, 6 Platoon, was also ordered to silence this outpost. Gostelow, on his own initiative, had decided to do the same.[26]

Peck had left Clarke and sent Rockliff, 4 Platoon, and Strickland's brother officer Jackson, 5 Platoon, forward as advanced guard but the two parties became separated climbing the southern end of Russell's Top.[27] En route, someone in Jackson's party cut a Turkish "telephone wire."[28] Perhaps this wire tapped into communications with Gaba Tepe. Uyar recorded that there was no phone between Ari Burnu and Faik's HQ on Second Ridge,[29] but the "Kabatepe Region Commander," reported to "9th Division Command" that "The telephone to Arıburnu is not working."[30]

To Peck and Everett's left, parties of the 12th Battalion under Lalor, Lieutenants I.S. Margetts, P.J. Patterson and E.Y. Butler also began climbing through the scrub towards the cliffs above. West Australian Corporal E.W.D. Laing, 12th Battalion, who had begun his ascent with Jackson of the 11th, soon came across the 57-year-old Clarke struggling up with his pack; Laing carried the pack for him. Lalor had brought from Australia a family heirloom, a sword which he now "carried with intense pride ... its bright hilt wrapped in khaki cloth."[31] Peck saw him advancing, sword in hand, and "shouted to him not to be a bloody fool."[32]

Turner, Cockburn and Lowson may have been with the platoon despatched by Peck to Plugge's Plateau. Lowson, 3 or 4 Platoon, silently clawed his way up "almost perpendicular cliffs,"[33] beneath "a heavy fire ... often losing each other ... on hands and knees ... bullets ... pierced my equipment ... confronted by a trench full of Turks with bayonets fixed but not looking over anxious to use them ... rushed straight into them inflicting heavy loss with our bayonets."[34]

From the crest he saw a "big army of Turks ... in full flight. Then we opened fire and gave them a terrible time."[35] This probably refers to the north face of Plugge's Plateau, but, given the chronology,[36] may describe fighting by 4 Platoon at the southern end of Russell's Top. Fighting here is not documented in the *Official History*, but is described by Faik. Faik's party, entrenched on the seaward crest of the Top, received news that "the enemy was coming up from Koku Dere [Shrapnel Gully]

---

23   Eastcott, manuscript, p.8.
24   Bean, *Official History*, Volume I (1921 and 1941), p.270.
25   *Ibid.*, pp.270, 327.
26   Gostelow, diary, 25 April 1915.
27   Jackson, Ellam-Innes Collection.
28   *Ibid.*
29   Uyar, p.99.
30   The Çanakkale (Gallipoli) Report of Major Halis, Major Halis, *Çanakkale Raparu*, Arma Yayinlari, Istanbul, 1975, the Gallipoli Centenary Turkish Archives Research Project, MacQuarie University, p.109, <http://www.mq.edu.au/about us/faculties and departments/faculty of arts/mhpir/research/research by staff/gallipoli centenary research project/project outcomes/translated turkish works on gallipoli/#halis>, 16 November 2015.
31   Bean, *Official History*, Volume I (1921 and 1941), p.291; Peck, 3DRL 606 item 25.
32   Peck, 3DRL 606 item 25.
33   Lowson, "Under Fire", n.p.
34   *Ibid.*
35   *Ibid.*
36   It seems likely the assault on Plugge's Plateau would have been well under way by the time Lowson's party arrived.

Figure 16. "X" placed by Charles Gostelow on a photograph taken from the beach beneath Ari Burnu, showing his landing point. Walker's Ridge descends right to left and terminates before reaching the beach. (Photograph by C. Gostelow, n.d., Gostelow Family Collection)

Figure 17. Plugge's Plateau and Ari Burnu from No. 1 Outpost,
showing the open ground crossed by Strickland, Rafferty and Gostelow.
(Photograph by J.P. Hurst, n.d., author's collection)

in our rear." Faik "sent two bombardiers under Sergeant Lapsekili Myharrem. They threw grenades from one of the trenches overlooking the valley. At that moment we came under fire from the enemy who was climbing ... a slope 100 m to our left."[37] This may refer to the parties climbing in the area of Reserve Gully. The Turks began to engage the enemy "on this side." Men began to fall: "Platoon OC Gallipoli Sergeant Suleyman"[38] received a nasty wound to the left foot.[39] Faik was hit "in the groin ... I could no longer command the platoon. I handed over command to ... Myharrem,"[40] ordered the men to stand their ground until the reserves arrived, and withdrew. "Dawn had not yet broken."[41]

Many men barely paused on Plugge's Plateau, pursuing their enemy or following orders to push on. Of C Company, Luke Taylor[42] pushed inland, as did Leane's observer[43] and Newham, who went on "without stopping, passing hundreds of Turks wounded and killed."[44] Such must be the reaction to a man's first victorious minutes in battle and the sight of battlefield dead – there were of course nowhere near this number of defenders in the area. Combs and six others, one of whom may have been Brodribb, as elements of their stories seem to match, "dashed down the hill," as "long as we saw a Turk in the thick scrub," they "chased him until he dropped. We must have passed hundreds of snipers."[45] Luttrell also chased "Jack the Turk" inland.[46]

On the crest above the zig-zag path lay two Turks, one dead, the other "mortally wounded in the brain."[47] The latter reached for his water bottle and an Australian placed it in his hand.[48] Brockman attempted to give him morphia, but the Turk, as unfamiliar with his new enemy as were the Australians and thinking they might be trying to poison him, "looked venom at him and spat it out."[49] Brockman, being "the senior officer present, assumed command of the position"[50] and began sorting out the intermixed companies by assembling the 11th on the left, sending the 9th Battalion men to the right and the 10th forward. Howe heard someone call out "What happened to the red-headed navy youngster – was he hit?"[51] Brockman replied "He was alright last time I saw him. I told him he had better stay with his boat."[52]

Mofflin found Darnell and was "ordered to dig."[53] Medcalf and Bunning also began digging.[54] Nearby lay three dead members of Faik's 2 Platoon.[55] Another, possibly one of those who shot at Batt and was killed by Howe's party,[56] "lay thirty feet below, legs wide ... head down-most ... the boys ... gave scarcely a moment's consideration to these gruesome sights," but seeing his "pal" Batt[57] being treated and in great pain, Medcalf found his attitude changing from "nervous" and uncertain to "angry and savage."[58] He tried to reassure the dying man, who was evacuated, but became one of the

37   Şefik, para. 36.
38   *Ibid.*
39   Uyar, p.102.
40   Şefik, para. 36.
41   *Ibid.*
42   724 Private Luke Benjamin Taylor, C Company, 22 at embarkation, butcher, of Kalgoorlie, born Gympie, Queensland. Taylor, letters to Mr G. Stack and Mrs R. Sharpen, mother, 15 May 1915 and undated, *Kalgoorlie Miner*, 7 July 1915.
43   Anonymous, Leane's observer, manuscript.
44   Newham, "Recollections of a Returned Soldier", n.p.
45   Combs, manuscript.
46   Luttrell, letter, 16 May 1915.
47   Howe, 3DRL 8042 item 7.
48   Bean, *Gallipoli Mission*, p.78.
49   Brockman, 3DRL 606, item 27.
50   Howe, "Sparks From an Old Controversy", p.7.
51   Howe to Churchill, 30 November 1962.
52   *Ibid.*
53   Mofflin, letter, 20 October 1915, p.16.
54   Medcalf, manuscript, p.63.
55   *Ibid.*, pp.63–64.
56   Howe, 3DRL 8042 item 7; Bean, *Official History*, Volume I (1921 and 1941), p.260.
57   Medcalf, manuscript, p.64.
58   *Ibid.*

many to die amidst the confusion of the overburdened medical services; he was probably buried at sea. Among his few possessions was his South Africa Medal ribbon[59] – like "Darkie" Williams, Batt had survived that war to become a casualty in the first minutes of this one.

The medical section worked "like Trojans," though could do little for many "poor fellows" other than give "quick first-aid, and leave them."[60] Brennan found his sergeant, which was "very fortunate, as two can do better than one, especially with fractures and bad haemorrhage cases."[61] Plugge's was under rifle fire from Russell's Top and Second Ridge,[62] and some of the 11th were firing at Turks retiring along tracks to Wire Gully, about 1200 yards distant.[63] Louch settled into the Turkish trenches on the inland side of the plateau, and a Turkish shrapnel shell "sang over" and flashed brightly in the fading darkness, throwing its pellets "into the water off" Ari Burnu. The men watched the shells exploding above the landing, "fascinated."[64] Fox had "a look round" and thought the Turkish trenches "excellent, stored with food and ammunition."[65]

Although suddenly immersed in the new and shattering experience of war and confronted by the realities of death and wounding, the men were still a community abroad, and "Everyone was as cheerful as possible."[66] "It was great to have done this,"[67] wrote Fox. When the brigadier reached the plateau, "he was that pleased that he couldn't keep his mouth shut for smiling."[68] Bean, who had not yet landed, wrote of the men's "excitement and surprise" at "being there and alive,"[69] and that some had "a notion that their work as a covering force was done,"[70] a perception he gained from Brockman.[71] Could the men, despite their many briefings, really have been this ignorant of their role, or was the comment a reflection of confusion about their location? Or was Brockman referring to the men's exultation at their success and the sight of their fleeing enemy, or their belief that getting ashore would be the most difficult part of the operation?

C.J. Bradley,[72] A Company, felt that "If we had been the defenders instead of the Turks … we would have held at the beach and bayoneted the lot."[73] John Turner also thought the Australians would not have lasted "long … if the Turks had any go or fight in them at all."[74] Everett also was surprised: "Whether it was the bayonets, the weirdness of the situation, or … no reply to the rifle fire, something started the Turks on the run."[75] Hearder thought "the uncanny silence and the fact that not a soul fired a shot got on his nerves in the dim light."[76] Such observations reveal an ignorance of the Turkish strategy and strength. Few Australians appear to have realised that they greatly outnumbered the Turks opposing them,[77] who were unlikely to have been able to stop them getting ashore, even if they had fought to the death. Nor that the Turkish troops stationed along the coast

59   B2455, Batt.
60   Fox, "I Was There", p.8.
61   Brennan, letter, 1915, Army Museum of Western Australia.
62   Brockman, 3DRL 606, item 27.
63   Howe, 3DRL 8042 item 7.
64   Louch, 3DRL 606 item 27.
65   Fox, "I Was There", p.8.
66   Brennan, letter, 1915, Army Museum of Western Australia.
67   Fox, "I Was There", p.8.
68   Mofflin, letter, 20 October 1915, p.16.
69   Bean, *Official History*, Volume I (1921 and 1941), p.262.
70   *Ibid.*
71   Brockman, 3DRL 606, item 27.
72   146 Private Charles James Bradley, A Company, 34 at enlistment, blacksmith, of Kwollyin, via Kellerberrin, born Wangaratta; "well-known round the WA timber districts as a champion sportsman and all-round good fellow."
73   C.J. Bradley, letter, *Sunday Times*, n.d.
74   Turner, letter, 25 June 1915.
75   Everett, talk, St. George's House, Perth.
76   Hearder, manuscript 3DRL 3959, p.12.
77   Şefik, para. 34.

Figure 18. Remains of a trench atop No.1 Outpost (right).
(Photograph by J.P. Hurst, n.d., author's collection)

were but a screen, to provide the first resistance and raise the alarm.[78] Such mistaken impressions on 25 April may have contributed to the "legend" of the Landing, but this impression of the limited fighting qualities of the Turkish soldier would not survive long.

On the beach Eastcott was "having to pull the dead off" some of the wounded before he could treat them. Shrapnel "was searching the beach and spraying over the boats. Most of this was coming from Gaba Tepe." As he moved towards Fisherman's Hut to dress others, Eastcott's breeches "started to come down" – a bullet had cut "through my braces." With the "intense nerve strain" and the pain from his other wounds he had not noticed this lucky miss.[79]

Some 500 yards to the north[80] of the northernmost tows of the 3rd Brigade was a 150 foot high "hump" on a spine descending from the main range, later known as "No. 1 Outpost" (Figures 18, 19). About 300 yards further north, separated by relatively flat, partly cultivated, ground, lay Fisherman's Hut, on the seaward side of a low knoll. The Turks here had seen the invasion fleet before moonset,[81] and watched "the landing craft … coming straight towards them," before veering off in the direction of Ari Burnu.[82] They saw the landings and the exchange of fire between the pinnace and the defenders and opened an "accurate" fire on the troops "north of Ari Burnu."[83] The Australian parties detailed to deal with this flanking fire from No. 1 Outpost and the knoll by Fisherman's Hut set out to do so.

Accounts of the Fisherman's Hut action are threadbare. Bean describes Rafferty's part in this operation, but tells us nothing of Gostelow and very little about Strickland, other than that the

78   Although Şefik had ordered his troops along the coast that there was to be no withdrawal, and they were to fight to the death. Uyar, p.67.
79   Eastcott, Manuscript, pp.9–10.
80   Bean, *Official History*, Volume I (1921 and 1941), p.323.
81   Şefik, para. 39.
82   *Ibid.*
83   Şefik, para. 39.

latter landed with a "platoon … with the battleship tows." Strickland had in fact landed with the destroyer tows. He was "ordered to proceed along the edge of the beach … Rafferty was to work next to him, inland."[84] We do not know who gave Strickland his orders, though it was probably Clarke. When Rafferty had reminded Clarke that his orders were to escort the Indian Mountain Battery, he received the curt reply "I can't help that."[85] Strickland requested that he be allowed to outflank the position, only to be told "there was no time, go straight at it."[86] The two commands are similar in tone.

Between No. 1 Outpost and the 3rd Brigade's left flank was a patch of open pasture[87] (Figures 17, 20). Bean records that Rafferty hesitated before committing his men to a charge across this exposed ground, until he saw four troop-filled boats approaching the beach near the hut. In an effort to prevent a slaughter, Rafferty charged. Twenty of his party of about 45 were hit.[88] On his left, Strickland's party were similarly "cut up."[89]

The boats contained 140 men, including Captain H.T.C. Layh, of the 7th Battalion.[90] Bean recorded that they came under shrapnel, rifle and machine gun fire (from what they believed to be two machine guns)[91] and suffered heavily, the survivors scrambling ashore under heavy fire from Fisherman's Hut (Figure 19). The Turkish fire eventually ceased. One of Rafferty's party managed to make contact with the few living men among the dead and dying in or beside the boats. Rafferty, unaware that a party of about 40 had made it ashore, withdrew to rejoin the 3rd Brigade and, with his few remaining men, to attempt to carry out his original orders.[92]

Gostelow had also advanced towards Fisherman's Hut. It is unlikely that Bean mistook Gostelow for Strickland, as he sourced his account from Jackson, a friend of Strickland's, and Belford states that Strickland and Gostelow both took part in the foray.[93] Belford wrote that a party under Strickland and Gostelow "dealt summarily with the machine gun crew. Some … managed to escape."[94] This is probably incorrect. Gostelow described coming "across another party of Australians who had landed further round than ourselves so we joined forces."[95] This was probably Rafferty's party, which comprised "twenty-three men" of Rafferty's "platoon and twenty stray men from other tows."[96] Gostelow continued that they located "an enemy trench" and poured "heavy rifle fire into it – we could see the Turks skip out and run for it – I think I accounted for one".[97]

It appears some disaster befell Strickland's platoon, the consequent heavy casualties explaining the lack of information about their fate. Rafferty and the 7th Battalion would doubtless have seen Strickland's party had they managed to cross the open between No. 1 Outpost and Fisherman's Hut and Turkish sources confirm that the Australians did not close with the garrison.[98] While racing for shore members of the 7th Battalion saw "a line of men" "shot down" "trying to advance towards them" across "a large open patch of green grass"[99] (Figure 17). As these advanced along or alongside the

84   Bean, *Official History*, Volume I (1921 and 1941), p.270.
85   *Ibid.*
86   Jackson, Ellam-Innes Collection.
87   Bean, *Official History*, Volume I (1921 and 1941), p.324.
88   *Ibid.*
89   Jackson, Ellam-Innes Collection.
90   Bean, *Official History*, Volume I (1921 and 1941), p.326.
91   *Ibid.*, p.327.
92   Bean, *Official History*, Volume I (1921 and 1941), p.328.
93   Belford, *Legs Eleven*, p.73.
94   *Ibid.*
95   Gostelow, diary, 25 April 1915.
96   Bean, *Official History*, Volume I (1921 and 1941), p.323. Some of these may have been from the 11th Battalion. No 11th Battalion men are known to be buried in cemeteries in this area, though the majority of the 11th Battalion's dead from the Landing have no known grave.
97   Gostelow, diary, 25 April 1915.
98   Şefik, para. 39 and footnotes.
99   Bean, *Official History*, Volume I (1921 and 1941), p.328.

beach, they may have been Strickland's party. Siefken belonged to Strickland's platoon. He landed with "a clear wheat field on our left and a cliff in front. We couldn't advance either way. A few who tried to charge across the wheat field did not get ten yards before they were dropped."[100] "Bandy" Turner, probably of the same platoon, wrote "We got chopped to pieces ... I thought my time had come, but I was lucky ... I did not see Scotty after we landed. I think he went out on the left flank with the officers, but only two came back."[101] Both accounts appear to refer to the Fisherman's Hut foray. Bandy was "hit just below the elbow" soon after and evacuated.[102] Siefken was "laying down shooting using a haversack ... for a rifle rest" when a bullet "punctured a tin of dog[103] and a tin of tea and sugar, then my cap" and "just" drew blood.[104]

An account by a member of Gostelow's platoon has recently come to light. Lance Corporal Beresford Everett Bardwell landed under:[105]

> a fearful hail of lead a great many of our men being hit in the boats and on shore ... flung off our packs and lay down on the beach. There seemed to be a hopeless mixture of Companies and Battalions boats from different ships landing at same place. Second boats landed further round to the left upon which machine guns played cutting up the men dreadfully ... After lying under heavy fire ... we worked in dribs and drabs in any order round into shelter of one of the hills. I thought it was time to move after a bullet landed just under my chin. ... The crowd I found myself with a mixture of our Battalion and 12th moved out to the left flank where we received rather a bad time ... We took up a position but there seemed to be a dearth of officers and after holding it for some time someone gave the order to retire. We retired a short distance ... and moved forward again.[106]

The location is vague, but reference to a mixed party of 11th and 12th Battalions and that Bardwell apparently saw Layh's party shot up, makes it possible that he was in the area.

Şefik records the local garrison numbering 60–70 men of 1 Platoon, 4/2/27th Regiment under command of Reservist Second Lieutenant Ibradili Ibrahim Hayrettin (also spelled "Hayreddin").[107] He describes them firing on the landings north of Ari Burnu before engaging "the forces" approaching them[108] and firing at troops "desperately trying to get ashore," forcing them "to flee under cover" and inflicting "further losses on them."[109] This refers to the 7th Battalion's experience and possibly to Strickland's. After the 7th Battalion had been dealt with, Ibrahim left a single squad to keep them pinned behind their sand bank, and took the remainder of the platoon to resist the flanking attacks. He also sent a small party with grenades to deal with an Australian party trying to "outflank them from a dry creek bed."[110] Gostelow, perhaps?

Hayrettin believed his party had defeated the landings in their area. With their ammunition almost exhausted[111] and the enemy on Yuksek Sirt [Russell's Top] apparently heading for Hill 971, 1 Platoon handed defence duties "to the pickets at the mouth of the Azmak Dere" and withdrew

---

100 Siefken, letter, 3 September 1915.
101 B. Turner, letter to parents, 28 May 1915, Ellam-Innes Collection, Perth.
102 Turner, letter, 28 May 1915.
103 Bully beef.
104 Siefken, letter, 3 September 1915.
105 Beresford Everett Bardwell, 24 at embarkation, solicitor's clerk, of Geraldton, born Elsternwick, Victoria.
106 B.E. Bardwell, diary, 25 April 1915, State Library of Western Australia, <purl.slwa.wa.gov.au/slaw_b3967614_35.pdf> (20 January 2016).
107 Şefik, para. 34.
108 Ibid., para. 39.
109 Ibid., para. 39.
110 Uyar, p.108.
111 Şefik, para. 39.

to Duz Tepe,[112] "following the Sazli Dere track," intending "to bar" the enemy's route to Hill 971.[113] Many years later, Ibrahim wrote an account of the morning's fighting, but apart from giving an insider's view of the action, sheds little further light on the event:

> [T]he English ... turned towards Ağıldere ... thinking that they would meet with less resistance ... we faced them with our few weapons and our faith, and thanks to the devastating fire we rained down upon them, within an hour's time we had felled and destroyed so many invading soldiers that the shores were covered with their bodies ... according to the ... English ... their losses ... were 100 soldiers; from what we saw, however, this number was definitely higher ... respecting the dictates of war whereby one must strive to hold the high ground, we went up to the hill of Kocaçimen.[114]

No doubt the advance of Gostelow's, Rafferty's and possibly Strickland's parties, and the firing and showing of bayonets over the sand dunes by the 7th Battalion survivors as though making ready to charge,[115] also contributed to the Turks' decision to withdraw.

1 Platoon had certainly "carried out its duties with success."[116] They caused about 100 casualties in the 7th Battalion, and more in Rafferty's and Strickland's parties.[117] Everett's boat on the left of the first wave had been sunk, the second wave had suffered casualties in their boats or before leaving the destroyers, and 1 Platoon's fire had drawn three officers and portions of their platoons away from the main landing. Blay refers to running "the gauntlet" of rifle and machine gun fire as he approached North Beach and Jackson and Siefken, among others, to men being hit on landing. Louch, beneath Plugge's Plateau, refers to fire from the left and Pittersen, of Gostelow's platoon, described machine gun fire from a "well entrenched" enemy,[118] probably referring to Fisherman's Hut. Many others describe flanking fire while on the beach. Fisherman's Hut was not the only source of fire on these parties, but was the only source of fire from the "left."[119] The experience here provides a very vivid demonstration of the dangers that would have beset the 3rd Brigade had they landed on Brighton Beach, exposed to flanking fire from the much stronger Gaba Tepe.

The Turkish survivors of 1 Platoon succeeded in climbing to the high ground to fight on. Had Strickland been permitted to outflank the position, he may have prevented this movement, with possible, significant implications for those who later fought on Russell's Top, Baby 700 and Battleship Hill. Instead, his orders forced his party to become targets for them – only "about 15 of us left ... about 14 were killed, the rest wounded."[120] Had ship to shore communications been better or this action occurred in a later war, naval gunfire could perhaps have annihilated the forces at Fisherman's Hut, and the parties of Rafferty, Strickland, Gostelow and Layh left fewer, if any, of their number littering the beach, scrub and bullet-splintered boats. In fact, in contrast to the supporting fire of ships like *Bacchante* further south, it appears *Ribble* would not open fire as "there were strict orders not to use" her after 12 pounders.[121] Many of those climbing the hills and ridges further south, like Goodlet, later commented on the sight of the dead and wounded in the boats near Fisherman's Hut.

---

112 Alternately written as Duz Tepe, DuzTepe, Duz tepe. Duz Tepe will be used here unless quoted otherwise.
113 Şefik, para. 39.
114 Ibdradili Ibrahim Hayrettiin, letter to Feridun Fazıl Tülbentçi, 1945, Great War Forum, <http://1914-1918.invisionzone.com/forums/index.php?showtopic=40505&page=718 Aug 2015>.
115 Bean, *Official History*, Volume I (1921 and 1941), p.327.
116 Şefik, para. 39.
117 Siefken, letter, 3 September 1915; Bean, *Official History*, Volume I (1921 and 1941), p.328.
118 Pittersen, letter, 4 May 1915.
119 There may also have been some fire from Russell's Top, but this does not match descriptions of fire from the "left."
120 Siefken, letter, 3 September 1915.
121 T. Travers, *Gallipoli 1915*, p.72.

Figure 19. Fisherman's Hut (centre left), and cottage of the Commonwealth War Graves Commission (centre right). Beyond Fisherman's Hut are No. 1 Outpost, Walker's Ridge and (on the horizon, left to right) Walker's Ridge Cemetery, The Nek, Russell's Top, the Sphinx, Razor Edge and Plugge's Plateau (part). (Photograph by J.P. Hurst, n.d., author's collection)

Gostelow set out to rejoin "our battalion and picked up another XIth officer and a few men – he, being senior, took charge."[122] Only one other 11th Battalion officer was present in this area and his seniority can be confirmed. Gostelow handed the reins to Strickland and the two, with an unknown number of men, made their way back towards the 3rd Brigade.

Six hundred yards to the south, Tulloch's party were making their way in the gathering light along Walker's Ridge, under rifle fire from Russell's Top, "loftier scrub-covered gullies on their left"[123] and the occasional sniper, at least one of whom was bayoneted during the climb.[124] This nagging fire, probably from Şefik's 1 and 3 Platoons, forced the party to climb in single file and dodge "from side to side of the crest."[125] Along the way there was "a bit of a fight against something," though Tulloch couldn't remember any more about it.[126] Whenever Hitch reached a point where he could "wave the flag" he tried to make contact but "didn't get any" replies; "we were out of touch."[127]

On Plugge's Plateau, MacLagan spread his map on the ground, lit his pipe and went into conference with Brockman.[128] There then took place a significant but poorly documented meeting whose importance has been overshadowed by MacLagan's later decisions. MacLagan's "first order" to Brockman was to "dig in where they were,"[129] which the troops were already doing. The 11th Battalion's ultimate objectives lay beyond the high ground of Baby 700 to their north-east. Brockman

122 Gostelow, diary, 25 April 1915.
123 Bean, *Official History*, Volume I (1921 and 1941), p.271.
124 Tulloch, 3DRL 606 item 206 – diaries nos. 192–205.
125 *Ibid.*
126 *Ibid.*
127 Hitch, interview, May 1974, p.9.
128 Medcalf, manuscript, p.64; Howe, "Sparks From an Old Controversy", p.7.
129 Brockman, 3DRL 606, item 27.

Figure 20. Commonwealth War Graves Commission cottage (left), Fisherman's Hut (centre right), No. 1 Outpost (right). (Photograph by J.P. Hurst, n.d., author's collection)

was ordered to "make good the left over Walker's Ridge [later Russell's Top] way. Brockman … decided to send his own and Leane's Company on to the left up towards Baby 700; Denton's and Barnes' Company to Quinn's and Courtney's."[130] Roughly, this meant that B and D Companies were to occupy the high ground on the right of the valley, while A and C advanced along Russell's Top on the left. Significantly, in the *Official History*, Bean words this slightly differently. He wrote that the "11th was responsible for the left of" MacLagan's force, rather than stating the objective was the high ground, and that MacLagan "decided to hold the far side of the valley and Baby 700."[131] He directed various company commanders to occupy key features on the ridge opposite.[132] The reference to company, rather than battalion, commanders is a little alarming – presumably 11th Battalion HQ had not yet arrived, but if not, why not? MacLagan also ordered Major Hilmer Smith's company of the 12th Battalion to proceed "due east"[133] to the opposite side of the valley; Brockman had the impression that this meant the area later known as "Bloody Angle."[134] Numerous accounts confirm that MacLagan wanted Baby 700[135] and Second Ridge occupied.[136]

A significant key to understanding the Anzac Landing is missing from Bean's account: the answer to the question "why?" A close reading of these movement orders reveals a dramatic but unacknowledged change of the plans. Why were the men digging in on Plugge's Plateau or proceeding directly inland instead of advancing to the high ground? Why was the bulk of the 11th Battalion's

---

130 *Ibid.*

131 Bean, *Official History*, Volume I (1921 and 1941), p.276.

132 *Ibid.*

133 *Ibid.*

134 Brockman, 3DRL 606 item 27.

135 For example, Bean, *Official History*, Volume I (1921 and 1941), pp.276, 282, and Selby, 3DRL 8042 item 7.

136 Bean, *Official History*, Volume I (1921 and 1941), pp.276, 282. Medcalf, an eyewitness to some of this conversation, recalled the brigadier, ordering the 11th Battalion to "take possession of the second ridge half a mile ahead." Medcalf, manuscript, pp.64–65.

strength being diverted from Sari Bair on the left to Second Ridge on the right, why did MacLagan decided to "hold" rather than advance and why was Baby 700, not Battleship Hill, to be held?

MacLagan's later decision, made at about 7:30-8:00 a.m., to divert the 2nd Brigade from its objectives on the high ground on the left to Second Ridge on the right, in effect converting the offensive battle into a defensive one, is central to recent debate about the Anzac Landing. Depending on whether MacLagan's decision is considered to be wrong or right, he is considered pessimistic or pragmatic, and as either losing the Anzac Corps the initiative very early in the battle, never to be regained, or saving the Corps from possible disaster from aggressive Turkish counter-attacks. His overlooked orders to the 11th Battalion on Plugge's Plateau precede this much debated change of plans by possibly two hours.

A number of factors appear to have influenced this earlier decision. Williams[137] and Roberts[138] have argued that MacLagan's later decisions were influenced by his concerns about the proximity and strength of Turkish reserves approaching from the south and that his first reaction was to protect his right flank. If so, his earlier decisions may have been similarly influenced. This will be discussed in more detail in later chapters.

A second factor is that the 11th Battalion had two objectives. If the battalion landed in the "correct" place, it was to advance to its first objective, 400 Plateau, before continuing to the second objective on Third Ridge, and "thence" to a section of Battleship Hill.[139] In this light the decisions made on Plugge's Plateau to divert half the 11th Battalion to Second Ridge could be viewed as little more than an attempt to reconnect with the original plan. The question then becomes whether MacLagan should have simply adopted a new plan to attain the objective, Battleship Hill, rather than follow this part of the original plan. Perhaps MacLagan was cautiously having a "bob each way" – securing Second Ridge before deciding about Third Ridge, proceeding to Baby 700 before deciding on Battleship Hill, and simultaneously guarding against the expected Turkish counter-attack from the right. This appears to reflect a cautious or defensive approach more than a thrust for the planned covering position and the high ground.

Professor Robin Prior appears to provide missing information that connects the range of unexplained events and unanswered questions outlined above. If Birdwood had instructed MacLagan to take Third Ridge "as a first priority for the covering force," and only then to turn his attention to "the heights of Sari Bair to the north,"[140] MacLagan was really only following orders when he diverted troops to the right – providing those troops kept going towards Third Ridge. Landing near Plugge's Plateau, at the foot of First Ridge, meant that he first had to send troops to Second Ridge (Map 5). As noted earlier, Bean states that occupation of Second Ridge was the aim at this stage, not advance.[141] In general terms, the conflicting priorities of vague pre-landing orders and dubious intelligence about the location and strength of the Turkish forces presumed to be massing for a counter-attack, may have taken the wind from the sails of the thrust for the strategic high ground before the troops even got ashore. These attitudes and decisions will be examined further in later chapters.

Following MacLagan's orders, the companies on Plugge's Plateau departed. Louch, of Buttle's platoon, was "pushed off behind Croly"[142] and slid "down the sheer sandy slope of Plugge's Plateau on our backsides, still clutching our box of ammunition."[143] Mason, of Reid's platoon, after being

---

137 P.D. Williams, "Z Beach, the Landing of the ANZAC Corps, April 25, 1915", Master of Arts, Northern Territory University, 2000.

138 C.A.M. Roberts, "The Landing at Anzac: A Reassessment", *Journal of the Australian War Memorial*, No 22 (April 1993). pp.25–34.

139 3rd Brigade War Diary, August 1914–June 1915, AWM4 Australian Imperial Force Unit War Diaries.

140 Prior, *Gallipoli, The End of the Myth*, pp.110–111. Based on Birdwood, "Operation Order No 1" 17/4/15, *Gallipoli Maps and Appendices VI*, Appendix 14, pp.37–41.

141 Bean, *Official History*, Volume I (1921 and 1941), p.276.

142 Louch, 3DRL 606 item 27.

143 Louch, manuscript, p.15.

ordered by "Denton to follow him," descended past the "mine,"[144] in fact a pick handle at "the foot of the track ... with a Turkish placard affixed." This was believed to be "a booby trap" and was left "severely alone – until some inquisitive soldier knocked it over with a bullet. Nothing happened."[145] "Private Pinktop," [i.e. Simcock] had been ordered by Mason to remain on the beach to guard the platoon's kit, but "refused to be left" and advanced with the others. Mason did not manage to entice anyone "to stop with the kits, nor could the other platoons of our company."[146] Mason's party wheeled "left across gully and then turned right into line and advanced up the gully to clear out snipers. As we turned left we saw 40 or 50 Turks well above us retiring … along top of ridge on left."[147] These were probably Faik's 3 Platoon withdrawing along Russell's Top.

Peck "left Rockliff and MacFarlane in charge" in Rest Gully, wrote Bean, and "disappeared inland" towards Second Ridge "in search of" battalion headquarters.[148] In fact, MacFarlane was probably heading for Plugge's Plateau.[149] Given that Peck must have realised that HQ had landed beneath Ari Burnu, it can only be assumed he intended to rendezvous with or establish HQ on Second Ridge as per the original plan. Alternatively, he may simply have gone where he thought he was needed. This is hinted at by Brockman, who told Bean that Peck "had got forward the first morning as soon as he realised that the CO was not moving further forward."[150] As Peck would later be described by Bean as "one of the best officers in the AIF" and by Newton Wanliss as "the ablest man who commanded a battalion of the AIF in France,"[151] it can be presumed his motives were justified.

Everett also arrived in Rest Gully, after crossing Razor Edge or the southern tip of Russell's Top and suffering casualties, probably from the fire of Faik's party. He was instructed by "the CO on Plugge's Plateau to dig in where he was."[152] The surviving record is a little garbled but it appears Johnston arrived on the plateau, sent a message for Everett to dig in on Russell's Top, and Everett moved to the "Nek to reconnoitre the position to dig."[153] The area was "most unsatisfactory for digging being commanded all round," and Everett returned to inform "the CO to that effect."[154] It will be noted that once again the stance is defensive.

Colonel Clarke somehow reached Russell's Top before his "young and active" subordinates, Margetts and Patterson.[155] "Near the Sphinx" they saw a trench "running across the Top like a neatly-opened drain." The parapet was flat and covered with dry "pinkish brown" bushes. "Every trench seen … at this date" was similar, and the men learned "by bitter experience what was meant by a brown streak through the scrub."[156] The trench was "full"[157] of Turks and the Australians, about 50, rushed it. The picture of what happened here is confused, but Margetts confirms the presence of "a trench overlooking the beach … fixing bayonets, we received the order to go for it … the Turks … cleared out in great disorder",[158] the Australians following and shooting some as they ran. These may be the Turks Mason saw retiring above him. Clarke shouted from behind to his men to "Get into some sort of formation and clear the bush as you go."[159]

144 G.F. Mason, 2DRL 301, Book 31, Australian War Memorial.
145 Howe, "Sparks From an Old Controversy", p.8.
146 Mason, 2DRL 301, Book 31.
147 *Ibid.*
148 Bean, *Official History*, Volume I (1921 and 1941), p.277.
149 Everett, interview, Ellam-Innes Collection, p.240; Peck, 3DRL 606 item 25.
150 Brockman, 3DRL 606 item 27.
151 I. Grant, *Jacka, VC*, p.93.
152 Everett, interview, Ellam-Innes Collection, p.239.
153 *Ibid.*
154 *Ibid.*
155 Bean, *Official History*, Volume I (1921 and 1941), p.272.
156 *Ibid.*, p.273.
157 *Ibid.*, p.272.
158 I.S. Margetts, letter to parents, 23 May 1915, 1DRL 0478/2.
159 Bean, *Official History*, Volume I (1921 and 1941), p.273.

The Turks, of 3 Platoon, had fired on the landing along North Beach or northern Ari Burnu until discovering enemy troops advancing from behind and to their left. Here their story runs cold, as the wounded Faik left the battle after passing command to Muharrem.[160] Despite Faik's and Şefik's orders to hold their ground these troops withdrew, and probably occupied a number of positions on Russell's Top. They may have fought at the southern trench, as possibly described by Lowson and Everett, before withdrawing to the second trench, which could also have been the movement Mason saw.[161]

Margetts thought "Every Turk appeared to be jabbering" as they, with an "officer," possibly in fact Sergeant Muharrem, crossed the Nek and sank into the scrub to establish a line on the seaward slope of Baby 700.[162] The Australians, under fire at a range of about 350 yards from Turks across the valley to their right, formed a line near the Nek. Clarke, standing by a track that still runs along the inland crest of Russell's Top, was killed, as was a Private Davis[163] beside him. Major C.H. Elliott, who had assumed the

Figure 21. The dip on Walker's Ridge that confronted Tulloch's party. The view is towards Russell's Top. (Photograph by J.P. Hurst, n.d., author's collection)

duties of 2IC 12th Battalion when Lieutenant-Colonel S. Hawley had been shot through the spine while landing, was wounded.[164] The 12th Battalion, the only one in the brigade to have two colonels on strength, had lost them both in its first hour or so in action.

Clarke's death pinpoints Blay's position. Blay had charged "up … cliffs," probably south of the Sphinx. "Many of us don't remember getting up to the top … we had to help each other up the last 20 feet with rifles … we could hear the Turks" retiring "through the scrub" and "ran into snipers planted under bushes."[165] He then came across "Clarke … shot through the mouth."[166] Mason and Bean believed the shots that killed Clarke and his batman were fired from the vicinity of Quinn's or Courtney's Posts,[167] but given the proximity of the survivors of Faik's 3 Platoon, the shot may have come from much closer. Blay thought so. The men held "a hat on a rifle around the bend in the path to draw" the sniper's fire, "then surrounded his lair … we could not take prisoners so he was shot. He had accounted for 5 or 6 of

160 Şefik, para. 36.

161 Based on his diagram, which is approximate and, given the situation, understandably inaccurate. Mason, 2DRL 301, Book 31.

162 Bean, *Official History*, Volume I (1921 and 1941), p.273.

163 Margetts, letter, 23 May 1915, 1DRL 0478/2.

164 Bean, *Official History*, Volume I (1921 and 1941), pp.273–274.

165 Blay, diary, 25 April 1915.

166 *Ibid.*

167 Bean, *Official History*, Volume I (1921 and 1941), p.273.

Figure 22. Walker's Ridge from the lip of a deep trench overlooking
North Beach, showing the dip Tulloch's party had to cross.

us."[168] Clarke's order to his men to clear the scrub as they advanced had been well-advised, but had not saved his life. Blay pushed "on all battalions mixed together," occasionally seeing the enemy and giving "them a few rounds rapid … passed their trenches overlooking the beach and understand what we had to face and consider how lucky we are to be alive."[169]

Tulloch's party, out of sight to the north and approaching the upper heights of the daunting Walker's Ridge, were confronted by a dip of about 20 feet, before the spur rose to Russell's Top. This dip was under fire but too narrow to be bypassed and "every man had to run fifteen yards, completely exposed" to rifle fire[170] (Figures 21, 22). Bean states this fire came from spurs to the north,[171] but today there is evidence of a deep trench on the seaward crest of Russell's Top with a field of fire covering the area from North Beach to Ari Burnu and, at much closer range, the dip confronting Tulloch; whether Faik's 3 Platoon were in occupation at the time is not known. Tulloch scrambled onto the Top. He noticed a party of Australians about 100 yards away; one of them was "bending over" a dead body – "Colonel Clarke."[172]

D Company was already below strength when they began their move inland. Buttle and Reid had arrived with parts of their platoons, but Gostelow was probably at that time near North Beach. Walker's 14 Platoon have left few clues, though Ashton[173] was probably still on the beach beneath Plugge's Plateau, as presumably were others. Below Ari Burnu, Ashton found some of the 11th

168 Blay, diary, 25 April 1915.
169 *Ibid.*
170 Bean, *Official History*, Volume I (1921 and 1941), p.271.
171 *Ibid.*
172 Tulloch, 3DRL 606 item 206 – diaries nos. 192–205; Bean, *Official History*, Volume I (1921 and 1941), p.271.
173 It is unclear whether Ashton belonged to 13 Platoon, or to 14.

Battalion HQ, including Johnston,[174] and with his "cobber," E.P. Davis,[175] one of the first in the Geraldton area to enlist, volunteered to carry a box of ammunition. They followed[176] the officers "up the winding"[177] "almost perpendicular path"[178] leading to Plugge's Plateau. The "terrible sight" of the body-filled 7th Battalion boats near Fisherman's Hut "made our blood boil."[179] If seen as described, this suggests 11th Battalion HQ climbed Plugge's relatively late. Between Ari Burnu and Plugge's Plateau, Ashton came across his first dead Turk, his face covered "with a greatcoat … satisfaction and … compassion" were mixed. "'Poor devil' we thought, as we carefully stepped over this pathetic form lying on the bottom of the shallow trench."[180]

Fox also suggests Johnston was on the plateau at some stage as "Our commanding officer came up, passed a word of promise and good cheer."[181] Neither Brockman nor Howe refer to seeing Johnston on the plateau. Roberts appears to have arrived on Plugge's some time after Brockman's meeting with MacLagan,[182] as no-one mentions him being there at the time and it would be expected MacLagan would have consulted him had he been present.[183] Roberts then ordered Leane's company to remain on Plugge's as reserve rather than advance with Brockman,[184] suggesting he was not present when MacLagan gave the orders to advance. Howe estimated he was on Plugge's for about half an hour before,[185] to avoid rifle fire falling on the exposed plateau,[186] Brockman led A Company, with some of Major S.B. Robertson's 9th Battalion company, down the zig-zag path "into the valley."[187]

Roberts' reason for holding C Company back is not known. Perhaps the loss of Annear and MacDonald – one third of the company's officers – had something to do with it. The AIF was an untried force and officers and men had yet to recognise or display their abilities on the battlefield, but this decision kept Leane, destined within two weeks to lead an operation that would earn him the Military Cross, and who would gain a reputation throughout the war as a dynamic and fearless infantry leader, out of the fight. Forty-eight hours later he was still there, and "fuming."[188] La Nauze, not the senior officer in the company but "as true as steel" and a personal friend and comrade of Leane's, was appointed company 2IC by Johnston.[189] McCleery took command of La Nauze's 11 Platoon.

Doctrine endorsed the holding of reserves, as the first commander to commit the last of his forces would probably lose his ability to influence the course of the battle;[190] but providing a reserve was not the role of the 11th Battalion. The brigade held a reserve – the 12th Battalion. Nor is it clear why a battalion 2IC would be making such decisions, nor even whether he was: perhaps Roberts was acting on instruction from Johnston. Roberts had many years' experience in the citizen's forces and had led a squadron of the 8th Commonwealth Horse to South Africa, but arrived after hostilities ceased. The C Company narrative for 25 April in Bean's notes of interview is very sparse, and the reason is not hard to find – Leane was the only C Company officer who landed that morning to survive the campaign.

174 F. Ashton, interview by S. Welborn, 14 September 1976, Reid Library, University of Western Australia, p.3.
175 774 Private Emanuel Percy Davis, 27 at embarkation, farmer and commercial traveller, of Geraldton and Perth, born Victoria.
176 Ashton, interview, Welborn, p.3.
177 Ibid.
178 Ashton, manuscript, p.15.
179 Ibid., p.16.
180 Ashton, manuscript, p.16.
181 Fox, "I Was There", p.8.
182 Brockman, 3DRL 606 item 27.
183 Mofflin recalls Roberts being on the crest early, though this does not imply he was there at the time of the meeting. Mofflin, letter, 20 October 1915, p.16.
184 Brockman, 3DRL 606 item 27.
185 Bean, Gallipoli Mission, p.79.
186 Bean, Official History, Volume I (1921 and 1941), p.277.
187 Howe, "Sparks From an Old Controversy", p.8.
188 Brockman, 3DRL 606 item 27.
189 R.L. Leane, letter to Mrs C.A. La Nauze, 4 July 1915, Ellam-Innes Collection, Perth.
190 General Staff, War Office, Field Service Pocket Book 1914 (London: His Majesty's Stationery Office, 1914), pp.136, 140, 141, 153.

D Company's numbers were further reduced when "a party of about 60" of "Reid's platoon and portion of" Buttle's were detached to "go and reinforce the 12th Battalion."[191] It is unclear how this move came about or who ordered it. Denton's account suggests he gave the orders,[192] Buttle's that it was Brockman,[193] and Mason's that "Tulloch came down for reinforcements after Colonel Clarke was killed."[194] Tulloch is unlikely to personally have backtracked along Russell's Top, though he had tried, unsuccessfully, he thought, "to get into touch with Major Roberts."[195]

One of those remaining with D Company was Louch, who was directed by Denton "to a position … covering Wire Gully."[196] Identifying some of the men who served in 16 Platoon and comparing their names to those who fought with Louch in the coming days, implies a portion of 16 Platoon went with him. Bean tells us that "Denton's company" then climbed towards Courtney's Post.[197] With Gostelow and an unknown number of his platoon on North Beach, Ashton and members of 14 Platoon still in the vicinity of Plugge's Plateau, Reid's platoon and a portion of Buttle's climbing Russell's Top, and an unknown portion of Buttle's platoon heading for Wire Gully, it is unclear who accompanied Denton. The version of events accepted since 1921 – that Denton took D Company to Courtney's Post – is correct in name only. D Company was already scattered from Fisherman's Hut to Wire Gully.

Of B Company's movements from Plugge's there is very little record. Barnes would not live long enough to leave an account of the Landing. Bean states that the company turned into a steep niche in the ridge "where a man could scarcely climb on hands and knees," later named "Steele's Post."[198] The only other existing B Company accounts that can be pinpointed to Plugge's Plateau and Shrapnel Gully are those of 7 Platoon's Darnell, Inman and Mofflin. Inman states only that as "No more Turks were handy … we formed up & set out again. We went about a mile, then got into a disused trench … A few fell and more were injured."[199] Darnell, as OC scouts, had been ordered to "take as many" of his scouts from Plugge's "as he could find … out on the left to reconnoitre."[200] He took Mofflin "with him … to send back signals."[201] Mofflin followed Darnell "into the gully" where they found Everett and Barnes. "Just then signals came from the other side of the gully 'reinforcements urgently wanted in centre'. So Captain Barnes ordered all who were there of B Company to go and reinforce the firing line."[202] Who requested the reinforcements and when is unclear. With "Arnold … Andrews … Jack Nelson" and others, Mofflin "set off," apparently climbing Bridges Road.[203]

Barnes' 2IC, Tulloch, was on Walker's Ridge or Russell's Top, Strickland was on North Beach, Jackson had been separated by Razor Edge and probably crossed Shrapnel Gully before Barnes arrived there, and of Newman's movements at this time there is no record. With the possible exception of Newman, who appears to have had few of his platoon with him and whose later movements suggest he was not with the company, Barnes appears to have had not a single officer of his company with him. With each of his platoon officers having at least a portion of their platoons with them, and members of Newman's platoon, like Blay, advancing on Russell's Top, not a single complete platoon under command of its officer remained with B Company. Like D Company, B Company appears at this time to have existed in name only. The perception of B and D Company moving to Second

191 Buttle, 3DRL 8042 item 7.
192 J.S. Denton, letter to C.E.W. Bean, 16 June 1920, 3DRL 8042 item 7.
193 Buttle, 3DRL 8042 item 7.
194 Mason, 2DRL 301, Book 31.
195 Bean, *Official History*, Volume I (1921 and 1941), pp.286–287.
196 Louch, manuscript, p.15.
197 Bean, *Official History*, Volume I (1921 and 1941), pp.284–285.
198 *Ibid.*, pp.282, 284, 285.
199 Inman, diary, 25 April 1915.
200 Darnell, 1DRL 233.
201 Mofflin, letter, 20 October 1915, p.16.
202 *Ibid.*
203 *Ibid.*

Ridge, and the second wave arriving in "good order"[204] behind the first are clearly, at least in the case of the 11th Battalion, not correct. What is also missing from the existing picture is an understanding of what was going on and why. If Denton's orders were to occupy Second Ridge, why, for example, were Buttle and Reid despatched to the left?

Brockman, Everett, Selby, Morgan, MacFarlane and Rockliff,[205] all the officers of A Company, assembled in Rest Gully. There the troops waited while "the senior officers, with a few men as escort,"[206] climbed Russell's Top to reconnoitre the terrain over which Brockman was expecting to take A Company. The officers remaining in Rest Gully spent the time reorganising, assigning the many "stray" men who had become detached from their companies into a provisional "company"[207] – in fact, about a half-company in strength[208] – with sergeants to lead its "platoons."

From Russell's Top, Everett described seeing "Lalor moving forward on his left … with about half a company." Lalor, having ignored Peck's advice, happily waved his sword at Everett, who "warned him about a machine gun" firing "from the high ground on the left of the Nek."[209] Lalor led "his troops … over the open ground by the Nek towards the scrub just beyond. He got driven back from the scrub and tried immediately to cross the open again – 2 or 3 times this happened."[210] It is unclear whether this occurred during Everett's first trip to Russell's Top or later with Brockman. The presence of a machine gun cannot be confirmed, the only contender being the Fisherman's Hut gun, if it existed.

During the estimated half an hour Brockman was away, the men in Rest Gully watched troops crossing to Second Ridge and a shell scatter "its shrapnel harmlessly over"[211] the inland slope of Razor Edge.[212] "The heroes – or villains – of the landing … the two men" carrying the platoon's box of reserve ammunition,[213] caught up with the advanced troops: "In cardboard packets of 5 rounds it had to be carried in cases – about the most awkward load possible in that country."[214] Howe, de Mole,[215] James Pettit[216] and Walter Genery[217] split a box's contents and put it in their sandbags.[218] "Within the next hour everybody had a turn at carrying the stuff – cursing it and the carriers who had brought it forward."[219]

The precise chronology of events on Russell's Top and orders given are unclear. At some point, Brockman instructed Lalor either to move along Russell's Top "towards the Nek,"[220] or to "move up the high land to Baby 700,"[221] and detailed S.B. Robertson to go to Pope's Hill.[222] Brockman then returned to Rest Gully. One of the waiting men, Private C.E. Bonavia,[223] "came up and asked de Mole for water," having drunk his own. The men had been ordered to preserve their water and as

---

204 Brockman, 3DRL 606 item 27.
205 Howe, 3DRL 8042 item 7.
206 Howe, "Sparks From an Old Controversy", p.8.
207 Bean, *Official History*, Volume I (1921 and 1941), p.283.
208 Everett, interview, Ellam-Innes Collection, p.240.
209 *Ibid.*
210 *Ibid.*
211 Howe, "Sparks From an Old Controversy", p.7.
212 Bean, *Gallipoli Mission*, p.79.
213 Howe, "Sparks From an Old Controversy", p.7. Battalion orders state that two ammunition boxes per company were to be carried forward, rather than one per platoon.
214 Howe, "Sparks From an Old Controversy", p.7.
215 216 Private Clive Moulden de Mole, A Company, 28 at enlistment, clerk, of Perth and Adelaide, born South Melbourne, Victoria.
216 220 Private James Paul Pettit, A Company, 26 at embarkation, dentist, of Boulder and Cloncurry, Queensland, born Sale, Victoria.
217 176 Private Walter John Genery, A Company, 26 at embarkation, printer, of Subiaco, born Yass.
218 Howe, 3DRL 8042 item 7.
219 Howe, "Sparks From an Old Controversy", p.7.
220 Brockman, 3DRL 606 item 27.
221 Bean, *Official History*, Volume I (1921 and 1941), p.283.
222 Brockman, 3DRL 606 item 27.
223 157 Private Charles Emanual Bonavia, 27 at the Landing, draughtsman, born Malta. Bonavia migrated to Australia from Malta three years earlier and in Egypt acted as an interpreter as he spoke "Arabic."

most had not yet touched theirs, Brockman told Bonavia "to fill his bottle from the creek." Possibly believing the creek to be poisoned, he would not do so. Bonavia "was not seen again."[224]

At this time A Company, having assembled and reorganised and with no officer casualties, was the closest to a full company that the 11th Battalion had assembled. They were joined by the battalion machine gun section.[225] Everett told Brockman "he wanted … to work across to the position later known as Courtney's."[226] From Russell's Top an insight can be gained into Everett's possible thinking. North of MacLaurin's Hill, Second Ridge dips slightly; occupation of this point would prevent enemy penetration through this "gap" and provide observation beyond the ridge. Brockman must have approved as Everett took the mixed "company" of 3rd Brigade men[227] to Courtney's Post. Bean states that "Duntroon cadet … Selby" was despatched with him,[228] but this was not so.[229] Brockman also ordered Rockliff and MacFarlane to take their platoons to Second Ridge with the intention that they climb in the vicinity of Steele's Post and then move north along it to "junction left."[230] This movement by 3 and 4 Platoons may have been intended to provide additional flank protection for Brockman's right as he moved up the valley, while not diverting strength from Baby 700; alternatively, "junction left" may simply have meant to make contact with the troops on their left on Second Ridge. Suddenly the troops in Shrapnel Gully and Rest Gully heard "an awful rattle of musketry and at once … Denton semaphored through for reinforcements."[231] Hearder and the machine gun section "hurried off" to Denton's assistance.[232]

Brockman had planned to take two companies, and possibly the machine gun section, to "make good the left,"[233] initially an objective for a whole battalion of 16 platoons, but now found himself with, at best, about two understrength platoons. In brief, the battlefield deployments described previously confirm that defence of the right had become a higher priority than the thrust for the high ground, and it appears that almost any development was allowed to bleed troops from the latter. The persistent concerns about the right flank are even more surprising when it is considered that fewer troops would be required for defence than attack.

Brockman signalled to Plugge's Plateau for reinforcements[234] and Leane despatched Cooke's 12 Platoon. As Cooke organised his platoon, his former comrades of the 1st Battalion, Lancashire Fusiliers, were probably landing in daylight under rifle and machine gun fire a dozen miles to the south. One wonders if he knew the battalion was participating in the campaign or had caught up with some of them in Lemnos; perhaps he heard the gunfire as they fought their way ashore. Had he remained with his regiment, there is a one in two chance he would have become a casualty and a one in four chance that he would have been dead by about the time Brockman called for assistance; Cooke's old battalion were awarded "six VCs before breakfast" this day. For the moment, Cooke's section of the peninsula, though under light rifle and shrapnel fire, was relatively quiet. Cooke joined Brockman in Rest Gully.

Bean's reconstruction accounts for the positions of most of the 11th Battalion's officers, but pieces of the puzzle remain logically disconnected. When Brockman requested reinforcements before beginning the climb to the high ground, his force did not consist of the assembled strength of the 11th Battalion, but perhaps two platoons, one of which would later be diverted to Second Ridge. This is significant, but not discussed. By not determining the links between the officers of B and D Companies and

224 Howe, 3DRL 8042 item 7.
225 Hearder, manuscript 3DRL 3959, p.12.
226 Everett, interview, Ellam-Innes Collection, p.240.
227 Bean, *Official History*, Volume I (1921 and 1941), p.283.
228 *Ibid*.
229 Selby, 3DRL 8042 item 7.
230 Brockman, 3DRL 606 item 27.
231 Hearder, manuscript 3DRL 3959, p.12.
232 *Ibid*.
233 Brockman, letter, 25 May 1915.
234 Brockman, 3DRL 606 item 27.

their platoons, the *Official History* and subsequent histories make the mutually exclusive placements of these companies on Second Ridge and their component officers and platoons elsewhere. The account Johnston gave Bean was so odd that Bean wrote "Surely this is wrong" in the margin alongside it, and later incredulously "The CO who gives this account didn't really know where his men got to."[235] By contrast, the report Johnston wrote for the brigadier, was brief, detailed and, when compared with the reconstruction and conclusions in this book, accurate. Historians who have for many decades drawn conclusions and proposed theories based on the image presented in the *Official History* have, in the case of the 11th Battalion, been using inaccurate data, or in other words, a flawed starting point.[236]

The holding back of C Company creates an opportunity to examine the extent of the fragmentation of the 11th Battalion. If C Company, minus Cooke's platoon, remained on Plugge's Plateau, then only about 25 percent of accounts by members of the company could be expected to describe fighting elsewhere, and these should be by members of Cooke's 12 Platoon. In fact, a first reading of C Company accounts suggests none were on the plateau, as all write of such things as the advance inland and heavy enemy fire: once again we have the phenomenon of the participants' accounts presenting a vastly different picture to the secondary sources of nearly 100 years. Equipped with the knowledge of Leane's experience on this and subsequent days, a closer examination reveals that descriptions of front line fighting sometimes refer to later events or to general accounts of the battle, rather than the writer's experience. Marshall, for example, describes the enemy bringing "up reinforcements quicker than we could land ours" and being "under a tremendous fire ... men were being hit all round."[237] This sounds like front line fighting, but he appears to have remained on the plateau as he describes the events offshore throughout the day and movements with Leane the following day. Gallaher, 11 Platoon, describes the fighting in some detail, but his account does not provide evidence that he was either forward or back – his letter describes the first three days, and it is not possible to tie with certainty any of his descriptions to the first day.[238] In other words, references to casualties and hard fighting do not necessarily refer to the front line, nor the first day, and closer examination of accounts is required.

By contrast, of others in C Company, Leane's observer and Brodribb, Combs, Luttrell, Newham, Stagles and J.T. Cook[239] pushed inland, the latter possibly with Cooke, as was Leslie Job.[240] Stan Williams, coincidentally Marshall's mate,[241] was sent forward with "the company scouts ... to watch for messages."[242] J.C. Hilliard fought on either Baby 700 or Second Ridge; and Luke Taylor and Webb fought somewhere in the front line. W.W. Scott was separated from the battalion soon after landing[243] and Aitken served "with strangers until Tuesday afternoon."[244] Percy Williams[245] is buried on Baby 700 and other members of the company, such as William George Price,[246] Walter Reeves[247] and Edward Coleman,[248] are recorded as killed on 25 April, but with no known grave. This suggests that they died

---

235 Bean, 3DRL 606 item 25.
236 Roberts, *The Landing at Anzac*, second edition, pp.99–101, p.129, p.142, provides examples.
237 Marshall, letter, 9 May 1915.
238 Gallaher, letter, *Kalgoorlie Miner*, June 1915.
239 639 Private (at embarkation) James Turnbull Cook, C Company, 19 at embarkation, labourer and formerly apprenticed to racing stables, of Kalgoorlie, born Bendigo, Victoria.
240 674 Corporal Leslie Job, C Company, 19, telephonist, of Boulder, born Fitzroy, Victoria.
241 Marshall, letter, 15 May 1915.
242 Williams, interview, Liddle Collection, pp.4–5.
243 Scott, letter, n.d.
244 Aitken, letter/diary, p.20.
245 738 Private Percy Williams, C Company, 21 at enlistment, grocer and miner, of Kalgoorlie, born South Melbourne.
246 704 Private William George Price, C Company, 19 at embarkation, jeweller, of Boulder, born Minimi, New South Wales.
247 711 Private Walter Reeves, C Company, 24 at embarkation, labourer, of Kalgoorlie, born Cambridge, England.
248 647 Private Edward John James Coleman, C Company, 23 at embarkation, railway porter and mechanic, of Kalgoorlie and Footscray, Victoria.

fighting inland,[249] as bodies were less likely to be recovered or identified if they fell on ground later held by the enemy. This cannot be assumed with certainty, as even Annear has no known grave. Two members of C Company mentioned earlier, Carroll and Edgar, are buried on Plugge's Plateau. These two aside, as they could have been killed in the early fighting, only two of 15 C Company men whose movements this morning can be traced appear to have remained on the plateau. Although accounts exist for only a fraction of the company, the C Company that remained on Plugge's Plateau probably comprised Leane, La Nauze and possibly Corley, with a low but unknown number of men.

Of parties from other companies, Darnell could find only 20 of the 35 scouts who had landed with him,[250] Gostelow appears to have taken only 20 of his platoon with him to attack Fisherman's Hut and Buttle and Reid had 60 men of their two platoons with them when they climbed to Russell's Top. Rockliff and MacFarlane mustered about 100 men[251] on landing, suggesting that on the beach their platoons were relatively intact, but this was before they began their climb through country that divided and scattered other parties. The impression gained is that, rather than the 11th Battalion platoons and companies existing as such but missing a small percentage of men who had become separated, the opposite was generally the case – platoons and companies were represented by only a fragment. This leads to a shift in the way secondary sources and the battle should be read – when Barnes and Denton took their companies to Second Ridge, when Newman, Darnell or Jackson are placed on a map, we are not seeing the dispositions of platoons, companies and a battalion, but fragments of each.

Other difficulties with interpreting primary sources are that we do not know what arrangements were made of which today there is no known record, nor how much writers or interviewees really knew about events, and the extent to which perception, memory, hearsay or personality influenced accounts.

The confusion on 25 April has been ascribed to the force being landed intermixed, compressed and on the wrong beach, to unfamiliar, rough and tangled terrain, enemy fire, and the men's orders and determination to push on. 11th Battalion accounts evidence all of these factors, but highlight one that is often underrated – the impact of the early resistance of the greatly outnumbered enemy. Şefik pays tribute to the "zealous defiance" of 4 Company, which "in all probability confused the aggressors so they hesitated to advance quickly to carry out their main task which was to capture before sunrise the high line of Artillery Range." The 3rd Brigade evidence suggested here would suggest this to be an accurate assessment. 4 Company's conduct was "worthy of the highest praise."[252]

The most visible impact of the Ottoman opposition was the casualties they inflicted. Within 30 minutes of getting ashore the 11th Battalion had suffered three officer and an unknown number of other rank casualties. Turkish fire from Fisherman's Hut caused great loss and drew the core of three platoons from the brigade. Harassed by fire from Russell's Top, Plugge's Plateau and "snipers" scattered through the scrub, men rushed inland to come to terms with their enemy, some of whom fought until killed or wounded. Others ran, dividing and breaking up their pursuers. Even after Plugge's Plateau had been taken, enemy fire continued to fall on its exposed crest, compelling A Company to reorganise in Rest Gully. From there, requests for reinforcements from Second Ridge drew off the machine gun section and others. In effect, since the first shot the 11th Battalion had been under fire of some sort – at long or short range, from small arms or artillery. How this affected decision-making will be examined in later chapters. Although the companies were intermixed on landing, the stretch of beach where they came ashore is not great and it would not have taken long to sort them out, if not prevented by enemy fire.

Although the popular imagination is today inspired by the dramatic image of troops scrambling ashore under fire, the 3rd Brigade's direct and initial impression in the first hours was that the

---

249 There is some evidence Coleman fought with Cooke.
250 Darnell, 1DRL 233.
251 Peck, letter to wife, n.d.
252 Şefik, para. 46.

Turkish defenders put up a great volume of fire but not much of a fight when confronted face to face. When the effects of the Turks' resistance, the early fragmentation of the 11th Battalion, exaggerated perceptions of Turkish numbers and their aggression in the face of such long odds[253] are considered, Şefik has every right to be proud.

The evidence in these chapters contrasts with another significant belief of the Landing – that the destroyer tows landed some time after the battleship tows, and sheds light on another issue – Turkish shelling of the first waves.

It is generally believed that the second wave of the covering force landed in good order between 10 and 30 minutes after the first. Bean describes in detail the battleship tows' landing, the assault on and consolidation of Plugge's Plateau, and the departure of the 9th and 10th Battalions for objectives inland. He then continues that "the second instalment of the covering force was already ashore and making inland"[254] and describes the arrival of the destroyer tows, creating the impression that Plugge's was taken by the troops of the battleship tows. Howe confirms this, writing that Plugge's "was captured by A and C Companies of the 11th Battalion ... with a platoon of the 10th and Major S.B. Robertson's company of 9th."[255] Bean confirms the impression with a range of other comments. Colonel Clarke landed "ten minutes" after "the last battleship tow."[256] By the time the destroyer tows carrying the 11th and 12th Battalions landed, the "Turks ... had been thoroughly awakened by the arrival of the battleship tows ... a quarter of an hour before ... Before the boats left the destroyers bullets were rattling against" their bows.[257] When the "first Turkish gun ... opened at 4.45 a.m., fifteen minutes after the landing ... The first destroyer tows had just landed."[258] In *Gallipoli Mission*, after describing Howe's ascent of Plugge's Plateau and Annear's death, Bean continues, "the second wave ... was just landing."[259] In *Anzac to Amiens* he describes the capture of Plugge's Plateau and departure of the scouts into Shrapnel Gully: "By this time part of the second wave from the destroyers was reaching" Plugge's, having begun "to get into the rowing boats just as the Turks began firing at the first wave, which must then have been scrambling ashore."[260] This version has been repeated in works published since.

Evidence compiled in this work presents a different picture. Men were shot alongside B Company's Mofflin during his ascent of Plugge's, and by the time he reached the top he was "well up" with the leading troops. He even prodded Brockman[261] in the buttocks with his bayonet during the climb. Mofflin then shot a Turkish soldier firing on the beach and Selby took his rifle.[262] Clearly Mofflin was as involved in the fighting for Plugge's Plateau as anyone.

By my research, Croly, Newman and Louch landed with the second wave, yet Belford wrote of Croly "sitting in one of the leading boats," at the first shot.[263] Newman's account of "the pinnace on my immediate left" shooting "up a flame from its funnel ... machine guns and rifles opened fire,"[264] matches accounts of the first wave. Louch described being in a boat approaching the shore when he saw the machine gun on Ari Burnu knocked out[265] and was on the beach when Johnston flopped down beside him, apparently after landing from *London*.

253 Three Turks choosing to charge Brockman in the face of an assault by hundreds of Australians provides one extraordinary example.
254 Bean, *Official History*, Volume I (1921 and 1941), p.263.
255 Howe, "Sparks From an Old Controversy", p.6.
256 Bean, *Official History*, Volume I (1921 and 1941), p.269.
257 *Ibid.*, p.268.
258 *Ibid.*, p.278.
259 Bean, *Gallipoli Mission*, p.77.
260 C.E.W. Bean, *Anzac to Amiens* (Canberra: Australian War Memorial, 1946), p.87.
261 Mofflin, letter, 20 October 1915, p.14.
262 *Ibid.*, p.15.
263 Belford, *Legs Eleven*, p.70.
264 *Ibid.*, p.68.
265 Steel & Hart, *Defeat at Gallipoli*, p.61.

In contrast to the established history, 11th Battalion evidence shows that the leading boats from the destroyers were close behind, if not amongst, those of the battleships. Johnston confirmed this in his report to MacLagan: "the tows from the Battleship" were "very little ahead of those from the Destroyers and all practically landed together."[266] This comment did not appear in the *Official History*, but appears to be accurate.

One reason for the misrepresentation is that the reality was more complex than presented in established histories. As it was not possible to land all 2,500 troops of the destroyer tows simultaneously, the boats landing the first wave were to return to the destroyers to assist with landing the second. Some of these men consequently had to wait some time, a delay Bean described as seeming to last for "ages."[267] Some, but not all – others got ashore early, from the boats already alongside the destroyers. Mofflin's boat rushed for shore soon after the first shot, without waiting to be filled or for a tow.[268]

For the second wave to have reached the beach so rapidly, the destroyers must have released their boats close to shore. This appears to be confirmed by Murphy, who thought his destroyer "about 50 yards from the shore … we could see the first … boatloads landing" when the "silence was violently broken by furious rifle and machine gun fire."[269] At the first shot some of the battleship tows, by their own accounts, were much further from shore. Dix also confirms the 11th Battalion evidence: as the first troops were landing, he turned to see "our destroyers almost as far inshore as our picket boats and the soldiers from them already on their way to land."[270]

This anomaly did not become visible until it became possible, using the reconstructed battalion roll, to assign accounts to companies and ships. It then became apparent that many anecdotes attributed for the past 90 years to the first wave,[271] actually belong to the second, making the latter invisible. One 11th Battalion destroyer appears to have been further north than any of the battleships tows,[272] which may have given her the opportunity to move closer to shore than had she followed them. A number of the first wave saw boats on the beach to their north. These are generally assumed to have been from the battleships, but may have been from this destroyer.[273] Accounts by men of other battalions, particularly the 12th Battalion, which was distributed over a number of destroyers, may reveal more.

The existing image of the 11th Battalion landing in two distinct waves, separated by 10 to 20 minutes, is incorrect. Some of the leading troops of the second wave may have landed ahead of some of the last troops of the first. Given the varying estimates of distance, the irregular shoreline and the scattered landing of the battleship tows, this would not be surprising. The experiences of the 9th and 10th Battalions may be similar.

Another contentious issue is whether the Landing was made under shell fire. Bean and others, such as Howe, note that the first enemy shell burst over the troops some time later. Bean wrote that Brockman's company saw their first shrapnel while reorganising in Rest Gully, which contrasts with his statement that "The first Turkish gun had opened at 4.45 a.m., fifteen minutes after the landing."[274] This is confirmed by Uyar, who wrote that "At 4.45 a.m., with improved visibility,"[275] the Gaba Tepe gun opened fire. Louch recalled seeing "the first shell to be fired" by this gun as he

---

266 3rd Brigade War Diary, August 1914–June 1915, AWM4 Australian Imperial Force Unit War Diaries, Australian War Memorial, Canberra ACT.
267 Bean, *Official History*, Volume I (1921 and 1941), p.265.
268 Mofflin, letter, 20 October 1915, p.12.
269 Murphy, letter, *Sunday Times*, 6 June 1915.
270 Dix, private papers, Imperial War Museum, p.8.
271 Such as those of Louch, Croly and Newman.
272 Bean, *Official History*, Volume I (1921 and 1941), Map 11, opposite p.256
273 Such as Gostelow's party.
274 Bean, *Official History*, Volume I (1921 and 1941), p.278.
275 Uyar, p.105.

climbed Plugge's Plateau,[276] yet Facey and others describe being shelled on the way to shore.[277] Could troops have been shelled on the destroyers, in their boats or on the beach?

Şefik suggests that only one gun fired on the Z Beach landing – the "Mantellie [sic] gun," emplaced "right on the beach in the side of the Gaba Tepe headland" to enfilade any landing "on the Ari Burnu beach."[278] This refers to a two-gun battery of 87 mm 1885 Krupp guns, only one of which was operational.[279] The functioning gun appears to have opened fire early, in response to machine gun fire "from the landing craft."[280] This suggests the Mantelli gun commenced firing earlier than Bean believed, apparently as the first wave were landing. Şefik wrote that "The Battalion CO Major Izmet … received news by telephone of the first landing from OC 4 Company at Ari Burnu … He replied with orders to launch an immediate attack … and gave instructions for the Mantelli gun … to open fire."[281] As these orders were relayed by phone, or if the Gaba Tepe CO opened fire on his own initiative, firing may have commenced early. That the gun opened fire earlier, possibly in response to the pinnace firing her machine gun, as noted in Ottoman sources, is confirmed by naval officer Dix, of the first wave, who recalled the picket boat's machine gun fire, then "shells began to come from Gaba Tepe way, and, turning to a 'bang' from behind us, we saw" the destroyers landing their troops.[282]

Şefik also mentions a "Nordenfeldt" gun[283] and its existence is confirmed by the later 11th Battalion raid on Gaba Tepe.[284] In fact there appear to have been two, 1 inch, multi-barrelled Nordenfeldt guns at Gaba Tepe, which had "already joined the firefight."[285] More curiously, Brockman later told Bean that when in the boats "Something went into water … possibly Hotchkiss shells – and threw up a spray – a number of these were falling about."[286] Keast also thought he was under fire from "two machine guns and one Hotchkiss 3 pounder."[287] For reasons explained later, the four Turkish mountain guns on 400 Plateau appear not to have fired on the landing beaches nor their approaches at this time.

If my timeline is correct in suggesting the landing of various boats was not as portrayed by Bean and others, it is possible Newham's recollection of a shell exploding near him, MacDonald's and Louch's of seeing an early shell burst, and even Brockman's of "things" hitting the water and throwing "up a spray,"[288] may ring true. As the destroyers took some time to land their troops,[289] it is possible Facey and others, had they landed later, did come under fire while aboard their destroyers.

Şefik's account of only a single, slow firing gun, makes it unlikely that the fire was "heavy," as often described, though it may have felt so to men exposed to it for the first time. The Mantelli gun "fired 144 shrapnel" and 37 high explosive shells.[290] Many accounts described *Bacchante*'s attempts to silence this "battery" as unsuccessful. Şefik disagrees, writing that a "ship which infiltrated between Ari Burnu and Gaba Tepe was able to silence this gun."[291] Another battery, of four "short barrelled 150 mm howitzers

276 Louch, manuscript, p.14.
277 Facey, *A Fortunate Life*, p.254.
278 Şefik, para. 17, and footnote 2.
279 Uyar, p.105.
280 As reported by Lieutenant Asim, CO of No. 3 Company at Gaba Tepe. Şefik, para. 37.
281 Şefik, para. 43.
282 Dix, private papers, Imperial War Museum, pp.7–8.
283 Şefik, para. 43.
284 Bean, *Official History*, Volume I (1921 and 1941), p.559.
285 Uyar, p.105.
286 Brockman, 3DRL 606 item 27.
287 Keast, diary, 24/25 April 1915.
288 Brockman, 3DRL 606 item 27.
289 Bean, *Official History*, Volume I (1921 and 1941), p.265.
290 Şefik, para. 45; Uyar, p.105.
291 Şefik, para. 45. Medcalf also noted that "The fleet soon reduced the fort to silence." Medcalf, manuscript, p.65.

deployed east of Palamutluk Ridge,"[292] and described by Şefik as "equally worthless"[293] opened fire early, but probably not until later and possibly not at the beach or landing boats.[294]

In summary, it may be that the single Mantelli gun opened fire earlier than acknowledged by western sources, to be joined later by the howitzers, creating perceptions of heavy fire. That the howitzers continued to fire despite the Bacchante's efforts against the Mantelli gun may have created the incorrect impression that the Navy failed to silence the initial Gaba Tepe gun. Given that the Australians could not have known what Turkish guns were firing at them, the reasons for their contradictory recollections are obvious. Those who described shells exploding on the beach or of the fleet reducing "the fort to silence," may have been closer to the truth than previously realised.[295]

---

292 Williams, *The Battle of Anzac Ridge*, p.103, citing Genelkurmay Baskanligi, *Birinci Dubya Harbinde*, p.92.

293 Şefik, para. 17, fotnote 2.

294 Şefik thought that this battery was "effective in keeping the transport ships away from the shore and thus delaying the landing." Şefik, para. 45.

295 Medcalf, manuscript, p.65.

5

Tulloch's Party on Battleship Hill

"Sometimes minutes seem like years …"[1]

Up the Range

Men converged on Russell's Top from a number of directions and most gravitated towards the Nek as the obvious route inland. It has not been possible, due to discrepancies between accounts as men from a number of units arrived at different times by a variety of routes, to determine precisely the details and sequence of events on Russell's Top early on that morning. The existing secondary sources are based on fragments of information, often taken in isolation, and the detail is sometimes inaccurate or contradictory.

After Clarke's death the Turks on the seaward slope of Baby 700 were either scared off by Tulloch's party climbing Walker's Ridge,[2] dislodged by half a dozen men sent forward by Lalor and Butler, two of whom were killed,[3] or dislodged by a party who crossed the Nek and outflanked and "probably shot them." The "firing had been nasty from these men."[4] This "left the coast clear."[5] It is likely there had been a number of Turkish parties in the area.

Near the Nek, Margetts and Patterson were joined by Captain L.E. Burt, 12th Battalion, and some men.[6] They assembled in "a hollow"[7] – probably in the area covered today by the cemetery at the Nek – and there met Tulloch. A rough reorganisation took place, with officers and NCOs taking "charge of" groups,[8] who were then considered to be "platoons" or "sections." Burt instructed Margetts to dig in[9] short of the narrowest part of the Nek – probably just short of where the Turkish monument stands today. There they were joined by Lalor with about half of his D Company. This brought the 12th Battalion strength to about five platoons – three quarters of A Company, under Burt, Margetts and Patterson, and about half D Company, commanded by Lalor, Booth and Butler. Margetts estimates about 50 to 70 men of the 9th, 10th and 11th Battalions[10] were there also. At this stage, even though the 12th Battalion platoons could be expected to be understrength, the reserve battalion greatly outnumbered the "assault" battalions on Russell's Top.

As the 11th Battalion's orders were "to get Big 700" (Battleship Hill) where the battalion "were to rendezvous,"[11] Tulloch's party dutifully "pushed on,"[12] crossing the Nek in groups and advancing

1   Şefik, para. 52.
2   Bean, *Official History*, Volume I (1921 and 1941), p.274.
3   Newton, *The Story of the Twelfth*, p.89.
4   Tulloch, 3DRL 606 item 206 – diaries nos. 192–205.
5   *Ibid.*
6   I.S. Margetts, AWM38 3DRL 606 Book 31.
7   Margetts, 3DRL 606 Book 31.
8   *Ibid.*
9   *Ibid.*
10 *Ibid.*
11 Tulloch, 3DRL 606 item 206 – diaries nos. 192–205. Bean confusingly wrote that the 11th were to rendezvous on Baby 700. Bean, *Official History*, Volume I (1921 and 1941), p.287.
12 Tulloch, 3DRL 606 item 206 – diaries nos. 192–205.

towards the scrub-covered Baby 700. Butler went with them, as Lalor had ordered him "to take his men forward to the next slope," presumably Baby 700, "to cover" Tulloch's "consolidation";[13] they appear in fact to have accompanied Tulloch to Battleship Hill.[14] Bean wrote that Tulloch was joined at about this time by "Jackson and Buttle" of his company, who "crossed Shrapnel Gully," "retired, and met their own half-company commander, Captain Tulloch."[15] In fact, Buttle and Reid belonged to D Company and had climbed Russell's Top from the vicinity of Rest Gully. It appears Buttle and Reid, believing they were to reinforce the 12th Battalion, arrived at the Nek soon after Tulloch left, and Lalor ordered them on. Buttle recalled his orders being to "follow the Turks retreating to the left front and to hold the ground while he [Lalor] was digging in."[16] Consolidation and support by Lalor, of the brigade's reserve battalion, make sense, but it is difficult to understand why Buttle would be ordered to reinforce the reserve battalion or to hold back the enemy while the reserve consolidated. It is difficult to establish who, if anyone, was ordered to "thrust" for the 11th Battalion's objective on Battleship Hill.

Private D.B. Robinson[17] accompanied Reid, and his account appears to describe their movement along Russell's Top. Due to sniping, Robinson was "sent ahead to scout" with Private B.J. Gannaway,[18] and came across Lalor, known "affectionately … as 'Puss-in-Boots', owing to his small stature and his habit of wearing riding boots." Robinson "sent word back to the party to come up." Lalor believed there was a party ahead requiring support – presumably Tulloch's. Robinson's party then "rushed" on through scattered fire.[19] This and the evidence examined above suggest Buttle and Reid did not meet Tulloch until after leaving Lalor and the Nek.

Buttle's party soon met B Company's Jackson "coming from the right on a similar mission to ours but told him that we were from the 12th and as his party was disorganised he did not come with us."[20] How Jackson happened to appear on the slopes of Baby 700 is unclear. Bean thought the time about 7:00 a.m.[21] When Jackson joined Tulloch he was ordered to go to the north of Baby 700 to prevent Turks infiltrating around Tulloch's left rear.[22] Jackson is stated to have had a platoon with him,[23] but appears to have had only about 20 men,[24] or less than half a full platoon. Herein lies one of the difficulties of reconstructing the battle of 25 April – a party of 20 men with their officer can be referred to as a platoon, even though more than half of the men are elsewhere; conversely, so many men were separated from their leaders, that personal accounts cannot necessarily be directly tied to the experience of others of their platoons.

The end result is that, despite the importance of Tulloch's foray and the number of times his story has been retold, at the time of writing there had been no attempt at establishing the strength of the party he took to Battleship Hill. They are variously described as a "platoon,"[25] several platoons,[26] a "handful"[27] and "about 60 men."[28] Later writers appear to take their figures from Bean, but there is confusion as to when the quoted figures applied. Carlyon, for example, noted 60 after the party was

13   Newton, *The Story of the Twelfth*, p.90.
14   *Ibid.*
15   Bean, *Official History*, Volume I (1921 and 1941), p.286.
16   Buttle, 3DRL 8042 item 7.
17   936 Private Daniel Bosworth Robinson, D Company, 24 at embarkation, clerk, of Williams, born Melbourne, Victoria.
18   903 Private Benjamin Joseph Gannaway, D Company, 29 at embarkation, labourer, of Wagin, born Preston, Victoria.
19   Belford, *Legs Eleven*, p.77.
20   Buttle, 3DRL 8042 item 7.
21   Bean, *Official History*, Volume I (1921 and 1941), p.275.
22   Tulloch, 3DRL 606 item 206 – diaries nos. 192–205.
23   Bean, *Gallipoli Mission*, p.84.
24   Tulloch, 3DRL 606 item 206 – diaries nos. 192–205.
25   *Ibid.*
26   Bean, *Gallipoli Mission*, p.84.
27   Bean, *Official History*, Volume I (1921 and 1941), p.275.
28   *Ibid.*, p.287.

joined by Reid, but[29] this number probably refers to Tulloch's strength before Buttle and Reid joined him. This figure may have come from *Anzac to Amiens*, which curiously reduces Tulloch's party to 60,[30] having on the previous page referred to them as a company.[31] The matter is further confused by the reorganisation on Russell's Top, statements that Tulloch had left the beach with a platoon of B Company, although as company 2IC he did not command a platoon, that Jackson and Buttle belonged to his half-company and had advanced inland together,[32] and that Butler had been with Tulloch "from the start,"[33] though it is unclear whether this means from the beach or the Nek, nor whether Tulloch's estimate of advancing across the Nek with 60 men includes Butler's party.[34] To compound the confusion, in *Gallipoli Mission* Bean refers to Reid but not Buttle,[35] and although Buttle stated that he and Reid had about 60 men with them, Bean changed this to 30 in the *Official History*.[36] Bean probably took this figure from an estimate by Tulloch, though it is likely Buttle's figure is more accurate as it refers to his own party, whereas Tulloch's is a guess of the strength of a party who had "probably ... followed across the Nek."[37] Tulloch, in fact, concentrating on leading his party through enemy territory and thick scrub, could not remember seeing Buttle at all during the advance. Buttle's and Reid's party could be expected to be relatively intact as, apart from sniper fire, the fighting on Russell's Top was over when they arrived.[38] The identity of the B Company "platoon" that accompanied Tulloch from the beach, if it was a single platoon, is not stated in any secondary sources. In Chapter 10, analysis of evidence from a range of sources makes it likely that this party consisted predominantly of men from Newman's 8 Platoon.

During the reorganisations on the Top, it can be assumed that the 11th and 12th Battalion officers drew their own troops into their fold, and that the smaller number of stray 9th and 10th Battalion men, whose objectives lay inland rather than with the brigade reserve, would have accompanied the 11th Battalion. Margett's estimate of 50–70 men of the 9th, 10th and 11th Battalions[39] is probably the most accurate reflection of the number with Tulloch before Buttle's and Reid's 60 joined him. To this Butler's platoon, thought to be at about half strength,[40] should probably be added: Sergeant E.R. Kidson, like Lalor and Butler a West Australian serving with the 12th Battalion, was killed on Battleship Hill,[41] suggesting that Butler was also there. Tulloch's party may consequently have numbered up to 150, many more than usually acknowledged.[42]

After crossing the Nek, Tulloch's party advanced into the dense scrub of the seaward slope of Baby 700, "extended into line"[43] with about "7–10 paces"[44] between men. "The sun was bright, the sky clear," and "the fresh air of spring was full of the scent of wild thyme."[45] The men disappeared over the southern shoulder of Baby 700[46] and ventured into the unknown. The sound of firing came from their right rear,

29   Carlyon, *Gallipoli*, p.157.
30   Bean, *Anzac to Amiens*, p.102.
31   *Ibid.*, p.101.
32   Bean, *Official History*, Volume I (1921 and 1941), p.286.
33   *Ibid.*, p.288.
34   Tulloch, 3DRL 606 item 206 – diaries nos. 192–205.
35   Bean, *Gallipoli Mission*, p.84.
36   Bean, *Official History*, Volume I (1921 and 1941), p.288.
37   Tulloch, 3DRL 606 item 206 – diaries nos. 192–205.
38   Belford, *Legs Eleven*, p.77.
39   Margetts, 3DRL 606 Book 31.
40   Newton, *The Story of the Twelfth*, p.89.
41   *Ibid.*, p.90, and B2455, Kidson.
42   With the exception of Roberts' Appendix 4, which was published a many years after I had undertaken the work decribed here. Roberts reached the figure of 190 though it is based on fewer sources. Regardless of which figure, 150 or 190, is closest to the truth, they demonstrate the unreliability of previous figures. Roberts, Appendix 4, p.173.
43   Bean, *Official History*, Volume I (1921 and 1941), p.287.
44   Tulloch, 3DRL 606 item 206 – diaries nos. 192–205.
45   Bean, *Official History*, Volume I (1921 and 1941), p.288.
46   *Ibid.*, p.287 refers to this as "rather on the inland side of the crest."

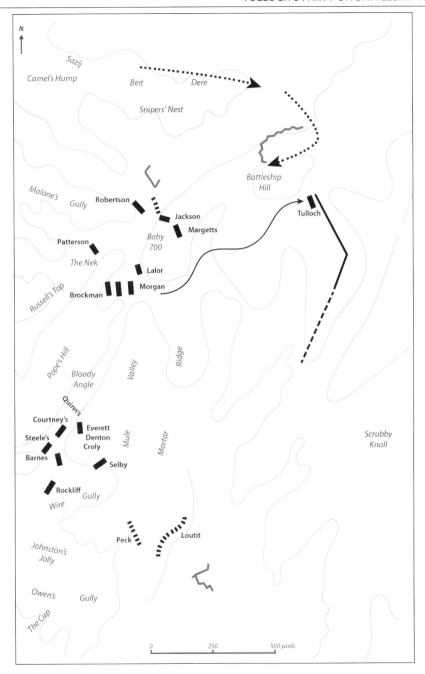

Map 7. Adapted from Bean's Map 13. Annotated to demonstrate possible extent of Tulloch's position. Solid line: Tulloch's possible position on Incebayir Ridge if his party numbered 100 men in single line at a spacing of five yards. Hatched line: additional ground if Tulloch had 150 men at a spacing of five yards. This is not to suggest that this is the actual position of Tulloch's line, but demonstrates that the party occupied a greater front than shown in the *Official History*'s Maps 12 or 13. The approximate route from Fisherman's Hut, roughly transferred from Şefik's map, of 1 Platoon, 4/2/27th Regiment, is depicted by dotted line. (Bean, Map 13, *Official History* (1921 and 1941), Volume I, precedes p.289)

and occasionally, when crossing crests or the exposed forward slopes, bullets "fired at long range lisped past."[47] The men's attention was focussed on the confusion of ridges and gullies ahead, where there as yet appeared to be no sign of life. As they crossed what appeared to be a "second crest,"[48] a crackle of rifle fire erupted from the scrub ahead and men began to fall. A line of about 60 Turks was firing from the scrub halfway up the next rise, about 400 yards away, supported by a machine gun, so Tulloch believed, firing from "behind them."[49] Tulloch's party threw themselves down and returned fire. A "stiff fire fight" developed as the Australians attempted to gain fire superiority. Lying "in the scrub," they kept "up a carefully controlled fire" and "beat down the Turkish fire."[50] The Turks "melted away."[51] About 10 of Tulloch's party had been hit. The line then "rose and advanced across the intervening dip and over the crest which the enemy had been defending."[52]

Soon bullets began to "zipp"[53] once more past the Australians, from a "well hidden"[54] enemy force somewhere ahead and machine guns firing at "very long range."[55] Under this fire, they dashed another 150 or 200 yards forward "by rushes."[56] Robinson saw "a large body of Turks in dark uniforms coming down the opposite ridge with 25-yard rushes, he thought about "a thousand," yards ahead, though it was probably closer to 500–800 yards. "We then lay down and opened fire."[57] A "prolonged fire fight" ensued as the Australians once more attempted to gain fire superiority.

Tulloch's accounts[58] suggest his party fought here for some time before the men, on an order passed down the line, crawled forward another 100 yards on their bellies.[59] The "men were doing everything they had been taught – firing only as directed – conserving ammunition."[60] They formed a firing line along the inland slope of a long narrow ridge, with five yards between men[61] and a valley separating them from the series of ridges apparently occupied by the Turks. To what Bean assumed to be to the party's left front rose a "still larger crest of the main ridge, its bare summit being about half a mile away."[62] Ten minutes after the men crawled forward, "heavy machine gun fire opened at short range on the line which they had left."[63]

Blay described "a deep valley" in front "before another ridge about ½ mile away" at "the farthest point the Australian and New Zealand troops reached." In the distance the "sea of Marmora" lay "glinting in the sun"[64] (Figure 23). Reid, with Robinson lying beside him, was on the right of the line,[65] "coolly" using his glasses to direct fire.[66] Mason and Simcock were probably near Reid, and members of B Company doubtless towards the left. Some somewhat abstract research into a range of records shows that G.L. Morris,[67] who had joined the battalion in the previous fortnight and

47   Ibid., p.288.
48   Tulloch, 3DRL 606 item 206 – diaries nos. 192–205.
49   Ibid.
50   Bean, Official History, Volume I (1921 and 1941), p.288.
51   Tulloch, 3DRL 606 item 206 – diaries nos. 192–205.
52   Bean, Official History, Volume I (1921 and 1941), p.288.
53   Ibid.
54   Tulloch, 3DRL 606 item 206 – diaries nos. 192–205.
55   Ibid.
56   Bean, Official History, Volume I (1921 and 1941), p.289.
57   Belford, Legs Eleven, p.78.
58   Tulloch, 3DRL 606 item 206 – diaries nos. 192–205; Bean, Gallipoli Mission, p.85.
59   Tulloch, 3DRL 606 item 206 – diaries nos. 192–205.
60   Ibid.
61   Ibid.
62   Bean, Official History, Volume I (1921 and 1941), p.288.
63   Tulloch, 3DRL 606 item 206 – diaries nos. 192–205.
64   Blay, diary, 25 April 1915.
65   Tulloch, 3DRL 8042 item 7.
66   Belford, Legs Eleven, p.78.
67   1674 Private (at embarkation) George Lambert Morris, 3rd Reinforcement, 22 at embarkation, clerk, born Castlemaine, Victoria. Interviewed 1st AGH, Heliopolis, 26 September 1915.

Signaller J.J. Ryan,[68] were also on Battleship Hill that morning, as probably was Charlie Braidwood[69] and possibly W.D. Lumsden.[70] A few anonymous Queenslanders and South Australians of the 9th and 10th Battalions probably also fought on Battleship Hill. Blay, remarkably, fell asleep, but was "rudely awakened by our bugler, he … thought I was shot."[71] The Australians' water bottles were "practically untouched,"[72] a sign of good discipline.

The bulk of the enemy force appeared to be lining the ridge ahead. "After firing on" them "for some time," Robinson received the order "that we were to entrench." This they did, "alternately filling our magazines and emptying them at the enemy."[73] Both sides were "very well hidden,"[74] but attempts at digging or moving brought down a "storm of fire."[75] Hitch pulled back into dead ground to "see if there was any possibility of a signal." He returned with a message, "hang on reinforcements coming," as "a heavy burst of firing broke out first on the left flank and then on the right."[76] Tulloch would later recall seeing a man "standing by a tree on the north shoulder of the hill" about 800–900 yards away, with runners "coming … and going to him."[77] Tulloch began sniping at what he assumed was a battalion commander, "but could not move him."[78]

The young captain, who had only recently joined the battalion, was fighting his first battle. He was responsible for possibly 150 men, most of whom he is unlikely to have known. Though he could not have known it, he was probably the only officer in the battalion, if not the brigade, to command a party occupying one of their objectives. It was an extraordinary position in which to find himself. Apart from a later comment in a letter to Bean, there is little to indicate how he felt or reacted. In most accounts men described the job rather than their reaction to it and Tulloch was probably too busy to focus on much but the work at hand. After the war, photographs taken of Battleship Hill in 1919 would still send "shivers down my neck for those look to me the identical bushes whose leaves amputated by machine gun bullets were falling"[79] on the prone men and working their way under their tunic collars.[80]

Tulloch could see, apparently to his right,[81] another line of Turks firing on some Australians "digging in" further south.[82] Although few Turks could be seen ahead, "increasing fire at short range" suggested they were massing in dead ground "under very good covering fire."[83] Bullets also began to whip among the Australians from the left rear. Jackson's party "could be heard fighting"[84] in that direction, but Turks appeared to be firing either from beyond Jackson's party, or between it and Tulloch's.

The Turkish fire continued to build and men continued to be hit. Tulloch heard that "Mr Reid" had been shot.[85] All accounts note that Reid was kneeling and observing through his binoculars directing the fire of his men when a Turkish bullet struck him in the thigh.[86] Tulloch thought Reid was hit

68   258 Private (at embarkation) James Joseph Ryan, Signaller, 20 at embarkation, telephonist, of Broome Hill, born Wilmington, South Australia.
69   409 Private Charles Braidwood, B Company, 24 at embarkation, tailor, of Fremantle, born Scotland.
70   924 Private William Deas Lumsden, D Company, 20 at enlistment, lumper/farm hand, of Albany, born Scotland.
71   Blay, diary, 25 April 1915.
72   Tulloch, 3DRL 606 item 206 – diaries nos. 192–205.
73   Belford, *Legs Eleven*, p.78.
74   Tulloch, 3DRL 606 item 206 – diaries nos. 192–205.
75   *Ibid.*
76   It is difficult to know what to make of this message, as it was reputedly "from Sedd-ul-Bar." Was the message meant for Tulloch? Hitch, interview, May 1974, p.10.
77   Tulloch, 3DRL 606 item 206 – diaries nos. 192–205.
78   *Ibid.*
79   Tulloch, 3DRL 8042 item 7.
80   Bean, *Official History*, Volume I (1921 and 1941), p.289.
81   Bean, *Gallipoli Mission*, p.86.
82   Tulloch, 3DRL 606 item 206 – diaries nos. 192–205.
83   *Ibid.*
84   *Ibid.*
85   Tulloch, 3DRL 8042 item 7.
86   Buttle, 3DRL 8042 item 7; Mason, 2DRL 301, Book 31.

about midway through what he later estimated to be a half hour fight, Buttle and Robinson that it happened during the later withdrawal, and Mason, for reasons that even Bean could not explain, that it happened during fighting near Fisherman's Hut. Reid's femur was probably shattered, and the thigh began "to swell perceptibly."[87] His pain must have been intense but he declined assistance from both Buttle[88] and Mason,[89] who were within calling distance on either side of him,[90] replying that as he could crawl he could "get into the gully"[91] behind. Leaving Buttle his equipment and taking only an automatic pistol and/or a revolver for protection, Reid began dragging his wounded leg back towards the ridge behind.[92] Most accounts state that he was alone, though Robinson thought a man assisted him.[93] Tulloch, under enemy fire and endeavouring to command his extended and mixed party, conceded to being "pretty well occupied at the time," but saw over his right shoulder "Mort crawling out, dragging one leg behind him."[94]

Reid's wounding is a valuable reference point as it ties witnesses to Battleship Hill. Goodlet saw Reid hit[95] but does not mention it in the account he wrote of the Landing 20 years later. Nor in that account does he mention that he was one of the select band who gazed briefly down on the Dardanelles from Battleship Hill on 25 April. Like most, he probably didn't know where he was.

Tulloch was isolated, the enemy were getting closer and their fire stronger. He was clearly being outflanked, appeared to be outnumbered, was forward of everyone else in the area and was responsible for many lives. There was no sign of support being sent his way from battalion, brigade or division; the only reference to anyone being aware of Tulloch's plight is Hitch's comment about a signal.[96] Turkish small arms fire was taking its toll on those who had accompanied him on the long climb from the beach far below and now lay in the scrub on this lonely, unnamed patch of foreign soil.

Tulloch decided that his only option was withdrawal. Word was passed along "to hang on for a little longer to give" Reid "an opportunity to get away."[97] Meanwhile Tulloch pondered his next challenge – extricating his force while engaging an aggressive and apparently numerically superior enemy. He ordered his party to retire in four sections, alternate sections doubling back, then throwing themselves to the ground to cover the withdrawal of the other two. Robinson recalled three "men on our left" being ordered "to crawl back to the scrub and retire, then three men on the right."[98] The "air was alive with bullets" recalled Hitch:

[B]y the time we reached the top of the next ridge all the others were in motion. We opened fire ... to keep the enemy from coming on too quickly ... ran back together for about another 150 yards and the order was passed along reform left, Turks advancing on the left ... They were a fine looking body of men ... but as they came under our fire they ran back and I had two shots at a running man and missed him.[99]

Hitch later earned a fearsome reputation as a sniper, and was surprised that these shots missed. He later discovered that the Turk owed his survival to an earlier shell burst damaging Hitch's rifle.[100]

87   Belford, *Legs Eleven*, p.78, quoting Robinson.
88   Buttle, 3DRL 8042 item 7.
89   Belford, *Legs Eleven*, p.76.
90   Brennan, Australian Red Cross Wounded and Missing Enquiry Bureau files, 1DRL/0428.
91   Mason, 2DRL 301, Book 31.
92   Buttle, 3DRL 8042 item 7.
93   Belford, *Legs Eleven*, p.78.
94   Tulloch, 3DRL 8042 item 7.
95   Goodlet, quoted in Reid's Red Cross file.
96   This was mentioned many decades after the Landing.
97   Belford, *Legs Eleven*, p.78.
98   *Ibid.*
99   Hitch, interview, May 1974, pp.10–11.
100 *Ibid.*, p.10.

Hitch tended a wounded man whose arm was hanging by a "little bit of muscle." He used a twig and the tape torn from one of his own puttees to make a tourniquet, and another man cut away "the rest of his sleeve," then "the rest of his arm." As Hitch returned to the line a pellet "came slashing though the scrub" and hit him on the back of the hand, but didn't "break the bone." The withdrawal had left him, and he leapt down a steep gully hoping to notify the unit to his right of the Turkish breakthrough. He injured himself in the jump, and found himself trapped in the gully until nightfall.[101]

There is no record of how many killed or wounded were left lying in the scrub at Tulloch's furthest point, nor their names, though in 1919 Bean probably found the remains of at least one.[102] Howe described men of the 9th and 11th reaching Baby 700, and seeing the party withdraw, "heavily engaged" but "in good order, carrying their wounded with them."[103] This implies that only dead were left on the slopes of Battleship Hill, though some may have been too badly wounded to move and others may have been missed in the scrub. The survivors called Reid's name as they passed the ground over which they had earlier advanced, but received no answer. In a cryptic account, Mason referred to Reid being seen in one of the gullies "moving inland," but "Saw no more of him."[104] It is unclear what was meant by "inland."

Retchford may also have fought with Tulloch, though there is too little information in his account to be sure. He "advanced about 2½ miles and took a position" but as "there were only about a hundred of us" they had to retire, bullets fairly raining "on us … We all got back alright, and then established a fairly good position, digging in for our lives."[105]

The 19th Division Deploys

For many decades Australian writers' perceptions of what happened on Battleship Hill that morning have been driven by the generally accepted version of what was happening on the Turkish side. This was based on the accounts of Kemal and Zeki. It has consequently been assumed by Australian historians that Tulloch's advance was stopped and his party pushed back by Kemal's 57th Regiment, and that this was a crucial turning point in the campaign. Although the story has been repeated many times, its anomalies have not been resolved, nor perhaps even identified. When Bean returned to Gallipoli in 1919, he considered Tulloch's advance "perhaps the most important that I had come to Gallipoli to investigate."[106] Apart from repetition, the story of Tulloch's band appears to have remained where Bean's endeavours left it. This version of the story, accepted from that day to this and reiterated in recent texts, may be incorrect.

Mustafa Kemal, in camp in or near Boghali, was woken by gunfire, but it was not until 6:30 a.m. that he received a report and orders from Colonel Hamil (or Halil) Sami Bey, commander of the 9th Division, "to send a battalion against"[107] the invaders landing at Ari Burnu. Kemal concluded that this "landing is not a mere demonstration" but "a main force," and his "whole division would be required,"[108] or, according to more recent sources, his whole regiment, the 57th.[109] On his own initiative, he marched to the sound of the guns, determined to reach the high ground of Koja Chemen

101 Hitch, interview, May 1974, pp.10–13.
102 Bean, *Gallipoli Mission*, p.98.
103 Howe, "Sparks From an Old Controversy", p.8.
104 Mason, 2DRL 301, Book 31.
105 Retchford, letter, 14 May 1915.
106 Bean, *Gallipoli Mission*, p.83.
107 R.R. James, *Gallipoli* (London, Sydney: Pan Books, 1984), p.112.
108 James, *Gallipoli*, p.112.
109 Broadbent, *Gallipoli – The Fatal Shore*, p.93; Carlyon, p.156.

Tepe before the "English," as the enemy were at this stage presumed to be.[110] This was "vigorous"[111] and decisive action, as the 19th Division was the reserve division of the Fifth Army and consequently under the orders of General Liman von Sanders, who was awaiting a landing at Bolayir, and Kemal had acted without "awaiting leave or instructions."[112]

There is some confusion in secondary sources as to Kemal's whereabouts, but R.R. James states that on reaching Koja Chemen Tepe, Kemal ordered his officers to "close the men up and give them a short rest."[113] He, "his ADC ... chief medical officer, an orderly," and the commander of the mountain battery,[114] then walked along the crest connecting 971 to Chunuk Bair to assess the situation. From Chunuk Bair the officers could see warships and transports off Ari Burnu, "but no signs of fighting from Battleship Hill towards Gaba Tepe."[115] The events of the next few moments have been extensively quoted and have become firmly established as part of both the history and legend of that day. Kemal encountered "fleeing towards, Chunuk Bair,"[116] a "detachment who had been placed on hill Point 261 to the south of Chunuk Bair to observe and cover the shore."[117] Broadbent[118] states that Hill 261 was Baby 700, Carlyon that it was "the southern shoulder of Chunuk Bair."[119] Maps show a "261" contour on Chunuk Bair,[120] but Şefik does not record any troops being stationed anywhere near there.

"Why are you running away?" demanded Kemal. ""Sir, the enemy' they said ... pointing out Hill 261."[121] He then saw a line of enemy "skirmishers" approaching "Hill 261 and ... advancing completely unopposed."[122] Kemal, between his regiment and the invaders, said "You cannot run away from the enemy." "We have got no ammunition," they replied. Afterwards Kemal could not say whether his reaction was "a logical appreciation or an instinctive action,"[123] but he issued his famous command:

> "You have your bayonets" ... I made them fix their bayonets and lie down ... I sent the orderly officer ... to bring up ... at the double those ... of the ... regiment ... on Chunuk Bair who could reach it in time. When these men fixed their bayonets and lay down on the ground the enemy lay down also. The moment of time that we gained was this one.[124]

Lord Kinross recorded that "this moment of hesitation by the Anzacs may well have decided the fate of the peninsula."[125] By these accounts, "Kemal had seen Tulloch's party and Kemal was probably the officer Tulloch saw ... and fired at."[126] Broadbent continues that "Kemal's units ... began to rain fire down towards Tulloch's party of fifty or so men,"[127] and Roberts that 57th Regiment's "Zeki closely engaged Tulloch's force."[128]

110 Bean, *Gallipoli Mission*, p.135.
111 *Ibid.*, p.133.
112 *Ibid.*, p.135.
113 James, *Gallipoli*, p.112.
114 *Ibid.*
115 James, *Gallipoli*, p.112.
116 *Ibid.*, pp.112–113.
117 *Ibid.*, pp.112–113.
118 Broadbent, *Gallipoli – The Fatal Shore*, p.93.
119 Carlyon, *Gallipoli*, p.157.
120 Fewster confirms Chunuk Bair's height as 260 m. K. Fewster, V. Basarin and H.H. Basarin, *Gallipoli: The Turkish Story* (Crows Nest, NSW: Allen and Unwin, 2003), p.65.
121 James, *Gallipoli*, pp.112–113.
122 *Ibid.*, p.113.
123 *Ibid.*, p.113.
124 *Ibid.*, p.113.
125 Kinross, *Ataturk*, p.90.
126 Carlyon, p.157; Broadbent, *Gallipoli – The Fatal Shore*, p.93.
127 Broadbent, *Gallipoli – The Fatal Shore*, p.93.
128 Roberts, *The Landing at Anzac*, 1st ed, .p.101.

Uyar's and other Turkish accounts present a more detailed picture. The quoted times are as stated in those accounts.

Kemal was woken by the sounds of gunfire and received his first information about a "landing north of Kabatepe and naval gunfire at 5:20 am."[129] Major Hayrettin (or Hayreddin), 19th Division's Chief of Staff, later wrote of being woken that morning by a lieutenant who showed him a signal sent by Halil Sami at 5:10 advising of the landings.[130] Kemal alerted his troops, advised his corps commander, Esad Pasha, and sent out cavalry patrols, as had been previously practised. Like Şefik, Kemal knew the importance of acting swiftly, but as the 19th Division was reserve for the Fifth Army, he could not move without orders. Unfortunately, Sanders had headed north to Bolayir, "without leaving any orders." Esad Pasha hesitated and was reluctant to act without Sanders's approval.[131] Kemal also faced other problems – he had phone communications with Gaba Tepe only via Maidos; these phone networks carried communications for the local division, the 9th,[132] consequently limiting the flow of information to 19th Division. More significantly, the corps commander was not at Maidos, which was the obvious fulcrum for command of the two divisions responsible for the southern defence of the peninsula.

At 7:30 a.m. Kemal's patrols reported that the "landing at Anzac was serious and there were already fierce clashes around Hill 971."[133] Kemal ordered the 57th Regiment to prepare to march. Also at 7:30 a.m., Halil Sami had requested Kemal to "send a battalion to support the 27th Regiment," whose story will be told subsequently. Halil Sami, commanding a neighbouring division, was not above Kemal in the chain of command, but Kemal used this request as the pretext to move. He sent a report to corps headquarters at 8:00 a.m. advising what he was doing, and headed for the coast "with his entire regiment – the 57th Regiment, the 57th Machine-gun Company and the 5/3rd Mountain Artillery Battery."[134] Kemal's force left camp at 8:10 a.m. and he later reported that they launched their counter-attack – by all accounts against Tulloch on Battleship Hill – at 10:00 or 10:24 a.m., depending on sources.

For many years what was missing from accounts that associated Tulloch's and Kemal's roles on the morning of 25 April, was the story of the 27th Regiment, and a chronology that effectively ties the various accounts together.

Deployment of 27th Regiment

Those of the 27th Regiment camped near Maidos were woken by gunfire – not from the Straits this time but the west, where their 2nd Battalion was on duty along the coast. Şefik rushed to the phone, discovered troops were being landed at Ari Burnu,[135] as he had long believed they would, and issued orders for his regiment to "assemble … load up the A echelon transport, distribute the troops' rations, feed the animals." Within 10 minutes his officers were reporting that the 1st and 3rd Battalions, Machine Gun Company and transport were ready to move.[136] No orders came. Şefik contacted the

129 Uyar, p.120.
130 Izzettin (Çalışlar), "Battle of Gallipoli Memoir", April 12 1331/April 25 1915, Askeri Mecmua 1920, Military Journal. The Gallipoli Centenary Turkish Archives Research Project (Macquarie University, Australian War Memorial), <https://www.mq.edu.au/about/about-the-university/faculties-and-departments/faculty-of-arts/departments-and-centres/department-of-modern-history,-politics-and-international-relations/research/gallipoli-centenary-research-project/project-outcomes/translated-turkish-works-on-gallipoli#izzettin>, 18 November 2015.
131 Uyar, p.120.
132 Izzettin, memoir.
133 Uyar, p.122.
134 Ibid., pp.122, 123.
135 By telephoning Gaba Tepe. Şefik, para. 52.
136 Şefik, para. 52.

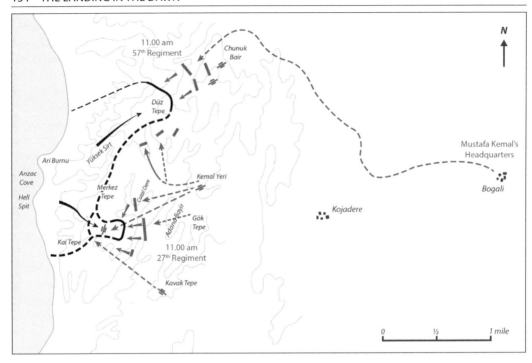

Map 8. Adapted from Şefik's Kroki (Sketch) 3, showing Kemal's route from Bogali to Chunuk Bair, annotated and printed in Örnek's and Toker's *Gallipoli: The Front Line Experience*. The annotation "11.00 am, 57th Regiment" was not Şefik's and may have been added for the Örnek/Toker volume. (Şefik, Kroki 3, 1:25,000, in T. Örnek and F. Toker, *Gallipoli: the Front Line Experience*, pp.30, 31)

Divisional Chief of Staff, Hulusi Bey, but was told to "Wait until you hear further from me." The men were told to drink their soup and wait, the sounds of small arms fire intermittently reaching them as their comrades fought along the coast. "Irritated beyond words," their colonel phoned 9th Division once more. "Hulusi Bey, our comrades are burning there under fire. How much longer are we going to wait?" Division, waiting to get a clearer picture of what was going on, and still concerned the Ari Burnu landing was a feint, would not be rushed. "Sometimes minutes seem like years,"[137] Şefik wrote. Hours later, an isolated Tulloch must have felt the same.

"Finally," at 5:45 a.m., 27th Regiment received its movement orders. They were to take a mountain battery of four 75 mm guns[138] from Camburnu, "halt the enemy landing … between Ari Burnu and Gaba Tepe" and throw them "into the sea."[139] Rather than wait the half hour it would take the mountain battery to join him, Şefik left a "company," probably platoon is meant, "from the 3rd Battalion,"[140] to escort it, despatched nine of the 17 mounted troops attached to the regiment to gather intelligence from the front,[141] and hurried to the battle area. Within "about 5 minutes of receipt of" their orders,[142] 27th Regiment was "on the march."[143] 1st Battalion took one of the newly

---

137 Şefik, para. 52.
138 8th Mountain Artillery Battery, 9th Field Atillery Regiment, 3rd Mountain Artillery Battalion. Uyar, p.113.
139 Şefik, para. 53.
140 *Ibid.*, para. 54.
141 *Ibid.*, para. 57.
142 *Ibid.*, para. 68.
143 *Ibid.*, para. 68.

made roads,[144] and the troops sheltered in ditches when enemy aircraft appeared (Map 9). Despite being exposed for nearly an hour to observation by allied aircraft and the *Manika*'s balloon,[145] not until 27th Regiment had passed the danger zone did the Navy begin bursting shells behind them, apparently firing blind, "traversing and sweeping over the plain which we had just passed."[146] Perhaps the allied spotters missed the marching column as they focussed on the known, old Maidos-Gaba Tepe road, while Şefik's troops marched on the newer, narrower road, "2–300m to the north."[147]

The regiment then advanced northwards along the eastern side of Third Ridge, which Şefik presumed would shield his columns from allied eyes, hiding a screen of small pickets along its top to protect his left. Although his columns may have been hidden from the bulk of the Australian force, a 9th Battalion party under Captain J.M. Dougall had reached Bolton's Ridge[148] and saw "a column of the enemy … marching steadily northward up the backbone of the ridge", after ascending "from the plain behind." Dougall, who had served with the Queen's Own Cameron Highlanders, "was greatly impressed" by the "orderly and excellent" deployment, and presumed them to be "well-trained … regular troops."[149]

As he moved northwards, Şefik gained information about the enemy's whereabouts from a wounded man of 4 Company, 2/27th Regiment. On Anderson Knoll [Kavak Tepe] he and his battalion commanders assembled and surveyed the battlefield. Sporadic firing could be heard, and the party saw their first enemy troops in the Karayurek Dere [Legge Valley] to their north; others could be seen on the 400 Plateau. The veteran soldier counted 26 transports from the "large number"[150] of ships visible offshore, multiplied this figure by 1,000 to gain a rough estimate of the enemy's possible fighting strength and scanned the scrub ahead to locate their flank. He deduced this to be the southern edge of the 400 Plateau and began making plans to attack it.[151]

Şefik wrote that his strategy of attacking "the enemy before he attacks you" and striking his flank, conformed to theoretical principles, "But there were certain obstacles."[152] Kanlisirt [Lone Pine] appeared to be occupied by a numerically superior enemy and dominated the intervening valley. Şefik's solution was to use his artillery and machine guns to suppress this point, but he could do little about the possible effects of naval gunfire on his exposed left flank. He was also concerned that, as he was outnumbered, his attack on the Australian flank would provoke an advance by their centre, resulting in the loss of Third Ridge and ultimately, by attack from flank or the rear, his regiment.[153] To counter this, he marched his troops northwards to select a better position from which to launch their attack; on reaching the southern crest of Scrubby Knoll [Kemal yeri[154] or Hill 165], he decided he had found it.[155] He ordered his battalions to assemble out of sight of the enemy, "immediately behind Hill 165 … 3rd Battalion on the left and the 1st Battalion on the right," though this appears to represent an error – elsewhere he states the positions reversed. With "binoculars in hand," he surveyed the ground ahead, looking and listening for the enemy. "At this point the sound of firing … became more frequent … machine gun fire was also heard … shells were passing above us."[156]

144 *Ibid.*, para. 55.
145 *Ibid.*, para. 60.
146 Şefik, para. 59.
147 *Ibid.*, para. 61.
148 Bean, *Official History*, Volume I (1921 and 1941), p.356.
149 *Ibid.*, p.357.
150 Şefik, para. 62.
151 *Ibid.*, para. 62, 64.
152 *Ibid.*, para. 64.
153 *Ibid.*, para. 64.
154 Generally spelt "Kemalyeri" in the translation of Şefik's manuscript, but "Kemal yeri" on his maps and those of The Turkish General Staff's "Brief History", Maps 53 and 54. "Kemalyere", "Kemal yere", "Kemal Yere", "Kemalyeri" and possibly others are used in western sources. Subsequently "Kemal yeri" will be used in this book unless quoted otherwise.
155 Şefik, para. 65.
156 *Ibid.*, para. 65.

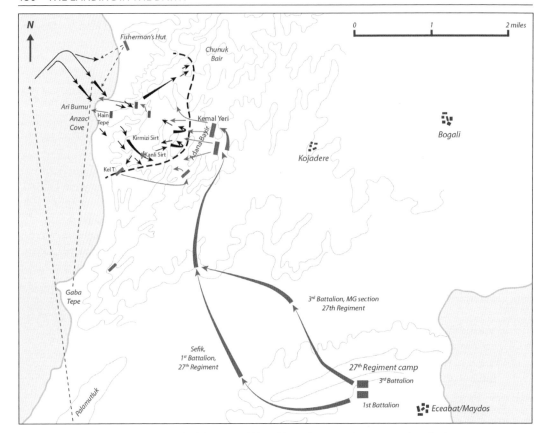

Map 9. Adapted from Şefik's Kroki (Sketch) 2, showing the routes taken by his two
battalions from their camp outside Maidos. (Şefik, Kroki 2, manuscript, n.p.)

Şefik reached Hill 165 at "0740 hours", the march from camp having taken "a little under two
hours."[157] By 7:55 a.m. he had sent Divisional HQ a report on his decision to attack.[158] The tail of
his column did not arrive "until after 0800 hours" when the "troops were given 15 minutes rest."[159]

What Şefik could not have known was that he had already achieved a great success – he had
beaten the enemy to Third Ridge. This was partly due to his planning, familiarity with the ground and
determination to act swiftly, but also to decisions made by his opponents. These will be discussed later.

The problem with comparing chronologies is that quoted times for 25 April 1915 are extremely
unreliable, and it cannot be assumed that Şefik's times correlate with western ones. In the allied
forces there was little synchronisation of watches; in the Ottoman forces, despite German officers
in the Ottoman Fifth Army complaining "bitterly and often,"[160] there was no standard approach to
timekeeping.[161] It is consequently necessary wherever possible to "anchor" accounts of the battle to
known events. Şefik states that a report of the landing "from the battalion CO at Gaba Tepe ... was
handed to the GOC at 0445 hours. My report to the Divisional Chief of Staff by telephone ... was

---

157 *Ibid.*, para. 66.
158 *Ibid.*, para. 68.
159 *Ibid.*, para. 68.
160 Williams, "Z Beach, the Landing of the ANZAC Corps, April 25, 1915", pp.55–56.
161 *Ibid.*, p.55.

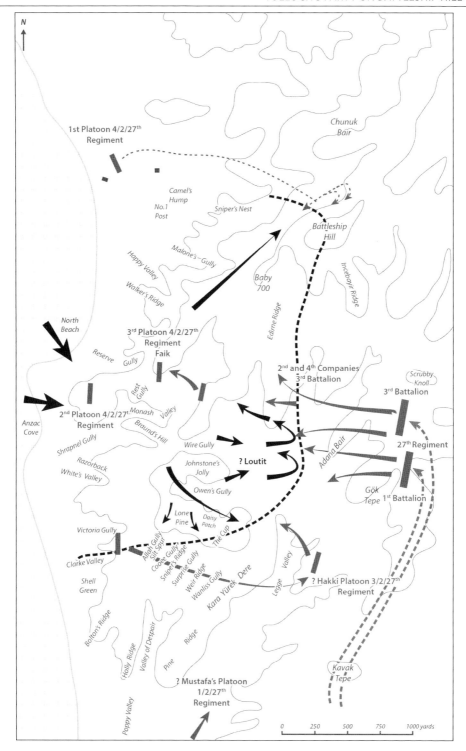

Map 10. Ottoman troop positions overlain on a section of Şefik's Kroki (Sketch)
2. Not shown is a group from 3 Platoon, 4/2/27th Regiment, despatched
early to Plugge's Plateau by Faik. (Şefik, Kroki 2, manuscript, n.p.)

… at the same time."[162] This was immediately after Şefik was woken by gunfire. This is surprisingly close to Bean's estimate of about 4:30 a.m. as the time of landing. Moreover, it was a member of Şefik's regiment who phoned the report through and Şefik's account includes recorded times from that point on, providing a continuous chronology. It would therefore appear that Şefik's times are comparable to western ones, and that, possibly for the first time, we can with some confidence directly connect an Ottoman and Australian chronology. It was not until 5:20 a.m. that the serious nature of the landing was reported and that "reinforcements are urgently needed … It was on receipt of this last report," by phone, "that GOC 9th Division gave the movement order to 27th Regiment."[163]

Şefik contrasts his account with that of Aspinall-Oglander's British history of the campaign,[164] and wrote that:

> News that Australian troops had landed was received one hour after the landing at 0530 hours by Sami Bey (GOC 9th Division) at Maidos … he sent two battalions of 27th Regiment to Gaba Tepe immediately … These men did not set out until 0730 hours and only at 0900 hours did the Australian troops and the Turkish troops clash.[165]

Şefik notes that these times "are incorrect."[166] There appear to be minor translation errors in this account, and Aspinall-Oglander actually states that at 9:00 a.m. 27th Regiment was first seen "filing up Gun Ridge from the south,"[167] meaning they would not have clashed with the Australians until some time later. Şefik's account is supported by a report that states that troops at Mal Tepe saw "a large group of Ottoman" troops "advancing on the eastern slope" of Third Ridge at "around 7.30 a.m.,"[168] which corresponds with Şefik's note of reaching Scrubby Knoll at 7:40 a.m. In other words, Şefik's account, which provides a continuous chronology from the approximate time of the first shots, has his troops arriving at the battlefield at least one and a half hours earlier than stated in western sources.

Şefik, by means of "observation, intelligence" and patrols,[169] established that the "enemy's left flank rested on Kalicbayiri [Baby 700] and his right flank on Kanlisirt [Lone Pine]. He believed their "front line" to lie "east of the line KilicDere – CatalDere – Karayurek Dere", that is, from the east of Baby 700 and Mortar Ridge to the east of Legge Valley, suggesting that he had seen the advanced Australian parties, such as those of Lieutenant N.M. Loutit, 10th Battalion (discussed in Chapter 6) and Tulloch.[170] Şefik and his officers correctly presumed the enemy's goal was the capture of the ridge line from Chunuk Bair to Gaba Tepe.[171] Within minutes of arriving on the battlefield, 27th Regiment's command had identified the location and objectives of the advanced elements of the covering force. "We set about the task of throwing the enemy into the sea."[172]

Şefik knew that his 2,000 men were insufficient to defeat what he believed to be a force "at least 4 or 5 times" larger and occupying a 2,000m front.[173] Via the Gaba Tepe telephone he contacted GOC 9th Division and reported that he thought it essential to engage the enemy on a wide front, but as this was impossible for two battalions, requested that 19th Division "be sent quickly to the

162 Şefik, para. 67.
163 *Ibid.*
164 C. F. Aspinall-Oglander, *Military Operations, Gallipoli*, Vol. I (London: Imperial War Museum, Department of Printed Books, 1929), p.185.
165 Şefik, para. 66, quoting an inaccurate translation of Aspinal-Oglander, *Military Operations, Gallipoli*, Vol. I, p.185.
166 Şefik, para. 66.
167 Aspinall-Oglander, *Military Operations*, p.185.
168 Uyar, pp.114, 115.
169 Şefik, para. 70.
170 *Ibid.*, para. 70.
171 *Ibid.*, para. 70.
172 *Ibid.*, para. 71.
173 *Ibid.*, para. 71.

Kocacimen mountains" to attack the enemy's left flank, while he attacked their right and centre.[174] "Kocacimen mountains" referred to the high ground from Ari Burnu to 971.[175] This was the message Şefik sent at 7:55 a.m. He adds that this message did not inspire Kemal to march to battle as he had left 10 minutes earlier.[176] Here we have another "anchor" to tie the movements of 27th and 57th Regiments to a chronology.

The *Brief History*[177] of the campaign produced by the Turkish General Staff states that Şefik's marching orders were sent by 9th Division at 5:00 a.m.[178] and Kemal's by 19th Division at 8:00 a.m.[179] Due to its brevity, translation errors and problems with quoted times, this source cannot be taken on face value, but of interest are its rough correspondence with Şefik's chronology and the three hour delay between Şefik's departure and Kemal's.

Şefik then explained the details of the attack to his officers, adding that until reinforcements arrived, their task was "to rush headlong at the enemy on a broad front, throw him into confusion, and hurl him back."[180] He reminded them of "the need for avoiding heavy losses due to carelessness, insecure actions or lack of liaison."[181] The 1st Battalion, minus a company held as reserve, was to attack 400 Plateau, and the 3rd Battalion the enemy's left flank (Map 10). The machine gun company, under Şefik's "orders and supervision" was to provide covering fire from Hill 165, as was the artillery battery, when it arrived. Arrangements were made for siting the first aid post and ammunition dump, thus freeing the echelon transport and pack animals to bring more from Boghali.[182] Although Şefik's account was written 20 years after the event, with all the benefits bestowed by hindsight, the image presented is of a trained and well-rehearsed regiment deploying for battle.

The 3rd Battalion, sitting behind the ridge in a wide column, was addressed by Şefik and their battalion commander, "to inspire confidence" and "stimulate" the troops. Şefik then addressed his 1st Battalion.[183] The men requested that they discard their knapsacks, as, unknown to them, had the 3rd Brigade. Şefik agreed, "provided that they have with them their ammunition, pickaxe, spade, flask and food bags."[184] The only thing now holding 27th Regiment's attack was the absence of artillery, as the mountain battery from Camburnu had not arrived.[185] Support appeared unexpectedly when "a mountain artillery convoy" approached from Kocadere village – it proved to be a single gun that had escaped from the four gun battery on 400 Plateau. Through binoculars Şefik could see the other three guns still in their positions. He ordered that "nobody was to go near those guns" and gave orders for the surviving gun to fire shrapnel "at the enemy troops" around them.[186]

The gun on Third Ridge opened fire at 1,500 m, scattering "in all directions"[187] the men near the guns on 400 Plateau. Turkish riflemen began to fire intermittently at targets. The Australians replied. The 1st Battalion's leading troops began to advance through the scrub and Şefik, his adjutant, machine

---

174 *Ibid.*, para. 71.
175 *Ibid.*, para. 71.
176 *Ibid.*, footnote to para. 72, p.42.
177 The Turkish General Staff, Ankara, *A Brief History of the Canakkale Campaign in the First World War (June 1914–January 1916)* (Ankara: The Turkish General Staff Directorate of Military History and Strategic Studies and Directorate of Inspection Publications, The Turkish General Staff Printing House, 2004).
178 *Ibid.*, p.69.
179 *Ibid.*, p.71.
180 Şefik, para. 74.
181 *Ibid.*, para. 74.
182 *Ibid.*, para. 74.
183 *Ibid.*, para. 75.
184 *Ibid.*, para. 76.
185 Şefik, para. 77.
186 *Ibid.*, para. 77.
187 *Ibid.*, para. 79

gun officers and gunners, resumed their scanning of the front with their binoculars, searching "for the key movements of the enemy and their density."[188]

2 and 4 Companies, 3/27th Regiment, advanced through the hills to the 1st Battalion's right. They "captured the Incebayir Ridge," then "the battalion CO ordered an attack" against Australians "in the middle of the Edirne Range" [Mortar Ridge]. The "riflemen on the left flank of the 3rd Battalion and ... on the right flank of the 1st Battalion encountered a little resistance from the Australians on the south western heights of Incebayir ... it was not sustained and they retreated in disorder suffering casualties."[189] An Australian was captured during this retreat.[190] At "the same time ... part of 2 Company under the command of Second Lieutenant Mithat" was ordered to secure their right flank against Australians "on the Duz Tepe [Battleship Hill] side."[191]

Earlier, at about 6:00 a.m., Major Izmet, commander of the 2/27th Regiment, had sent a platoon of 1 Company from Gaba Tepe to make contact with the embroiled 4 Company. This platoon, under Second Lieutenant Mustafa, met the wounded Faik, continued on to Artillery Range [Third Ridge] and "made plans to halt the enemy advance north of Kemalyeri" [Scrubby Knoll].[192] When the 3rd Battalion began operations on the high ground in the vicinity of Incebayir and Edirne Ridges, this party joined forces with them. Halis assigned this platoon (i.e. Mustafa's, 1/2/27th Regiment) to Mithat's party, ordering Mustafa's platoon to "a defensive position" on the right flank. "This force captured a position, opened an attack in the Duztepe direction and began to exchange fire."[193]

Comparison of Bean's and Turkish maps shows Incebayir Ridge to be the ridge occupied by Tulloch at his most advanced point. The only known Australian party advancing in this area was Tulloch's.

This presents a side of the battle overlooked and invisible to Australian writers for most of the past hundred years. The eyewitness evidence and chronology suggest that 27th Regiment, not 57th Regiment, engaged and forced back Tulloch's party. It appears that 27th Regiment arrived on the battlefield at about the time 57th Regiment was beginning its march and was in action some time before it. Until recently, those western historians who noted 27th Regiment's presence, generally divided the battlefield into two halves – 57th Regiment in the north and 27th Regiment in the south.[194] This may have been the situation later, but initially 27th Regiment was on the battlefield alone.

Did 27th Regiment Evict Tulloch from Battleship Hill?

From Third Ridge, before moving to Scrubby Knoll, Şefik noticed the enemy advancing in the "GokTepe, Kemalyeri, and ConkBayiri" area.[195] This suggests that he saw Tulloch's party advancing toward or on Battleship Hill. After examining the British *Official History*, Şefik concluded that his troops[196] in the Incebayir/Duz Tepe area exchanged fire with "Tulloch's detachment."[197] This matches Tulloch's account, as Tulloch does not refer to being stopped by the sight of an enemy line fixing bayonets and lying down ahead of them, as described by Kemal, but to being forced to ground by

---

188 *Ibid.*, para. 79.
189 *Ibid.*, para. 104.
190 *Ibid.*, para. 104, fn. 1. The prisoner's possible identity and fate are discussed in later chapters.
191 *Ibid.*, para. 106.
192 Şefik, para. 44.
193 *Ibid.*, para. 106.
194 Zeki also told Bean that 27th Regiment was "Farther south" than 57th Regiment. Bean, *Gallipoli Mission*, p.138.
195 Şefik, para. 64(c).
196 2 and 4 Companies of his 3rd Battalion, and the platoon from the 2nd Battalion at Gaba Tepe.
197 Şefik, footnote 3, para. 106.

Figure 23. Battleship Hill and Incebayir Ridge. Bean presumed Tulloch's party, facing left, lined the area in the vicinity of the post-Landing road. The grey triangle on the left is the water of the Dardanelles. Incebayir Ridge can be traced by the road as it bends to the right and continues down the ridge. If Tulloch had occupied this position, Chunuk Bair would have been to his front and the Dardanelles and Scrubby Knoll, marked by the memorial on the right, to his right and right rear. (Photograph by J.P. Hurst, n.d., author's collection)

small arms fire of increasing intensity[198] and bodies of Turks advancing in rushes towards his party.[199] In fact, except when the Turks were advancing, it was very difficult to see them at all.[200]

By the times established above, Şefik was on Scrubby Knoll preparing for battle as Kemal was leaving Boghali.[201] If it took 57th Regiment one and a half hours to arrive within a kilometre of Battleship Hill, as estimated by some sources,[202] after which they had to climb the range, concentrate and deploy, Kemal's troops would clearly not have been in a position to attack Tulloch until 2–3 hours after 27th Regiment.

According to Uyar, Kemal began his march with 57th Regiment at 8:10 am. "There were no roads or suitable paths … so they were forced to cut a track through the dense scrub and low vegetation."[203] Kemal's report "claimed that the 57th Regiment launched its counter-attack at 10:00 am. The distance to be covered was six kilometres as the crow flies and would take at least one and a half hours with probably only the fittest soldiers completing the march." Uyar continues that "Kemal's

---

198 Bean, *Gallipoli Mission*, p.85; Bean, *Official History*, Volume I (1921 and 1941), pp.288–289.
199 Belford, *Legs Eleven*, p.78, quoting Robinson.
200 Tulloch, 3DRL 606 item 206 – diaries nos. 192–205, p.90.
201 Şefik, para. 66. As noted earlier, a message Şefik sent at 0755 arrived 10 minutes after Kemal departed Boghali; he also states that he received a report from GOC 9th Division, "that 57th Regiment had been despatched with GOC quarter of an hour earlier (written 0825)." Şefik, para. 87.
202 Williams, "Z Beach, the Landing of the ANZAC Corps, April 25, 1915", p.88.
203 Uyar, p.123.

account appears reasonable," but does it allow time for assembly of troops, Kemal's reconnaissance, battlefield assessments and planning? Huseyin Avni "informed the division that the main marching group was passing Abdal Geçidi (mountain pass) at 10.00 am";[204] maps reveal this to be on the inland side of 971, approximately ¾ mile from Chunuk Bair.

The 1st Battalion, meanwhile, "had lost its way" and "arrived at the ridge half an hour late."[205] Kemal had sent a report "to Corps Headquarters at 10:24 a.m. that he had launched an attack. Six minutes later he sent a message informing headquarters that the 27th Regiment had arrived."[206] This latter comment may have led historians to presume 27th Regiment reached the battlefield later than the 57th, but probably refers to contact being made between the two regimental commands. "Huseyin Avni reported to Mustafa Kemal at 11.30 a.m. that the 2nd Battalion had launched a counter-attack with two companies with the 1st Battalion following from the south."[207]

Uyar and Roberts have interpreted these conflicting times as meaning that the earlier timing, of 10:24 a.m., in Mustafa Kemal's report "may well have referred to the time of the initial clashes of the forward elements of the 57th Regiment with the Anzacs well before the start of the counter-attack."[208] Perhaps. Or perhaps it referred to Kemal ordering the attack: issuing orders to his battalion commanders to attack is in effect "launching" an attack, which perhaps got underway at 11:00 or 11:30. In other words, Avni's 11:30 report could have been confirmation that Kemal's 10:24 order to attack had been carried out. This would seem to be supported by Şefik's account, which recorded that Kemal's "advance guard started to attack at 11:00 hours."[209] Alternatively, as noted previously, quoted times need to be approached warily until verified by other sources. Kemal's own account describes attacking an enemy "gun line," presumably meaning a firing line, on "the hill with an altitude of 216" and "walking forward in complete freedom" at 10:00 a.m.[210] It is difficult to align this with other accounts.

One of the keys to resolving these issues is to connect these disconnected events via a single time line – Şefik's account makes this possible. By Şefik's account Kemal "reached the front of Chunuk Bair before the vanguard" of his regiment at "a little after 1000 hours"[211] and his advance guard started their "attack at 1100 hours."[212] Şefik's account provides a continuous time line that shows his troops evicting an enemy force from Incebayir ridge possibly two hours before Kemal's first troops attacked; this corresponds with previously quoted times showing 27th Regiment committing to battle two to three hours before 57th regiment. As noted earlier, Şefik's sequencing of the movements of 57th and 27th Regiments makes it clear that as 57th Regiment departed Bogali, 27th Regiment was already on the field and deploying to attack.

Unfortunately, Şefik confuses the issue in a summary that states that between 11:00 and 12:00, "one platoon from" 2nd Company, 3/27th Regiment and one "from 2nd Battalion were opposing the advance of the Australians' left flank which held Duz Tepe north of Incebayir."[213] This timing conflicts with nearly all accepted times of Tulloch's withdrawal. It also seems to contradict Şefik's earlier account, and represents another example of the difficulties of interpreting participants' varying

---

204 *Ibid.*

205 Uyar, p.123.

206 *Ibid.*, p.124.

207 *Ibid.*, p.124.

208 Uyar, pp.123, 124; Roberts, *Landing at Anzac*, 2nd edition, pp.126, 136. Roberts doesn't mention the time, but states the "head" of his column attacked and held Tulloch's party while he organised the rest of the regiment for the main attack; this is presumably an interpretation of the signals mentioned.

209 Şefik, para. 113.

210 *The Collected Works of Ataturk*, Volume 1 (1903–1915), Translated excerpts. Translated by Banu Senay. Kaynak Publishing, 1998. The Gallipoli Centenary Turkish Archives Research Project, MacQuarie University <https://drive.google.com/file/d/0B5l4v9YR6fd3aWRaRHdJQV9aeWM/view?pli=1>, accessed 13 December 2015.

211 Şefik, para. 113.

212 *Ibid.*, para. 113.

213 *Ibid.*, para. 111.

versions of events. Presumably Şefik's account was written from notes in the 27th Regiment's records; to attempt to do the same from the 1st Division's War Diary, which includes notes on signals and reports, would create a very patchy picture indeed.[214] Perhaps one explanation is that Şefik's platoons were positioned as stated, but engaging Australians on or forward of Baby 700? As will be seen, there were numerous advances and withdrawals there throughout the day.

Other accounts confirm that 27th Regiment's troops were in action long before 57th Regiment. Halis was wounded during fighting in the vicinity of Mortar Ridge. Before his departure he "enjoined his brother officers that until the arrival of 57th Regiment nobody … [was] to fall back a single pace … if necessary they should all die where they stood."[215] Halis's replacement in command, 20-year-old Second Lieutenant Mucip reinforces the point. According to Broadbent, Mucip was fighting on Baby 700. Mucip describes fighting successive lines of Australians,[216] then Broadbent describes "his actions after he had bid to his farewell to … Captain Halis". Mucip sent a patrol to check his left flank, then the Australians attacked his right. "I went to that side … firing on our left flank became more intense. I … went to the left. The enemy had been reinforced. Time passed and no word came from" the patrol on the left. Another patrol was sent, and returned to report the three men had been killed:

> Isolated hand to hand fighting continued … As the hours passed, our losses mounted … a messenger came from the CO of the Regiment … telling us … "the 57th Regiment is advancing on our right flank and a Battalion, is coming to reinforce us." But time passed and there was no sign of either the Battalion or 57th Regiment … We struggled on stubbornly … it seemed as though our ammunition would give out. We used, with economy, the ammunition of our dead and wounded."[217]

According to this version of events, the Ottomans were fighting on Baby 700 before 57th Regiment arrived, presumably after evicting Tulloch from Battleship Hill.

Şefik wrote that, the "more our attack developed and … got into a delicate and dangerous situation, the more our eyes drifted involuntarily to the eastern slopes of Kocacimen mountain,"[218] looking for 57th Regiment.

According to the Australian *Official History*, Tulloch moved forward from the Nek at or before 7:00 a.m.,[219] began his last advance of 100 yards "after 9 o'clock"[220] and withdrew at least half an hour later. These times are estimates only. Tulloch's line would have been forced to negotiate difficult ground but enemy opposition was minimal for most of the advance.[221] Although it is not possible to make direct comparisons between walking a bitumen road today, and the time taken to lead a skirmish line of wet, heavily laden soldiers through dense scrub into unknown enemy territory, it is difficult to see how this advance could have taken two hours or more. More significantly, it is difficult to believe that in less time than it took Tulloch to advance roughly 1,000 yards, a full regiment marched from Boghali, climbed the main range, prepared a battle plan, deployed for battle and launched an attack. One wonders if Bean would have recorded different times if he had had access to Şefik's account, as he appears to have interpreted Tulloch's account from 57th Regiment's perspective, as told to him by Zeki. Examination of the resulting versions of the story appears to open a yawning gap in the established chronology.

---

214 1st Division War Diary, April 1915, Part 1, 25 April 1915.
215 Şefik, para. 107.
216 H. Broadbent, *The Turkish Defence: The Story from the Turkish Documents* (Carlton, Victoria: The Megunyah Press, 2015), p.383.
217 Mucip, 27th Regiment War Register, quoted Broadbent, *The Turkish Defence*, pp.383, 384.
218 Şefik, para. 113.
219 Bean, *Official History*, Volume I (1921 and 1941), p.275.
220 *Ibid.*, p.289.
221 *Ibid.*, p.288.

Another apparent anomaly with Bean's reconstruction is that he wrote that at "about" 9:15 a.m.[222] Margetts, on Baby 700, heard "a call for reinforcements" from his left in response to Turks he soon saw advancing along a trench running down "the seaward shoulder of Battleship Hill." This creates the impression that the 3rd Brigade on Baby 700 was by then already hard-pressed by a Turkish counter-attack, presumably by 57th Regiment, but by Bean's chronology 57th Regiment was not yet on the field, and Tulloch was advancing over or fighting on Battleship Hill.

The simplest answer is that the troops Margetts saw were not the counter-attacking 57th Regiment, but the platoon from Fisherman's Hut. Their obvious route, Sazli Beit Dere, is confirmed by Şefik's map, which shows them turning right towards Battleship Hill, along the western side of Chunuk Bair, as they reached the crest. This would place them in the area and moving in the direction indicated by Margetts, and to Tulloch's north east, possibly explaining the rifle fire Tulloch heard to his left or left rear (Map 7). This march appears quite a feat, but the presence of a track, familiarity with the ground and absence of enemy interference would have hastened progress. This platoon had probably begun their withdrawal soon after the 7th Battalion's arrival, as neither 7th Battalion nor Rafferty mentions coming to blows with them. As the only evidence of the garrison suffering casualties comes from Gostelow,[223] many of the platoon's initial strength may therefore have joined the fight on Sari Bair.[224]

The platoon were also joined by a few men from the 2nd and 3rd Platoons.[225] Their OC, Hayreddin, saw 27th Regiment's battle "raging to the south," confirming that he made the high ground, and confirming that 27th Regiment was fighting before 57th. On reaching the high ground, Hayreddin left some men behind, presumably to guard his back, before surging "forward towards the enemy, getting close enough so that our weapons would be effective and stopping them by engaging them with our intensive fire." They were bluffing, "pretending" they had been reinforced, and the enemy "could only stop in their tracks." Hayreddin continued that "we were advancing towards a landing force 100 times more numerous than us."[226] In general terms, this may be correct, but they may initially have been opposed by only Jackson's party of about 20. Their audacity paid off, and 27th and 57th Regiments "finally" approached.[227] Hayreddin believed this move lost the enemy "four hours."[228] Once again, times are relative, and it is unclear whether Hayreddin meant "four hours" since the firing of his platoon's first shots. Uyar believed that this platoon had been fighting "there for more than three hours" when Kemal arrived.[229]

At some point Hayreddin sent two patrols to make contact with other forces and to bring forward ammunition.[230] They returned with Kemal, "and his personal staff followed by the advance guard of 57th Regiment," which they joined,[231] confirming that they were operating in the area before 57th Regiment arrived. The troops Kemal met are generally regarded as "fleeing"[232] and at least one account refers to them as a "company … in full retreat."[233] Many different parties moved over the slopes of Sari Bair on this morning, but Şefik confirms that the troops Kemal met were the

222 *Ibid.*, p.293.
223 Gostelow, diary, 25 April 1915.
224 Apart from those detached earlier and mentioned previously. Uyar, p.108.
225 Uyar, p.109.
226 Letter, İbradılı Ibrahim (Hayreddin), to Feridun Fazıl Tülbentçi, 1945 <http://1914-1918.invisionzone.com/forums/index. php?showtopic=40505&page=7>, 18 Aug 2015.
227 *Ibid.*
228 *Ibid.*
229 Uyar, p.123.
230 Şefik, para. 39.
231 *Ibid.*
232 James, *Gallipoli*, pp.112–113.
233 Kinross, *Ataturk*, p.90.

Fisherman's Hut garrison.[234] When Şefik reached Scrubby Knoll he sent north three pack animals with ammunition for whatever remained of 4 Company, but whether this reached them or not, by the time Kemal arrived, 1 Platoon had apparently exhausted their ammunition.[235]

History has done a disservice to this platoon. The troops of 1 Platoon were far from beaten. In addition to their achievements near the beach, it may well have been this platoon that fought Jackson. They may also have forced Tulloch's withdrawal – their route would have enabled them to get past Tulloch's left flank, and it is difficult to see how any other party could have done so. Some of the withdrawing Russell's Top garrison also fought in the area, and appear to have joined 1 Platoon.

Evidence from the Australian side matches Şefiks account more closely than it does Kemal's.

Howe later wrote that as he reached the high ground from Shrapnel and Monash valleys at about 9:00 a.m., he saw Tulloch's party withdrawing to Baby 700.[236] The value of Howe's account lies in first hand experience and observation, and the fact that he retraced his movements of 25 April with Bean's Historical Mission in 1919. Some decades later he wrote an account of the battle.[237] On some of the larger issues it is unreliable, such as stating that Kemal took 27th (instead of 57th) Regiment to Chunuk Bair,[238] and his time of 9:00 a.m. has to be treated with the same caution as other times noted on the day, but it would have to be assumed to be roughly right. Four and a half hours had elapsed since A Company had stepped onto the beach and begun their assault on Plugge's Plateau; it is difficult to believe it could have taken them any longer than this to arrive at Baby 700, and indeed, it is difficult to account for these hours. They belonged to the covering force, and the high ground was their objective.

Mason thought Tulloch's withdrawal began about 8:00 a.m., and heard there had been a sighting of Reid at about 11:00 a.m., or "two hours after the retirement"[239] – these times are roughly consistent with Howe's. In other words, Howe's and Mason's timing would have Tulloch's party pushed back an hour or two earlier than believed by Bean, and several hours before 57th Regiment's attacks between "10.24" and midday.

Bean appears to have based his reconstruction of events largely on Zeki's account. After being ordered by Kemal to attack, Zeki saw a line of Australians advancing "on the inland slope of Dus Tepe" [Battleship Hill],[240] suggesting Tulloch's party. Zeki continues: "Some soldiers of my battalion had crossed" a valley, "I think it was Dik Dere." These men "attacked the Australians so closely" it seemed "bayonets might be used." Opposite a line of Zeki's men "was a line of Australians … an officer was standing, pointing with what looked to me like a sword … men of my battalion … were retiring."[241] Zeki watched a "lieutenant of my battalion … fall and his men retire … I shouted to the men with me to shoot at the Australian who seemed to be encouraging his men to go forward after my retiring men. On reaching the valley my soldiers moved southwards along it."[242] It will be noted that this description does not match those of any of Tulloch's party. Apart from the references to Battleship Hill and Dik Dere, this account resembles fighting on Baby 700 or Mortar Ridge. Bean states that, despite being wounded, Zeki crossed the valley to rally these men. They were not rattled and he was not needed, so he went in search of medical treatment at about 4:30 p.m.[243]

234 Şefik, para. 113, FN1, p.59.
235 *Ibid.*, para. 39, 84.
236 Howe, "Sparks From an Old Controversy", p.10.
237 *Ibid.*, pp.4–21.
238 *Ibid.*, pp.7–8.
239 Mason, 2DRL 301, Book 31.
240 Bean, *Gallipoli Mission*, p.136.
241 *Ibid.*
242 *Ibid.*
243 Bean, *Official History*, Volume I (1921 and 1941), pp.451, 452.

It initially appears from this account that Zeki's troops attacked Australians on Battleship Hill immediately after arriving on the battlefield, but the subsequent narrative appears to describe fighting later in the day, including Zeki's evacuation wounded at "4 o'clock or 4.30."[244] Zeki continues that the "troops from Dus Tepe [Battleship Hill] retired to the seashore and remained there covered by the fire of their warships. The Turkish troops got about to Jessaret Tepe [The Nek]."[245] From Battleship Hill Tulloch's party in fact withdrew towards the Baby 700 area. In the late afternoon, when Baby 700 fell, some men withdrew down the northern gullies to the sea.[246] The Turks did not reach the Nek until evening. Zeki's account is therefore a condensation of events from the day as a whole, and contains errors and assumptions similar to other accounts – "the usual inconsistencies,"[247] Bean phrased it. Much of Zeki's account appears to describe neither Tulloch's party nor Battleship Hill.

Of note is that Bean, despite Zeki's and battlefield evidence, does not state in either the *Official History* or *Gallipoli Mission* that Kemal and Tulloch locked horns. He initially recorded that Zeki, heading for Baby 700 and Mortar Ridge, saw his first Australians on Battleship Hill "in the position reached by Tulloch,"[248] but, as noted, the chronology is awry.

This section of Bean's narrative is essentially a compilation of fragments of descriptions provided by Zeki, with consequent difficulties in determining time and place. It is not until many years later, in *Anzac to Amiens*, that Bean mentions that after Kemal climbed Third Ridge north of Scrubby Knoll "Captain Tulloch's men, several ridges away, by Battleship Hill could then be seen."[249] This was presumably an assumption, based on the little Turkish information he had. He continues that it was the attack of one of 57th Regiment's battalions down the seaward side of the main range that "eventually drove the Australians from *Baby 700* [my italics]" i.e. not Battleship Hill.[250]

There are many contradictions in these accounts, probably consequences of gaps in the written record, assumptions, errors in memory or chronology or in identification of ground. Bean took his account from Zeki in "imperfect French,"[251] combined information from different conversations to reconstruct events and chronology, interpreted Turkish place names, changed the narrative from third person to first and added to his notes from memory, "when my memory is certain."[252] Zeki's account is supported by his selection in 1919 of "the place where he had first sighted Australian troops,"[253] but if he had not mentioned Battleship Hill and Dik Dere, it would be easy to assume the Baby 700–Mortar Ridge fighting was being described. Zeki states, "I *think* it was Dik Dere"[254] [my italics] and Bean added in a footnote that he thought some of Zeki's timings may have been incorrect.[255] In other words, the established history of this clash was created by Bean, in large part from the best or only Turkish source he had, which covers the whole day and not just the time when Tulloch may or may not have been on Battleship Hill. Modern perceptions of what happened on Battleship Hill that day originated with this fragmented collection of contradictory evidence.

Recently Uyar observed that:

Mustafa Kemal realised that he could not wait for the rest of his regiment to arrive. He ordered the 2nd Battalion's commander, Captain Mehmed Ata (Erçikan), who had just arrived, to launch an immediate

---

244 Bean, *Gallipoli Mission*, pp.136–137.
245 *Ibid.*, p.140.
246 See Chapter 10.
247 Bean, 3DRL 8042 item 7.
248 Bean, *Official History*, Volume I (1921 and 1941), pp.450–451.
249 Bean, *Anzac to Amiens*, p.115.
250 *Ibid.*
251 Bean, *Gallipoli Mission*, p.129.
252 *Ibid.*, p.128.
253 *Ibid.*, footnote, p.137.
254 *Ibid.*, p.136.
255 *Ibid.*, footnote, p.138.

attack in the direction of Battleship Hill. He then placed the mountain battery in a fire position in a small creek on the eastern side of Chunuk Bair … He looked for the 1st Battalion … but could see no sign of it. He angrily sent orders to its commander, Captain Ahmed Zeki (Soydemir), to join the attack immediately from the south. The hasty piecemeal attack achieved its aim and drove the forward elements of the Australians (a composite company under … Tulloch) off Battleship Hill, but the attack lost its momentum under increasing enemy fire from Baby 700.[256]

He continues that Kemal's main counter-attack did not begin until 11:30 a.m. or so. Various accounts confirming that Zeki's battalion was half an hour late suggest that, even if an early, piecemeal 57th Regiment attack had been made on Tulloch, Zeki was not with them. If he was, then it makes it even more unlikely that Kemal's attack could have been made as early as assumed.

One piece of evidence that requires examination is one of Şefik's maps (here Map 8), which confirms that his troops fought on Incebayir Ridge, but also shows 57th Regiment advancing from Chunuk Bair, apparently against an Australian line on Battleship Hill.[257] This and another of his maps (here Map 9) show the right of 27th Regiment deploying forward (west) from Scrubby Knoll and then attacking in a north or north-westerly direction towards Baby 700 and Mortar Ridge. This would appear to be supported by a map in Uyar's book, whose origin was Serdar Ataksor, presumably a descendant of 27th Regiment's Halis.[258] This shows the attack of 57th Regiment "about noon," with an Australian party occupying the northern side of Battleship Hill.

None of this is easy to understand or explain. The representation of the Australians' position matches neither Tulloch's descriptions of his location nor chronology, the discovery of Turkish cartridges described by Bean,[259] the accepted Australian histories, or the earlier assertion that Kemal's advance guard attack had thrown Tulloch from the hill long before noon. The only known Australian party to have occupied ground in the vicinity shown on Uyars' map was Jackson's, though there is no evidence that this party made it as far forward as shown, and it is unlikely they could have been there at midday. Şefik's maps also appear to misrepresent the Australian positions in the vicinity of Mortar Ridge.

How can such anomalies be reconciled? As this area was outside Şefik's area of operation, it is possible the Australian presence here was assumed, in the same way Australian troops and historians assumed the presence of Ottoman troops, and machine guns, on the battlefield. The same argument could be applied to the map in Uyar's work as it also originated with 27th Regiment; it may even have been the one on which Şefik based his map, or vice versa. Either way, the Australian presence on these maps is not supported by other evidence, and in places doesn't accurately reflect the Australians' position as we know it.

That these 27th Regiment maps may misrepresent the situation appears to be supported by two other pieces of evidence. Firstly, Uyar believed Tulloch had been forced from Battleship by a "hasty piecemeal attack" launched about 10:30 a.m. A 27th Regiment map that appeared recently in H. Broadbent's *Defending Gallipoli: The Turkish Story*,[260] also shows their counterattack at "midday," but clearly shows the allied line to have been pushed back from Incebayir Ridge. The text supports this, stating that a dotted line showing the advanced Australian positions "earlier in the day, from which they had been pushed back", passes through Incebayir Ridge. Another advanced line, on Third Ridge, appears to represent Loutit's earlier position. In other words, this 27th Regiment map directly contradicts the earlier 27th Regiment map, as it shows the Australian line on Baby 700 at the time of

256 Uyar, pp.123, 124.
257 See Map 8. Reproduced in Örnek's and Toker's *Gallipoli: The Front Line Experience*, second edition (Strawberry Hills: Currency Press, 2006), pp.30–31.
258 Uyar, p.125.
259 Bean, *Gallipoli Mission*, p.97.
260 Broadbent, *Defending Gallipoli: The Turkish Story* (Carlton, Victoria: Melbourne University Press, 2015), p.49.

the midday attacks, and Incebayir Ridge and Adana Bair abandoned. It also contradicts assertions in recent Australian books that Tulloch was still on Incebayir Ridge at "midday" or "1300"[261] (1:00 p.m.):[262]

One option is that Tulloch was first engaged by 27th Regiment, and later pushed back by 57th Regiment. Roberts and others have explained the contradictions between Turkish chronologies and Australian by claiming Tulloch held Battleship Hill for four hours, until pushed off by Kemal's counter attack around noon or even "after 1 p.m."[263] He interprets Tulloch's comment about fighting for half an hour as meaning that he fought for half an hour after Reid's wounding. Perhaps, but this is speculative. Tulloch actually said "They fought there for half an hour,"[264] and "about ¼ of an hour before we retired, word was passed up to me 'Mr Reid is hit'."[265]

Accounts by the Australians who were there do not give the impression they fought for four hours, and one wonders how their ammunition would have lasted that long. Tulloch mentioned being on Battleship Hill "about noon probably," but this time needs to be treated as warily as others – it is common for people who have been up all night, or who rose particularly early, to imagine it to be much later than it is, and this time actually contradicts Tulloch's own chronology; nor did Bean conclude "noon" to be correct. The most convincing evidence that this timing is incorrect is the events on Baby 700, covered in a later chapter. Put simply, a battle was raging on Baby 700 throughout the morning, with Turks swarming forward to the attack from Battleship Hill; how could this have happened if Tulloch was still on Battleship Hill, and how could he have withdrawn through such a battle? Nor does he mention doing so.

Can we really accept that Tulloch waited on Battleship Hill for three to four hours[266] while troops behind him on Baby 700 did likewise? As will be seen, none of the 11th Battalion troops who arrived on Baby 700 behind Tulloch describe sitting around waiting for the enemy; rather, as will be seen, they were in action immediately. It seems highly unlikely that Tulloch fought on battleship Hill for three to four hours or more to be pushed back by 57th Regiment at noon, and there is no reliable evidence that he did.

Uyar believed that Kemal's 10:24 a.m. message about launching a counter-attack referred to the "hasty piecemeal attack" that drove Tulloch from Battleship Hill, with the main attack not being launched until 11:30 a.m.[267] Once again, perhaps, but apart from Kemal's message, is there any evidence? The description of this attack does not appear to gel with any Australian accounts, nor match the maps described, which show Australians still in occupation of the hill at noon.[268]

A similarly difficult piece of evidence is that Tulloch reputedly fired at an officer on the northern slope of Chunuk Bair. As none of Şefik's officers are likely to have been near this point, the assumption must be that the man was a member of 57th Regiment,[269] generally assumed to be Kemal himself.[270] In the *Official History* Bean wrote that the "higher hill, of which the lower slopes faced" Tulloch's party "was the shoulder of Chunuk Bair … On its skyline … about 900 yards away … was a solitary tree. By the tree stood a man … Tulloch … fired at him."[271] Later Bean describes Kemal climbing "the Third Ridge north of Scrubby Knoll"[272] rather than the north shoulder of Chunuk Bair. In *Gallipoli Mission*,

261 Broadbent, *The Turkish Defence*, p.95.
262 Roberts claims "sometime [*sic*] after 1pm," Roberts, *Landing at Anzac*, second edition, p.152.
263 Roberts, *Landing at Anzac*, second edition, pp.126, 140, 152–153.
264 Tulloch, 3DRL 606 item 206 – diaries nos. 192–205.
265 Tulloch, 3DRL 8042 item 7.
266 Roberts states "four hours," Roberts, *Landing at Anzac*, second edition, p.152.
267 Uyar, p.124.
268 *Ibid.*, p.125.
269 Carlyon, *Gallipoli*, p.157, wrote "probably."
270 Olson suggested the target may have been Zeki Bey. W. Olson, *Gallipoli, The Western Australian Story* (Crawley, WA: University of Western Australia Press, 2006), p.63.
271 Bean, *Official History*, Volume I (1921 and 1941), p.289.
272 *Ibid.*, p.448.

Bean reworded his account slightly, omitting Chunuk Bair and stating "Tulloch noted on the 'northern shoulder' (apparently of a farther hill, in front) was a solitary tree."[273] In other words, the story is vague: Bean was doing the best he could to work out what had happened, with ground that remained forever after in enemy hands and many features being at the time unnamed; all were unfamiliar.

Kemal's and Tulloch's descriptions do not match. The chronology presented here suggests it is highly unlikely that the events on Battleship Hill happened as previously believed.

An Alternate History

Is there a credible alternate version of events that better matches and reconciles the great mass of evidence presented in this chapter? Could Tulloch have been evicted by 27th Regiment? Could he have been further down the ridge than Bean presumed, facing Scrubby Knoll, rather than Chunuk Bair? Of the 11th Battalion's three objectives, Tulloch's assumed position approximated that on the left; the central one was to his right front. As Incebayir Ridge bends back towards the sea, it faces both.

Tulloch may have been engaged before the arrival of 57th Regiment by a number of parties of 27th Regiment converging on him from several directions, as shown above. The first party was probably a portion of the Russell's Top garrison, 3 Platoon, 4/2/27th Regiment, conducting a fighting withdrawal after being driven from their trench by Margetts and others. These Turks had probably fired on the beach, withdrawn, killed Clarke, fought from the seaward slopes of Baby 700, delayed Tulloch, then withdrawn again. Tulloch's party were then probably forced to ground by the fire of either this party again; the Fisherman's Hut garrison (1 Platoon, 4/2/27th Regiment); the platoon from Gaba Tepe (1 Company, 2/27th Regiment); or parties from Şefik's recently arrived force advancing from Scrubby Knoll (2 or 4 Company, 3/27th Regiment). The approach of enemy troops from a number of directions would explain the outflanking and sporadic engagements experienced by Tulloch.

Tulloch saw a Turkish line, apparently to his right.[274] Turks in this area were probably from the beach garrisons and outposts; the Gaba Tepe garrison (1 Company, 2/27th Regiment); 2 or 4 Company, 3/27th Regiment; or even some of 1/27th Regiment who were fighting in this area during the morning.[275] Some of these troops had been despatched early and reached Mortar Ridge while 57th Regiment was on the march. A combination of these events with the advance of 27th Regiment down the ridge to Tulloch's front and an increasing fire as various parties joined the fight, could have given historians the impression that these were all part of a single event – 57th Regiment's counter-attack.

Where was Tulloch? What was to his front – was it really Chunuk Bair? Or could it have been Scrubby Knoll? Tulloch himself was unsure of his position[276] Bean's map, reproduced in many works since, was apparently based on one torn from *The Anzac Book*[277] on which Tulloch had "traced what he believed to be his course".[278] Assuming that this accurately depicts Tulloch's route, his front, if it was 100 or 150 men strong at five yard spacing in a single line, would have extended for half a kilometre or more, far longer than the approximately 50 yards shown on Bean's Map 13[279] (as shown here in Map 7) or 150 yards on his Map 12.[280] If the line's left lay as depicted, its right may have extended well down Incebayir Ridge, with the men on the right of the line being closer to Scrubby

273 Bean, *Gallipoli Mission*, p.85.
274 Bean, *Gallipoli Mission*, p.86; Bean, *Official History*, Volume 1 (1921 and 1941), p.290.
275 Şefik, para. 111.
276 Bean, *Gallipoli Mission*, p.94.
277 *The Anzac Book*, between pp.90 and 91.
278 Bean, *Gallipoli Mission*, p.84.
279 Bean, *Official History*, Volume I (1921 and 1941), between pages 288 and 289.
280 *Ibid.*, between pages 268 and 269.

Figure 24. Photograph taken from further down Incebayir Ridge than indicated by Bean, demonstrating that the Dardanelles is visible to the "direct front" from this point. Scrubby Knoll is concealed by the foliage on the right. It can be seen how from this position the view matches Tulloch's description: from here Tulloch may have seen the "field gun," actually the single 75 mm mountain gun with Şefik, "which seemed to me on a skyline to my almost direct front … somewhere near the bottom right edge of the glimpse of water;" Scrubby Knoll would have been "near the bottom right edge of the glimpse of water." (Photograph by J.P. Hurst, n.d., author's collection)

Knoll than those on the left were to Chunuk Bair; it is also possible the left of the line was further down the ridge than depicted.

Possible evidence of this is that, in correspondence with Bean, Tulloch mentioned a "field gun which seemed to me on a skyline to my almost direct front," positioned in a photograph sent to him by Bean "somewhere near the bottom right edge of the glimpse of water" (Figures 23, 24).[281] Initially, Şefik had only a single mountain gun in action, while Kemal had a battery of four guns, later placed in a creek bed closer to Chunuk Bair, and it is unclear whether Tulloch could have seen any of them.[282] Tulloch did not mention being shelled. He saw one gun, near the glimpse of water; Şefik had a single gun, at Scrubby Knoll, and it didn't fire at Tulloch, but at 400 Plateau.[283]

Was the Dardanelles, Tulloch's "glimpse of water", visible from further down Incebayir Ridge? In 2015, photographs taken from near the point at which Incebayir Ridge bends back towards the sea, revealed that water was indeed visible, immediately above and to the left of Scrubby Knoll (Figure 24). Australian troops in the area would have faced either Scrubby Knoll or the ridge connecting it to Chunuk Bair. The view from this point matches Tulloch's description ("almost direct front") far more accurately than from opposite Chunuk Bair: from the latter, the Dardanelles are to the right.

281 Tulloch, 3DRL 8042 item 7.
282 Uyar, pp.104, 124.
283 Hitch did describe being shelled by three or four guns. His account was transcribed from a 1974, and like Zeki's, appears to condense events. It is difficult to determine the accuracy of the chronology, as other accounts from Battleship Hill do not mention shelling. Hitch, interview, May 1974, p.10.

Figure 25. Photograph taken from Incebayir Ridge, in between the previous two photographs. Scrubby Knoll is indicated by the mast in the centre. The photograph in Figure 24 was taken from a point further down the ridge, directly opposite Scrubby Knoll. In conjunction, these three photographs demonstrate how the perspective changes significantly – had Tulloch been further down Incebayir Ridge than Bean realised, Scrubby Knoll would have been to his direct front (Figure 24), rather than his right rear (Figure 23). (Photograph by J.P. Hurst, May 2015, author's collection)

In Tulloch's first "stiff fire fight" on Baby 700 he described "about 60 Turks" with "one machine gun." It is disputed that there were any guns in this area at this time, but there were guns at Scrubby Knoll, and these may also have been the guns he described firing on him "at very long range."[284] The troops attacking him may have been 27th Regiment from Scrubby Knoll, rather than 57th Regiment from Chunuk Bair. They could have deployed northwards from there to occupy the ridge crest where Bean found their cartridge packets in 1919, or these may have been left there at another time.[285]

If Tulloch was facing Scrubby Knoll, Şefik's maps of his troop movements reflect Tulloch's experience, showing that 27th Regiment deployed from Scrubby Knoll and occupied Incebayir Ridge.[286] It is difficult to explain how they could have done this without first evicting Tulloch. Şefik described 2 and 4 Companies, 3/27th Regiment capturing Incebayir Ridge before attacking Mortar Ridge, and the 2nd Battalion party from Gaba Tepe capturing "a position," attacking "in the Duztepe direction" and exchanging fire with, he assumed, "Tulloch's detachment."[287]

It is also reasonable that Tulloch's party may have reached this section of Incebayir Ridge. The route Tulloch drew for Bean is not along the spine of the ridge but further south, and negotiated a number of gullies. Bean confirms that "In the valleys" during their advance, "not a shot came near them."[288] This advance could have ended facing Scrubby Knoll or the ridge to its north as easily as Chunuk Bair. Moreover, Tulloch does not state that the enemy he opposed came from Chunuk Bair. Bean based this in part on Zeki's account, and evidence of a Turkish firing line he found on a ridge

284 Tulloch, 3DRL 8042 item 7.
285 Bean, *Gallipoli Mission*, p.97.
286 Şefik, footnote 3, para. 54.
287 Şefik, para. 106, footnote to para. 106, para. 111.
288 Bean, *Official History*, Volume I (1921 and 1941), p.288.

opposite Tulloch's assumed position,[289] but there were also Turks firing on Tulloch from his right front and Mason's somewhat confused account refers to enemy "fire from ridge on right"[290] – possibly Scrubby Knoll or nearby. Troops firing at the left of Tulloch's line could still have left the traces of their presence that Bean found in 1919.[291]

It is drawing a long bow to attempt to rewrite a history of over 90 years' standing, yet the accepted version of what happened on Battleship Hill that morning contains many contradictions of evidence, is not supported by the chronologies or eyewitness accounts presented in this chapter, and appears to be based on assumption. Most writers who propose that Tulloch was stopped by 57th Regiment and Kemal's "you have your bayonets" command, and that it was Kemal he shot at, have drawn this conclusion from their interpretations of Bean's account. These assumptions appear to stem primarily from the fact that Tulloch advanced from the sea, Kemal from inland, and they must consequently have collided on Battleship Hill. Bean separately interviewed Tulloch and Zeki,[292] combined their accounts, walked the ground to determine where the engagement probably took place and reconstructed the history from this viewpoint. His version has been generally accepted since. Yet in neither the *Official History* nor *Gallipoli Mission* does Bean make the assumptions of later years and later writers.

From the perspective of timing, the idea that Kemal arrived on Chunuk Bair at much the same time as Tulloch reached Battleship Hill is difficult to accept. Similarly, it seems impossible that Tulloch could have remained on Battleship Hill until midday or "after 1 p.m."[293] Şefik's unbroken chronology presents a plausible alternative and correlates well with a range of 11th Battalion evidence, some of it provided in a later chapter. Western writers were unaware that Ottoman troops were fighting in Tulloch's vicinity before 57th Regiment arrived.

The established history is but one possible reconstruction. It may be correct, or it might be the product of a shortage of information in Bean's time and a lack of investigation since. The arguments presented in this chapter are based on a greater body of evidence and deeper examination than previously, and reveal many flaws in the accepted, simplistic picture. If the story is reconstructed with 27th Regiment included and modern assumptions excluded, a different history is allowed to emerge. The apparent increasing size of the enemy force and the confusing range of stories about parties of Turks to Tulloch's front, right and left rear, can be better understood as being contacts with a number of 27th Regiment parties rather than as a large counter attack from 57th Regiment.

This argument is not without flaws, but provides a closer correlation with the chronology and eyewitness accounts of Tulloch, Howe, Margetts, Şefik and others, which will be examined further in later chapters. When examined, the original story and its supporting evidence are also greatly flawed, so much so that modern writers have sought to reconcile the contradictions by assuming, against the bulk of Australian evidence, that Tulloch simply stayed on Battleship Hill for four hours. The icing on the cake is to stand on the ground opposite Scrubby Knoll, and feel one is seeing what Tulloch described seeing in 1915.[294]

Nor does Kemal claim that he stopped Tulloch. This was a later assumption by western historians. The skirmish lines Kemal saw going to ground may have been those of Margetts, Robertson or others advancing over the inland slopes of Baby 700 – by James' wording, the enemy skirmishers Kemal saw

289 Bean, *Gallipoli Mission*, p.97.
290 Mason, 2DRL 301, Book 31.
291 Bean, *Gallipoli Mission*, pp.95–100.
292 Bean, *Gallipoli Mission*, p.84.
293 Roberts, *Landing at Anzac*, second edition, p.152.
294 So ingrained is the existing story that despite the evidence presented here, it was not until visiting the ground and seeing the photographs taken in May 2015 that the 1915 battlefield seemed to "appear" and the argument seem credible. If the Dardanelles were not visible the argument would have fallen flat without further debate. Tulloch's story can be told from this point on Incebayir Ridge.

were in fact approaching, rather than on, "Hill 261."[295] Şefik was in no doubt that without Kemal's "quick appreciation … this daring attack of ours could have ended in disaster."[296] With great relief the 27th Regiment commander eventually saw "the force we were expecting … 57th Regiment … with the brave Divisional GOC … leading from the front."[297] Şefik was aware he had a tiger by the tail, knew his aggressive assault was only a holding action, and that he could not do it alone; had Kemal not responded with strength and speed, his weakness would have been identified and the enemy have rallied and launched a co-ordinated assault.[298] Essad Pasha later endorsed Kemal's actions.[299] Whether or not 57th Regiment evicted Tulloch's party is irrelevant to assessment of Kemal's achievements.

Moreover, Tulloch's eviction from Battleship Hill was more of a symbolic than strategic defeat. Once Kemal occupied the high ground of Chunuk Bair or Hill 971, Tulloch's unsupported position would have become untenable. His objective on Battleship Hill was but a stepping stone to the all important high ground, the taking of which was not his job. Tulloch may have been holding open the door, yet neither 2nd Brigade nor anyone else came to his support – the decision to divert these troops elsewhere will be discussed in later chapters. This is where Şefik's key contribution to the Ottoman victory that day has been overlooked. Certainly Kemal barred progress to the high ground, but if not for Şefik's early and aggressive attack, would the Australians have beaten him there and denied him the opportunity? As has been seen, and will be shown, the Australians were being drawn away from the high ground before 57th Regiment arrived on the field.

A great many men died on the slopes of Baby 700, Mortar Ridge and Battleship Hill that day, and their stories accompanied them to their unmarked graves. We cannot know who else fought over those slopes, what they did and saw, or which Turks saw them. Bean, for example, describing 3rd Battalion troops advancing to Mortar Ridge, notes "Probably some of the 3rd Brigade … had already been there; here in the story may exist a gap that will never be filled."[300] We know of Tulloch's story because he survived to tell the tale. Any number of unidentified parties, Turkish and Australian, may also have fought in this area.

In summary, there is much evidence that Tulloch was evicted from Incebayir Ridge before 57th Regiment arrived. Tulloch's and Kemal's eyewitness accounts do not match; there are deep chronological problems with the existing story; it would seem the case in Australian sources for 57th Regiment, has not previously been seriously examined and its flaws identified; Australian testimony and chronologies match more closely with 27th Regiment's experience; Tulloch's story can more easily be told from opposite Scrubby Knoll than Chunuk Bair; and, significantly, it seems impossible that Tulloch's party could have been on Battleship Hill while the Turks vigorously attacked Baby 700[301] behind them, nor did they see thousands of troops getting past their flanks to do so.

As to who fought whom on Battleship Hill that morning, Bean may already, unwittingly or otherwise, have shed some light. He wrote of Tulloch's withdrawal being forced by Turks moving "round the seaward side of Battleship Hill" to occupy abandoned trenches.[302] What Bean did not know was that these troops may well have belonged to 4 Company, 2/27th Regiment. Bean did not have all the pieces. His legacy lies in leaving us as many as he could collect.

Battleship Hill would remain in Turkish hands for the remainder of the campaign.

295 James, *Gallipoli*, p.113.
296 Şefik, para. 113.
297 *Ibid*., para. 113.
298 *Ibid*., para. 90.
299 Bean, *Official History*, Volume I (1921 and 1941), p.449.
300 Bean, *Gallipoli Mission*, p.91.
301 This is discussed in a later chapter.
302 Bean, *Official History*, Volume I (1921 and 1941), p.294.

6

Adana Bair

"Keep going, you are the covering force"[1]

Early on the morning of 25 April, 3rd Brigade men led by Lieutenant N.M. Loutit, 10th Battalion, reached a spur of Third Ridge, a 3rd Brigade objective, only to be pushed back by the enemy. As with Tulloch, the brigade did not attempt to follow Loutit's party to its objective, but instead began a defensive battle on a ridge closer to the beach. This change of plan contradicted the briefings emphasising a rapid advance and is pivotal to the outcomes of the fighting this day, yet is poorly understood. Given that the main Turkish counter-attack did not strike the Australians on Second Ridge until five or six hours after the first troops crossed the beaches, it would appear that there was a period of several hours during which the initiative was lost. Roberts has argued that the decision to stop the advance was premature and led to the covering force's failure to achieve its objectives, condemning the Anzac Corps to an eight month campaign.[2] Peter Williams, equally convincingly, argues the opposite – that the decision was the correct one under the circumstances.[3]

Such debate is confused by discrepancies between sources. Even Loutit's various accounts tell different stories – or more correctly, different versions of his story. Clues in accounts by three 11th Battalion members suggest they fought with Loutit, meaning that their stories can contribute evidence to discussion on the battle at Third Ridge. This and the two subsequent chapters will reconstruct and examine these hours, predominantly from the viewpoint of those on the battlefield, to determine what happened and, if possible, why.

Carrying guns, tripods, ammunition, water and spares, "slipping and scrambling and sliding," the 11th Battalion Machine Gun Section laboured towards Second Ridge to reinforce D Company, while "the enemy poured in rifle fire and shrapnel."[4] Hearder was struck on the back of the knee but continued the climb; one of his men, wounded in the head, was left behind. "By the Lord I do not want another such trip,"[5] wrote George Henderson Smith[6] to his father, "slipping down the steep slopes on the seat of one's trousers and toiling up steeper slopes."[7] They were climbing the sometimes sheer seaward side of Second Ridge behind MacLaurin's Hill (Figure 27). When Hearder paused to assemble his men, "just about done up from the stiff" climb,[8] he discovered three more were missing, including his corporal,[9] probably Murphy.

The section "dashed over the ridge"[10] but could discover no sign of D Company. They set up their guns "and opened fire, immediately a terrific fire opened on us, but we were lying pretty close to

1   Şefik, para. 52.
2   Roberts, "The Landing at Anzac: A Reassessment", pp.25–34.
3   P.D. Williams, "Z Beach, the Landing of the ANZAC Corps, April 25, 1915."
4   Hearder, manuscript 3DRL 3959, pp.12–13.
5   Smith, 3DRL7247.
6   618 Private George Holt Henderson Smith, Machine Gun Section, 19 at enlistment, clerk, of Perth, born Adelaide.
7   Smith, letter to father, 3DRL7247.
8   *Ibid.*.
9   Hearder, manuscript 3DRL 3959, p.13.
10 *Ibid.*

the ground and they could not actually see us."[11] Hearder's missing NCO soon rejoined them.[12] The Australians began reversing the parapets of Turkish trenches, possibly recently vacated by Faik's men, to face the direction of the expected threat – inland.[13]

Everett's party climbed the steep slope behind Courtney's Post and was probably the 11th Battalion's northernmost party on Second Ridge.[14] Everett kept a number of men beneath the seaward crest, but "the moment" the others started to crawl forward into the scrub, "they were fired at."[15] He could only "guess" where the fire came from, but thought the Turks "had run back … across the valley," where some "got into a trench … about 300 yards across the plateau."[16] This account suggests the Turks were survivors of 4 Company, 2/27th Regiment from Russell's Top or even Plugge's Plateau, withdrawing to Mortar Ridge to continue the fight. Members of 1 or 3 Companies, 3/27th Regiment[17] and a platoon of 1 Company, 2/27th Regiment, probably also fought Everett's party at various times during the morning. Everett managed to establish a firing line about 10 yards in from the seaward crest and made contact with Denton.[18] Later, the two stood in minor gullies behind the ridge and directed reinforcements to the front line.[19]

Selby and some of 1 Platoon climbed onto Second Ridge in this area, but did not, as stated in the *Official History*,[20] see Everett.[21] The two parties fought near each other but Selby did not manage to contact his company 2IC until some days later.[22] Medcalf, of Selby's platoon but acting as Brockman's observer, at some stage spied his section mates Albrecht[23] and Harvey struggling forward with ammunition; Harvey shouted and waved his cap "indicating a bullet hole."[24] Enemy fire, which Selby believed came from his left, made digging on the crest impossible.[25] He was then told, though by whom is not stated, "to take his men out and support" a party visible "out ahead to his right," but when about "a hundred yards out" could see "no men nearer than Johnston's Jolly." His party lay down but suffered "casualties – it was a hopeless position and so after a few minutes he brought them back."[26]

Enemy fire thus prevented Selby's and Everett's parties digging on the exposed crest of the ridge, from where they could have dominated Legge Valley and made life difficult for the attacking Turks. This enabled the Turks to establish themselves on the inland side of Second Ridge, where they remained for the duration of the campaign.

Several others of A Company appear to have fought in this area. John Turner probably fought near the Machine Gun Section.[27] Wood's account of static, defensive fighting suggests he was on Second Ridge as well. Wood "advanced … to the third ridge … we drove the Turks back to their main position" and "were ordered to hold the ground we had taken until our supports arrived. We made a stand."[28] A number of men refer to Second Ridge as being the "third."[29] Perhaps, as they had

11 *Ibid.*
12 Murphy, letter, *Sunday Times*, 6 June 1915.
13 *Ibid.*
14 Everett, interview, Ellam-Innes Collection, p.240.
15 *Ibid.*
16 Everett, interview, Ellam-Innes Collection, p.240.
17 Şefik, para. 111.
18 Everett, interview, Ellam-Innes Collection, p.240.
19 *Ibid.*
20 Bean, *Official History*, Volume I (1921 and 1941), p.283.
21 Selby, 3DRL 8042 item 7.
22 Everett, interview, Ellam-Innes Collection, p.242.
23 136 Private (at embarkation) Frederick Albrecht, A Company, 21 at embarkation, school teacher, of Perth.
24 Medcalf, manuscript, p.65.
25 Selby, 3DRL 8042 item 7. Bean notes that Denton came under fire from the Chessboard when he arrived at Second Ridge. Bean, *Official History*, Volume I (1921 and 1941), p.426.
26 Selby, 3DRL 8042 item 7.
27 Turner, letter, 25 June 1915.
28 S.M. Wood, letter to J.S. Seddon, 3 May 1915, collection of E. Rose, Toodyay, Western Australia.
29 John Turner is one. Turner, letter, 25 June 1915.

Figure 26. Legge Valley and Adana Sirt [Adana Ridge] and Third Ridge from Wire
Gully. The knoll occupied by Peck is marked by the monument at the end of the
road (upper centre). (Photograph by J.P. Hurst, n.d., author's collection)

been briefed to hold Third Ridge, when ordered to defend Second Ridge, they presumed it to be their
objective; alternatively, they may have simply been confused by the tangled and unnamed terrain.
Cockburn[30] and Murray[31] also appear to have occupied Turkish trenches on Second Ridge and "kept
the Turks back when they attacked."[32]

After catching their breath on Plugge's Plateau, a number of C Company men raced inland.
Combs "had the good fortune to get one of the Turkish Officers, also got his glasses [binoculars]."[33]
Brodribb may well have been one of six with Combs, as he recorded a "Turkish officer in a striking
uniform" being "riddled with bullets. One of the chaps … took a liking to his field glasses. Therefore
he took them."[34] Leane's observer may also have been with this party as in many respects his story
matches those of Combs and Brodribb.[35] Combs thought the dead man "a fine big fellow, and I
thought if he is the type of man we are to meet we are in for a rough time." They "got a fair mob
in front of us, going for their lives"[36] and came across a Turkish camp. The Turks had left behind

30   Cockburn, diary, 28 April 1915.
31   Murray, letter, 16 May 1915.
32   *Ibid.*
33   Combs, manuscript.
34   Brodribb, letter, 17 July 1915.
35   Anonymous, Leane's observer, manuscript.
36   Combs, manuscript.

"everything rifles, ammunition, food, clothing … While we were looking through this stuff, up came one of our officers with about fifteen more men."[37] The combined parties pushed off inland.

B Company's Mofflin, Ed and Jack Inman and others of 7 Platoon, had also settled into Turkish trenches on Second Ridge. Mofflin could see "for about 2,000 yards. On our right was a gully and the other side of that a flat table land … On our left the ground gradually rose for about 200 yards then we couldn't see any more"[38] (Figure 28). This resembles the view from the southern slopes of MacLaurin's Hill, with the view ahead to Third Ridge, to the right across Wire Gully to the 400 Plateau, and with the mass of MacLaurin's Hill to the left.

As detailed earlier, the image of D Company occupying Courtney's Post and B Company the area of Steele's[39] is a simplification. The portion of D Company that was present was spread from Wire Gully to Battleship Hill, with the Machine Gun Section and an unknown number of B Company and others of the 3rd Brigade scattered amongst them.

Mofflin "could see a thin khaki line of our lads lying down firing. Then they got up and retired a bit and fired and retired again" with "Turks coming over the hills … in hundreds."[40] The retirement was probably of one or more parties of the 3rd Brigade who had advanced quickly towards Third Ridge. The Turks were probably the counter-attacking 27th Regiment. Mofflin and those with him set their sights to fire over the heads of the withdrawing men and opened fire.[41]

Loutit, 1 Platoon, A Company, 10th Battalion, had landed in Anzac Cove from the destroyer *Foxhound*.[42] His party hurried across Shrapnel Gully, killing some of Şefik's 2 Platoon, 4/2/27th Regiment, withdrawing from Plugge's Plateau, en route,[43] and were joined by Brand, the Brigade Major. From Wire Gully they could see, on the crest of 400 Plateau but only a few yards from the head of Owen's Gully,[44] a battery of Turkish guns.

The story of these guns is a confused one. Witnesses from various parties panting inland through the scrub and tangled terrain from different directions at different times[45] described seeing from two to four[46] "Krupp field pieces,"[47] "Hotchkiss guns … probably 12 pounders"[48] and field guns.[49] They appear in fact to have been four 75 mm Krupp mountain guns.[50] Some crew and horses were shot, possibly two of the guns fired a round each, one managed to escape and the breech blocks were removed from the others. Brand arrived, examined papers found on an "officer" shot attempting to engage the Australians with his pistol, and prevented the men from firing on "a string of Turks with mules," "hurrying northward up Legge Valley and over the Third Ridge."[51] This was presumably the gun that later joined Şefik. One of the 9th Battalion saw Turks loading machine "guns which had been firing on the advancing Australians"[52] onto mules, but this may in fact refer to the escaping mountain gun, which could be dismantled for transport by mule.

37 *Ibid.*
38 Mofflin, letter, 20 October 1915, p.17.
39 Bean, *Official History*, Volume I (1921 and 1941), pp.284–285.
40 Mofflin, letter, 20 October 1915, p.17.
41 *Ibid.*
42 Loutit, interview, D.A. Wilson.
43 N.M. Loutit, Official History, 1914–18 War: Records of C E W Bean, AWM38 3DRL 606 item 227 [2] – diaries nos. 206–215.
44 Loutit, 3DRL 606 item 227.
45 Such as Lieutenant D. Fortescue, 9th Battalion, 3DRL 8042 item 7; Corporal P.W. Harrison (9th Battalion), Bean, *Official History*, Volume I (1921 and 1941), pp.341–2; and Loutit.
46 Bean, *Official History*, Volume I (1921 and 1941), p.342; Fortescue, 3DRL 8042 item 7.
47 Bean, *Official History*, Volume I (1921 and 1941), p.342.
48 D. Fortescue, letter, 3DRL 8042 item 7.
49 Bean, *Official History*, Volume I (1921 and 1941), p.342.
50 The 7th Mountain Artillery Battery, 3th Mountain Artillery Battalion, 9th Field Artillery Regiment. Uyar, p.103.
51 Bean, *Official History*, Volume I (1921 and 1941), pp.342–343.
52 Corporal P.W. Harrison. Bean, *Official History*, Volume I (1921 and 1941), p.342.

Why had these guns not fired on the landing and why had they allowed themselves to be surprised and overrun? Bean's account[53] is probably more accurate than he could have realised. Şefik recorded that the battery was only to fire on orders from the battalion commander, 2/27th Regiment.[54] Faik requested fire support, but the battery commander, still expecting a landing at Gaba Tepe, and without orders from the battalion CO, would not open fire. Thus the guns were initially on the crest of the plateau, but did not for some time engage the landing. When the battery commander learned that "the enemy was getting close," he tried to withdraw the guns into the pits, but three fell into enemy hands after their "horses" were "struck down."[55] Uyar notes that the battery commander escaped with one gun and most of the ammunition, but that most of the battery's equipment was lost.[56]

The battery had been positioned in the Cup, at the head of Owen's Gully. Near the bottom of the gully was "a camp," with "eastern lamps ... still burning." Australians rummaging "through the tents" brought out "odd articles – watches and leather pouches."[57] Loutit went "right through" the camp, destroying "a telephone evidently communicating with Gaba Tepe,"[58] then, with "the Turks on the run,"[59] he dragged the men away and "pushed on down the valley."[60] Clues in Combs' and Leane's observer's accounts suggest they may have been among those Loutit recruited in the camp.

The party was joined by Lieutenant J.L. Haig, 10th Battalion, a nephew of the general.[61] As they emerged into the expanse of Legge Valley they noted a horse or horses in the lines of a battery in a paddock.[62] Ahead were "the scrub-covered folds of the Third Ridge", "lifeless under the morning sun."[63] Loutit recalled, "few Turks were about except snipers," shooting "from behind and everywhere",[64] elsewhere, the battle continued spasmodically, the sound of "desultory ... shooting" being audible on "all sides."[65]

Loutit's 32 men, from the 9th, 10th and 11th Battalions,[66] climbed a 200 feet high spur to discover that they were not on "the backbone of the Third Ridge, but a spur ... not shown on the original maps, known later by the Turks as Adana Bair"[67] [Adana Hill] or Adana Sirt [Adana Ridge].[68] Third Ridge lay 400 yards beyond and Scrubby Knoll about 500 yards to Loutit's left front. The *Official History* states that the Australians, confronted by "Turks in large numbers"[69] on the summit of Third Ridge, threw themselves down and opened fire. The enemy replied with a "hot"[70] rifle and machine gun fire. Loutit took two men and reconnoitred to the left as far as Scrubby Knoll, noticing on the way the water of the Narrows glittering in the morning sun.[71] Enemy fire was heavy, and, after having one of his party wounded, "Loutit and the other, carrying the wounded man as best they could, made

53   Bean, *Official History*, Volume I (1921 and 1941), p.340.
54   Şefik, para. 42.
55   *Ibid.*
56   Uyar, p.104.
57   Bean, *Official History*, Volume I (1921 and 1941), p.340.
58   T.L. Loutit, letter from T.L. Loutit to C.E.W. Bean, 20 September 1919, quoting a letter from 948 R.A. Rayney, A Company, 10th Battalion, 3DRL 6673/110, Australian War Memorial.
59   N.M. Loutit, letter to father, 22 May 1915, quoted T.L. Loutit, letter to C.E.W. Bean, 23 May 1919, 3 DRL 6673/110, Australian War Memorial.
60   Bean, *Official History*, Volume I (1921 and 1941), p.340.
61   T.L. Loutit, letter, 20 September 1919, 3DRL 6673/110.
62   Bean, *Official History*, Volume I (1921 and 1941), p.345; Loutit, interview, D.A. Wilson.
63   Bean, *Official History*, Volume I (1921 and 1941), p.345.
64   Loutit, 3DRL 606 item 227.
65   Bean, *Official History*, Volume I (1921 and 1941), p.345.
66   Loutit, 3DRL 606 item 227. Belford, *Legs Eleven*, p.79, confirms 11th Battalion men with this party.
67   Bean, *Official History*, Volume I (1921 and 1941), p.345.
68   Şefik, para. 102.
69   Bean, *Official History*, Volume I (1921 and 1941), p.346.
70   *Ibid.*
71   *Ibid.*

their way back towards their party."[72] After attempting to carry the apparently mortally wounded man, Loutit realised it "was hopeless" and "he was left."[73]

The Turks opposing Loutit on Third Ridge were doubtless men of 27th Regiment, but which ones? If Bean's description of large numbers of Turks occupying Third Ridge as Loutit crested Adana Ridge is correct, Loutit's party must have been confronted by 27th Regiment's counter-attack, but if so, would not their presence have made Loutit's reconnaissance to Scrubby Knoll impossible? Şefik thought his lead elements reached Scrubby Knoll at 7:40 a.m., but the tail of the column did not arrive until about 8:00 a.m.[74] They probably engaged the enemy at, by Şefik's estimate, 8:30–9:00 a.m.[75] It is difficult to reconcile Loutit's account with Şefik's. How could Loutit have been confronted by 27th Regiment on Third Ridge, yet, some time later, have approached Scrubby Knoll without colliding with their HQ and lead elements, their northernmost battalion or their counter-attack? How could Loutit, moving quickly from the beach, have been beaten to Third Ridge by a regiment marching from the other side of the peninsula?

Many years later, without the benefit of a detailed knowledge of 27th Regiment's movements, Loutit gave another insight into the events of that morning. As his party arrived, he "realised that we had outrun the main body, so I decided to wait for them to come up."[76] This is supported by a member of his company, R.A. Rayney, who wrote that the party "halted and waited for their flanks."[77] Until then Loutit had been chasing – a term also used by Combs[78] – the retreating Turks who "were in scattered groups which when dispersed did not hold us up."[79] In hindsight, Loutit did not support the official version which stated that he had been stopped by Turkish resistance, and presumed "the Turks came back when they realised we had stopped chasing them." He added that, had he continued to advance, he believed the enemy "would have kept running inland, there were not too many of them."[80] This account appears to contradict those he gave Bean, Bean's notes stating that "These Turks stopped them there with rifle and machine gun fire. They had lost many men."[81] This account appears to be supported by a letter Loutit wrote from Gallipoli, which described having to "stop because the hill was lined from end to end with enemy."[82]

There are clearly discrepancies between these accounts. One reason Loutit's experience is of importance is for the possible clues it may contain about the time of arrival of Şefik's forces and the progress of the 3rd Brigade. Whether Loutit was stopped by 27th Regiment's counter-attack, or he got there first and waited, is central to debate about whether or not the 3rd Brigade's halt on Second Ridge was justified.

One possible explanation for these anomalies is that, as with interpretations of Tulloch's battle on Battleship Hill, a number of events may have been simplified, assumptions made and incidents amalgamated. Although there is little doubt that Şefik's 1st and 3rd Battalions were the troops who ultimately forced the retirement of Loutit's small force, and were seen from Second Ridge streaming over the ridges in pursuit, they may not have been the troops Loutit first encountered on Third

---

72   *Ibid.*
73   N.M. Loutit, letter to C.E.W. Bean 4 June 1920. 3DRL 8042 item 7, Australian War Memorial.
74   Şefik, para. 68.
75   *Ibid.*
76   Roberts, "The Landing at Anzac: A Reassessment", p.31.
77   T.L. Loutit, letter, 20 September 1919, 3DRL 6673/110.
78   Combs described chasing "the blighters a little further." Combs, manuscript.
79   C.A.M. Roberts, "The Landing at Anzac: A Reassessment", p.31.
80   *Ibid.*
81   Loutit, 3DRL 606 item 227.
82   Loutit, letter, 22 May 1915.

Ridge.[83] These may have been survivors of the scattered parties of 4 Company, 2/27th Regiment, conducting a fighting withdrawal, or other parties.

Second Lieutenant Ismail Hakki's 80-odd men[84] of 3 Platoon, 3/2/27th Regiment, was at Kel Tepe [Kal[goorlie]] when the landing commenced.[85] Hakki engaged any enemy he saw and sent runners to make contact with friendly forces and take back information on the enemy; in response, he received orders from "Lieutenant Asim" at Gabe Tepe to hold his area "at all cost."[86] As the Australians pushed inland, this party came under fire from their right and rear, suffering one dead and two wounded, after which they withdrew to Pine Ridge and then Anderson Knoll,[87] from where they "halted the enemy advance with rifle fire."[88] They later fought on the left flank of 27th Regiment's attack at 400 Plateau.[89] This platoon appears to be the force shown on Şefik's map on the south eastern slopes of Adana Bair (Map 10). Şefik presumed actions described in "British documents," apparently Aspinall-Oglander's history, referred to this party.[90] Şefik described them firing on "Two companies of Australians … sent for mopping up operations in the direction of Gaba Tepe," preventing the Australians reaching Gaba Tepe and wounding "several" of their officers.[91]

Bean's account reveals that it was not quite as dramatic as this. Hakki's platoon did not repulse the attack of two companies. The companies referred to were those of the 9th Battalion's Captains I. Jackson and J.A. Milne. Jackson had been wounded earlier. Milne's company were confronted by what appears to be Hakki's platoon at the head of Bolton's Ridge, but Jackson's company was at the time near the Cup. Milne was wounded, possibly by fire from Hakki's party, but sent a section and some scouts to outflank the Turkish trench, which was soon taken, "the few Turks who were left in it being killed or captured."[92] Bean's account appears to be confirmed by Şefik's map (here Map 10), which shows this platoon withdrawing to Adana Ridge. As the Australian section who evicted them was led by a Corporal P.W. Harrison, who "afterwards attacked the Turkish guns"[93] at the Cup, it can be presumed Hakki's platoon began their withdrawal before Loutit commenced his advance to Third Ridge, and to have beaten him to Adana Ridge.

Second Lieutenant Mustafa's platoon, 1/2/27th Regiment, from Gaba Tepe, also operated in, or travelled through, this area early in the morning. By Şefik's chronology they were sent at about 6:00 a.m. to gain information on the fighting in the Ari Burnu region. On "the ridges to the west of the village of Koca Dere" they met the wounded Faik withdrawing from Russell's Top. Faik continued on to hospital, while Mustafa's platoon "passed on to Artillery Range" [Artillery Ridge, Third/Gun Ridge], planning to fight in the area "north of Kemalyeri." They later fought with 3/27th Regiment.[94]

Any, or none, of these troops may have fired on Loutit's party. Loutit's reference to suffering many casualties and being held up by enemy rifle and machine gun fire, does not contradict this if his account is viewed as a summary of events – when Şefik's main force arrived they did cause casualties and force Loutit's withdrawal. Moreover, to a small band of Australians advancing into enemy territory, a

---

83   A civilian, S. Dilman, visited and stayed with an uncle, a company commander in 27th Regiment, on 24 April. Dilman claims he accompanied the regiment when Şefik marched his two battalions to the sound of the guns the following morning. Dilman later recalled that "When I arrived on the ridge I saw Australians retreating. I think they belonged to a company which occupied part of Third Ridge." S. Dilman, typed transcript of interview with Peter Liddle, July 1972, Tape 46, TU01 item 4, Liddle Collection, Brotherton Library, University of Leeds.

84   Uyar, p.106.

85   Şefik, para. 34.

86   Uyar, p.107.

87   *Ibid.*

88   Şefik, para. 41.

89   Uyar states that they had joined Şefik, who ordered them to provide flank security. Uyar, p.114.

90   Aspinall-Oglander and Becke, Military Operations, Gallipoli, Vol I, p.178.

91   Şefik, para. 41.

92   Bean, *Official History*, Volume I (1921 and 1941), pp.355–356.

93   *Ibid.*, p.355.

94   Şefik, para. 44.

single, organised enemy platoon may have represented a superior force lining the ridge from "end to end." Perhaps 27th Regiment then arrived on Third Ridge as Loutit conducted his reconnaissance to Scrubby Knoll, and the majority of his party, remaining on Adana Ridge with Haig, began to engage them. This would explain the contradiction in that Rayney does not describe Third Ridge being lined with enemy, but "comparatively flat country swarming with the enemy"[95] – probably Şefik's battalions approaching from Maidos. That Loutit's account to Bean is a condensation of the action is further evidenced by the fact that it did not include a description of his patrol to Scrubby Knoll, nor did a letter to his father.[96] Such omissions give the impression that incidents separated by time are a single event, and many contradictions in Loutit's accounts can be reconciled by a closer study of their wording and context, and comparison to other accounts, including Turkish ones.

Combs also condenses the action into a few words. A "large force" held them "up … one of our naval sea planes flew over at a couple of hundred feet … the Turks opened fire on it… the roar of rifles … was the fiercest we had heard up till that time, and I shall never forget it."[97] The fire became "too hot" for Loutit's party on Adana Ridge to dig, and they were forced to return fire while lying behind nothing more substantial than bushes, suffering casualties.[98] Perhaps one of them fired the bullet that hit Captain Galib in the arm, about "ten paces in front of" Şefik.[99] That the fire on Loutit's party was heavy and increasing is not surprising. They had probably been visible to 27th Regiment for some time: the enemy troops that Şefik saw in Legge Valley when he arrived at Kavak Tepe,[100] and later "on the western foothills of Artillery Ridge,"[101] were probably Loutit's party.

Earlier, when Brand had told Loutit to "keep going" inland from 400 Plateau he "promised" to send others to follow.[102] Under fire on Adana Ridge, Loutit looked back over his shoulder, but, although men could be seen "digging in" or "cruising round potting snipers" on Second Ridge and 400 Plateau, none were crossing the valley to join his dwindling band.[103] Outflanking was probable, and Loutit sent back to one of the parties behind "to come up" on his right flank.[104] This group, "about one platoon of 9th Battalion" under command of Captain J.F. Ryder, formed a line on Loutit and Haig's right. Soon Turks, apparently having moved north along Gun Ridge and begun their advance, were infiltrating to Loutit's left from Scrubby Knoll, and were firing into the backs of Ryder's men. Ryder sent a messenger back for reinforcements.[105]

Peck had crossed to Second Ridge in a "fruitless"[106] search for battalion HQ, which was probably on Plugge's Plateau. At "Maclaurin's Hill Corner" he found various parties of the 10th Battalion digging in under Major E.C. Oldham, Captain M.J. Herbert, and Lieutenants J. Hamilton and H.R. Heming.[107] Peck "noticed men about half a mile in front."[108] He had previously sent Jackson's party forward and thinking these might be them, hurried to investigate. Instead he found "isolated fellows – cooks etc."[109] and after "gathering them together"[110] was contacted about "halfway down Wire

95   T.L. Loutit, letter, 20 September 1919, 3DRL 6673/110.
96   Loutit, letter, 22 May 1915.
97   Combs, manuscript.
98   Loutit, 3DRL 606 item 227.
99   Şefik, para. 78.
100 *Ibid.*, para. 62.
101 *Ibid.*, para. 80.
102 Bean, *Official History*, Volume I (1921 and 1941), p.339.
103 Loutit, 3DRL 606 item 227.
104 *Ibid.*
105 Bean, *Official History*, Volume I (1921 and 1941), p.348.
106 Peck, letter to wife, n.d.
107 Peck, 3DRL 606 item 25.
108 Peck, letter to wife, n.d.
109 Peck, 3DRL 606 item 25.
110 Peck, letter to wife, n.d.

Gully"[111] by a messenger who "rushed up calling for reinforcements for Ryder."[112] This messenger is probably the sergeant referred to in the *Official History*[113] who had been sent back by Ryder on a Turkish horse.[114] The sergeant afterwards "let the horse go"[115] and it dutifully trotted back towards the Turkish lines.[116] Peck pushed forward. Bean states that one of those with him at this stage was Newman,[117] though it is not clear from Peck's accounts when Newman joined him. As these reinforcements advanced across Legge Valley, Ryder's party pulled back.

Years later, Loutit implied Ryder's withdrawal was "premature" and forced him to "abandon his position."[118] In 1920 Loutit wrote to Bean of Haig "doing some very fine work. Ryder sorry to say did not at the point furthest out."[119] Only those on the ground, Loutit, Haig, Ryder and the men with them, could know the truth. There were a number of Turkish parties, unidentified in Australian sources, operating in the area and these may have threatened Ryder's right or rear.

Loutit would no doubt have been unaware that Brand had halted the advance on Second Ridge. Brand had been entrusted by MacLagan to prevent "the enemy forestalling us on 400 Plateau" but had done the opposite, deciding "it was hopeless to try to reach and effectively hold the covering positions originally assigned."[120] The advanced parties would instead act as a defensive screen while 400 Plateau and Second Ridge were established for defence.[121] MacLagan supported Brand's decision, possibly having reached the same conclusion himself.[122]

With the 3rd Brigade already having decided not to reinforce the ridge, the outcome was inevitable – 27th Regiment began to swarm forward. Combs recalled the Turks starting "to advance on us, so we held them up long enough for the men at our rear to take up a position. After lying there for about an hour they came on with a rush."[123] This tends to support Brand's comments on the value of the advanced parties acting as a screen[124] to cover the troops digging on Second Ridge, but whether this represented "the best role"[125] for these men is less certain.

Twenty-one-year-old Loutit, seeing his right flank "going for all they were worth down the slope,"[126] enemy troops infiltrating around his left, hundreds of Turks advancing on his front, his own small party reduced by casualties, and with little support coming from behind, was, like Tulloch, forced to make a difficult but urgent decision. He ordered his force to withdraw. The party retired in small groups, alternately providing covering fire and running to cover, with the pursuing Turks close on their heels.[127]

Combs may not have been the only 11th Battalion man to advance with Loutit and live to tell the tale. Leane's observer's account is similar to those of Combs and Brodribb and matches the ground. He eventually "found we could not hold the third high ridge … forced to … retire to the second ridge. We were loath" to surrender ground "but it was unavoidable."[128] The observer was apparently unaware of the arrival of 27th Regiment and, as did a number of other men, ascribed the Turkish

111 Peck, 3DRL 606 item 25.
112 Peck, letter to wife, n.d.
113 Bean, *Official History*, Volume I (1921 and 1941), p.348.
114 Peck, 3DRL 606 item 25.
115 *Ibid.*
116 *Ibid.*
117 Bean, *Official History*, Volume I (1921 and 1941), p.348.
118 Roberts, "The Landing at Anzac: A Reassessment", p.32.
119 N.M. Loutit, letter to C.E.W. Bean, 5 April 1920, 3DRL 8042 item 7.
120 Brand, "Memories of ANZAC Day", p.4.
121 Bean, *Official History*, Volume I (1921 and 1941), p.344.
122 *Ibid.*; Brand, "Memories of ANZAC Day", p.4.
123 Combs, manuscript.
124 Bean, *Official History*, Volume I (1921 and 1941), p.344.
125 *Ibid.*
126 Loutit, 3DRL 606 item 227.
127 Bean, *Official History*, Volume I (1921 and 1941), p.348.
128 Anonymous, Leane's observer, manuscript.

counter-attack to "German Officers" who "now managed to rally the Turks."[129] Stagles may have been another member of C Company to have reached Adana Bair, as his account matches key features of others'. He saw the water of the Narrows and the enemy marching "towards us." An officer "said the only thing you can do boys is to get your ammunition out in front of you. Pump everything into them and get back the best you could."[130] Forbes, "separated from" A Company probably also fought on Third Ridge: "the Turks began to come on in far superior numbers so we had to get back as quickly as our legs would carry us. There were only about 25 of us and there were some hundreds of Turks."[131]

Peck, hurrying forward from Wire Gully, received a message from Ryder, stating "that he was going to get back to a hill on my right rear, and accordingly I waited to cover the retirement."[132] With fire intensifying, Peck took up a position on a small knoll at the toe of Mortar Ridge, and as "men drifted back, I drew them into my fold"[133] (Figure 26). As the survivors of Loutit's and Haig's parties arrived at the knoll, some possibly before Peck, they turned to do battle.[134] At the same time, Turks occupied the position Loutit had just vacated. They brought a machine gun into action and "fire became very heavy."[135]

Many reports of the presence of enemy machine guns early on the morning of 25 April cannot be verified, but Şefik's account appears to confirm the presence of this gun – "to cover the 1st Battalion's attack we moved a machine gun platoon [i.e. two guns] on to the Adana Ridge."[136] Peck's party on the knoll, apparently on the receiving end of this fire, did their best to keep under cover and most of the bullets passed "over our heads."[137] Peck "was about to write a message asking for reinforcements,"[138] when he "felt something like a salute from the business end of a mule on my right arm."[139] Clarke had been killed while writing a message, and Brand noted that at this stage of the battle, "the casualties were chiefly among the officers or anyone recognised as leaders."[140] Peck's arm "went quite "dead" … but I felt no pain"[141] and he was assisted to the rear.[142] He later recalled he had been hit at "exactly" 10:00 a.m.[143] He was treated at Brennan's aid post for "a bullet through the shoulder. It had just missed the bone."[144]

Newman, who had been acting as Peck's 2IC, assumed command.[145] Brodribb was beside him,[146] though it is unclear whether he had withdrawn from Adana Bair, or had advanced with Peck's party.[147] Eventually Brodribb said to Newman "no good to Gundi. Let's get out of this."[148] "Alright, Broadie," Newman replied. "Pass the word along to retire."[149] Newman and Brodribb belonged to different companies, but their familiarity may have originated in their pre-war lives in the goldfields. Once more the few survivors of Adana Ridge ran back over open ground through a heavy rifle,

129 *Ibid.*
130 Stagles, interview, Liddle Collection, p.11.
131 Forbes, letter, 29 May 1915.
132 Peck, letter to wife, n.d.
133 *Ibid.*
134 Bean, *Official History*, Volume I (1921 and 1941), p.348.
135 *Ibid.*, p.349.
136 Şefik, para. 102.
137 Peck, letter to wife, n.d.
138 *Ibid.*
139 *Ibid.*
140 Brand, "Memories of ANZAC Day", p.4.
141 Peck, letter to wife, n.d.
142 Loutit, 3DRL 606 item 227.
143 Peck, 3DRL 606 item 25.
144 Brennan, letter, 1915, Army Museum of Western Australia.
145 Brodribb, letter, 17 July 1915.
146 *Ibid.*
147 Brodribb, interview, *Kalgoorlie Miner*, 24 August 1915.
148 Brodribb, letter, 17 July 1915.
149 *Ibid.*

machine gun and, as it seemed to the men, shrapnel fire,[150] and once more it became a race between them and the Turks. When they had covered only half the distance to Second Ridge the enemy occupied the knoll they had just left.[151] Combs, "chased" through "intense" fire by a machine gun, ran harder than ever "before in my life." In addition to carrying rifle, ammunition, equipment and "soaking wet" rations, he "was drenched."[152] Forbes marvelled that "we ever got back … I came out of it with only a shrapnel hit in the back."[153]

Most of the party ran up the "scrubby, broken, and narrow" Wire Gully, which provided a degree of cover.[154] Bean and Belford mention Newman bringing with him an 11th Battalion "machine-gun … which was set up … at the head of Wire Gully."[155] This appears unlikely, as both the battalion's guns appear to have fought with the Machine Gun Section. Newman ended up on Second Ridge near Lieutenant E.J.C. Stopp, 10th Battalion. Loutit and Haig "climbed a steep gutter" to Johnston's Jolly, turned once more to do battle and began to dig in.[156] Combs "reached our own line … dead beat" and was ordered to "rest awhile" behind the lines; he believed those who withdrew to the "flanks … never returned."[157] Brodribb, "very much distressed,"[158] reported to headquarters, probably MacLagan's 3rd Brigade headquarters situated behind MacLaurin's Hill,[159] and was also told to rest.

The reason for Brodribb's "distress" was the loss of "50 to 60 men,"[160] including 21 of Loutit's 32.[161] Nineteen years later, Loutit wrote that the "fact remains" that these men "did their job, and … materially assisted others at an extravagant price."[162] Perhaps here Loutit was choosing to avoid comment on the decision that left his party unsupported after being ordered forward. Brand later wrote that "the problem" had been how "to acquaint the small advanced parties on distant ridges (Mortar Ridge and Battleship Hill)" of the decision not to support them. "Some got back, others did not."[163] It will be noted that Brand, writing in 1935, the year after Loutit's letter about the incident was printed, did not mention Adana Ridge, nor that, as messages were arriving from Loutit, replies could no doubt have reached him. Brand noted that the forward parties who fought, died, were wounded or captured, "nevertheless did good work in diverting the enemy's attention for a precious hour or so" but were "eventually ignored" by the Turks who "advanced up the ravines" to be engaged by the Australian defences.[164] Loutit, Peck, Combs and Brodribb certainly did not suggest that they felt ignored by the enemy. It is not known whether Brand's reference to Battleship Hill implies that 3rd Brigade HQ was aware of Tulloch's party but had decided against supporting it.

Many must have fallen in the path of 27th Regiment, and Brodribb believed some men had been taken prisoner,[165] though no Australian who might have fallen into enemy hands during this withdrawal survived to tell of it. Şefik stated that the Australian prisoner referred to earlier had been retreating from fighting on the "south western heights of Incebayir"; some "Australians withdrew from the valley between Kanlisirt and Kirmisisirt and some to the valley west of the Edirne Ridge."[166] It is unclear

---

150 Brodribb, letter, 17 July 1915.
151 Bean, *Official History*, Volume I (1921 and 1941), p.349.
152 Combs, manuscript.
153 Forbes, letter, 29 May 1915.
154 Bean, *Official History*, Volume I (1921 and 1941), p.349.
155 *Ibid.*, p.353; Belford, *Legs Eleven*, p.80.
156 Bean, *Official History*, Volume I (1921 and 1941), p.349.
157 Combs, manuscript.
158 Brodribb, letter, 17 July 1915.
159 Bean, *Official History*, Volume I (1921 and 1941), p.359.
160 Brodribb, letter, 17 July 1915.
161 Loutit, "The Tragedy of Anzac", p.8.
162 *Ibid.*
163 Brand, "Memories of ANZAC Day", p.4.
164 *Ibid.*
165 Brodribb, letter, 17 July 1915.
166 Şefik, para. 104.

whether this reference to withdrawal "from" is correct or a translation error – if correct, it is possible the prisoner was one of those Combs mentioned as withdrawing to the "flanks." If a translation error, the correct word being "to," which appears likely given the references to Incebayir and Edirne ridges, the prisoner was probably a man fighting with some forward party higher up the range. In this case the prisoner may have been one of Tulloch's party who had withdrawn southwards from Battleship Hill or a survivor from some party whose story has not been recorded; on the other hand, the fact that the prisoner was escorted by 2 Company, 1/27th Regiment suggests he was not captured on Incebayir Ridge.[167] The only member of the 1st Division to have fallen into enemy hands this day and survived, was Fred Ashton, 11th Battalion, who was captured in the Baby 700–Mortar Ridge area and was to endure the remainder of the war in captivity. Ashton's account suggests he was not the prisoner to whom Şefik refers, as it states that he was captured later in the day. This will be discussed in Chapter 9.

If Peck's 80[168] men had reached Adana Ridge they could perhaps have extended one of the flanks and added their firepower to the defence of the ridge. This may have disrupted or slowed the advance of 27th Regiment, or have convinced Şefik that a stronger force was in occupation than was the case. It is difficult to imagine what impact 80 more rifles would have had against Şefik's regiment and guns, and the Australians may well have found themselves stranded regardless of numbers: Şefik used his support weapons to isolate the forward parties,[169] and Turks elsewhere could have hindered the movement of reinforcements. Nor were 80 more men likely to have caused MacLagan and Brand to reverse their decision – the attack had been deprived of momentum and time had been lost. On the other hand, had stronger, organised Australian forces occupied Adana Bair or Third Ridge when it appears Loutit's band did, Şefik's options would have been drastically reduced and his advance over the open ground beyond the ridge possibly disrupted. But they did not, leaving any advanced Australian parties to find their own way back, or to wither and die on whatever ground they had reached.

Nearly two decades after his advance to Adana Ridge, Loutit appeared still to have been deeply affected by the impact of that morning's battle. He was by then a veteran of four years of war, during which he had watched the men of the AIF serve with "a courage that cannot be described."[170] As he reflected on the approach of another 25 April, he wrote of "the doings of a wonderful little band of men … who did their job as only one who saw them doing it can really appreciate."[171]

With Third Ridge in enemy hands, Second Ridge became the Anzac line of defence. Everywhere, from 400 Plateau to Baby 700, Australians were peering into unfamiliar enemy territory. Combs, railway servant from Northam, and Brodribb, of the Kalgoorlie Gold Mine, exhausted after the landing, fighting, and withdrawal, were catching their breath on the seaward side of MacLaurin's Hill. Those who had been fortunate enough to have had time to use their entrenching tools once more took up their rifles. Bullets cracked overhead or whipped through the scrub. Hundreds of Turks in organised bodies were making good use of cover and advancing across the valley, gullies and ridges. Şefik had committed his troops to battle. 27th Regiment's assault had begun. Along the lines of riflemen scattered through the scrub on Second Ridge and 400 Plateau, the order was passed by word of mouth "not to move an inch."[172] "Then there was a battle indeed."[173]

---

167 *Ibid.*, footnote 1 to para. 104, p.54.
168 Brodribb, *Kalgoorlie Miner*, 24 August 1915.
169 Şefik, para. 102.
170 Loutit, "The Tragedy of Anzac", p.8.
171 *Ibid.*
172 Luttrell, letter, 16 May 1915.
173 Cockburn, diary, 28 April 1915.

7

Hammer and Anvil: The Fighting on Second Ridge

The importance of Second Ridge can be easily appreciated by standing on Plugge's Plateau and looking inland. A commander who had come from the sea on 25 April would have had the beach to his right and rear, and a solid ridge to his front. Unseen, somewhere beyond that ridge, lay the Turkish Fifth Army. If held, Second Ridge became a rampart from which to resist the enemy counter-attack. It provided cover for the beach and the main supply route to the firing line. If it fell, the only place the landing force could run was to their boats, or more likely, the sea.

By Bean's and subsequent accounts the Australian advance ended when the troops dropped into the scrub or whatever cover they could find and hastily formed lines to resist the Turkish counter-attack. As the attack approached Second Ridge, the battle there all but disappears from most narratives – focus shifts elsewhere, and much of the fighting on Second Ridge on 25 April is all but invisible.[1] As the fighting here was static for much of the day, this omission may appear of little consequence, other than creating a nagging gap in the narrative. But a great many men became casualties in this "gap," and as troops were diverted throughout the day from objectives elsewhere to defend the ridge, the significance of the fighting here may lie in what it reveals about the battle as a whole and what the Turkish forces were doing during this period. Şefik's account of 27th Regiment's battle adds a valuable counterpoint to Australian sources and provides a template against which to test Australian perceptions.

Often the only clues to tie a man to an event or place are similarities between accounts that suggest common incidents or places. In contrast to the back and forth fighting on and loss of Baby 700, a stationary line and successful defence of a prominent ridge tend to indicate the fighting along Second Ridge. Second Ridge accounts are often brief, as the pattern of the battle changed little throughout the day. Other themes were common to the experience of the battle elsewhere – shrapnel, endurance, mixing of units, a stream of casualties, perceptions of being greatly outnumbered, a confusion of time and place, and the limited perspective of participants.

The largest *documented* portion of the 11th Battalion appears to have fought on Second Ridge, though as will be revealed, this interpretation is probably not correct. Fragmentation significantly lowered the numbers present with their units, and affects the way the battle has been read: writers tend to derive their figures on how many men were at certain points at certain times from the full strength of platoons and companies. Conversely, it will be revealed in a later chapter that the number who fought on Baby 700 was probably higher than presumed by Bean and writers since.

A Company's Selby, Rockliff and MacFarlane took whatever portions of their platoons they could assemble and Everett a party of detached men to Second Ridge. According to the published histories, B and D Companies were despatched to Second Ridge, but in fact it was only B Company's Barnes, Darnell and ultimately Newman, and D Company's Denton and Croly, and the Machine Gun Section, who established themselves there. Most of the battalion's platoon officers had some portion of their platoons with them, though evidence suggests these officers were often accompanied by only about a third or a half of their platoons.[2] Newman appears to have had few, if any, of his platoon with

---

1   Williams, *The Battle of Anzac Ridge*, is an exception.
2   Some of this is detailed in earlier chapters. Jackson refers to having "about 50 of B & A Coy" accompanying him and Buttle (a D Company officer); Tulloch suggests Jackson had about 20 with him; Buttle refers to about 60 with him and Reid, Darnell to being accompanied about 20 of his scouts.

him when he fought on Second Ridge,[3] and Darnell was with the scouts, not his platoon. None of D Company's platoon officers were on Second Ridge. There was therefore not a single intact platoon of B or D Company under command of its own officer on Second Ridge, though an unknown number of these companies are likely to have attached themselves to Barnes and Denton. C Company, less Cooke's platoon, was supposed to remain on Plugge's Plateau, but as revealed earlier, most appear to have moved inland.

After covering the withdrawal of what appear to be Loutit's or Peck's parties, Mofflin "got to work" enlarging the narrow and shallow Turkish trench and building a parapet of sandbags. Bullets were:

> thudding against the bank or pinging overhead … we stood up to give them a few rounds rapid now and again we could see the Turks coming towards us in hundreds over the skyline … I prayed then for reinforcements … I made the first entry in my diary. 10 a.m.[4]

"Some time" later "we got a solid reinforcement … CAPTS Burns and Miller of the 3rd Battalion."[5] The 3rd Battalion history confirms that by "approximately 10 a.m.," "every man" was "in action reinforcing the 3rd Brigade."[6] Mofflin was soon under machine gun fire, the enemy guns starting "on the right" of the trench and pumping "lead into us," taking "the tops of [*sic*] the sandbags right along."[7] The fire came from the ridge opposite, where 27th Regiment's officers, binoculars in hand, directed their four machine guns.[8] One of Şefik's aims was to silence the Australian machine guns[9] and his guns may have been searching for Hearder's section, which was somewhere near Mofflin.

"Still clutching" a box of ammunition, Louch had struggled up the ridge to occupy "a position" near the upper end of Wire Gully but "some way down the slope."[10] Others of D Company, including C.S.M. R. Hemingway,[11] Lance Corporals C. Thompson[12] and N.A. Clayden,[13] Private J. Marfurt[14] and M.E. "Dick" Clarke,[15] appear to have accompanied him, suggesting that a portion of 16 Platoon had deployed to Second Ridge, though others of this platoon were on Battleship Hill with Buttle. Croly was believed to be "somewhere to" Louch's "left. There were Turks (no-one knew who they were at first) to the right front."[16] The men were "Soaking wet and very uncomfortable," "could see no enemy" and "did not seem to be doing any good where we were."[17]

Reinforcements from other battalions squeezed into the shallow trenches and the units became "properly mixed up."[18] This further evidences the pressure to which the Australian commanders believed they were being subjected: the 2nd Brigade had earlier "been diverted to MacLagan's right," and when the 1st Brigade landed, its leading troops were sent "to strengthen his left."[19] Members of the 3rd Battalion were diverted to reinforce "the 11th Battalion," in the centre, "on MacLaurin's

---

3   Lock, *The Fighting 10th*, pp.213–214.
4   Mofflin, letter, 20 October 1915, pp.17–18.
5   *Ibid.*, p.18.
6   Eric Wren, Randwick to Hargicourt, The History of the 3rd Battalion A.I.F. (Sydney: Ronald G. McDonald, 1935), pp.48–49.
7   Mofflin, letter, 20 October 1915, p.18.
8   Şefik, para. 74.
9   *Ibid.*, paras. 79, 80, 102.
10   Louch, manuscript, p.15; 3 DRL 606 item 27 – 206–215.
11   914 Company Sergeant-Major (on 1 January 1915) Reginald Hemingway, D Company, 25 at enlistment, bank manager of Perth, born Albany..
12   952 Lance Corporal Charles Thompson, D Company, 29 at embarkation, labourer, of Wagin, born Sheffield, England.
13   881 Lance Corporal Norman Albert Clayden, D Company, 19 or 22 at embarkation, mercantile clerk, of Pingelly and Wagin.
14   1106 Private Joseph Marfurt, 26 at embarkation, labourer, born Switzerland.
15   879 Private (at embarkation) Mervyn Ephraim Clarke, D Company, 20 at embarkation, farmer, of Bunbury, born Bunbury.
16   Louch, 3DRL 606 item 27 – 206–215.
17   Louch, manuscript, p.15.
18   Mofflin, letter, 20 October 1915, p.18.
19   Bean, *Official History*, Volume I (1921 and 1941), p.430.

Hill ... almost immediately"[20] after landing: even at this early stage the divisional reserve,[21] the 1st Brigade, was being committed to a defensive battle on Second Ridge. Somehow, an energetic thrust for the high ground had evolved into commitment of a whole division to a defensive battle for a ridge and hill short of the objectives.

So many reinforcements crowded into the 11th Battalion positions that "some went down to the bottom of the gully where they dug a few rifle pits."[22] This may have been the movement described by Bean, in which two 3rd Battalion officers "dived into the bed of Wire Gully" and established a post "about fifty yards in front of the line."[23] Louch's party "remained where we were and suffered casualties,"[24] partly through being enfiladed "from our left."[25] In 1999 the author found empty Mauser rifle charger clips on the inland southern shoulder of German Officers' Ridge. The only ground possibly occupied by ANZAC troops and visible from this position is the southern slope of Wire Gully, and April 1915 was the only time during the campaign that this area was occupied by allied troops. The clips may be therefore be relics of the Landing. If so, the Turk or Turks who fired from this spot may have belonged to 27th Regiment's advancing 3rd Battalion, or to withdrawing survivors of the original garrison (2nd Battalion). The range is very short.

Mofflin's position was also exposed to enfilade fire, "the most dangerous in warfare,"[26] from an enemy with a better knowledge of the ground. A party of Australians "straight across the gully from us ... hung on like grim death ... a sniper ... only a few yards in front of them" gave "us a hot time."[27] One bullet "whizzed in front of" Mofflin's "nose, caught the next man ... passed the next man and killed Captain Burns."[28] Nearby, Ed Inman had a "wonderful escape," when a bullet "cut the roof" of his "cap in two", grazing his head.[29]

Andrews was "crouching ... calm and cool as a cucumber"[30] near Mofflin. Every "time a bullet came near him" Andrews "would say 'Did you get me Guy?' and every now and again he would have a shot ... A bullet grazed his shoulder. 'Did you get me ...' Poor old Rajah, he never finalised his old saying, he got it just above the eye. Killed!"[31] The last Mofflin would see of his friend was his body being "passed out of the trench"[32] that night; Andrews has no known grave. Sergeant Arnold was at some stage also wounded in the hand, leaving Mofflin in charge of the platoon.[33]

Ed Inman's brother Jack had clambered into the trench with him, but, possibly as a consequence of intermixing of the reinforcements, "disappeared a few minutes later."[34] The brothers passed verbal messages along the line to each other, but after about 10:00 a.m. Ed received no reply. Soon after, three "of us were shot together. Young Paine[35] ... was shot dead. Jack Nelson got a bullet through the butt of his rifle, through his cheek and out his throat." Inman was hit "on the knuckle ... came out my wrist."[36]

20   *Ibid.* The decision to divert troops to support MacLagan is discussed further in the following chapter.
21   Bean, *Official History*, Volume I (1921 and 1941), p.228.
22   Louch, manuscript, p.15.
23   Bean, *Official History*, Volume I (1921 and 1941), p.431.
24   Louch, manuscript, p.15.
25   *Ibid.*
26   Mofflin, letter, 20 October 1915, p.19.
27   *Ibid.*
28   Mofflin, letter, 20 October 1915, p.19. Wren, *Randwick to Hargicourt*, p.54, confirms that the 3rd Battalion's adjutant, Captain Ronald Burns, was shot while directing fire.
29   Inman, diary, 25 April 1915.
30   Mofflin, letter, 20 October 1915, p.18.
31   *Ibid.*
32   *Ibid.*
33   Mofflin, letter, 20 October 1915, p.18.
34   Inman, diary, 25 April 1915.
35   Henry Arthur Paine, 22, labourer, or Torbay Junction, born Wagin. Official documents state that he was 22 at death, except for his enlistment papers which state that he was nearly 23 when he enlisted.
36   Inman, diary, 25 April 1915. 1203 Private Henry Arthur Paine, B Company, 22 at embarkation, labourer, of Torbay Junction, born Wagin.

Despite his wound, Inman did his best to bandage Nelson "but could not stop the bleeding."[37] He was forced to remain where he was, enduring everything the Turks threw at them, until nightfall, when it became possible to evacuate him. When he returned to Gallipoli in August he was stunned to discover that his brother had been missing since the Landing. Everyone "was surprised I did not know of Jack, they all thought he was with me."[38] Ed would search fruitlessly for information about his brother's fate or whereabouts. The only real clue lies in Mofflin's letter. Mofflin had written at the time that Andrews' "chum … Jack Inman got it in the head seriously wounded alongside him."[39] Sadly, Mofflin's family therefore knew more about Jack's fate than the Inmans, who would receive neither correspondence nor definite news about him. Jack Inman appears to have died after being dragged unconscious from the firing line and may be buried in an unmarked or unnamed grave behind Second Ridge.[40]

Nelson survived, was returned to Australia and discharged from the AIF. Henry Paine has no known grave. Two others named Pain in the 11th Battalion, William Pain[41] and George Pain,[42] were also wounded this day. Both Pain and Paine served in B Company. William Pain would return to Gallipoli to be wounded again at Leane's Trench.

Darnell positioned a forward patrol of scouts to observe 27th Regiment's arrival on the battlefield, then appears to have fought on Second Ridge, where the men dug "like fury … mere holes … but cover … We repulsed attack after attack," while subjected to lethal shell and machine gun fire.[43] "At last the 2nd Brigade arrived," then "the rest of the Division" and ammunition.[44] Darnell believed his forward patrol was later "wiped out by shrapnel."[45] Another member of B Company, L.A. Parsons,[46] despite "bullets flying at us" and men falling, reached "our objective on the second line of ridges, and held same for all we were worth until reinforcements came up."[47] Parsons' reference to Second Ridge as "our objective" reinforces the impression that the other ranks were either unaware of their true objectives, were confused by the terrain, or that their objectives had changed.

Newham's account also suggests Second Ridge to be their objective. He pushed forward early and "gained the point that we had started out to get … made our firing line, every second man digging … until every man was in … a little cover … I was ordered to go and fetch reinforcements."[48] Newham was attempting to return to the firing line when "a smash … laid me low … I tried to move but could not." He later spotted and called out to "my old mate," 26-year-old Wyalkatchem farmer "Bert Hamilton."[49] Newham later learned he had suffered six wounds from a single bullet, which "Bert" dressed "to the best of his ability … gave me a smoke" and a drink, and "shook hands … 'goodbye Sid [sic] old boy keep a good heart and you will be alright', I said 'Right ho Bert old bloke I'll do my best' … it was about 10:30 a.m.." Hamilton was shot in the side later that day but survived to serve until discharged in 1917.[50]

Denton established D Company's HQ behind the ridge in the vicinity of Courtney's Post. His men "were on the crest," one of his "platoons" being "out with Barnes … under Captain Croly,"[51]

37   Inman, diary, 25 April 1915.
38   *Ibid.*
39   Mofflin, letter, 20 October 1915, p.18.
40   J.P. Hurst, "A Mother's Pain", Wartime: the Official Magazine of the Australian War Memorial, Issue 30, 2005, pp.32–33.
41   1398 Private William Henry Pain, B Company, 25 at enlistment, miner, of Day Dawn, born Essex, England.
42   339 Private (at embarkation) George Harvey Pain, B Company, 23 at embarkation, fireman, of West Guildford, born Shropshire, England.
43   Darnell, PR82/175.
44   *Ibid.*
45   *Ibid.*
46   1168 Private Leslie Alfred Parsons, B Company, 25 at embarkation, farmer of Korrelocking, born South Australia.
47   Parsons, letter to Mr Williams, 4 August 1915, private collection.
48   Newham, "Recollections of a Returned Soldier", n.p.
49   1016 Private (at embarkation) Herbert Hamilton, C Company, 26 at embarkation, farmer, of Wyalkatchem, born London, England.
50   He also survived being torpedoed aboard the SS *Strathallan* on 21 December 1942.
51   Bean, *Official History*, Volume I (1921 and 1941), p.429.

though which platoon this could have been is not known: perhaps some of the wounded Walker's 14 Platoon had come forward. The question Bean raises is whether "Denton's men should be pushed further forward or retained to line the side of Monash Valley."[52] If Denton's "company" advanced "its only possible objective would be Mortar Ridge," whose toe lay directly opposite him, but "Denton understood ... his objective" to be "the edge of Monash Valley."[53] This reaffirms that attack had become defence. The logic behind the assumption that Mortar Ridge could be the only objective appears to be that, "when the Turkish attack began … from Scrubby Knoll ... it lapped onto Mortar Ridge," where a "Turkish line lodged itself, and from which it poured in its fire at only 300 yards' range upon the troops in front of Courtney's and Steele's."[54] Digging in Denton's area became impossible "from that moment," but withdrawing the line to the Monash Valley side of the ridge would have deprived it of observation and a field of fire. The troops were consequently left "lying on the forward slope," where they "could use their eyes and their rifles." Their "task was not to advance, but to hold on ... From 10 a.m. ... they were involved in a heavy and continuous contest of rifle-fire."[55]

At about 10:00 a.m. Brand "came along" and Denton "told him that I intended to defend the position I was on."[56] Denton "got a message" at about 11:30 a.m. "addressed to me as OC Left Flank to hold the ridge at all costs."[57] The Turks kept up "a murderous rifle and machine gun fire" and attacked "strongly from the left and in our centre."[58] To meet these attacks Denton "managed to secure about 3 machine guns and got as much ammo as I could."[59] The impression is clearly of a determination to hold Second Ridge, as confirmed by Bean, who described a "definite line" "of large posts" being established along "the edge of Monash Valley."[60]

Denton's account contains a jumble of incidents over several hours, but examination raises the question: what stopped Denton, the change of plans discussed in earlier chapters, or enemy pressure? By Bean's account, Second Ridge was made untenable by fire from Mortar Ridge after 57th Regiment's attack,[61] yet by his own timing, 3rd Brigade troops should have reached the area long before 57th Regiment.

If enemy fire forced Denton and others to ground on Second Ridge, it must have come initially from survivors of the area garrison (4 Company, 2/27th Regiment), and later from the counter-attacking 1st and 3rd Battalions, as confirmed by Bean's reference to the attack coming from Scrubby Knoll. Once again, it appears the fighting withdrawal of the survivors of the initial Australian onslaught, followed by Şefik's strategy of attacking early and on a broad front, paid dividends.

Very little is known of the experience of MacFarlane's and Rockliff's 3 and 4 Platoons. No accounts by either officer have come to light, but accounts by others may be linked to them. John Turner, probably 3 Platoon,[62] and Guy and Cockburn, both of 3 or 4 Platoon, appear to have fought in the vicinity of Second Ridge. Turner "dropped down and just held on, keeping the enemy back" while "in our spare time digging ourselves in,"[63] "in one long, thin line which neither shrapnel … machine gun … or rifle fire could shift."[64] Everyone "acted real well … especially our machine gun

---

52 *Ibid.*, p.426.
53 *Ibid.*, p.427.
54 *Ibid.*, pp.428–29.
55 *Ibid.*, p.429.
56 Denton, letter, 16 June 1920.
57 *Ibid.*
58 *Ibid.*
59 Denton, letter, 16 June 1920.
60 Bean, *Official History*, Volume I (1921 and 1941), p.429.
61 *Ibid.*, p.289.
62 Turner was a member of the original A Company. MacFarlane counter-signed a letter Turner wrote about the Landing, and wrote to his parents after his death at Leane's Trench, suggesting Turner belonged to MacFarlane's 3 Platoon.
63 Turner, letter, 25 June 1915.
64 J.W.G. Turner, letter to father, 14 May 1915, Ellam-Innes Collection.

sections. Their fire was very deadly indeed."[65] Cockburn also appears to have occupied a trench well inland, "which we held until reinforcements came up."[66] The ensuing battle was "something terrible. I never wish to be in as hot a place again with bullets. We hung onto this trench all day … showered" with shrapnel. The "worst of it was we didn't know whether we were hitting the enemy … couldn't see them … all we could do was to fire into the scrub. They knew we were occupying their old trench and they knew just where to fire."[67]

Cockburn's description could refer to many parts of the battlefield, but certainly matches the fighting on Second Ridge and echoes the common experience of strain, endurance, heavy small arms fire and shrapnel. Guy may have been further south as he fought with the 10th Battalion: "we found the main body of the enemy and we had to dig in … not … easy" as "we were in a veritable hell of lead and shrapnel."[68] "Everyone was separated from his comrades and his company, but we took orders from the nearest officer."[69] Guy's "thoughts were occupied – as much as the enemy would let them be" with the fate of his company, but he "could not leave my hole owing to the fire … Men were dropping all around and the stretcher bearers and Medical Staff did prodigious valour."[70]

Ottoman bullets and shrapnel forced the more fortunate men into trenches, holes, gullies or other indentations and the others to keep low, where many found they could see little but a wall of scrub. Tangled terrain and the smoke of battle added to the impression of isolation of such parties. Hearder became increasingly concerned about his flanks. For the first "half hour," "our boys appeared some distance" away "on our right. Eventually a small body came up about 100 yards on our left rear … but I did not know what battalion … nor their number."[71]

After leaving Plugge's, Brennan passed "a lot of wounded Turks … they had no field dressings like our men carry. I gave some morphia to a few of them, but most of them spat it out."[72] Brennan, Wright and an unknown number of their section made the stiff climb to Second Ridge, believing "lots" of "Turks lay down under bushes and sniped our men off after they had passed."[73] The "Turks were reinforcing strongly" when Brennan reached the ridge, and the Australian units "fearfully mixed up." Denton "and about half a dozen of our men" were nearby; the others were from "a mixture of battalions. I found myself in [a] trench with some machine gun supports, and borrowed a bit of their trench to haul wounded into and to dress there."[74] Here, "just below Courtneys," Brennan established the 11th Battalion's Regimental Aid Post (RAP).[75] Wright, who was "a little further along the line,"[76] would later be Mentioned in Despatches for "conspicuous gallantry or valuable service," which included managing the available stretcher-bearers, who retrieved and evacuated the wounded under fire in very trying circumstances.[77]

After retiring from Adana Bair, Leane's observer was determined to withdraw no further "and we did not." Then commenced "that tremendous rifle fire … fearful and everlasting … wonderful in its awfulness."[78] After resting near HQ, Brodribb returned to the line, shrapnel bursting "right along … The stretcher bearers worked themselves to a standstill, some of the poor chaps being shot down right

65   Turner, letter, 14 May 1915.
66   Cockburn, diary, 28 April 1915.
67   *Ibid.*
68   Guy, letter, 10 May 1915.
69   *Ibid.*
70   *Ibid.*
71   Hearder, manuscript 3DRL 3959, p.13.
72   Brennan, letter, 1915, Army Museum of Western Australia.
73   *Ibid.*
74   *Ibid.*
75   Everett, interview, Ellam-Innes Collection, p.242.
76   Brennan, letter, 1915, Army Museum of Western Australia.
77   Gill, Fremantle to France, pp.370–71. MID *London Gazette* 29354, 5 November 1915.
78   Anonymous, Leane's observer, manuscript.

and left whilst carrying their burdens."[79] Combs also returned to the line at "about 11.00 a.m. ... The enemy" was attacking in strength, "the only thing we could do was to fight to a finish ... we were not very strong ... other brigades were still landing. We opened on to these large masses of Turks with our rifles as fast as ever we possibly could."[80] Rifles "became so hot, we could hardly move the bolts."[81]

In such accounts may lie the seeds of one thread of the legend and myth of 25 April. The perception of fighting hordes of an outnumbering enemy is almost universal. Murphy wrote that "the Turks could have overrun us had they had enough courage"[82] and Brodribb thought the "odds 10 to 1."[83] This perception is probably due to battle stress, pre-battle briefings, fragmentation, inexperience, poor visibility and the nature of the battle. Many men could see the enemy advancing, not only to their front, but from Baby 700 in the north and 400 Plateau in the south, but their own side, dispersed and prone in the scrub, were often invisible.

To Combs' relief, "the *Queen Elizabeth* ... put" two "14 inch shells fair into" the advancing Turks "and a more terrible sight one will never see ... pieces of Turk and dirt were blown everywhere, rifles, pieces of shrubs." Those shells "saved us ... we would never have been able to hold them back ... after ... we pretty well got the lot with rifles and machine gun fire."[84] Combs was then "sent away" for reinforcements. As he returned, "a stream" of Turkish fire divided his party and he was forced into "another part of the line."[85]

Looking back, probably from the vicinity of Pope's Hill, Medcalf could see transports, battleships, pinnaces, boats and destroyers supporting the landings. A "continuous stream of reinforcements continued to land and advance to the help of those" clinging to the ridges. "Things were fearfully hot at times, and the noise was deafening."[86] Casualties continued to mount. Medcalf recalled "many still forms ... past human aid"[87] and Cockburn "a terrible lot of dead, dying and wounded."[88] The stretcher bearers worked as Medcalf "had never seen men work before,"[89] yet many wounded had to be left "in the firing line until dark."[90] In Everett's section some wounded could be dragged by "their heels" to the seaward edge of the ridge where they could be "pulled over the sudden drop."[91] They were replaced by "1st, 3rd, 7th and 8th"[92] Battalion men arriving from the gully behind.

Everett eventually occupied a forward trench, about "50 to 80 yards in"[93] from the seaward crest, from where he had good observation of enemy movements inland from Second Ridge, particularly of the left flank. Throughout the day he would send "exceedingly accurate reports"[94] to 3rd Brigade HQ, and in coming days would consolidate his position and, despite frequent casualties, continue the good work. The reports were passed back to Denton, who passed them by phone to the brigade, and as a consequence Denton was later decorated. Denton was not "so far forward" as Everett, but "got the DSO."[95]

---

79   Brodribb, letter, 17 July 1915.
80   Combs, manuscript.
81   *Ibid.*
82   Murphy, letter, *Sunday Times*, 6 June 1915.
83   Brodribb, letter, 17 July 1915.
84   Combs, manuscript.
85   *Ibid.*
86   *Ibid.*
87   Medcalf, manuscript, p.66.
88   Cockburn, diary, 28 April 1915.
89   Medcalf, manuscript, p.66.
90   Cockburn, diary, 28 April 1915.
91   Everett, Ellams-Innes Collection.
92   *Ibid.*
93   Brockman, 3DRL 606 item 27.
94   *Ibid.*
95   *Ibid.*

The cries of "Stretcher-bearer wanted on the right" and "Stretcher-bearer wanted on the left" imprinted themselves on Brockman's memory that day.[96] "Considering the risks" "Doc" Brennan took, "he ought to have been outed a hundred times, but he never got a scratch."[97] Brennan's courage and dedication were admired by many, one man writing that he "deserves the DSO for the work he did under fire. The stretcher bearers are all heroes."[98] Brennan was also "indefatigable in hauling up food," ammunition and water and "passing it over the top."[99] He ensured "that everyone who came up brought some. He took rations and ammunition from the wounded and stored them in the first aid post, passing them up as required."[100]

The casualties and increasing pressure were due only in part to the arrival of more Turkish infantry on the field. When Kemal arrived in mid to late morning, he effectively took command of the Turkish forces in the area. A relieved Şefik relinquished command[101] and with 57th Regiment attacking on his right and Kemal taking responsibility for the front as a whole, was able to focus on his primary intention of driving the invaders to his front into the sea.

The passing of noon had little relevance to the course of the battle and appears to have had little significance to the men fighting it. A midday meal was impossible for most. Howe referred to men in the vicinity of Baby 700 being fortunate enough to "brew up" during a morning lull in the fighting, but most later noted having little interest in food. Mofflin dealt with the morning's stresses by smoking, which created a great thirst but he remained disciplined and "would not touch my water."[102] Medcalf wrote that with "every nerve and particle of energy ... concentrated on keeping the Turk at a respectable distance," nobody "thought of eating or drinking;" nor was there time to feel "nervy."[103]

Newman had joined Stopp and spent the remainder of 25 April with the 10th Battalion.[104] A reference to Stopp in Bean's notes illustrates the nature of the fighting in the area. A 12th Battalion party isolated at the head of Owen's Gully could see "men in a trench about 600 yards north" – Lieutenant Stopp's party. Turks were "concentrating" nearby, and the Australians launched a local bayonet charge. The men were seen to parry and "mix" with the Turks, who "ran back ... our men retired. A little later 2 white flags came up from Turkish side ... one minute our men were signing to Turks to put down their arms ... next minute they were out 'mixing it' again with [the] line of Turks behind."[105]

Şefik describes a similar incident, though from his observation it was the Australians who attempted to surrender. On the 400 Plateau, two parties "attacked one another with bayonets and some sprang to their feet and fired. Other Australians jumped up waving handkerchiefs and beckoning with their hands ... Our men assumed ... the Australians ... were surrendering ... Our naïve but brave men ... told the Australians, by signs, to surrender." The Australians indicated that the Turks should surrender. When a Turk seized an Australian's rifle "another Australian fired at our man" and "a bombardier from Ankara, Ismail Oglu Ahmed" concealed nearby, threw a grenade. The Australians leapt for cover, some fell wounded and others "ran off. This deceitful handkerchief waving trick was repeated" later that day.[106]

Wounded and in great pain, Newham lay surrounded by the "horrid noises of the dying the moans and groans of those who were fighting with death, for the last few drops of lifes [sic] blood." With shrapnel "bursting all around" and "bullets ... chopping up the ground," he waited "for the next one"

96   Brockman, letter, 25 May 1915.
97   Ibid.
98   Anonymous scout, letter, 15 May 1915.
99   Everett, interview, Ellam-Innes Collection, p.242.
100 Ibid.
101 Şefik, para. 115.
102 Mofflin, letter, 20 October 1915, p.18.
103 Medcalf, manuscript, p.65.
104 Lock, The Fighting 10th, pp.213–14.
105 3DRL 606 item 143.
106 Şefik, para. 137.

to "finish me off."[107] Through the noise, he heard a familiar voice and called out to "Harry Bauswell." H.G. Buswell,[108] was a well-known footballer in Bunbury and a lumper on the town's docks. Newham had also worked as a labourer in Bunbury, which may explain how the two knew each other. "By God Woodward it is you Newham," replied Buswell. Buswell "put his finger down" Newham's "throat and took out a lot of congealed blood, then washed my mouth out and gave me a drink." Buswell returned with two stretcher bearers who, "under a heavy shower of bullets and shrapnel," endeavoured to get the wounded man into a trench. Eventually, Newham began walking and with "the blood flowing out of my wounds, and my mouth," frequent faints, rests, and the assistance of the bearers, "pegged along" until reaching the end of the trench. His estimate of having his first rest "after going about a hundred yards or so, which I thought was a mile or so in my weak state," evidences the extent of the Turkish trenches dug in this area before 25 April. Newham somehow reached an aid post,[109] where his case was assessed as hopeless until protests from stretcher bearer and patient convinced the doctor otherwise. Blood-soaked bandages were cut away, wounds cleaned and bound and morphia injected.

Despite the morphia and doing "all in my power to keep from making a noise," the agony of "raw wounds" aggravated by "strong Iodine" proved too much. Newham "begged the attendant to give me something to put me out of the way and out of pain but he tried to cheer me up the best he could."[110] Newham would spend the remainder of the year in hospitals and be invalided to Perth with bullet wounds in the right forearm, a compound fracture of the "chest wall … fractures left arm, through both lungs." His war was well and truly over and he was discharged the following year, aged 26. In 1931 he confided in a letter that "my health is failing fast and I am expected to go out any time."[111] Boer War veteran Buswell survived the Gallipoli campaign but was killed at Pozieres the following year. He did not live to hear of the Military Medal he would be awarded for fighting at Leane's Trench on 1 August 1915.[112] One of his brothers would also be killed on the Western Front.

Fahey spent the first day ministering to the spiritual and physical needs of wounded near the beach. He thought the wounded and dying Australians "splendid":

> I am so glad to be associated with them. Nothing could excel their courage and reckless daring and their cheerfulness in the most trying positions. Those men who found discipline irksome in camp, and growled about small things, will now face death with a smile, growl at nothing and bear the most cruel wounds … I have seen men come in with very little face left, but the little that they had was decorated with a cigarette, and a faint attempt at a smile. I have never heard a wounded man groan.[113]

One of four scouts establishing an observation post on Second Ridge wrote that observing was "trying work," as bullets and shrapnel cut the leaves from the "trees around us." "Scout Porter was hit in the head. It was my first sight of blood … tied him up as best we could … forced to retire with Porter."[114] Perhaps this describes the true fate of the post Darnell believed had been wiped out by shell fire.

All three men named Porter serving with the 11th Battalion were wounded at the Landing. John Porter,[115] B Company, was wounded in the left thigh and evacuated.[116] William Porter,[117] a veteran of the Royal Irish Rifles, had been among the first recruits to travel to Perth from Geraldton. On 25 April

107 Newham, "Recollections of a Returned Soldier", n.p.
108 859 Private Henry George Buswell, D Company, 31 at embarkation, lumper, of Bunbury.
109 Newham, "Recollections of a Returned Soldier", n.p.
110 *Ibid.*
111 B2455, Newham.
112 Gill, *Fremantle to France*, pp.102–103.
113 J. Fahey, letter to archbishop of Perth, Patrick Clune, Advocate 31 July and 7 August 1915, quoted McKernan, Padre, pp.51–52.
114 Anonymous scout, letter, 15 May 1915.
115 1013 Private (at embarkation) John Porter, B Company, 20 at embarkation, carpenter of Jolimont, born London, England.
116 His wounds forced his discharge from the AIF.
117 820 Private William Porter, D Company, 33 at enlistment, labourer, of Geraldton, born Londonderry, Ireland.

he was probably with 13 Platoon when he was hit in the arm and evacuated.[118] Thomas Hedley Porter[119] served 18 months in South Africa with the 4th Contingent, West Australian Imperial Bushmen. His experience on the veldt would probably have been an asset to the scouts of a newly formed battalion, and, as he was wounded in the head on 25 April, appears to be the "scout Porter" referred to.[120]

"After seeing" the wounded Porter "safely on his way … we made our way safely up the valley … [past] many wounded, all trying to look brave." "Arundle," probably R.L. Arundale,[121] "and I met Corporal Hughes[122] of the platoon"[123] and "decided to remain together … went into the firing line on our right. It was warm work." A "machine gun in front of us," presumably one of 27th Regiment's, was "singing" "like a sewing machine," "but the bullets were just a foot too high." Three days later, while stalking Turkish snipers, Arundale was shot through the head and killed alongside the narrator. The two had been "the best of pals."[124] The location of Arundale's body is today unknown.[125] Lance Corporal Hughes was wounded in the ankle in mid-May. He returned to Gallipoli to succumb to influenza and was returned to Australia the following year.

From Second Ridge many men could see fragments of the bitter struggles raging elsewhere and spare a thought for those fighting them. Cockburn watched Anzac troops, probably on Baby 700, getting "it terrible hot" and retreating "about 200 yards."[126] Mofflin watched the Turks "trying to force our right flank," presumably 400 Plateau:

> Our lads charging them, then retiring … a red cross man helping two wounded … through a perfect hell … a shell burst near them and I saw no more … a wounded man limping back … I saw him go shooting up in the air spreadeagled … a shell burst under him … Our trench would have been untenable if our right flank had fallen back.

A small party, probably in Wire Gully, "saved us … they hung on like grim death till an Indian Mountain Gun" arrived.[127]

Cockburn thought this mountain battery "came up about midday" and "was a great help" until "knocked out but they got it going again."[128] This was the 26th (Jacob's) Indian Mountain Battery which, according to Bean, came ashore at 10:30 a.m., made its way to 400 Plateau and opened fire from "close behind the crest" at five minutes before noon.[129] For the men in the firing lines, the "mere sound of" these guns "came … like a draught of cool water to one perishing from thirst."[130] Many men consequently refer to the valiant efforts of this battery, though its value as a geographical reference point is diminished by the fact that it was visible from much of the battlefield – including the Turkish positions on Battleship Hill and other heights.

---

118 William Porter had served in India, Africa and Burma during nearly 16 years with the Royal Irish Rifles. He returned to the battalion in July, was badly wounded in the left shoulder, hip, right arm and head in the fighting for Leane's Trench, and died of his wounds in Alexandria.

119 204 Private Thomas Hedley Porter, A Company, 38 at enlistment, miner, of Fremantle, born Yorke Peninsula, South Australia.

120 T.H. Porter returned to the unit on 5 May. He later served with the 44th Battalion, was commissioned and badly wounded on the Western Front, but survived the war to return home in 1919 with the "1914 men."

121 10 Private Rupert Louis Arundale, A Company, 22 at embarkation, civil servant of North Perth, born Manchester, England.

122 55 Lance Corporal Arthur Hughes, A Company, 24 at enlistment, stereotyper of Como, born Durham, England.

123 Anonymous scout, letter, 15 May 1915.

124 *Ibid.*

125 In July 1916 Arundale's identity disc was sent to his next of kin. Perhaps his body was lost in the chaos of the Landing, or was unrecoverable but his "pal" managed to retrieve his identity disc; or perhaps the grave's location was lost after the evacuation, as the Turkish garrison used the wooden crosses for firewood.

126 Cockburn, diary, 28 April 1915.

127 Mofflin, letter, 20 October 1915, p.19.

128 Cockburn, diary, 28 April 1915.

129 Bean, *Official History*, Volume I (1921 and 1941), p.393–94.

130 *Ibid.*, p.394.

The "first reinforcements" Cockburn recalled were New Zealanders. These were probably predominantly of the Auckland Battalion, New Zealand Infantry Brigade, New Zealand and Australian Division. The Auckland troops were supposed to be reinforcing "the Australians on the left,"[131] but some of them responded "to cries of 'reinforcements'" from "the hard-pressed"[132] Second Ridge. Historian Christopher Pugsley adds that it was the threat of Turkish soldiers "advancing in open formation" against German Officer's Trench, Johnston's Jolly and Lone Pine Plateau and the "intensity of the Turkish counter-attack against Second Ridge,"[133] that "drew New Zealanders piecemeal into the defence of Second Ridge."[134] Bean thought the first New Zealand troops reached Monash Valley after noon.[135]

This confirms that the battle was getting out of hand. The commanders of a force larger than a division, opposed by probably only five battalions, thought they were fighting for their lives against a superior force attacking their whole front, and continued to divert troops from their prescribed objectives to fighting elsewhere. The course of the battle had been dictated early by Şefik's strategy of vigorous attack and difficulties in accurately determining what was happening on the battlefield.[136] There may also be a simple geographical reason why New Zealand troops drifted to Second Ridge. Troops ordered to reinforce the left[137] tended on reaching the end of Shrapnel Gully to begin climbing the hillside ahead of them. This is not the seaward side of Baby 700 but Second Ridge, as the valley changes direction and continues on as Monash Valley. Some troops who made this error were sent on by MacLagan or his staff,[138] but some joined the battle here, depriving the troops on the high ground of support.

Aitken left a graphic and much quoted account of the Landing but it is unclear where he fought. In the "first rush" he had lost "Macs,"[139] possibly Daniel McCallum,[140] "and in fact the whole Battalion."[141] In the afternoon Aitken's party "had to take up an entrenched position forward for we knew they would come back with reinforcements."[142] The reference to only a single move during the day suggests Second Ridge, though losing the battalion makes 400 Plateau a possibility. Aitken also endured the relentless, "deadly and awful" shrapnel:

> [A] single well placed shot will wipe out dozens and it inflicts the most terrifying gaping wounds … It's no good saying I wasn't afraid after the 1st intoxication had died down, for I was; at first the shrapnel had me shivering and the hail of bullets made me duck, but I think I'm over all that now.[143]

Bean wrote that Brockman, after arriving at Second Ridge, "went around the position as far as it concerned him."[144] There must have been more to this, from a military perspective, than stated. Did

---

131 C. Pugsley, *Gallipoli: The New Zealand Story* (Auckland: Hodder and Stoughton, 1990), p.117.
132 *Ibid.*, p.136.
133 *Ibid.*
134 *Ibid.*
135 Bean, *Official History*, Volume I (1921 and 1941), p.302.
136 The information about Turkish troops advancing from Third Ridge was probably many hours old before the New Zealanders reinforced the firing lines, and demonstrates the "blurring" of events and chronology in western sources; without the benefit of Şefik's account, it would be assumed that the Ottoman infantry were continually reinforced by troops advancing to the attack across Legge and Mule Valleys.
137 Pugsley, *Gallipoli: The New Zealand Story*, p.117.
138 Bean, *Official History*, Volume I (1921 and 1941), p.302.
139 Aitken, letter/diary, p.20.
140 687 Private (at embarkation) Daniel McCallum, C Company, 11 Platoon, 21 at embarkation, bank clerk, of Kalgoorlie, born Bendigo.
141 Aitken, letter/diary, p.20.
142 *Ibid.*, p.19.
143 Aitken, letter/diary, pp.18, 20.
144 Brockman, 3DRL 606 item 27.

Brockman, for example, confer with Denton or MacLagan? Why wasn't he fighting for the objectives on the high ground, especially as, after the diversion of the majority of the brigade to Second Ridge, his company was the only one officially despatched that way? The answer is probably that three of his platoons had ended up on Second Ridge, and we can only presume Brockman was trying to make contact with his scattered parties, determine the tactical situation and establish the state of the 11th Battalion. It is also unclear whether the words "went around the position" are Brockman's or Bean's, but either way, the latter's notes suggest those of a man preparing to write a narrative rather than an examination, and Brockman's and other officers' actions to organising for defence rather than attack.

Brockman's movements for the remainder of the day are unclear, but as his and Bean's references from that time on refer only to Second Ridge, it can be presumed he served there for the afternoon, planning the defence of the ridge. Despite having to "either … run or crawl"[145] to reach the forward 11th Battalion posts, Brockman twice "endeavoured to confer with" Croly "in the rifle pits on" German Officers' Ridge. During his second attempt Company Sergeant Major G.F. Charles[146] "was hit through the chest."[147] Charles was "with difficulty got back,"[148] apparently to Brennan's aid post, and evacuated the following morning.[149] "Movement over Second Ridge, wrote Bean, "was clearly impossible during daylight."[150]

A conflict of command developed here, with important consequences for the future of this portion of the front. 11th Battalion headquarters appears to have remained on Plugge's Plateau, and 3rd Brigade headquarters was on the seaward slope of Second Ridge. According to Bean, individual posts were commanded by the "officer who first occupied" the area, "so long as he kept alive."[151] Brockman, arriving at MacLaurin's Hill shortly before noon, was "the senior officer on the ridge during the midday hours"[152] and believed that, as the senior major in the 3rd Brigade, he was the ranking officer forward of MacLagan's HQ. He thought the Australian line along Second Ridge should have been on the inland crest, "overlooking Mule Valley," rather than "hanging … by its finger-nails along the rim of" Shrapnel and Monash Valleys.[153] He consequently "had several mixed platoons under Lieutenant Darnell … and other officers ready to push out over the crest after dark in order to form this line. But," adds Bean, "between the detachments of the 11th Battalion there were now a greater number of the 3rd."[154] The 3rd Battalion's second-in-command, Major A.J. Bennett, arrived during the afternoon and from that time "there were two separate commanders issuing orders to two different sets of troops on the same sector of MacLaurin's Hill." Bennett "was senior" to Brockman and did not approve of Brockman's plan.[155] Colonel R.H. Owen, who moved his 3rd Battalion headquarters from Plugge's Plateau to Steele's Post in the afternoon, summoned Brockman and "told him that he would not send the men out to form a line" forward:

> until he had himself reconnoitred the place. From that time Colonel Owen definitely assumed the command on MacLaurin's Hill … He received his instructions from MacLagan … 400 yards away … his

---

145 *Ibid.*

146 162 Company Sergeant Major George Frederick Charles, A Company, 37 at embarkation, labourer of Perth, born Birmingham, England.

147 Bean, *Official History*, Volume I (1921 and 1941), p.438. Charles was apparently wounded at about 8:00 p.m.

148 Brockman, 3DRL 606 item 27.

149 Charles continued to serve, and in the Second World War attempted to enlist in 1941, at the age of 63, by claiming to be 48. He was discharged in November 1941, but re-enlisted the following day.

150 Bean, *Official History*, Volume I (1921 and 1941), p.438.

151 *Ibid.*, p.438.

152 *Ibid.*, pp.438–39.

153 *Ibid.*, p.438.

154 *Ibid.*,.p.439.

155 *Ibid.*, p.439.

own orders were carried out mainly through his three majors immediately behind the front line – Brown at the southern end ... Bennett in the centre; Lamb at the northern end ... and through Major Denton.[156]

Brockman is not mentioned.

It is difficult to know whether Bean's overview evidences diplomacy, a journalist's background or other factors, but this issue is probably of greater significance than it suggests. In essence Bennett had "clearly thought that Brockman would go on with his plans and got Owen to stop him."[157] Brockman "was very keen" to get "the line forward ... their present position was militarily absurd ... He had grabbed a company of the 16th to help. When Bennett took over he took these from him,"[158] and "nothing was done that night to get the line out."[159]

Whether it was possible to advance the line and hold it as Brockman planned is not known, but the possible consequences of moving the line forward were great. The seaward crest of Second Ridge was an inferior position to the forward one. Gaining a field of fire over Mule Valley could have altered the course of the battle in this area, both that day and throughout the coming months. During the campaign many lives would be lost in raids, attempted advances and defence of such places as the Chessboard and Quinn's Post. These might have been saved if the line had been pushed forward early and held. Commanding the valley may also have threatened Turkish access to 400 Plateau, with unknown consequences on the future of Lone Pine. But it was not to be.

Brockman wrote to his wife that:

[it] fell to me to organise the leaderless, get them into the firing line, and do what was possible, to do the impossible, until reinforcements came. It was awful and yet grand the way that all ranks lay down in the open under a merciless rain of shrapnel, machine gun, and rifle fire ... I longed for the night in order that we might scratch holes ... Until we could get dug in I was desperately afraid that we would be swept out by sheer weight of numbers.[160]

His own "narrow escapes" were[161] "too numerous to mention ... Some tell me I am foolhardy ... I had to be ... a display of anything but absolute assurance, callous indifference to bullets, dead and wounded and the display of a sort of sporting enthusiasm, might have meant disaster."[162]

This might not be just bravado on Brockman's part. Fox wrote that "Our officers were great ... to see Major Brockman ... smoking a cigarette and calmly walking up and down the line, was something to inspire at the time."[163]

Brockman recalled the "dead and wounded and dying, the truly awful sights, the heroic actions of individuals and whole bodies of men"; the "rattle of musketry, the infernal rat-tat-tat of the machine guns, the bursting of shrapnel, lyddite, hand grenades ... guns of the warships, and the terrible explosions ... on the other side."[164] Of interest is the Australian reference to grenades. Grenades had not been issued to the Australians, who were not trained in their use. Later they would be synonymous with Turkish trench fighting, but references in Australian sources to their use at the Landing are rare. The noise of the fighting left Brockman "deaf for days."[165] Alvie Clifton,[166] of

156 Bean, *Official History*, Volume I (1921 and 1941), p.439.
157 Brockman, 3DRL 606 item 27.
158 *Ibid.*
159 *Ibid.*
160 Brockman, letter, 25 May 1915.
161 *Ibid.*
162 *Ibid.*
163 Fox, "I Was There", p.8.
164 Brockman, letter, 25 May 1915.
165 *Ibid.*
166 155 Private Alvared Roe Cecil Clifton, A Company, 24 at enlistment, labourer, of Perth.

Medcalf's section, was also rendered "stone deaf" from "midday on Sunday" by noise, including "heavy rifle fire."[167] Clifton's section lost him mid-morning in Shrapnel Gully and presumed him to have been "bowled over early in the piece;"[168] he rejoined the battalion the following Friday.

11th Battalion accounts reflect a determination to hold Second Ridge, regardless of punishment. Medcalf described Turkish artillery and infantry "from the direction of Hill 971" trying to "break our left wing. The country rose inland from the left," enabling "the enemy to bring enfilade fire onto … our line … musketry rose in an increasing crescendo" and shrapnel inflicted "much damage."[169] He had seen enough of the battlefield to add ominously that "The Turks appeared to be getting the upper hand."[170] He "lost touch" with Brockman and found himself fighting at what would become Courtney's Post. "A shallow trench had been dug; two machine guns were close by; and good rifle practise was to be had on the enemy" advancing in short rushes "at 400 or 500 yards distance,"[171] possibly referring to Mortar Ridge.

The enemy's successful advances in the vicinity of Baby 700 also enabled them to threaten the rear areas of the ANZAC position. Brennan's post behind Courtney's "got very warm" later in the "afternoon … Turks got round … our left," from where their bullets "could get" the front and rear of the position "and we had to dig in as quickly as possible." This added to Brennan's difficulties with "removal of the wounded … We could do practically nothing till dark, and even then there were snipers about. Many stretcher bearers were wounded … all day … the valley was swept by shrapnel."[172] Steep terrain presented an added difficulty for the hard-working bearers.

Denton's section was attacked "strongly from the left"[173] and from the front "we were repulsing … Turkish charges. But our rifle fire … broke them each time. I refrained from going out to them … as were just on the ridge with I did not know what behind us." Had the Turks forced their way across Second Ridge, "they would have split us in two",[174] probably resulting in disaster for the landing forces. "Altogether it was a very anxious time from the middle of the afternoon until next morning."[175]

Darnell, somewhere nearby, described the Turks coming "on in dense mobs and we simply mowed them down."[176] Cockburn thought the enemy "like rabbits in the scrub and very artful"[177] and Wood, possibly with Selby, that they were "so well entrenched and concealed that it was very difficult to see them."[178] Wood described standing "fast" all day, "the fire was terrific."[179] Harvey and "Dick" Pleydell,[180] also possibly with Selby, were "hanging like flies on to a cliff with the enemy about 50 yards away."[181] Harvey had been shot through the hat for the second time and was "very wild about it."[182] At some time during the day, while he and Pleydell were firing "as fast" as they "could load and aim," Harvey was shot in the shoulder.[183] He was evacuated but lost his left arm.

167 Clifton, letter, n.d., Ellam-Innes Collection, Perth.
168 Medcalf, manuscript, p.83.
169 *Ibid.*, pp.65–66.
170 *Ibid.*, p.66.
171 *Ibid.*, p.66.
172 Brennan, letter, 1915, Army Museum of Western Australia.
173 Denton, 3DRL 8042 item 7.
174 *Ibid.*
175 Brennan, letter, 1915, Army Museum of Western Australia.
176 Darnell, PR82/175.
177 Cockburn, diary, 28 April 1915.
178 Wood, letter, 3 May 1915.
179 *Ibid.*
180 218 Private Arthur Deacon Pleydell, A Company, 23 at embarkation, clerk, born Mortlake, Victoria.
181 Medcalf, manuscript, p.82.
182 *Ibid.*
183 Medcalf, manuscript, p.82.

Figure 27. The Chessboard, Second Ridge and 400 Plateau from the seaward approaches to Baby 700. The large Turkish monument (centre) marks the position of the Chessboard. The white monument on the knoll beyond and to its right marks Courtney's Post, and the large white pillar in the background (left) is at Lone Pine on 400 Plateau. Gabe Tepe is the point just visible above the trees to its right. (Photograph by J.P. Hurst, n.d., author's collection)

Hastings, probably also on the left of Second Ridge, wrote of shrapnel "cutting our men up terribly."[184] 1 Platoon's Forbes was detached from A Company, and his reference to being on the right with "another lot" suggests he fought[185] on MacLaurin's Hill, 400 Plateau or the ridges to the south. Forbes was hit in the back by a shrapnel ball while trying to advance during the afternoon. Soon after "I was in the small 'dug-outs' with another platoon," when hit by "shrapnel in the right wrist."[186] With no control of his hand, Forbes "put a ligature round my biceps to stop the bleeding, bandaged the wrist as well as I could" and was evacuated to "one of the transports."[187] The references to advances and "small dug-outs" provide clues as to Forbes' possible whereabouts. Frank Loud, 9th Battalion, had been forward with men from a number of battalions in "an old bomb proof shelter," and also[188] fought in or around the Turkish gun positions at the junction of Pine Ridge and 400 Plateau,[189] suggesting Forbes did also. References to enemy trenches are numerous, but dugouts rare.

Loud described a machine gun, "doing excellent work until put out of action by a shell."[190] Şefik also referred to "the broken parts of a machine gun which the Australians had used" in this area until suffering "a direct hit from our artillery." Here, "both sides had fought fiercely."[191] Şefik appeared to be describing 400 Plateau, and Loud the positions at the top of Pine Ridge. Whether the two accounts refer to the same gun is not known.

Two men now buried at Shell Green probably also fought in this area. David Lees[192] was originally buried on 2 May 1915 "over 3rd Inf Brigade HQ," presumably on the seaward side of Second Ridge. T.W. Stokes[193] was buried "by foot of Artillery Road on Shell Green," suggesting he too fought

---

184 Hastings, letter, 10 June 1915.
185 Forbes, letter, 29 May 1915.
186 *Ibid.*
187 Forbes, letter, 29 May 1915.
188 F. Loud, diary, *Journal of the Australian War Memorial*, April 1990, p.68.
189 Unpublished paper, J.P. Hurst, "'Did anyone see a gun?', The vexed question of Ottoman machine guns at the Gallipoli Landing, Z Beach, 4.30 a.m., 25 April 1915".
190 Loud, diary, p.68.
191 Şefik, para. 137.
192 318 Lance Corporal David Lees, B company, 45 at enlistment, engine driver of Kununoppin, born Goulburn.
193 946 Private Thomas William Stokes, HQ and D Company, 20 at embarkation, engine cleaner, of Bunbury, born Geraldton.

Figure 28. Second Ridge, the reverse view to Figure 27, showing Wire Gully (in the foreground), the Chessboard, Baby 700 (marked by the solitary tree on the skyline), Battleship Hill and Chunuk Bair (the trees and monument on crest, right). MacLaurin's Hill is marked by the ascending road (centre). (Photograph by J.P. Hurst, n.d., author's collection)

on Second Ridge, 400 Plateau or further south.[194] Boer War veteran Henry Riekie[195] also appears to have fought in this area. At some stage during the day he was wounded, and as he lay behind the firing lines, must have realised he was dying. Australia and loved ones must have seemed very remote indeed; among Riekie's last words to a wounded West Australian of the 12th Battalion lying nearby, was a request to look after his family. The 12th Battalion man survived to return to Western Australia, married Riekie's widow and became father to and provider for Riekie's five children.[196]

One recurrent theme in 11th Battalion accounts of the day is the intensity and severity of Turkish artillery fire. Darnell described the "shell … and machine gun fire" as "Hell, no other word for it"[197] and Denton as "a hell" he never wanted "to go through" again.[198] Leane later wrote to David Crisp's[199] sister that "no-one who was not there can realise just what everyone went through during the first three days."[200] Aitken wrote of "carnage" that "was simply awful and I saw sights that sickened me Mother."[201] Newham described "the screams" of shrapnel shells being "like a little child getting beaten

194 B2455, Stokes. Two more, Sergeant F. Matthews and Lance Sergeant W.J. Garland, were killed on 3 May. Garland was killed when the 11th Battalion occupied trenches in the area.
195 1170 Private Henry John Riekie, A Company, 36, grocer, of Subiaco, born Fitzroy.
196 Correspondence between N. Riekie and J.P. Hurst, 2011–2013. B2455, Riekie; B2455, J.W. Wood.
197 Darnell, PR82/175.
198 Denton, 3DRL 8042 item 7.
199 641 Private David Harold Crisp, C Company, 26 at embarkation, miner, of Boulder, born Maryborough, Victoria.
200 R.L. Leane, letter to M. Crisp, *Kalgoorlie Miner*, 17 August 1915. The letter was written after Crisp's death in June.
201 Aitken, letter/diary, p.19.

badly," while larger shells were like "a woman screaming … as though she was being murdered."[202] Fahey thought shrapnel "horrible," its wounds "awful," tearing and mangling "men … in the most cruel manner."[203] "It explodes with a fearful noise and literally ploughs the ground. It makes strong men quail. I have seen men come in untouched, but complete idiots, nerve-wracked from the effects of shrapnel fire."[204] He saw "strong men" temporarily deranged by shells "bursting near them and tearing men to pieces."[205]

The infantry, "completely unsupported by artillery," were, "struggling against a weapon which was out of their range. A deep catching of the breath, a cry after each shower of shrapnel, told where its pellets had gone home. The stream of wounded was incessant. The rest could only hold on, hoping – though without believing – that the torture would soon end."[206] Throughout the day the Anzac commanders were concerned about the demoralisation this incessant fire could cause the untried Australians and New Zealanders.

Williams established that, according to Turkish sources, 44 Turkish guns in 11 batteries[207] were present at Anzac during the day: eight at Sari Bair; four at Gaba Tepe; four at Palamutluk (Olive Grove); 25 at Third Ridge; three (not in action) on 400 Plateau; giving a total in action of 41. Not all these appeared on the battlefield early and not all were in action throughout the day, but these figures are considerably higher than Aspinall-Oglander's estimate of 24 guns[208] or Bean's of 16–20 guns in 4–5 batteries.[209] According to Williams, the mountain and field guns, 75 mm or 77 mm,[210] directed their fire on points to be attacked by the infantry. The heavier guns (mostly 150 mm howitzers) bombarded the transports. Once the transports were forced offshore in the afternoon, these howitzers switched their fire to land targets,[211] including "the valley through which the Turks knew … must … pass our" reinforcements, wounded, ammunition, water, provisions, and onto which they "poured a constant rain" of shrapnel. This became known as "the "Valley of the Shadow of Death," or "Shrapnel Gully.""[212]

By contrast, Uyar determined a much lower number, noting that only nine 75 mm mountain guns could fire on the Anzac firing lines. A battery of six short 150 mm howitzers had four guns at the Olive Grove and two at Cam Tepe. Only the Olive Grove guns were within range of the Anzac landing points, and these "began firing on naval vessels and coastal positions at around 6:00 a.m.;" due to their positions and lack of forward observation, these guns did not fire at targets inland.[213] Only one of the two 87 mm "Mantelli" field guns at Gaba Tepe was operational. Of the four 75 mm mountain guns on 400 Plateau, only one escaped to later rejoin the battle. Şefik initially had no guns at his disposal, but was soon joined by the gun from 400 Plateau and later, the four mountain guns of the 8th Mountain Artillery Battery,[214] giving him a battery of five; two of these were later moved to Anderson Knoll. Kemal then positioned his four 75 mm mountain guns of the 6th Mountain Artillery Battery to the south of Chunuk Bair.

202 Newham, "Recollections of a Returned Soldier", n.p.
203 McKernan, *Padre*, p.51.
204 *Ibid.*
205   J. Fahey, letter, private collection.
206 Bean, *Official History*, Volume I (1921 and 1941), p.393.
207 Williams, *The Battle of Anzac Ridge*, pp.101–104.
208 Aspinall-Oglander, Becke, *Military Operations*, Vol 1, p.100.
209 Williams, *The Battle of Anzac Ridge*, p.100, states Bean thought 4–5 batteries = 16–20 guns.
210 *Ibid.*, p.101.
211 *Ibid.*, pp.99–101.
212 Hastings, letter, 10 June 1915.
213 Uyar, p.103.
214 Uyar, pp.104, 113.

The allies noticed that most of these guns formed an arc from Battleship Hill to Anderson Knoll,[215] and so obvious was the massing of guns behind Third Ridge that it became known as Gun Ridge.[216] If Uyar's lower figures are correct, the Turks were hardly "massing" guns, but their dispositions still reflect allied perceptions. Williams' work revealed that during the afternoon most of the Ottoman guns fired on Baby 700 or 400 Plateau to soften up the key points Kemal intended his infantry to attack, but Second Ridge was also subjected to a persistent shelling that increased in intensity throughout the day.[217] Bean wrote that Turkish guns on Chunuk Bair enfiladed Second Ridge, and "had only to increase or shorten the range in order to play on the backs of the Australians … as a fireman plays with a hose."[218]

Clausewitz wrote that "Artillery is the principal agent of destruction,"[219] and on 25 April this power was committed to achievement of Kemal's strategic goal of annihilating the invaders or pushing them from their ridges and hilltops. The Anzacs' best defence should have been counter-battery fire, but none of their own field batteries were ashore and there was little effective fire to slow or harass the Turkish gunners. Infantry in the open were defenceless against shrapnel, and with skilful, deliberate and well directed use of the enemy guns, it is little wonder the Australians described 25 April as "pure Hell."[220] Gostelow spent much of 25 April taking ammunition to the front lines, possibly in Shrapnel Gully, before reinforcing Second Ridge[221] on 26 April, where his position "was simply raked by shrapnel, machine guns and rifle fire. I laid in a hailstorm of shrapnel."[222]

Artillery could also be used as a tactical weapon. When the CO of the 2nd Battalion at Gaba Tepe interpreted an Australian advance from the south eastern slopes of Lone Pine as a "move against" him,[223] Şefik responded with artillery support rather than reinforcements. He moved two of his five guns from Hill 165 to Kavak Tepe, to "stop by gunfire any moves that the Australians might make on the southern slopes of Kanli Sirt,"[224] and when there were no such moves, these guns were to fire on Kanli Sirt, in effect keeping the plateau under a cross fire. Şefik was so confident the enemy infantry would be thus held, that he did not send an infantry guard with these guns as was customary in British, and probably Ottoman, doctrine. When he launched his outnumbered infantry in their attack across Legge and Mule Valleys, he used his machine guns and mountain guns to cover and enable their crossing.[225] This begs the question of whether the 3rd Brigade would have made similar advances if similarly supported.

Şefik's guns bought him the freedom to use his infantry as he wished, a force multiplier which helped him to retain the initiative and control the battle. Williams notes that one of the great tactical lessons of this war was that infantry can neither capture nor hold ground without sufficient artillery support.[226] For the Australians and New Zealanders at Anzac on 25 April, there was next to none. With no field guns to relieve pressure on their front, suppress enemy artillery fire, break up enemy attacks or disrupt communications, reinforcements or supplies, they could neither cover movements of their infantry nor create opportunities by reaching beyond rifle range. They were forced instead to send fragments of infantry to meet every perceived threat, further disorganising their force.

---

215 Williams, *The Battle of Anzac Ridge*, p.99.
216 Bean, *Official History*, Volume I (1921 and 1941), p.450.
217 Belford, *Legs Eleven*, p.82.
218 Bean, *Official History*, Volume I (1921 and 1941), p.391.
219 Quoted Williams, *The Battle of Anzac Ridge*, p.100.
220 Darnell, 1DRL233. Charlie Gostelow's daughter recalled seeing a diary entry he had apparently written between 25 and 28 April, stating "this is Hell on earth." J.P. Hurst, conversation with Mrs M. Forsythe, n.d.
221 Belford, *Legs Eleven*, p.82.
222 Gostelow, diary, 25 April 1915.
223 Şefik, para. 130.
224 *Ibid.*, para. 131.
225 *Ibid.*, paras. 125 and 128.
226 Williams, *The Battle of Anzac Ridge*, p.100.

The early deployment of 11th Battalion to Second Ridge, the calls for reinforcements that deprived Baby 700 of support and the stream of casualties, give the impression that the fighting on Second Ridge throughout the day was close, critical and desperate. The *Official History* describes Turks advancing "like a flood over the whole of this countryside," "wave after wave" "advancing in skirmishing formation from Scrubby Knoll … crossing the green flats towards the foot of German Officers' Ridge and the Jolly," "skirmishing up every hollow and round every spur."[227] Darnell described repulsing "attack after attack … I can't say enough for the men's pluck they weren't men they were fiends and nothing could withstand their charges."[228]

Probably only five Turkish battalions and remnants of a sixth were on the field. Six battalions of 72nd and 77th Regiments, of 57th Regiment, were nearby but not engaged, and lower numbers of other troops, such as cavalry and Gendarma, were seen, or believed to have been seen, on the battlefield. The ANZAC troops were being pounded by a relentless artillery fire, but Şefik did not have enough troops to have launched attacks against Second Ridge throughout the day, and once 57th Regiment arrived, 27th Regiment's main objective became eviction of the enemy on 400 Plateau. Three companies of Şefik's 1st Battalion and one company of his 3rd Battalion attacked 400 Plateau;[229] one company of the 1st Battalion was held in reserve. Two 3rd Battalion companies supported 57th Regiment on the southern slopes of Battleship Hill and Baby 700,[230] and the third fought on the southern toe of Mortar Ridge, supporting the attack on 400 Plateau and preventing an allied advance from Second Ridge.[231] A platoon of 2nd Battalion was ordered to attack the "southern slopes" of the Pine to secure that flank and prevent Australians venturing south.[232] In summary, both Şefik's troop dispositions and his explanation of them make it clear that his two objectives were the high ground on the ANZAC left and 400 Plateau on its right. The ground in between, Second Ridge, was not a priority for infantry assault.

Examination of 11th Battalion accounts also presents an image at odds with the existing one. Casualties, enemy pressure and attacks appeared relentless, but evidence of assaults on Second Ridge beyond 27th Regiment's initial advance in the morning is elusive. Everett noted that "On Sunday the main effort of the Turks was on the left … [they] made no serious counterattack till after dark."[233] Louch later recorded that "No enemy appeared" to his front in Wire Gully, "and we passed the day without having fired a shot."[234] How can such differences in perceptions or depictions of the battle be reconciled?

Firstly, bayonet charges were often made to clear ground to one's immediate front and in some areas, particularly 400 Plateau, groups, large and small, continually manoeuvred, charged and withdrew through the scrub. This may attest to the ferocity of charges described by Darnell, but does not provide evidence of sustained, closely pressed Turkish attacks. Denton wrote of attacks in his area, but he was on the left, where the pressure was real but distant, as Turks advanced over Baby 700 to his left and Mortar Ridge to his front. Mortar Ridge in fact shielded much of Second Ridge from direct assault, but it also enabled the Turks to bring effective small arms fire to bear on the defenders of Second Ridge; it also provided cover where Turks could have, or have been imagined to be, massing for an assault. Şefik also noted the confused, face to face fighting on 400 Plateau. Darnell,

227 Bean, *Official History*, Volume I (1921 and 1941), pp.433, 434.
228 Darnell, AD82/175.
229 Şefik, para. 119.
230 *Ibid.*, para. 117.
231 *Ibid.*, para. 118.
232 *Ibid.*, para. 120.
233 Everett, interview, Ellam-Innes Collection, p.241.
234 Louch, manuscript, p.15.

Facey[235] and others may have witnessed or taken part in bayonet charges, but this does not confirm continuous, close and aggressive attacks on Second Ridge.

Enemy advances may have been seen, but which Turks and when? The obvious answer is 27th Regiment during their initial advance. Later Şefik's main focus was elsewhere, but the Anzacs, not realising this, continued to reinforce Second Ridge. The impressions of those in the firing lines, "gaps" in the written histories of the battle, the sight of many advances by both sides on Baby 700 and 400 Plateau, and lack of clarity in time and chronology in many sources, create the impression that attacks on Second Ridge continued throughout the day.

The early morning decisions to divert troops to Second Ridge may have been influenced by the disorganisation of the landing force. When unable to send intact units under known leaders, as Şefik could do, Australian commanders instead ordered as many rifles as possible into the firing line, thereby drawing a large portion of the 11th Battalion to a ridge that was not their main or final objective. The battle then developed some of the characteristics of the hammer and anvil. The hammer is mobile, the anvil is not. The Turkish infantry pushed the Australians into a defensive line on the anvil of Second Ridge and pinned them there with fire and the threat of direct assault. The ridge was then pounded by the hammer of shrapnel and small arms fire that caused a stream of casualties. As Second Ridge was bled of men, the Anzac commanders, under the impression that the ridge was under constant attack, continually diverted troops there. With the 1st Division's reserve reinforcing the 3rd Brigade, the division lost its flexibility and the initiative, and unwittingly condemned itself to fight there for the remainder of the campaign. Although attacking the ridge itself was not a priority for 27th Regiment, the Anzacs, believing they were under threat from a numerically superior enemy, were compelled to hold it. And allied command was denied one great advantage of their Ottoman counterparts – artillery.

Fighting among strangers, Medcalf felt the strain "could not last much longer."[236] The "position seemed hopeless" and while awaiting the expected "final attack," he pondered:

How can man die better
than facing fearful odds
for the ashes of his fathers
and the temples of his Gods?[237]

A "speck" appearing "in the sky to the left over by Hill 971"[238] revealed a British biplane, which, despite Turkish fire, "flew unhurt from one end of the line to the other." Eight such flights appear to have been made that day, though not all were over Anzac.[239] The fire on the infantry "slackened a little" as the aircraft "sailed serenely on, and shortly after … we were greatly cheered by the shots from the ships firing over our heads."[240]

"Broadsides came from each" of five battleships "in quick succession. A tongue of flame," a "report; and a cloud of smoke rolled forward … Masses of debris … and guns could be observed flying skywards."[241] Aitken confirmed seeing "trees, men, guns, rocks and so on all mixed in the air."[242] Everett, Hearder and the *Official History*[243] record similar stories.

---

235 Facey, *A Fortunate Life*, p.258.
236 Medcalf, manuscript, p.66.
237 *Ibid*. The quote is from T.B. Macaulay, *Lays of Ancient Rome*.
238 Medcalf, manuscript, p.67.
239 Williams, *The Battle of Anzac Ridge*, p.107.
240 Hastings, letter, 10 June 1915.
241 Medcalf, manuscript, p.67.
242 Aitken, letter/diary, p.19.
243 Bean, *Official History*, Volume I (1921 and 1941), pp.501–502.

Turkish sources dispute that naval counter-battery fire destroyed any of their guns,[244] and Bean wrote that "The ships' guns ... were so useless ... that they had almost ceased to fire."[245] This is the generally accepted view, the main reasons being that: the front lines were in many cases fluid or in close contact; the low trajectory of naval shells reduced their ability to hit targets in such terrain; and there were problems with accuracy,[246] "spotting" and communication.[247]

Battlefield accounts suggest possible reasons for the belief that the naval fire was more effective than other evidence suggests. The moral support to strained men expecting imminent annihilation, provided by the guns of what they believed to be the greatest navy in the world, must have been immense. Medcalf's "dismal reflections ... were replaced by pleasing ruminations on the might of Britain."[248] Hastings recalled the shells being "hurrahed ... as comrades and friends"[249] as they passed overhead, and Clifton that "we would have been driven" out if not for the Navy.[250] To infantrymen who could not have known the true effectiveness of this fire, nor whether the ships were hitting their targets, the sight of any damage to the enemy would have been a tonic. Perhaps what they perceived to be destroyed enemy guns were carts or wagons; or guns apparently knocked out may have been returned to action when repaired or re-crewed.[251] Alternatively, there may be errors in Turkish sources, as men from other Australian battalions also claim to have seen Turkish guns hit.[252] Rumour also added to the men's impressions. "We ... were cheered by messages" that the approaching Turkish reinforcements "were suffering terribly."[253]

A compounding factor may once again be chronology. A closer reading of Clifton's account suggests that it refers to the following day,[254] and those of Everett, Hearder, and Aitken may also refer to Turkish attacks made on 26 or 27 April. Perhaps the naval fire was sporadically effective. On 27 April, Everett relayed information about a party of Turks assembling for an attack from the Nek. The first shrapnel from the ships' guns burst about 10 minutes after Everett's report, "caught them beautifully ... and scattered them in every way. A second attempt was made about an hour later and they were caught in the same way – a couple of lyddite shells lodging fair in the middle of them."[255] Bean's conclusion may be correct in general terms while references in individual accounts may describe single events.

The 11th Battalion's Machine Gun Section was also fighting hard. Murphy wrote that, "all day ... they tried to blow us out with shrapnel. We had any amount killed and wounded out in the open and I have to thank God that I never got a scratch ... we thought the end was coming."[256] Despite all, wrote Forrest,[257] "our crowd hung to it like Britons."[258] In a move to "enfilade the Turks," Walther grabbed the tripod, "Webster the gun,"[259] Murphy "two boxes of ammunition," and all rushed "over the hill under heavy rifle fire." When Murphy caught up "Webster was lying on the ground and so was the gun, and Walther was trying to drag Webster into a shallow trench." Murphy helped drag

244 Williams, *The Battle of Anzac Ridge*, p.107.
245 Bean, *Official History*, Volume I (1921 and 1941), p.392.
246 Prior, *Gallipoli, The End of the Myth*, pp.39–41, p.45.
247 Strachan, pp.117–118, provides a good summary. H. Strachan, *The First World War: A New Illustrated History* (London: Simon and Schuster, 2003).
248 Medcalf, manuscript, p.67.
249 Hastings, letter, 10 June 1915.
250 Clifton, letter, n.d.
251 D.M. Horner, *The Gunners* (St. Leonards, NSW: Allen and Unwin, 1995), pp.89–90.
252 Bean, *Official History*, Volume I (1921 and 1941), p.484, provides one example.
253 Fox, "I Was There", p.8.
254 Clifton, letter, n.d.
255 Everett, interview, Ellam-Innes Collection, p.241.
256 Murphy, letter, *Sunday Times*, 6 June 1915.
257 431 Private Christopher Frank Forrest, 20 at embarkation, clerk, of Osborne, born South Australia.
258 Forrest, letter, 3DRL7247.
259 499 Private Frank Unwin Webster, 20 at embarkation, assayer, of Kanowna, born Brighton, Victoria.

Webster a few more "feet but it hurt him too much, although he was cracking jokes all the time."[260] They "had a lot of trouble getting" Frank "out of the fire zone. The bullets were whistling round us in thousands and raising the head a few inches meant stopping one … It's marvellous how we got him through … we ran 10 or 20 yards under the fiercest fire."[261]

The strain and intensity of the fighting along Second Ridge soon reasserted itself. Medcalf recalled the fire getting "hotter and hotter," until it appeared "the 1st Australian Division would be wiped out by the overwhelming fire from the left."[262] Presumably this was a consequence of the advance of 57th Regiment over the inland slopes of Baby 700 and of Şefik's men on Mortar Ridge. Men fell "backwards more frequently"[263] while the survivors "kept up a steady fire on every Turkish form that presented itself … All bayonets were fixed."[264] The field of fire in front was very short,[265] and "it seemed a force could easily mass under cover" and "charge the position." Medcalf "was rather hoping they would; anything would be better than this terrific tension which was becoming more severe as the enemy fire developed."[266]

By 6:00 p.m., the remnants of the 3rd Brigade had been under fire for over 13 hours. Cockburn was hit at about this time. With a wounded foot, he "had to lie where I was until" dark, then "crawled out somehow. But I was nothing to some of the poor buggers shot early in the day [who] had to lay where they were all day we put them under cover as well as we could." Cockburn was evacuated to a ship: there were "a terrible lot of deaths on board," one of whom was a Turkish prisoner who had "tried to knife a stretcher bearer" and been "plonked over the head" with a rifle butt. "There are some dreadful cases … Some with their arms and legs blown off, some shot through the mouth."[267] Cockburn would not reach hospital for four days.

Towards dusk "the copper round the barrel" of Henderson Smith's gun melted due to constant firing, "soldering it to the muzzle attachment" and "jamming" the gun.[268] The noise of battle made communication by shouting impossible and the machine gunners flicked each other with a finger on the neck or ear to attract attention. The crew got the damaged gun "cleared away and whilst getting back into position,"[269] Sergeant Wally Hallahan responded to what he thought was the flick of a finger to discover he had been shot through the neck. Incredibly, the bullet had passed between windpipe and spinal column, putting Hallahan "out of action for some days," rather than permanently. Another member of the section "was wounded through the chest" soon after.[270]

To the best of Murphy's knowledge "nobody … in our section" was killed on 25 April "although Walther and Webster have accounted for 600 or 700 Turks."[271] Throughout the day the strain and intensity of fighting along Second Ridge produced a stream of casualties, though in the main without close fighting or bayonet attacks.

That would change with the descent of darkness.

260 Murphy, letter, *Sunday Times*, 6 June 1915.
261 B.H. Walther, diary extract, printed *Sunday Times*, 19 April 1998.
262 Medcalf, manuscript, p.66.
263 *Ibid.*, p.66.
264 *Ibid.*, p.66.
265 Presumably as a consequence of placing the firing line along the seaward crest.
266 Medcalf, manuscript, p.66.
267 Cockburn, diary, 28 April 1915.
268 Smith, 3DRL 7247.
269 *Ibid.*
270 *Ibid.*
271 Murphy, letter, *Sunday Times*, 6 June 1915.

8

Where Did the Hours Go?

Whether the decision to halt the 3rd Brigade on Second Ridge was right or wrong revolves around the time it was made and the location of the various forces at that time.[1] The work presented here has created a body of evidence missing from the existing debate, including a chronology that reveals that Şefik's two battalions may have arrived at Scrubby Knoll about one and a half hours earlier than believed, yet the reconstruction presented in Chapter 6 suggests Loutit still beat him to Adana Bair. Does this new chronology resolve any of the outstanding questions of this morning's battle? Why did the 3rd Brigade establish itself on Second, instead of Third, Ridge?

Roberts has argued that there was a gap of possibly three hours between the 3rd Brigade's occupation of Second Ridge and the counter-attack of 27th Regiment,[2] that this was due to MacLagan's premature decision to fight a defensive action, a decision that "threw away any chance of the 1st Division securing its objectives ... surrendered the initiative to the Turks and committed the corps to a costly defensive battle on terrain of little military value."[3]

Williams argued that MacLagan's decision was the correct one, as it established on Second Ridge a defensive perimeter to absorb the attacks of the Turkish reserve. The landing at Z Beach was intended as a diversion to prevent the Turkish reserves from hindering the main landings at Helles, and when the Turkish counter-attack arrived earlier than previously believed, Second Ridge was a good defensive position at which to hold them, as confirmed by the course of the battle later in the day.[4]

Given the importance of this decision and the volume of material published on the Gallipoli campaign, it is extraordinary that such issues remain unresolved.

Was There a Lull in the Fighting?

11th Battalion accounts can be examined for anecdotal evidence of a lull in the fighting between the 3rd Brigade's occupation of Second Ridge and the counter-attack of 27th Regiment but, given problems with quoted times, the most difficult part of reconstruction is getting the chronology right.

Conclusive evidence of a lull is difficult to find in soldiers' accounts. Perhaps the most obvious example is that of Tulloch. Bean wrote of "no sign of life"[5] during Tulloch's advance over Baby 700 and Battleship Hill, although bullets lisped into the scrub at long range.[6] It would be unwise to assume that the battle had ceased altogether – Tulloch was still meeting occasional opposition, and troops to his south may at the time have been watching 27th Regiment's deployment. Tulloch makes no reference to a lull.

The chronology is confused by the fact that events presumed to represent the Turkish counter-attack may not have. It is easy to assume that the Machine Gun Section's deployment to Second Ridge after an outburst of fire and Denton's request for reinforcements, was in response to Şefik's

---

1   Roberts, "The Landing at Anzac: A Reassessment", pp.25–34; Williams, "Z Beach, the Landing of the ANZAC Corps."
2   Roberts, "The Landing at Anzac: A Reassessment," p.33.
3   *Ibid.*, p.30.
4   Williams, "Z Beach, the Landing of the ANZAC Corps, April 25, 1915."
5   Bean, *Official History*, Volume I (1921 and 1941), p.288.
6   Bean, *Gallipoli Mission*, p.85.

counter-attack, yet this means that the section would inexplicably have been sitting inactive in Shrapnel Gully for several hours. The firing they heard could in fact have been in response to other factors, including firing at any point along the line. Denton's request for reinforcements could have been a response to any number of events – the first sight of Şefik's approaching columns or the realisation, on cresting Second Ridge, probably before 6:30 a.m., that Denton's drastically reduced "company" was inadequate for either defence or attack. Hearder's and Walther's accounts of coming under fire immediately their guns opened or as they got into position, suggest that 27th Regiment was present,[7] but Murphy noted the Turks did not fire a shot until an allied aircraft flew over.[8] Combs noted this flight when he was on Adana Bair, and Margetts whilst digging at the Nek, the latter placing the flight between 7:00 a.m. and 8:30 a.m.

Retention of MacFarlane's and Rockliff's platoons on Second Ridge[9] would be assumed to have been in response to Şefik's counter-attack, but may also have been for other reasons – a decision by higher command to defend rather than advance, or weakness of the other 11th Battalion parties there. Everett, Selby, Mofflin and most others recalled being under fire from the moment they arrived on the crest of Second Ridge, but this was probably before 27th Regiment's counter-attack. What is significant is that regardless of when these parties arrived on the ridge, they stopped.

Newham implied there was a delay and that reinforcements were requested before the enemy attack began in earnest.[10] Mofflin's letter gives the impression the battle was in full swing when he arrived, yet Loutit's withdrawal apparently ended at "about 11 a.m."[11] and Peck believed he was wounded at 10:00 a.m.,[12] opening a gap of possibly three hours between the accounts of those like Mofflin and the *Official History*, with little explanation of what happened to the hours between 5:00 a.m. and 10:00 a.m. B and D Companies' early despatch to Second Ridge from Plugge's Plateau is confirmed by Mason, who reported there were still Turks withdrawing along Russell's Top as his platoon advanced through Shrapnel Gully. Mofflin was initially despatched with Darnell, who recorded that at about "9 a.m. got in touch with the enemy coming on to the attack in thousands."[13] This is confirmed by another scout who entrenched at "9 a.m." as the advanced parties, "repulsed by large reinforcements," were retiring.[14] This probably refers to 27th Regiment's counter-attack.

Mofflin's chronology raises the possibility that Peck's and Loutit's times may be incorrect. Mofflin covered their withdrawal, spent possibly "half an hour" digging, fired on the clearly visible counter-attack and then made his first diary entry, "10 a.m.".[15] He may therefore have reached Second Ridge and covered the retirement at about 9:00 a.m. or thereabouts. This corresponds with the accounts of Darnell, the anonymous scout and the 3rd Battalion history[16] and suggests that the withdrawal from Adana Bair was earlier than Bean appreciated. Şefik's chronology supports this, as his men began firing at targets while Loutit was still visible on the "the western foothills of Artillery Ridge,"[17] between 8:00 and 9:00 a.m.[18] Loutit's and Peck's recollections were recorded some time later, Mofflin's at the time. If Mofflin's times are correct, an hour or two can be shaved from the "lull" or gap in the chronology.

Irrespective of the evidence presented above, by 9:00 a.m. roughly four hours had passed since the 3rd Brigade had captured Plugge's Plateau. It is difficult to believe the 11th Battalion troops sent to

7   Walther, diary, 25 April 1915.
8   Murphy, letter, *Sunday Times*, 6 June 1915.
9   Bean, *Official History*, Volume I (1921 and 1941), p.286.
10   Newham, "Recollections of a Returned Soldier", n.p.
11   Loutit, 3DRL 606 item 227.
12   Peck, 3DRL 606 item 25.
13   Darnell, AD82/175.
14   Anonymous scout, letter, 15 May 1915.
15   Mofflin, letter, 20 October 1915, p.18.
16   Wren, *Randwick to Hargicourt*, pp.48–49.
17   Şefik, para. 80.
18   *Ibid.*, para. 79.

Second Ridge did not arrive there long before the Turkish counter-attack. If there was a protracted lull that morning, why is it not more visible in the men's accounts?

One reason may be that it simply was not of interest – letters sent home after the Landing, were initially limited to a single, censored page[19] and events were condensed and abbreviated. The men may been more inclined to write about things that happened, than a period when little was happening. Most men may not have been aware of a "lull," as they were occupied with one task or another throughout this period. Those who weren't scouting, advancing, fighting or withdrawing, may have been digging "like fury"[20] or carting ammunition, and those in Shrapnel Gully could hear fire beyond the ridge lines, suggesting the battle was still in full swing. There was also confusion about the local terrain, with some men believing all was proceeding according to plan as they dug in on Second Ridge, believing it to be "our objective."[21] If so, they would have seen little reason to advance further or have been concerned by any delay to do so.

It is likely the Turkish garrison's aggressive fighting withdrawal and the presence of more Turkish parties in the area than previously realised, played a major role by so effectively blurring the line between the two phases of the battle, that most men were unaware of any "lull." There is ample evidence of a sustained Turkish pressure on the invaders. Brockman was forced from Plugge's Plateau by a scattered long range fire, Hearder's section suffered casualties crossing Shrapnel Gully, Tulloch's party fought several times during the advance to Battleship Hill, Everett and Selby came under fire as they reached Second Ridge. Everywhere men commented on enemy sniper fire and at least one gun burst its shrapnel over the battlefield. None of this gives the impression of a "lull," even if the counter-attack had not yet begun.

Most Australians would recognise at some point that they had come up against the enemy's main body, but how many correctly identified this point? Many did not perceive the enemy counter-attacks as a separate event; some believed the retreating Turks rallied and turned on their scattered attackers. That 27th and 57th Regiments entered the battle at different times further blurred the sequence of events. Howe, unaware of the role of Şefik's regiment in the battle, wrote that the "retiring Turkish outposts" went "to ground on Third Ridge … maintaining brisk fire on anything which moved."[22] He may be right. Hakki's withdrawing platoon had temporarily dug in on Pine Ridge and Anderson Knoll and fired on any targets that appeared.[23] Another major factor was the sight of Şefik's columns advancing beyond Third Ridge some time before he launched his attack, though who in command might have seen or heard of the approaching columns, and from when and where, are more difficult to determine. The first step is to identify, if possible, the time the decision to halt on Second Ridge was made and by whom.

Bean's overview of these decisions states that MacLagan intended the 3rd Brigade's advance to continue when the 2nd Brigade arrived. After crossing Shrapnel Gully he saw 2,000–3,000 Turks on Third Ridge, and decided that "the 3rd Brigade should dig in temporarily" on Second Ridge or 400 Plateau. At "9 a.m., when the advanced parties reported that the Turks were pushing forward and trying to outflank them on the north," and with the 2nd Brigade "coming up in strength," MacLagan ordered the advance of Salisbury's line on 400 Plateau. Almost immediately afterwards, he "gave up all idea of reaching" Third Ridge.[24] This represents a confusion of events from different times, although the reference to Turks pushing forward at 9:00 a.m. supports Mofflin's and Şefik's chronologies.

---

19   Turner, letter, 14 May 1915.
20   Darnell AD82/175.
21   For example, Parsons and Newham believed Second Ridge was their objective. Newham, "Recollections of a Returned Soldier", n.p.; Parsons, letter, 4 August 1915.
22   Howe, "Sparks From an Old Controversy", pp.7–8.
23   The context of Howe's comment, made alongside a brief description of the 1st and 2nd Brigades' dispositions in the firing line, implies that this was later in the morning, long after 27th Regiment had entered the battle; but, given previously noted problems interpreting chronologies, it may not have been.
24   Bean, *Official History*, Volume I (1921 and 1941), pp.359, 360.

Elsewhere the *Official History* states that while "about two companies" of the 9th Battalion under Major A.G. Salisbury dug in, on MacLagan's orders,[25] on 400 Plateau,[26] nearby Brand decided "that, if the small advanced parties pushed on to the … silent … Third Ridge, they would run a great risk of being cut off."[27] Bean's notes state "Brand sent back to MacLagan … 'Enemy advancing from Gun Ridge. Shall I keep advance company forward?'"[28] These are intriguing statements as Brand had recently sent Loutit forward, and it is unclear why he would believe the 9th Battalion had more chance of being cut off than Loutit, which enemy was present to do so on the "silent" ridge, who the enemy advancing from "silent" Gun Ridge were, and which company is meant. At about 6:15 a.m., Brand had ordered Haig, on 400 Plateau, not to "go too far forward. Don't go up that hill,"[29] apparently referring to Third Ridge. In other words, Brand may have decided as early as 6:15 a.m. to hold the advance. MacLagan had apparently already made the same decision – between 5:30 and 5:50 a.m. he had begun telling the 2nd Brigade the plan had changed and they were to proceed to the right flank.[30] Soon after, he told the 2nd Brigade's commander, Colonel J.W. McCay, that if his whole brigade did not proceed to the right, MacLagan's "right will be turned," adding that the move was urgent.[31] Apart from MacLagan's 9:00 a.m. sighting of Turks on Third Ridge, all these decisions were clearly made long before Şefik's battalions arrived on the field.

The following account by Major Beevor, 10th Battalion, is included as it quotes MacLagan directly and ties his words to a time and place. Its significance has been overlooked by historians examining this issue. After landing from the destroyer *Foxhound*, and before leaving the beach, Beevor reported to MacLagan, Brand and Ross. MacLagan ordered Beevor to "move … not too far, to the southward, and then to select a defensive position facing inland, and dig in."[32] The "defensive position" referred to was on the 400 Plateau.[33] A defensive posture had therefore been decided on long before Şefik, listening to the distant sounds of battle from the other side of the peninsula, had received orders to leave camp. Surely the reserve, landing from the same destroyers, could have dug defensive positions, while the other battalions advanced to their objectives, if the latter was intended?

A second factor in determining the impact of the Turks on the decision to remain on Second Ridge is their positions at the time decisions were made. MacLagan later told Bean that he "saw the enemy thick upon Gun Ridge and decided … to dig … until reinforcements came up … He meant to push on as soon as reinforcements came."[34] At what time these Turks were seen is not stated. A range of evidence suggests MacLagan reached 400 Plateau somewhere around 6:30 a.m., 20 minutes to one hour after telling Salisbury to dig in.[35] At this time he could not have seen the 2,000 men of 27th Regiment on Third Ridge. Bean's wording is intriguing. MacLagan "could see Turks on the Third ridge, and they presently appeared there in numbers – judged to be between 2,000 and 3,000. To MacLagan it had seemed obviously unsafe to continue the advance against the Third ridge while such slender numbers were reaching the Second, and with no troops at all on his right."[36] It is difficult to make any sense of this, nor to understand who was reacting to what and when.

By Aspinall-Oglander's account, when MacLagan reached 400 Plateau, he was "unaware that any troops had … penetrated to Gun Ridge," and with his "brigade so dislocated" he decided it would be "unsafe at present" to attempt to occupy the broad frontage allotted to him, and to entrench instead

25   *Ibid.*, p.344.
26   Bean refers to their position as "400 Plateau" and "Second Ridge." Bean, Official History, Volume I, p.344.
27   Bean, *Official History*, Volume I (1921 and 1941), p.344.
28   9th Battalion at the Landing, unidentified interviewee, possibly Haig, AWM38 3DRL 606 Item 25.
29   AWM38 3DRL 606 Item 25.
30   Bean, *Official History*, Volume I (1921 and 1941), p.363.
31   *Ibid.*, p.365.
32   Beevor, "My Landing at Gallipoli", pp.13–14.
33   Bean, *Official History*, Volume I (1921 and 1941), p.353.
34   E.G. Sinclair MacLagan, J.H.Peck, A.M. Ross, AWM38 3DRL 606 Item 25.
35   Bean, *Official History*, Vol. I (1921 and 1941), p.357; Brand, "Memories of ANZAC Day", p.4; unidentified, 3DRL 606 Item 25.
36   Bean, *Official History*, Volume I (1921 and 1941), p.359.

on Second Ridge.[37] Turks on Third Ridge are not mentioned. The "precious hours during which Gun Ridge was almost undefended" were meanwhile "slipping away."[38]

Could Turks have been seen on Third Ridge at this early hour, and if so, who were they? The main Turkish force in the Anzac area early on 25 April was approximately 250 men of 4 Company, 2/27th Regiment.[39] Although two thirds of the company were reputedly annihilated during the fighting, it is not safe to assume that this happened in the initial clash. Numerous 3rd Brigade accounts refer to the enemy's retreat along Russell's Top or across Shrapnel Gully, or their later appearance at various places on the battlefield.[40] In addition, comparison of Australian with Turkish accounts reveals that Australians over-estimated the numbers of Turkish casualties. A greater number of Turks may consequently have survived the initial clashes than previously assumed, though 2 Platoon does appear to have suffered heavily during their withdrawal from Plugge's Plateau and Ari Burnu.[41]

The impact of the relatively low number of Turks fighting early in the morning may have been great in proportion to their size. Fewer troops are required for defence than attack, and can inflict disproportionate losses on an outnumbering enemy forced to leave cover to advance. It did not require a great number of marksmen with Mauser rifles to cause casualties and the impression of heavy fire. The riflemen firing at Everett and Selby may have been doing so at the short range of several hundred yards, and numerous accounts during the day refer to Turks shooting from much closer. Added to the impact of this fire are the perceptions by inexperienced troops of exaggerated enemy numbers, and Şefik's orders to his outposts to fight to buy time for the counter-attack. The heavy fire initially reported by various Australians may consequently have been from small Turkish parties, not the counter-attack.

1 Platoon, having suffered relatively lightly at Fisherman's Hut, joined the fight on the high ground.[42] The survivors of 2 and 3 Platoons also withdrew and fought on. Hakki's platoon of 3 Company, 2/27th Regiment at Kel Tepe conducted a fighting withdrawal to Third Ridge, where they turned and fought.[43] A platoon from 1 Company, under command of Second Lieutenant Mustafa, was sent northwards from Gaba Tepe and eventually served on Şefik's right flank.[44] Even had such troops not participated in the early fighting, they may have been seen by the 3rd Brigade. From 400 Plateau, at "about 6.30 or 7," Weir, 10th Battalion, saw enemy troops "on the [far] ridge."[45] Bean thought these Turks to be "the same by whom the advance of Loutit's party was presently barred."[46] They may have been Mustafa's or Hakki's platoons.[47]

Evidence compiled in previous chapters makes it possible to establish a model which is inclusive and accounts for many of the noted discrepancies. The *Official History* refers to a "lull" of "a quiet hour" that Loutit's party, as a forward screen, created for the 10th Battalion on 400 Plateau. Only once was this interrupted, by an outburst of rifle fire caused by a "movement of the Turks, probably against Loutit."[48] Bean also refers to "very heavy firing" breaking out "in front of the 10th Battalion," to the left of the 400 Plateau, at "about 9 a.m."; and to MacLagan announcing at the time that "a serious counter-attack was developing."[49] The men of the 9th Battalion who rushed forward to meet

37   Aspinall-Oglander, Becke, *Military Operations, Gallipoli*, Vol. I, p.182.
38   *Ibid.*
39   Şefik, para. 34–35.
40   Bean, *Official History*, Volume I (1921 and 1941), p.375, provides one such example on Johnston's Jolly.
41   Loutit, 3DRL 606 Item 227 [2].
42   Şefik, para. 39.
43   *Ibid.*, para. 41.
44   *Ibid.*, para. 44.
45   Williams, "Z Beach, the Landing of the ANZAC Corps, April 25, 1915", p.54.
46   Bean, *Official History*, Volume I (1921 and 1941), p.351.
47   Williams also believed these troops came from Gaba Tepe. Williams, "Z Beach, the Landing of the ANZAC Corps, April 25, 1915", p.54.
48   Bean, *Official History*, Volume I (1921 and 1941), p.351.
49   *Ibid.*, pp.357–358.

this attack were met by a destructive "whirlwind of fire" "from unseen rifles and machine-guns."[50] At this stage, according to western sources, Loutit was apparently on Adana Bair and Peck unwounded and moving forward.[51] Weir thought he arrived at 400 Plateau by "about 6.30 a.m."[52] and saw Turks on what we presume to be Third Ridge, but may have been Adana Ridge, at "about 6.30 or 7."[53] If so, there is a delay between the arrival of his company at about 6:30 a.m. and the counter-attack of 27th Regiment at possibly 9:00 a.m. So, why did the advance not continue?

The outburst of fire Bean noted during the "quiet hour" could have been caused by any number of Turkish parties, and whether it was "against Loutit"[54] or not, should not be confused with Şefik's counter-attack. In other words, if the decision to halt on Second Ridge had in fact been due to the presence of Turks on Third Ridge, as noted by Weir at about 7:00 a.m. or by other accounts possibly an hour earlier, they were not Şefik's counter-attack.

The decision to halt and dig on Second Ridge could not have been forced by the presence of 57th Regiment or 27th Regiment's 1st and 3rd Battalions. If Turks were visible on Third Ridge they were probably small parties from the coastal garrison, whose fighting withdrawal, combined with movement of small formed bodies through the area, may have effectively masked the true situation from the Australian commanders and have been misinterpreted as the Turkish counter-attack.

In other words, the 3rd Brigade's advance appears not to have been halted by 2,000 reinforcements of the 27th Regiment, or the 12,000 Darnell mentioned, but by the sight of some other body of Turks – perhaps a single platoon from Gaba Tepe under Mustafa, who happened to be marching through the area, or Hakki's platoon firing at targets from Anderson Knoll.

The decision to dig in was made even earlier, perhaps on the beach or Plugge's Plateau. Although separate from the decision not to proceed to Third Ridge, the delay caused by initially adopting this stance ultimately prevented the force from doing so. The question at the heart of these deliberations then is, could the 3rd Brigade have pushed on and reached Third Ridge before 27th Regiment, had they not stopped? Could the "precious hour or so"[55] bought by the sacrifice of Loutit's and other parties have been better used?

The men on the 400 Plateau and Second Ridge had time to begin scratching holes, but this does not imply that there was time for a battalion to have assembled and advanced across Legge Valley to establish a defensive position before 27th Regiment arrived in force. 27th Regiment, arriving in much better shape than the 3rd Brigade, still took possibly an hour to assemble, prepare and relay orders, deploy for battle and commence its attack. Nor was there an assembled Australian battalion on 400 Plateau ready to begin the advance. Although the 9th and 10th Battalions have not been subjected to similar scrutiny in this work as the 11th Battalion, they appear to have been in better shape, though still far from whole. In addition, Third Ridge breaks into a number of spurs and any 3rd Brigade troops attempting to reach its main spine would have been advancing against the grain of the land – being caught part way across could have been disastrous. They may have been concerned about coming under fire from the batteries near Gaba Tepe, which had not been knocked out by the 9th Battalion as planned, though it is unclear whether these guns were in a position to fire this far inland. Significantly, the advancing troops did not have effective, land-based artillery support to provide covering fire or disrupt their enemy's plans; this may have enabled Hakki's platoon to have inflicted significant loss.

On the other hand, the impact on the battle of even two Australian companies reaching Third Ridge or Adana Bair before 27th Regiment would have been dramatic. Their presence would

50 *Ibid.*, p.358.
51 Bean thought 27th Regiment began their march at 7:30 a.m., nearly two hours later than Şefik's recorded time. Bean, *Official History*, Volume I (1921 and 1941), p.447.
52 Williams, "Z Beach, the Landing of the ANZAC Corps, April 25, 1915", p.54.
53 *Ibid.*
54 Bean, *Official History*, Volume I (1921 and 1941), p.351.
55 Brand, "Memories of ANZAC Day", p.4.

probably have wrested the initiative from Şefik, though the arrival of 57th Regiment on the high ground to their north would have made their tenure difficult. For whatever reason the orders were given, when the troops of the 3rd Brigade stopped to fight on Second Ridge, the attack was deprived of its impetus and the assault force lost the initiative.

In summary, the decision to dig on Second Ridge was independent of Şefik launching his counter-attack. Put simply, the Australian commanders may have misread the battle, misinterpreting the movements and resistance of platoons as the counter-attack of battalions. The result was that long before 57th Regiment reached the field, a force of nearly a division was preparing to defend against attack by less than a brigade, and before that, by several platoons. Perhaps MacLagan intended to regain the initiative by first breaking 27th Regiment on the anvil of Second Ridge, or waiting until order was regained or his artillery arrived. Australian commanders landing later subordinated their orders to these early decisions.[56]

That Şefik's reserve battalions arrived considerably earlier than appreciated by Roberts, Bean[57] and Aspinall-Oglander,[58] and were visible for some time before they began their ascent of Third Ridge, greatly reduces the supposed "gap" of three hours. Sightings of enemy parties on the battlefield – platoons or fractions of platoons withdrawing, fighting or moving – occurred within this "gap," masking the transition from one phase of the battle (withdrawal of the garrison) to another (the counter-attack).

Williams argues that the "task of the Anzac Corps … was one of strategic offence and tactical defence."[59] The offensive strategy was to get ashore and pin down or destroy the Turkish reserve to allow the main Landings at Helles to succeed. The tactical defence was adoption of a position from which to engage this reserve. Whether or not this was the intention, the latter was what happened, though occupation of the tactically "absurd" seaward side of Second Ridge, with little or no ability to dominate Legge Valley, shows that it was the enemy who seized the initiative. The Australian commanders give the impression they were not controlling the battle, but reacting to it.

MacLagan and Şefik had been dealt different hands. Şefik commanded an organised, intact and committed force, marching along known roads or relatively easy ground. MacLagan's force was disorganised and pushing through dense scrub into unknown territory against the grain of a steep terrain. One of the mistakes in attempts to understand this battle is to assume that "the Third Brigade was relatively intact", and "three quarters" of the 11th Battalion "had assembled in Rest Gully, while many of its B Company were converging on the main range."[60] The inaccuracy of such assumptions in the case of the 11th Battalion, has been shown in previous pages, and fragmentation of the force would continue as later waves arrived.

Battlefield evidence, there is little or no direct evidence, supports Prior's view about changes in the force's orders. MacLagan appears to have been responding to contradictory orders and priorities on difficult ground. Şefik and many of his force had seen battle before,[61] while MacLagan's was untried. For all his belief in his brigade, MacLagan did not know how they would perform in battle. His confidence must have been further undermined by the scattering of his units and the absence of field artillery. In this light, the landing of the 3rd Brigade around Ari Burnu, the disorganisation of the force and its subsequent fragmentation, as established here for the 11th Battalion, are significant. The Australian leaders would learn, but on 25 April they had very little experience to help them fight a skilled enemy on the ridges of Sari Bair. Had this battle taken place after the fighting on the western front, the veterans of those battles would probably have read this one differently. Şefik by contrast,

---

56 This is examined in greater detail in a paper to be published in *Gallipoli: New Perspectives on the Mediterranean Expeditionary Force*, to be published by Helion and Company.

57 Bean, *Official History*, Volume I (1921 and 1941), p.447.

58 Aspinall-Oglander, Becke, *Military Operations, Gallipoli*, Vol. I, p.185.

59 Williams, "Z Beach, the Landing of the ANZAC Corps, April 25, 1915", p.34.

60 Roberts, *Landing at Anzac*, second edition, p.100. 1st edition.

61 E.J. Erickson, *Gallipoli: The Ottoman Campaign* (Barnsley, South Yorkshire: Pen and Sword Books, 2010), p.40.

conducted a tactical appreciation, issued his orders, and manoeuvred to achieve them, with the added advantage of having access to limited artillery support.[62] Şefik's experience, preparation, training and a knowledge of the ground gave his decision-making speed and commitment; the Australian leaders' appear hesitant and cautious by comparison.

Birdwood insisted on taking Third Ridge, but stressed establishment of a defence on the right before advancing up the range on the left. The 11th Battalion's first objective was on Second Ridge, and MacLagan sent much of the battalion there. The sight of small parties of Turks ahead met apprehensions of an attack from the right, and the force was ordered to stop and reorganise. Before the advance recommenced, Şefik's columns were seen approaching.

This is as close as we get from existing secondary sources; Beevor's evidence of being told to dig as soon as he came ashore suggests caution even before Turks were seen on Third Ridge.

27th Regiment's role has previously been underrated and MacLagan's choices were not as clear-cut as believed. Before MacLagan is judged too harshly, the roles of Brand, Bridges and Birdwood should be investigated more closely.

Şefik's account of the battle as it concerned 27th Regiment has not been subjected here to the same scrutiny as Australian accounts, but it appears to be based on records created during the campaign, and presents the image of an experienced, educated commander and his staff developing an appreciation of the situation into which they had been thrust. It is written with hindsight, but its detail, insights into Şefik's reasoning and correlation with western sources when comparisons are possible, are indicative of accuracy. By way of balance, a report in the 1st Division's Unit War Diary of "Prisoners of war taken near Kaba Tepe 25.4.15" reveals interviews with three members of the 1st and 2nd battalions of the 27th Regiment. They "surrendered willingly. They were called up 3 months ago and recently came up from Chanak … They are tired of war having been fed only twice daily on wheat porridge and beans. They have had no pay. They were unarmed as telephonists. The telephone has broken down."[63] This image contrasts with Şefik's account of military efficiency and motivated, committed, patriotic and religious troops. There are many sides to every story, and many stories within.[64]

The 27th Regiment launched a classic counter-attack. The enemy assault had lost its momentum, its troops were scattered and beginning the process of rallying and consolidating to meet the attack, a "state of expectancy"[65] defined by Clausewitz. The attack would be made aggressively and on a broad front, before the enemy could find their feet, to keep their leaders off balance and prevent them realising the Turks' numerical inferiority. The intention was to hold the enemy's advance until the 19th Division arrived. By choosing to defend, the 3rd Brigade had played into Şefik's hands. The risks of attempting an advance to Third Ridge were great, but so was the prize; the results could have been spectacularly successful or disastrous. The decision to stop on Second Ridge removed the attack's momentum and began a defensive action that was to last eight months.

The troops scattered in the scrub and trenches of Second Ridge knew nothing of such deliberations. All they could do was keep their rifles working and their minds alert, obey orders, often given by strangers, fight when necessary, dig when they could and hug "the earth closer than I ever hugged a girl"[66] when shrapnel or bullets demanded it. Theirs was not to reason why; the problem was, without an accurate understanding of what was happening on the battlefield, their leaders were probably little better off.

62 Şefik, para. 80.
63 1st Division War Diary, Sub-class 1/42/3 Part 2, AWM4, Australian Imperial Force Unit War Diaries, 1914–18 War, Australian War Memorial.
64 Uyar's *The Ottoman Defence Against the ANZAC Landing* provides a broader and more detailed study.
65 C. von Clausewitz, *The Essential Clausewitz: Selections from On War* (New York: Dover Publications, 2003), p.86.
66 Aitken, letter/diary, p.20.

9

The Battle for Baby 700

The 11th Battalion should feature prominently in the fighting on Baby 700, but are generally only glimpsed in the background to others' stories. This and the following chapter will attempt to reconstruct their experience on Baby 700 from the shards of information that can be found.

As a result of earlier deliberations, the only portion of the 11th Battalion ordered to the high ground was Brockman's meagre party. Could they have reached Baby 700 more quickly and in greater strength than they did? Reconnaissance is prudent before any major troop movement, but Brockman's reconnaissance of Russell's Top cost time, and the information gleaned may have been available from Everett.[1]

Brockman then decided to advance up the valley. His reasoning is not stated. Avoiding the Nek may have been desirable, but his party was not large and Tulloch had already cleared the way. Perhaps Brockman was influenced by Lalor's experience,[2] and of the perceived presence of a machine gun in the area.[3]

Howe and Louch described single shrapnel bursts, rather than salvoes, over the valley, suggesting the single "clumsy slow firing" Mantelli gun at Gaba Tepe.[4] One account noted that "No battalion would go up the Nek from Plugges ... Battalion after battalion ... met shrapnel" and "went up Monash" Valley,[5] but this appears to have been later in the day. Brockman's reasoning is probably straightforward: Russell's Top is very exposed, and if Brockman could see Gaba Tepe, the Turkish observers on Gaba Tepe[6] could see the Top, and his company advancing along the skyline. Proceeding via the valley presented its own problems: if the Turks arrived on the ridges in force, the valley would have become impassable.

Had Brockman taken his men across the Nek, they would have reached the high ground in strength, and possibly early enough to assist Tulloch's party. These are difficult "what ifs" to address, as we cannot even be clear about A Company's objective. Where was Brockman heading? There are no references to the company being ordered to take the objectives covered by the map references in the battalion orders. Direct evidence is scant or non-existent, but a number of comments reinforce that Baby 700 was the objective. In *Anzac to Amiens* Bean wrote that MacLagan had decided 9th Battalion's occupation of Third Ridge to be "a completely impossible task," and "to make sure of the northern flank," sent 11th Battalion troops to Second Ridge and, apparently, Baby 700.[7] In *Volume I* Bean tells us that Morgan proceeded "towards Baby 700" in accordance with orders and troops were "directed from Plugge's against Baby 700."[8] Another account stated that "MacLagan had seen that Baby 700 was the key" and later "begged battalion after battalion to go up that way."[9] None of this suggests a thrust for Battleship Hill: if the aim was to defend Second Ridge, Baby 700 had become

1   Everett, interview, Ellam-Innes Collection, p.239.
2   *Ibid.*, p.240.
3   *Ibid.*, p.240.
4   Şefik, footnote to para. 17.
5   3DRL 606 item 25, pp.7–10.
6   Bean, *Gallipoli Mission*, sketch, p.263.
7   Bean, *Anzac to Amiens*, pp.92–93.
8   Bean, *Official History*, Volume I (1921 and 1941), p.286.
9   3DRL 606 item 25 pp.7–10. It is unclear who said this – MacLagan, Peck or Captain A.M. Ross.

THE BATTLE FOR BABY 700 197

the left flank, and Battleship Hill lay beyond the line of defence. The existing evidence suggests Baby 700 as Brockman's objective and that Battleship Hill had disappeared from the plans, as had Third Ridge. Such gaps in the evidence would have been filled had Bean asked different questions.[10]

We are also left to ponder other questions - what would have happened if A and C Companies had reached Baby 700 or Battleship Hill, before enemy reinforcements reached the battlefield? Had they been despatched with haste from Plugge's, it is difficult to believe they would not have beaten the Turks to the crest.

Hedley Howe's separation from de Mole, Pettit[11] and Morgan evidences the terrain's role in fragmenting advancing parties of Australians on 25 April. With a few others, probably of his platoon, Howe reached Russell's Top slightly inland of the Nek, but from here his various accounts of the next moments diverge.

In 1965, Howe described pausing "on top of Baby 700," from where could be seen Battleship Hill, the crest of Hill 971, and, on "the lower spurs of Battleship Hill," Tulloch's withdrawal.[12] Admiration "of the scenery was cut short by two shells right" on target, bursting "about 20 feet above ground and about 50 yards ahead of" A Company's "line, killing and wounding about 20 men."[13] "Very smartly" the line moved forward down the inland slope of Baby 700:

> into more trouble. Machine guns, about 300–400 yards away, opened fire on either flank. In a clearly visible line right across the ridge … leaves and twigs from the scrub flew into the air … the advancing troops walked right into the fire. Casualties were heavy, but the lesson was learned. The troops moved through the fire, but stopped before reaching a second line of fire about 100 yards ahead.[14]
>
> Four machine guns … swept the crest … their firing perfectly co-ordinated. While the second pair barred any further advance, the first pair started to traverse the ground between … In a few minutes Brockman's two platoons and Robertson's company had lost nearly half their strength.[15]

"The surviving officers" ordered a retirement to the gullies about 100 yards behind, "shallow extensions of the heads of Legge Valley … and Malone's Gully," each running to "within about 25 yards" of the crest and providing cover "from rifle and machine-gun fire for about 400 men". "In twos and threes the men made their way back to this position, collecting ammunition from the dead … dragging their wounded with them." All "immediately began to organise for the day's battle ahead — as calmly and efficiently as at any time later in the war." Howe recalled that "the solid matter-of-fact common-sense of officers and men," applied to problems "as they developed," was of more value than their limited training.[16] The "dead wood from the scrub burned without smoke," and some men "made tea, which was passed along the line."[17] A "battalion" of Turks was seen advancing in open order over "the lower slopes of Battleship Hill, about 500 yards" distant. The Australians hit the

---

10 An exception is Bean's correspondence with Denton, who he may have asked about orders as he received the reply "With regard to the orders given on Plugge's Plateau to the other companies of the 11th I cannot remember, only my own and those of the General." Denton to Bean, 16 June 1920, 3DRL 8042 item 7.

11 Pettit and four others were "cut off" at some stage while carrying ammunition. Pettit "heard a yell behind him and believed Gennery was shot. He did not see him afterwards. Things were very much mixed up." Genery has no known grave. Pettit, inertviewed, No 26 General Hospital Etaples, date unclear, probably 30 May 1916, Australian Red Cross Wounded and Missing Enquiry Bureau files, 1DRL/0428.

12 Howe, "Sparks From an Old Controversy", p.8.
13 *Ibid.*, p.8.
14 *Ibid.*, pp.8–9.
15 *Ibid.*, pp.8–9.
16 Howe, "Sparks From an Old Controversy", p.9.
17 *Ibid.*, p.10.

Figure 29. The Nek, beyond trees, from the seaward slope of Baby 700. Photograph taken from the ridge on the seaward side of the "U" trench. (Photograph by J.P. Hurst, n.d., author's collection)

advance with a brisk rifle fire that forced the Turks into cover. "Every shot was aimed and Zeki Bey later informed the writer the Turks were surprised at the effectiveness of the fire."[18]

The Turkish advance continued, small parties dribbling forward "to a position about 300 yards in front of the Australian line."[19] The Australians were soon "engaged in a classic fire fight – attempting to check the enemy advance and beat down his fire so they themselves could move forward."[20] Howe then describes being in a party of two officers and about 40 men who attacked a U-shaped trench.[21]

In another account, which Howe gave Bean, on reaching the top of Monash Valley, Howe and the men with him crossed the narrow neck connecting Russell's Top to Baby 700. He and two companions then moved off to their right, searching for their battalion and the firing line. A party of troops lining the ridge on the far side of the gully called to them "to come on" and the three men crossed the gully head to join the party of "20–50" there.[22]

Howe's party "hopped over the top" of the ridge and "ran suddenly into a Turkish trench."[23] The Australians shot some of the occupants and leapt in. "There was a fight."[24] Some Turks were shot, others bayoneted.[25] It is not known whether any escaped, but about a dozen dead, probably survivors of the Russell's Top garrison, lay in the trench.[26] One was armed with a sword and presumed to

18 *Ibid.*, p.11. Howe and Zeki may well be describing the same event, but with 27th Regiment troops moving in the area before 57th Regiment's arrival, and Margetts seeing Turks advancing over Battleship Hill as early as 9:15 a.m., this cannot be assumed.

19 *Ibid.*, p.11

20 *Ibid.*, pp.10–11.

21 *Ibid.*, p.11.

22 Howe, 3DRL, 8042 item 7.

23 *Ibid.*

24 *Ibid.*

25 *Ibid.*

26 Bean, *Official History*, Volume I (1921 and 1941), p.311.

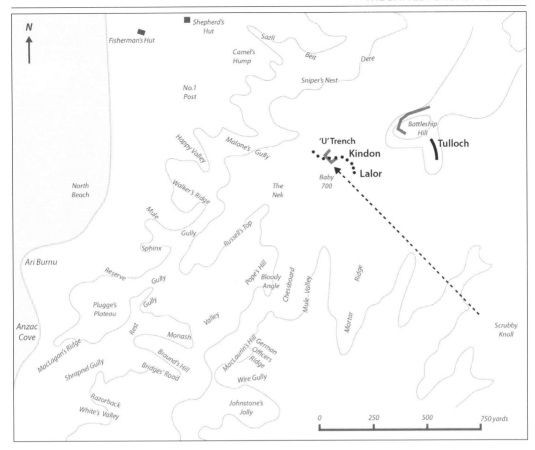

Map 11. Adapted from Bean's Map 12. Approximate position of "U" trench (the location of this trench varies slightly in Bean's various maps), relative to Scrubby Knoll. (Bean, Map 12, *Official History*, Volume I (1921 and 1941), after p.268)

be an officer.[27] "Joe" Adlam,[28] "claimed to have shot him and took" the sword.[29] A number of dead Australians from earlier parties also lay in and around the position.[30]

The trench was curiously constructed, being "absolutely straight"[31] for about "70 to 80 yards," with from "each end ... a communication trench" curving "for a few yards and then" running "straight back to the crest behind."[32] Remarkably, given the extent of the later entrenchments on Baby 700, this trench appears to still be visible. It lies beneath the crests of Baby 700 and the ridge on its seaward side, enabling observation only towards the north, and, to an unknown extent, inland to the north east or east; its purpose is a mystery. In Howe's time the trench was only three feet[33] deep and, because of its shape, became known as "U" trench (Map 11).

27   Howe, 3DRL 8042 item 7.
28   11 Private James Reginald Adlam, A Company, 21 at embarkation, labourer of West Perth, born Geraldton.
29   Howe to Churchill, 30 November 1962.
30   Howe, 3DRL 8042 item 7.
31   *Ibid.*
32   Howe, "Sparks From an Old Controversy", p.11.
33   *Ibid.*, p.11.

The shallow, untraversed trench soon proved a deathtrap when "a machine gun" opened fire "from the right."[34] This deadly enfilade forced the survivors into the communication trenches, from where Turks were soon seen advancing "over the level ground … about 500 yards"[35] inland. Howe and his companions were probably watching Turks advancing over the seaward side of Battleship Hill.

Some of the wounded survivors clambered "back over the parapet" and began crawling over the exposed ground to the gully head behind. The Turks:

> let them go … unwounded men … started lifting the seriously wounded from the trench and carrying them back – they too were unmolested … probably the first occasion on which the Turks permitted clearance of wounded.[36]

The trench was indefensible and under fire, no Australian firing line was visible and the enemy were advancing in force. No officers were with Howe's party, and it was agreed by "general consent"[37] to abandon the trench and have "a pow wow." They "decided to dig in … on the reverse slope and wait."[38]

There are contradictions between Howe's accounts. Did he advance over Baby 700 until forced back by machine gun fire and shrapnel, as described in his 1965 account, after which he attacked "U" trench, or did he advance to "U" trench from Monash Valley as he told Bean? Examination of Howe's various accounts suggest he is in fact describing two separate parties: his, which attacked "U" trench, and another, which made the doomed advance over Baby 700. If so, the latter appears to represent the only account of the fate of the party under Brockman, Morgan, Cooke and Robertson. There are further complications in the story of "U" trench. In one account Howe refers to no officers being present with the attacking party,[39] and in another refers to two.[40] Bean describes an earlier attack on the trench by the 9th, 11th and 12th Battalions,[41] though Howe refers to only one during the morning. In both attacks, if in fact there were two, the enfilading machine gun caused abandonment of the trench.

In *Gallipoli Mission*, Bean states that Margetts retired from his position on Baby 700 at about 10:00 a.m., after the death of Major Robertson "and many others."[42] In the *Official History* he states that Margetts' withdrawal was forced by the sight of a party withdrawing from "U" trench.[43] Seeing this, MacLagan, urgently requested reinforcements be sent there[44] to prevent a Turkish advance onto Russell's Top, and elements of the 1st Brigade were immediately sent. *Gallipoli Mission* continues that in Monash Valley the lead elements of these battalions became mixed with some of Brockman's party advancing from Rest Gully, among whom was Howe, though Howe's accounts do not mention this.[45] By this timing, Howe would have arrived on Russell's Top long after the withdrawal from "U" trench that forced Margett's retirement.

Bean's account is a muddle. By his own chronology, Kemal had not yet attacked Tulloch, or was just beginning to do so.[46] If Tulloch was still on Battleship Hill, could Turks really have been fighting behind him, advancing towards "U" trench and forcing Margetts' retirement? How could Turks have got past Tulloch? Tulloch describes withdrawing before, not through, the Turkish forces, yet Bean

34 Howe, 3DRL 8042 item 7.
35 *Ibid.*
36 Howe, "Sparks From an Old Controversy", p.11
37 Howe, 3DRL 8042 item 7.
38 *Ibid.*
39 *Ibid.*
40 Howe, "Sparks From an Old Controversy", p.11.
41 Bean, *Official History*, Volume I, p.294.
42 Bean, *Gallipoli Mission*, p.88.
43 Bean, *Official History*, Volume I (1921 and 1941), p.294.
44 Bean, *Gallipoli Mission*, p.88; Bean, *Official History*, Volume I (1921 and 1941), pp.294–295.
45 Bean, *Gallipoli Mission*, pp.88, 90.
46 Bean, *Official History*, Volume I (1921 and 1941), p.294.

wrote that Tulloch learned of the struggle in this area after returning from Battleship Hill. It is more likely that 57th Regiment had not yet arrived at Baby 700, and any pressure in the Baby 700 area was from parties from 27th Regiment. If so, the 1st Division's reserve brigade, the 1st, was being committed to a defensive battle before 57th Regiment's arrival on the field.

Bean's chronology is difficult to accept for other reasons. Brockman's two platoons were among the first ashore, with orders to push inland and secure the high ground. It is difficult to believe that they did not commence their approach to their objective until the same time as troops from the last brigade of the division to land, nor why this brigade, the divisional reserve, would be dispatched to the 11th Battalion's objective before the 11th Battalion got there. Why would it have taken A Company from four to six hours to reach Baby 700, and why did they advance so late? Who fought who on Battleship Hill and Baby 700? The aim of analysing the mess of detail in the preceding paragraphs is to establish a chronology to answer such questions.

Firstly, who were the advancing Turks Howe's party saw from the "U" trench? The assumption for most of the last century has been that it was 57th Regiment, pushing forward behind Tulloch's party, by recent accounts as late as 1:00 p.m.[47] This again begs the question of what Brockman's company had been doing for the previous hours. If Tulloch was not forced back until early afternoon as recently proposed, Brockman's party had somehow procrastinated for about seven hours – hardly feasible, and not recorded by anyone who was there. Could A Company really have been beaten to the high ground by 57th Regiment, who had marched several miles, assembled, deployed, climbed the heights and launched a regimental, or brigade sized, attack? Such a chronology would also imply that Brockman's party had been sitting idle during 27th Regiment's counter-attack. This chronology and its implications do not seem reasonable.

Examination of Howe's accounts suggests a less simple picture than Bean's but allows establishment of other scenarios. By Howe's estimate, Tulloch's party rejoined the firing line at about 9:00 a.m.,[48] some hours earlier than claimed in the *Official History* and other sources. If so, Brockman's party may have begun their advance over Baby 700 between 8:00 and 9:00 a.m., at which time Howe was in the vicinity of Malone's Gully.[49] Margetts' withdrawal may have been prompted by the retirement of Howe's, Brockman's, Tulloch's or some other, unrecorded, party.

The machine gun that fired into "U" trench was, Bean thought, positioned nearby on Baby 700,[50] implying it belonged to 57th Regiment. Study of the ground today is hampered by foliage taller than head height, but it is difficult to understand how the Turks could have had a tripod mounted, water-cooled, medium machine gun on the inland slope of Baby 700 between 8:00 and 10:00 a.m. that morning, on or near ground supposedly occupied by Margetts, directly behind Tulloch's party and to the right of Jackson's. Moreover, by the chronologies established above, 57th Regiment had not yet arrived. In addition, when Margetts' party withdrew, it was due to the cry "The left are retiring,"[51] in response, according to Bean, to the withdrawal from the "U" trench after it had been enfiladed by the machine gun. In other words, Margetts was on Baby 700 at the time this gun was supposedly firing from his immediate vicinity. This gun must surely have been visible to someone.

According to the chronology established above, Şefik arrived before 57th Regiment. He positioned his four machine guns, in two "platoons," near Scrubby Knoll.[52] No other Turkish machine guns are confirmed to have been on the battlefield at the time.[53] Şefik's guns opened fire between 8:00 and

47   Roberts, *Landing at Anzac*, second edition, p.152.
48   Howe, "Sparks From an Old Controversy", p.10.
49   Howe to Churchill, 30 November 1962.
50   Bean, *Official History*, Volume I (1921 and 1941), p.294.
51   *Ibid.*
52   Şefik, para. 102.
53   Unless the Fisherman's Hut or other guns existed; this is denied by several modern historians, but there is much eyewitness evidence to suggest otherwise. Hurst, 'Ottoman Machine Guns at the ANZAC Landing'; Ewen, "The Gallipoli Maxims".

9:00 a.m., which correlates with Howe's estimates of Morgan's and Cooke's advance over Baby 700. "U" trench lies in a direct line from Scrubby Knoll (Map 11).[54] It was invisible to these guns, but may have been marked on their maps and perhaps they even possessed range cards for it. Alternatively, Turkish officers, scanning the front through binoculars[55] and firing on "the smallest movement,"[56] may have seen the Australians charging over the ridge before disappearing into the gully head; perhaps the guns had fired at these men or have dropped bullets over the ridge and into the gully. If so, the halting of Turkish fire for evacuation of the wounded may have been a coincidence. What is not known is whether the 1915 topography would have allowed bullets from Scrubby Knoll to clear the ridge and fall into this trench.

Evidence against this possibility is that later in the day Howe again described accurate, apparently observed and aimed fire into the trench. Perhaps this fire came from a different gun – when members of the 1st Battalion and the 3rd Brigade charged over Baby 700 some time after 11:00 a.m., the Turks "ran, one of them lumbering back over the shoulder of the hill with a machine-gun packed upon a mule."[57] Whether this really was a gun is not known – Şefik had sent mules loaded with ammunition to this area, and troops had on other occasions reported seeing machine guns when it appears none were present.

Machine gun fire from the other flank is less easily explained, though it is possible perceptions of fire from the left flank may have been a mistake by inexperienced troops, and Howe appears to have acquired this information second hand. His description of fire opening "on either flank" may referred to fire falling on either flank of the Australian line, by one gun or pair of guns sweeping left to right, and the other right to left.[58]Howe's description of "perfectly co-ordinated" fire suggests the guns were co-located, rather than on separate flanks. Given the confusion of the fighting on Baby 700 and evidence available today, the matter will probably remain unresolved unless Turkish sources one day reveal more.[59]

Howe's 1965 account, despite anomalies, is significant for a number of reasons. Although it cannot be proved beyond doubt that 57th Regiment was or was not on the field when Tulloch withdrew, it is known that Şefik's machine guns were positioned on Scrubby Knoll before 57th Regiment's arrival, and Howe described fire coming from the right, rather than the front.[60] Howe also notes that when the 11th Battalion parties reached the head of Monash Valley and advanced onto the slopes of Baby 700, Turks on Third Ridge "were maintaining brisk fire on anything which moved." These were assumed to be "retiring Turkish outposts" who "had evidently … gone to ground,"[61] but may also have been 27th Regiment from Maidos. In other words, Şefik's chronology ties in with Howe's and others, and the time and direction of his machine gun fire accords with Howe's description of Morgan's and Cooke's parties receiving fire from the right. If this reconstruction is correct, it means that 27th Regiment may not only have played a major role in halting the advance of the Anzac right flank on 25 April, but also of their left, on the all important high ground of Sari Bair. Their fire may not only have stopped Tulloch, but have prevented Brockman's reinforcements getting forward to support him. 57th Regiment, usually credited with stopping Tulloch, may not yet have been on the field.

54   Bean, *Official History*, Volume I (1921 and 1941), Maps 12 and 13.
55   Şefik, para. 79.
56   *Ibid.*, para. 102.
57   Bean, *Official History*, Volume I (1921 and 1941), p.296.
58   Mofflin noted these guns methodically working from one end of his trench to the other. Mofflin, letter, 20 October 1915, p.18.
59   "Completing the Story – Researching Gallipoli in the Turkish Military Archives", Gallipoli Centenary Research Project, Macquarie University, The Australian War Memorial and Turkey's Middle East Technical University.
60   Howe, "Sparks From an Old Controversy", p.8.
61   *Ibid.*, pp.7–8.

Brockman's account sheds little light on these events and is difficult to follow, but suggests he was not in the advance described by Howe. He told Lalor, on the seaward slope of Baby 700,[62] "to stay where he was and dig in to protect the left flank"[63] and "went back over Popes and came across Major Kindon" of the 1st Battalion. When Brockman at some stage attempted to rejoin his men on Baby 700, "he met some" of them "coming back. The men said that they had gone on," he thought "under Lalor's orders," but later learned "it was on Robertson's." They had been "overwhelmed with numbers" and forced back. This may be the advance Howe described or a later one. Brockman then organised a firing line on Pope's and "got the men to dig … This must have been about 11 a.m."[64]

Brockman appeared surprised that his men had advanced, suggesting he had placed them on Baby 700 to defend it rather than advance to Battleship Hill. There is also a deal of confusion about Robertson's movements. Neither he nor Lalor survived to give their version of events. Medcalf, Brockman's observer, left only a general description of this period which does not describe his or the major's movements.[65] It is consequently not possible to be certain which withdrawal of his men Brockman witnessed, nor from where they were pushed, but given their final position at Pope's Hill, it seems likely that the withdrawal was the one in which Morgan was wounded.

Morgan's platoon was being hard pressed by the advancing Turks, and he gave the order to retire. He and Ayling held their ground until the men were clear, then Morgan gave Ayling "the tip" and the pair leapt up and ran for cover. Ayling was "going full speed" when a shrapnel burst knocked Morgan "head over heels."[66] The sergeant called him "and he groaned." With the enemy only "about 150 yards off" and "coming at us like mad," Ayling "hoisted" Morgan onto "his shoulder" and, with "a hail of lead" ploughing the ground, "carried him" back, expecting a bullet to hit him at every step. After about 50 yards he reached "the shelter of a dip in the ground," "dead beat." Their platoon and a few others returned with an officer, opened fire and checked the Turks while Ayling carried Morgan back[67] and "handed him over to the care of our bugler."[68] T.J. Davis[69] appears to have been in Morgan's party and Bugler W.T. Jamieson[70] was probably one of those who "carried him in."[71] Morgan was evacuated to England with some "very nasty wounds"[72] in his left shoulder and, in the confusion of 25 April, was reported missing.[73] Ayling received the DCM, being one of the first NCOs in the 11th Battalion to do so, for this rescue and subsequent handling of his platoon. "Not bad for a Yuba cocky, is it?,"[74] he proudly wrote to his wife.

When the 16th Battalion arrived at Pope's that evening, they found a "small party there," commanded by a sergeant of the 11th. This was probably Ayling, who told them that "his men formed the extreme left flank; no officers near them were left alive: their losses in the retirement had been heavy."[75] Ayling's party of "about 50" had arrived at Baby 700 with "an officer," but "when we got out of it there were only 18 men and myself left."[76] These disconnected accounts – Brockman's, Howe's, Ayling's and Bean's – probably tell a little of the missing story of Morgan's platoon.

62 Bean, *Official History*, Volume I (1921 and 1941), p.294.
63 Brockman, 3 DRL 8042 item 7.
64 *Ibid.*
65 Medcalf, manuscript, p.65.
66 Ayling, letter, *Sunday Times*, 1 August 1915.
67 Richards, manuscript, 2DRL 301, pp.39–40.
68 Ayling, letter, *Sunday Times*, 1 August 1915.
69 31 Private (at embarkation) Thomas John Davis, A Company, 23 at embarkation, clerk, of Brighton, Victoria, born Brighton.
70 63 Bugler William Thomas Jamieson, A Company, 20 at enlistment, civil servant, of Laverton, born Gippsland.
71 Australian Red Cross Wounded and Missing Enquiry Bureau files, 1DRL/0428.
72 Ayling, letter, *Sunday Times*, 1 August 1915.
73 B2455, Morgan.
74 Ayling, letter, 1 August 1915.
75 Bean, *Official History*, Volume I (1921 and 1941), p.469.
76 Ayling, letter, 1 August 1915.

It is unclear who, if anyone, was in overall command on Baby 700 throughout this day. S.B. Robertson, senior company commander of the 9th Battalion,[77] initially commanded at least a portion of the firing line, including men of the "9th, 10th and 11th."[78] According to Bean Robertson was killed late in the morning,[79] though other accounts have him killed later in the day.[80] It appears unusual that Brockman, who for "quite a while … was the senior officer on the front line,"[81] did not assume command on Baby 700,[82] especially as the 11th Battalion was responsible for the left and the 9th Battalion the right. If the aim was defence, as implied by Bean[83] and as appears repeatedly in this work to be the case, Brockman's actions in working around the posts at the head of the valley and along Second Ridge and his surprise that his men had advanced over Baby 700 make sense.

Bean's various accounts of the fighting on Baby 700 portray the critical, confused, fragmented, back and forth nature of the battle there. Implied is the gradual annihilation of the 3rd Brigade parties who first crossed its slopes. To its participants, it was "a soldier's battle," one of limited visibility and communication, of isolation, confusion and immense strain. Information came to men in fragments, forcing assumptions. Firing lines were broken by shrapnel, bullets, charges and hasty withdrawals over unnamed topography. Sometimes advances were made into a withering fire that limited rushes to only two yards at a time.[84] Men fighting among strangers thought themselves the only survivors of their battalions, and leaders found themselves commanding an area and whoever stumbled into it, rather than a platoon or company.[85] Howe, at the head of Malone's Gully, was joined at some stage by "a couple of wounded men," leading him to presume, as he couldn't see, that "there were evidently troops on the half-right front."[86] The fighting to his "half-right front" was the bitter battle for Baby 700. Parties were isolated on a small battlefield swept and fought over by many hundreds of men. Into this confusion Australians and, later, New Zealanders were rushed piecemeal, becoming fragmented and mixed as they filled gaps in the firing lines, advanced, withdrew and were slowly annihilated. Such fragmentation and confusion are mirrored in our attempts at reconstructing the battle. Often the to and fro nature of this fighting is the only clue in men's accounts to indicate that they fought here.

Men of the 1st, 2nd and 3rd Battalions were sent as urgent reinforcements to Baby 700.[87] "It was nearly 11" when a 1st Battalion company reached "the remnants of Robertson's and Lalor's line, which had been driven in from the forward slopes … There were probably about seventy of the 3rd Brigade at this place, but only a handful of ten or twelve was visible."[88] Most of the estimated 70 would have belonged to the 9th, 11th and 12th Battalions, the 11th to Tulloch's, Cooke's, Morgan's, Jackson's, Buttle's and Reid's parties. More were probably scattered over the hill in small, isolated groups. With "the remnant of the 3rd Brigade," a 1st Battalion company "charged the Turks who were on the seaward slope in front of them. The Turks ran."[89] Such charges further thinned the ranks of the survivors of the morning's advances. In such stories lie the missing experiences of the 11th Battalion on Baby 700.

In some cases the Turks withdrew to trenches,[90] and the Australians lay down in the scrub and returned fire, bullets whipping[91] amongst them, killing and wounding. On the left of Baby 700 the

77   E.A.D. Brockman, letter to Bean, 1920, AWM, 8042 item 7.
78   T. Gordon Robertson, letter to Bean, AWM38, 3 DRL 8042 item 7.
79   Bean, *Official History*, Volume I (1921 and 1941), p.298.
80   F. Coe, 18 August 1918, 3 DRL 8042 item 7.
81   Brockman, letter, 25 May 1915.
82   Brockman, 3DRL 606 item 27.
83   Bean, *Official History*, Volume I (1921 and 1941), p.285.
84   Robertson, letter, 3 DRL 8042 item 7.
85   *Ibid.*
86   Howe, 3DRL 8042 Item 7.
87   Bean, *Official History*, Volume I (1921 and 1941), p.295.
88   *Ibid.*, p.296.
89   *Ibid.*, p.296.
90   *Ibid.*, p.296.
91   *Ibid.*, p.296.

advancing troops were at some stage exposed to fire from its northern spurs[92] and on the right from those to its south. Turkish artillery showered the men with shrapnel.[93] Without artillery, all the men could do was "lie there," and the Turks "couldn't come on while we were lying there."[94] Their battle became one of enduring salvoes of enemy shrapnel and waiting to become a casualty, or rising from concealment to risk shrapnel, rifle and machine gun bullets, pushing back the enemy infantry when numbers allowed it and withdrawing when they demanded it. The longer one fought here, the lower the odds of survival. Into this confusion men were pushed in dribs and drabs. The strain here was "much the heaviest trial of the day,"[95] and as the hours wore on, the attacks continued and the lines thinned, "the torture" of enduring the artillery "fire increased."[96] By the afternoon, it was by "the strength of their determination, and by that alone," that "officers and men" clung to Baby 700.[97]

The New Zealand Auckland Battalion and some of the Canterbury Battalion[98] were despatched to Baby 700 and the battle's pattern – advance, hold, withdraw – was repeated. When the dwindling parties on Baby 700 were forced back, they rallied in gully heads or "the neighbourhood of the Nek."[99] The hill was starved of men as reinforcements were drawn en route into the fighting on Second Ridge, but, when troops trickled through to Baby 700, "another brave advance" would force back the opposing infantry. The fighting continued "furiously, hour after hour"[100] throughout the day. Officer casualties were heavy.[101]

An added problem was that once the men lay down in the scrub, they immediately lost contact with all but those alongside them, and leaders lost their ability to control the battle. The only means of communication was by word of mouth, but as the lines were invariably broken by casualties, this also became ineffective. Eventually, most of those who "had charged so gaily ... in the morning, and had gone up the hill so lightheartedly when the day was young," had been killed or wounded.[102] Many of Baby 700's stories were buried on its slopes, in the gullies and ridges nearby or, elsewhere – Egypt, France, England, Australia. Some survivors would never recall the "sweet smell of the crushed thyme" without a shudder.[103]

At some stage Ashton was despatched to the vicinity of Baby 700. He and E.P. Davis were part way up Second Ridge when they were ordered to the left by a "British staff officer,"[104] probably a member of MacLagan's staff.[105] Ashton believed he then joined New Zealanders advancing to the high ground[106] – if so, this would have been in the early afternoon, and many morning hours are missing from his account. His party "formed a firing line, as we had been trained." Dense scrub restricted "our view to just a few yards," and their left extended:

> more and more ... into the unknown ... feeling rather helpless ... no field of fire, no enemy to shoot at
> ... a regular hail of bullets whipping through the leaves, to our excited imaginations no more than two

92 *Ibid.*, p.298.
93 *Ibid.*, p.303.
94 *Ibid.*, p.303.
95 Bean, *Anzac to Amiens*, p.109.
96 Bean, *Official History*, Volume I (1921 and 1941), p.299.
97 *Ibid.*
98 Pugsley, *Gallipoli: The New Zealand Story*, pp.117, 131, 133.
99 Bean, *Anzac to Amiens*, p.107.
100 *Ibid.*, p.106.
101 Bean, *Official History*, Volume I (1921 and 1941), p.297.
102 *Ibid.*, p.298.
103 *Ibid.* Margetts would never again smell thyme without "recalling that horrible day." Margetts, 3DRL 606 Book 31.
104 Ashton, interview, Welborn, pp.3, 4.
105 Bean, *Official History*, Volume I (1921 and 1941), p.302 refers.
106 *Ibid.*, p.302.

inches above our heads … confusion of thought and movement … adjusting my sights up to 500 yards, I fired some dozen or so rounds at some figures.[107]

"Four times during the day" Howe's party "pushed forward over the crest of Baby 700" and four times "were pushed back,"[108] with Adlam still carrying his sword. Officers had been ordered to leave their swords behind, and within "Ten minutes" of Adlam souveniring his, Howe "knew why." Adlam "had become the greatest nuisance on the battlefront. Some Turks evidently" concluded that "he was the Australian Regimental commander – and detailed a machine gun especially to take care of Joe."[109] Lalor also carried a sword; he was killed during the afternoon. A Turkish story recounts that:

An Australian officer with a sword in his hand was seen ordering a party … to attack a group of 20 to 25 Turks … the Turkish troops stood up and charged … a large number of the enemy and a few Turks were killed.[110]

This is sometimes surmised to describe Lalor's death.[111] Perhaps this "officer" was not Lalor, but Joe Adlam.

Baby 700 claimed many officers during the day. By late afternoon Tulloch, Morgan, Butler (12th Battalion), Fogden (1st Battalion), Scobie and Richardson (2nd Battalion), had been wounded. Lalor, Patterson (12th Battalion), Gordon (2nd Battalion), Swannell (1st Battalion) and S.B. Robertson (9th Battalion) had been killed. History had lost sight of Cooke. Many dead and wounded littered the scrub.

On the left of the line there were "practically no officers" left.[112] Bean describes a party near the head of Malone's Gully, presumably Howe's, numbering "about fifty men of all units without any officer at all."[113] Howe recalled "a busy day … pretty constantly on the move" accompanied by "Joe and his sword, followed everywhere" by the machine gun, "which didn't hit him but got nearly everybody else in the neighbourhood … Dozens of times we told him to 'Throw the damned thing away!' but he persisted in hanging on to it."[114]

Evacuating the wounded was an added difficulty. Walking cases could find their way to the beach, but "no one had the faintest idea of the location of aid posts" and terrain and enemy fire made it almost impossible for stretcher-bearers to carry out the large number of wounded. The men had to improvise. Howe's party used "web equipment straps" as slings and the wounded were passed "down the precipitous slope from one pair of men to other pairs … and finally left with a small party in attendance in a sheltered gully about 200 yards above the beach."[115] "Walking wounded officers" took maps marked with troop positions and artillery targets, and "signed reports from senior officers … detailing the situation. Each and every one urgently requested artillery support and picks and shovels – but not one shell of ours landed in front of Baby 700 and not one pick or shovel came forward throughout the day."[116]

Howe was "in and out" of "U" trench "three times – until we finally decided to stay out of it." If Malone's Gully was held, "U" trench was useless to the Turks[117] – they could not "raise their

107 Ashton, manuscript, p.18.
108 Howe to Churchill, 30 November 1962.
109 *Ibid.*
110 James, *Gallipoli*, p.114n; C. Coulthard-Clark, "From Eureka to Gallipoli", p.47, *Defence Force Journal*, No.44, January/February 1984, pp.44–48.
111 Bean, *Official History*, Volume I (1921 and 1941), p.291.
112 *Ibid.*, p.310.
113 *Ibid.*, p.310.
114 Howe to Churchill, 30 November 1962.
115 Howe, "Sparks From an Old Controversy", p.9.
116 *Ibid.*, pp.9–10.
117 Howe to Churchill, 30 November 1962.

heads … without being shot" and a "virtual armistice prevailed between "U" trench and Malone's Gully."[118] At, by Pugsley's estimate, about 3:00 p.m.,[119] but in one account Howe thought "about 11:00 a.m.,"[120] a party of New Zealanders "came up a gully from the sea."[121] Howe's party, including some unidentified officers, told the New Zealand major that "it was no use taking the trench,"[122] but he insisted on "an immediate attack" by "about twice as many men as were needed."[123] The Australians advised the New Zealanders to "make for the communication trenches – and stay there."[124] The Turks ran.[125] The majority of the attackers "jumped into the straight trench. It seemed as if the Turkish machine gunners waited for them to get nicely lined up before opening."[126] The major was one of the first killed, and "every man in the trench was either killed or wounded – most of the latter seriously as the long bursts hit several times."[127] Howe sheltered in one of the communication trenches with two New Zealanders until "things quietened down."[128] Once again men "from Malone's Gully ran forward and started lifting the wounded … the Turks did not interfere."[129] Perhaps this reasserts that the guns were firing from Scrubby Knoll, with the charge over the skyline provoking long, blind bursts into the gully head, and the evacuation of wounded not so obvious or tempting a target.

Pugsley believed the New Zealand officer to be Major D. Grant, whose body was found in Malone's Gully during the 24 May armistice.[130] Bean believed Grant to have commanded a force on Kindon's former line and to have been killed there late in the afternoon.[131] In 1919 Bean found the rank insignia of a New Zealand major on Baby 700.[132] As no other New Zealand major appears to have been killed in this area at the Landing, the fate of Grant and his body are unclear.

With the "constant shifting … backwards and forwards," Ashton lost touch with Davis and found himself "on the extreme flank" beside "a young New Zealander, just a boy he seemed to my 22 years." The young soldiers did their best to "follow our training and rifle drill." A bullet or shrapnel pellet shattered the New Zealander's wrist and Ashton began bandaging it, when the boy "screamed … he had been shot again … in the stomach … I lay there badly shaken, with his cries in my ears, imploring me to shoot him." Feeling "terribly inadequate" and alone, Ashton went in search of a stretcher party "or even any troops."[133]

The "sun, well down by this time in the west, gave me some idea of where the beach lay." Keeping below the streams of machine gun bullets "bringing the leaves down in showers,"[134] Ashton tried to find the gully he had climbed earlier, but descended the wrong one (Figure 30). He assisted a wounded man of the 1st Brigade,[135] "who had crawled as far as he could towards help, as he thought," until "he finally collapsed." Once again Ashton sought help. He "came under fairly accurate rifle fire," heard a shout and:

118 Howe, "Sparks From an Old Controversy", p.11.
119 Pugsley, *Gallipoli: The New Zealand Story*, p.132.
120 Howe, "Sparks From an Old Controversy", p.11.
121 Howe, 3DRL 8042 item 7.
122 *Ibid.*
123 Howe, "Sparks From an Old Controversy", p.13.
124 *Ibid.*
125 Howe, 3DRL 8042 item 7.
126 Howe, "Sparks From an Old Controversy", p.13.
127 *Ibid.*
128 Howe, 3DRL 8042 item 7.
129 Howe, "Sparks From an Old Controversy", p.13.
130 Pugsley, *Gallipoli: The New Zealand Story*, p.132n.
131 Bean, *Gallipoli Mission*, pp.92–93.
132 *Ibid.*, p.102.
133 Ashton, manuscript, p.19.
134 *Ibid.*
135 Ashton, manuscript, p.20; Ashton, interview, Welborn, p.4.

Figure 30. Mule Gully, down which Ashton and others may have stumbled on 25 April.
Mortar Ridge is on the left. (Photograph by J.P. Hurst, n.d., author's collection)

found myself ... looking into the barrels of half a dozen Turkish rifles – the soldiers half hidden in a sort
of cave ... curiously dreamlike and nightmarish ... this was the end ... of so much enthusiasm and hard
work, of ambitions and dreams ... Turks came at me with fixed bayonets ... a crashing blow to the back of
the head with a rifle butt ... I sank down on my knees ... dragged along to a slight rise to the left, where
a couple of German officers in charge of a machine gun post had seen what had happened.[136]

Bean presumed Ashton wandered down Mule Valley. This may well be correct, though Chatal
Dere is also a possibility. There do not appear to be any natural caves in the area, but scrub and many
erosion channels and minor ridges scouring the ridge sides provide ample concealment. Ashton's
is not the only case of men becoming confused by that tangled geography – Major R. Scobie, 2nd
Battalion, presents one documented case[137] and Ashton's wounded 1st Brigade man another.

In "utter dejection" Ashton "waited for them to shoot me ... convinced that I owe my life to the
two German officers ... The Turks, generally speaking, took no prisoners, killing all those who fell
wounded ... into their hands." He was marched away, assuming his escort to be a "shooting party."[138]
Stripped of his equipment he was instead taken to "a sort of HQ" where a Turkish officer stood
"with his pants down – he'd been shot through both legs ... his orderly was attending to him." The
Australians were not the only ones to rat prisoners – the officer beckoned to Ashton and "whipped
off my wrist watch." He was eventually "put in a tent and given an overcoat to sleep in."[139]

136 Ashton, manuscript, pp.20, 21.
137 Bean, *Official History*, Volume I (1921 and 1941), p.316.
138 Ashton, manuscript, p.22.
139 F. Ashton, interview, 14 September 1976, 1976FA.

The machine gun post was probably 27th Regiment's. Şefik's account conflicts with Ashton's as it implies his prisoner was taken during the Australian withdrawal from Battleship Hill during the morning, but contradicts this by stating that the prisoner was escorted by 2 Company, 1st Battalion, suggesting that he was not captured on Battleship Hill.[140] There are some nagging coincidences. Şefik's prisoner was a "tall young … Western Australian," aged 22: Ashton turned 22 nine days before the landing.[141] The prisoner "seemed tired and cautious" but accepted a cigarette and relaxed a little, "crossed his legs, calmly smoked the cigarette and listened." The guard showed Şefik "a handful" of the prisoner's "metal money," which Şefik instructed be returned. The prisoner was sent "with a letter to Divisional HQ at Maydos."[142] If this man was not Ashton, he must soon have come to grief, as allied sources contain no further record of him.[143]

By about 4:00 p.m., various parties of New Zealanders and members of many Australian battalions, including survivors of the 3rd Brigade,[144] lay scattered through the scrub, clinging to what ground they could in defence of Baby 700. Further back, near the Nek, were New Zealanders under the recently arrived Lieutenant-Colonel D. McB. Stewart. Stewart was killed soon after.

Howe and other survivors were in the arms of "U" trench waiting for the fire to subside, when Turks were seen advancing over Battleship Hill and "the depression between" it and "Baby 700. This betokened … an attack on some considerable scale."[145] Howe's party began "to lose heavily,"[146] and to avoid being cut off, once more abandoned the useless trench. They decided to join a line of Australians to their right rear. Howe and a New Zealand corporal remained together but lost most of the others.[147]

"Even on the 400 Plateau" men embroiled in their own battles began to notice "great numbers" of Turks "in company column," deploying "into line as they topped the summit" of the "main ridge," then disappearing "behind Baby 700."[148] Clearly, the Turks were advancing for a major assault. At "about 4 p.m." they attacked."[149] Howe recalled the Turkish artillery building to "a rapid fire."[150] The Indian Mountain Battery had long since been silenced, and "the enemy's salvoes alone could now be heard."[151]

"About 4.30 on an arc extending over half a mile from the Chessboard on the right rear to the crest above the "U" trench on the left … about 300 yards in front … the Turks came forward in open order in three lines, each about 30 yards behind the one in front."[152] It must have been a daunting spectacle. Bean described the assault descending upon the "worn remnant"[153] defending Baby 700 and its flanks, and the "brave line which had held" the hill "through the long day finally broke."[154] The troops further back suddenly found the survivors of the front lines "running back on them. 'Get to b-!' … 'The Turks are coming on – thousands of them!' … The slopes of Baby 700 were left bare."[155] "The line had gone,"[156] its survivors dropping into the gully heads and lining the crests at Pope's Hill, the Bloody Angle and the vicinity of the Nek.

140 Şefik, footnote 1 to para. 104, p.54.
141 Ashton was five feet eight inches tall.
142 Şefik, para. 104, p.54, footnote 1.
143 In the 27th Regiment War Register, Şefik notes that the prisoner was handed over to an officer attached to 19th Division General Staff at Mal Tepe. 27th Regiment War Register, ATASE File 5338, Dossier H10, Index 001–11, Broadbent, Turkish Defence, p.464.
144 Bean, *Official History*, Volume I (1921 and 1941), p.313.
145 *Ibid.*, p.312.
146 *Ibid.*, p.312.
147 Howe, "Sparks From an Old Controversy", p.13.
148 Bean, *Official History*, Volume I (1921 and 1941), p.313.
149 *Ibid.*
150 Howe, "Sparks From an Old Controversy", p.14.
151 Bean, *Official History*, Volume I (1921 and 1941), p.315.
152 Howe, "Sparks From an Old Controversy", p.14.
153 Bean, *Official History*, Volume I (1921 and 1941), p.315.
154 *Ibid.*
155 *Ibid.*
156 *Ibid.*

The allied line did not break that easily, according to one of the few known survivor/chroniclers, Hedley Howe. As the leading Turks were "about half way to the Australian positions their artillery ceased fire." Despite the strain and demoralising attrition of the day, the survivors on Baby 700 remained full of fight. "Almost simultaneously, all along the line, the Australians and New Zealanders rose … and, kneeling or standing," opened fire. "The Turks went to ground … it appeared that their attack had been halted," but "Very quickly," they resumed the advance, "kneeling or standing to fire, and then crawling forward through the thick scrub."[157] The infantry of both sides were still fighting hard for Baby 700, but the Australians and New Zealanders were "Slowly and steadily" forced back, "fighting all the way."[158]

Howe's "40 or 50 men around the head of Malone's Gully stood fast. They were in an excellent defensive position and if compelled to retire could drop out of sight into the gully … They had easily halted the Turkish attempts to cross the skyline … shooting down any of the enemy who showed themselves."[159] Troops were then heard on the far side of the spur. Several "figures came over the skyline 150 yards away." A "Turkish officer, stood out at full height and looked through his glasses. Howe rested his rifle on a bush, took steady aim, and shot him."[160]

"Two corporals," Laing, 12th Battalion, but "well known to all the West Australians in the group," and a New Zealander of the Canterburys, "had taken command. The men had agreed among themselves that there would be 'no nicking off' – that all would clear out together when the word was given." This happened soon after.[161] Some of the party "slid down the … gully"; Howe, the Canterbury corporal, and three 11th Battalion men decided instead "to make a run for it across the Nek." They "emptied their magazines" once more "into the oncoming Turks," then "bolted."[162] Adlam was probably with this party, but in the rush disappeared "down Monash Valley."[163] These were "probably the last of the Anzac forces to cross the Nek alive during the campaign,"[164] and in one account Howe wrote that they suffered heavily in the retirement, with "more dead than alive."[165] He estimated they "must have had nearly 2,000 casualties on Baby 700 that day"[166] – in another account he suggests about 1,000[167] – "but Joe and his sword – and I – came through unscathed."[168]

Howe's account suggests that the withdrawal from Baby 700 was not the headlong flight it is often depicted as being. He recalled "It took the Turks the best part of an hour to cover the 500 yards from their start-line to the head of Monash Gully,"[169] and as "an exercise in retirement the Australian movement would have won full marks."[170] In one account he recalled that it was the fire of three New Zealand machine guns on Russell's Top that stopped the Turkish advance. He also believed "the majority of the seriously wounded had previously been carried back," few, if any, being left.[171] Bean wasn't so sure, writing that "in some places many of the wounded had to be left behind. Except for two officers and a private … Ashton was the only Australian" to survive falling into Turkish hands

157 Howe, "Sparks From an Old Controversy", p.14.
158 *Ibid.*, p.14.
159 *Ibid.*, p.15.
160 Bean, *Official History*, Volume I (1921 and 1941), p.315.
161 Howe, "Sparks From an Old Controversy", p.15.
162 *Ibid.*
163 Howe to Churchill, 30 November 1962.
164 Howe, "Sparks From an Old Controversy", p.15.
165 Howe, 3DRL 8042 item 7.
166 Howe to Churchill, 30 November 1962.
167 Howe, "Sparks From an Old Controversy", p.15.
168 Howe to Churchill, 30 November 1962.
169 Howe, "Sparks From an Old Controversy", p.14.
170 *Ibid.*, p.15.
171 *Ibid.*, p.15.

this day.[172] The advancing Turks then disappeared "into the thick scrub and broken ground of the valley slopes."[173]

"Still … moving fast," Howe "fell into the rifle pits" around the three machine-guns on Russell's Top, "already occupied by about 40 or 50 men from Baby 700 and the half-dozen New Zealanders" with the guns. An Auckland machine gun sergeant,"[174] probably Sergeant M.J. McLean,[175] "was in command. There was room for all in the rifle pits," arranged in a rough semicircle, "each of which was about two feet deep" and occupied by about five men.[176] The sergeant told Howe "You're in a damned bad place,"[177] but Howe thought it "a home from home"[178] after the trials of the day. Bean thought that these guns belonged to the Auckland and Canterbury battalions.[179] They appear to have been sited defensively, to prevent a Turkish advance over Baby 700 and the Top. Their firepower might have been of great value on Baby 700 during the day, particularly during the final Turkish attack; perhaps tripod-mounted machine guns would have made too easy a target on those exposed slopes.

Someone had earlier called "out Snowy Howe!" but, Howe, being "under fire at the time," had to wait until "things quietened down" before he and another man could crawl out to investigate. They found Private Ferguson, who had been at "U" trench, "shot through the lung" and with a broken leg.[180] Two Fergusons fought with the 11th this day; to confuse matters, both belonged to A Company and became casualties on 25 April. Ernest Leslie Ferguson[181] suffered a gunshot wound in the foot, and John James Ferguson[182] disappeared and is commemorated on the Lone Pine Memorial. Howe's party recovered whichever Ferguson it was[183] and put him behind their line with "about 50" wounded recovered during the withdrawal.[184]

The men confidently "settled in" to continue the battle.[185] Their post could only be attacked from the front, via the Nek, or by climbing the ridge from its flanks, which would only have been possible at certain points.[186] It was connected to the rear by a track, the "gunners had sixteen belts of ammunition," and most of the men had replenished their pouches "continuously during the day from the dead and wounded."[187] Gunfire to their left rear indicated heavy fighting, as unknown parties defended posts along Walker's Ridge and elsewhere.

"At dusk," 57th Regiment's 3rd Battalion "was ordered … to carry the attack to the sea" and later reported that they had reached The Nek.[188] These troops appear to have collided with Howe's party. Howe recalled a "strong force of Turks" attempting "to cross the Nek" just before sunset, "moving carelessly, bunched closely together."[189] It is difficult to match Howe's various accounts with certainty, but it appears these Turks were "heard before seen, yelling 'Allah! Mahommed!'"[190] There "was great excitement among the machine guns. Men whispered to each other: 'Let the bastards come'. The

172 Bean, *Official History*, Volume I (1921 and 1941), p.316. They were members of the 16th Battalion, captured that evening. *Ibid.*, pp.469, 470.
173 Howe, "Sparks From an Old Controversy", p.14.
174 *Ibid.*, p.15.
175 Pugsley, *Gallipoli: The New Zealand Story*, pp.141, 404.
176 Howe, "Sparks From an Old Controversy", p.15.
177 Howe, 3DRL 8042 item 7.
178 Howe, "Sparks From an Old Controversy", p.15.
179 Bean, *Official History*, Volume I (1921 and 1941), p.317.
180 Howe, 3DRL 8042 item 7.
181 37 Private Ernest Leslie Ferguson, A Company, 31 at embarkation, pastry cook of Fremantle, born Carlton.
182 169 Private John James Ferguson, A Company, 19 at embarkation, labourer of Perth, born North Melbourne.
183 Bean thought E.L. Ferguson, but Howe's notes do not say who. Bean, *Official History*, Volume I (1921 and 1941), p.317.
184 Howe, 3DRL 8042 item 7.
185 Howe, "Sparks From an Old Controversy", p.16.
186 *Ibid.*, p.15.
187 *Ibid.*, p.15.
188 Zeki Bey to Bean. Bean, *Gallipoli Mission*, pp.138–139.
189 Howe, "Sparks From an Old Controversy", p.16.
190 Howe, 3DRL 8042 item 7.

sergeant ordered everyone to hold fire until the machine guns opened."[191] When the "leading Turks were less than 20 yards distant" the guns let fly and stopped the attack "dead, the relatively few unwounded enemy escaping by jumping into the valleys on either side."[192]

A message, signed by all in Howe's party, was sent to the rear for reinforcements. They received the reply "Hang on at all costs. Reinforcements are on their way," but "They never came."[193] A party of New Zealanders were partly dug in "about 70–80 yards to the rear."[194] At about 8:00 p.m., Turks again advanced over the Nek and attacked the post from the front, while a larger party worked "their way along Monash Valley" and attacked its flank.[195] Beneath a moon "nearly full but obscured by cloud,"[196] the Turks attacked. Yelling, they got "right in among the party."[197] Many were "shot at close range (none bayoneted)"[198] but the attack was "easily beaten off."[199] The sergeant was wounded during the fight, leaving the two corporals in charge. A man sent back to check on the New Zealanders returned with the news that "the mob behind us has cleared out."[200] Another "strong party" of Turks from Monash Valley attacked Howe's "post from flank and rear. The movement had been heard and the men were ready and waiting … Invisible in the rifle pits … men and machine guns again kept silent, opening fire only at point-blank range. It was impossible to miss. The Turks fired a few rounds – mostly at each other – and the attack faded."[201]

Some of the attacking Turks were probably members of 3rd Battalion, 57th Regiment, who had penetrated along the Monash Valley side of Russell's Top. Bean wrote that this had been possible because they were assumed to be Indian troops, a belief held by "a surviving group of the 11th Battalion" at "the head of Monash Valley"[202] – possibly Ayling's party. Others may have been from the 72nd Regiment, who "Towards evening" were sent to support the attack in this area.[203] The 72nd was one of two Arab regiments in the 19th Division. They commanded little respect and had a reputation for firing wildly on their own side. Zeki felt the attack on Russell's Top might have gone "better, but the troops on" the "left were Arabs, and they panicked."[204] This matches Howe's description.

Howe's post was almost encircled and after "a brief discussion in which all participated, it was decided to fall back."[205] All but four of the "20–30 badly wounded" were evacuated, some by being carried on crossed rifles,[206] though Ferguson "could not be moved."[207] In another account Howe wrote that "Three very badly wounded men refused to allow themselves to be moved" but were "picked up by a counter-attack" towards morning.[208] If the wounded Ferguson was recovered and survived, he must have been E.L. Ferguson. Belonging to the relatively intact 3 or 4 Platoon, he was less likely to have fought on Baby 700, though some members of these platoons did fight in the area. His record makes no mention of the lung wound described by Howe.[209] J.J. Ferguson, 1 or 2

191 Howe, "Sparks From an Old Controversy", p.16.
192 Ibid., p.16.
193 Howe, 3DRL 8042 item 7.
194 Howe, "Sparks From an Old Controversy", p.16.
195 Ibid.
196 Ibid.
197 Howe, 3DRL 8042 item 7.
198 Ibid.
199 Howe, "Sparks From an Old Controversy", p.16.
200 Ibid.
201 Howe, "Sparks From an Old Controversy", p.16.
202 Bean, Gallipoli Mission, p.141.
203 Ibid., p.140.
204 Ibid., pp.140–141.
205 Howe, "Sparks From an Old Controversy", p.16.
206 Howe, 3DRL 8042 item 7.
207 Ibid.
208 Howe, "Sparks From an Old Controversy", pp.16–17.
209 E.L. Ferguson returned to Australia for discharge, but re-enlisted and was sent to France, only to have his old wound force his return to Australia.

Platoons, was more likely to have known Howe and to have fought on Baby 700. H.D. Guthrie,[210] 3 or 4 Platoon, describes the wounds of "a man named Ferguson … a drummer … with both his legs shattered … he looked as though he would die very quickly … we had to retire … about four hours later … This occurred up through Shrapnel Gully near Pope's Post."[211]

This may well refer to Howe's Ferguson. An unusual clue adds a little weight to this possibility. John Ferguson had had an unfortunate life. His mother left her husband because of his "cruel treatment" and took her two daughters to Western Australia. Some time later, John and his brother were taken from their father for neglect, made wards of the state and sent to an orphanage.[212] In the early 1900s the home had a fife and drum band[213] – perhaps John Ferguson was the drummer referred to by Guthrie, and the man who died on 25 April. John's brother also enlisted and served overseas. After twice being returned to Australia he died in a military hospital in 1919.[214]

Turks were heard following Howe's party and advancing out of sight along Monash Valley. The party, carrying the machine guns on their tripods as no-one knew how to dismantle them,[215] turned once more, formed up around the guns, and "blasted" the attack "at point blank range."[216] The impact of the fire from three Maxims and many rifles firing along the narrow Russell's Top must have been devastating. The retirement continued until near the Sphinx, when the party "dropped into a good trench overlooking the beach from which a Turkish machine gun had fired … early that morning."[217] Here Howe's party remained, fighting "an enemy detachment which" lay "in the scrub in front … Exposed as" the Turks were, "they got … the worst of the fire exchanges which continued throughout the night."[218] Howe's party's stance was defensive, but they were still full of fight. During the withdrawal Howe had picked up a pack – it was Colonel Clarke's.[219]

In penetrating this far, the Turks on Russell's Top had advanced further and "done better" than their commanders realised.[220] They, like the Anzacs, "were weak, about 80 or 90 men" and there were concerns that, "if attacked, they might not be able to hold … But," it was thought, "the 'English' were too exhausted to attack."[221] The stress of the intense fighting throughout the day was not confined to the Anzacs – the "general impression was that the commander" of 57th Regiment's 2nd Battalion, fighting in the Walker's Ridge – Fisherman's Hut area, "had lost his head, while the CO of the 3rd Battalion, Hairi Bey," some of whose men were presumably fighting Howe's party, "had kept his."[222]

An unknown number of other parties were fighting nearby. About half-way up Walker's Ridge, Captain A.C.B. Critchley-Salmonson of the Canterbury Battalion commanded a party of possibly 50 New Zealanders and Australians, the latter mostly 3rd Brigade men from Baby 700.[223] Another party, predominantly Aucklanders and members of the 1st and 3rd Brigades, occupied a post higher up. Jackson was with these, confirming that he too had withdrawn in this direction after Baby 700.[224]

---

210 44 Private (at embarkation) Henry David Guthrie, A Company, 28 at enlistment, clerk, of Perth.

211 Australian Red Cross Wounded and Missing Enquiry Bureau files, 1DRL/0428.

212 In later decades this orphanage, St. Vincent's Boys Home, South Melbourne, would be associated with sexual abuse of young boys.. Child Abuse Inquiry papers, Appendix 10, <http://www.parliament.vic.gov.au/images/stories/committees/fcdc/inquiries/57th/Child_Abuse_Inquiry/Submissions/Anthony__Chrissie_Foster_Appendix_10.pdf>, 10 January 2013. Broken Rites Australia, website, <http://brokenrites.alphalink.com.au/nletter/page205-elmer.html>.

213 Former St. Vincent De Paul Boys Orphanage, Victorian Heritage Database, Heritage Victoria website, <http://vhd.heritage.vic.gov.au/places/result_detail/27209?print=true>, 10 January 2013.

214 B2455, 903 G.H. Ferguson.

215 Howe, 3DRL 8042 item 7.

216 Howe, "Sparks From an Old Controversy", p.17.

217 Ibid.

218 Ibid.

219 Howe, 3DRL 8042 item 7.

220 Bean, Gallipoli Mission, pp.140–141.

221 Ibid., p.139.

222 Ibid., p.139.

223 Bean, Official History, Volume I (1921 and 1941), p.333.

224 Ibid., p.333.

Lieutenant-Colonel G.F. Braund, with a party centred on two companies of the 2nd Battalion, held the junction of Walker's Ridge and Russell's Top.

Bonavia, who had tried to cadge a drink from de Mole, probably belonged to Morgan's 2 Platoon and may have fought on Baby 700. Retchford, who possibly accompanied Tulloch, saw Bonavia alive and well "between 10 and 11 o'clock." George Dick[225] believed he saw Bonavia "killed outright by a bullet. They never went over that piece of ground again."[226] Perhaps this implies that Dick, a B Company reinforcement, had accompanied Tulloch.

Mason joined a collection of 3rd Brigade men on some "lower ridge in front of Walker's." "Jackson sent a message by Private Waldy," actually Corporal G.W. Waldy,[227] 3 or 4 Platoon, "Do you want reinforcements?" Mason did, but they appear not to have come. He estimates he had "Turks within about 40 yards" and about 75 men under his command; some of these were probably survivors of Howe's "U" trench party. How several members of 3 or 4 Platoon ended up in this area is something of a mystery; perhaps they had climbed to Russell's Top from the beach with other 3rd Brigade parties.

Simcock was with Mason. He was determined to find and recover a wounded man he knew to be lying out in the scrub, and during the evening crawled from cover and ventured into the gloom. He did not return.[228] The loss of such an identity as Simcock in the first day's fighting shocked many in Western Australia. Grief sought solace, and fuelled the emergence of heroic stories. One had it that in May "while leading a charge against the Turks after his company commander had been killed," Pink Top "had his head blown away" by "shrapnel."[229] Others reported that "Pink Top ... took command. He gave the order to charge and they did not stop until poor Pink Top had just gained the top of the hill. Just as he said 'Come on boys' he was hit full in the face by shrapnel and blown to pieces ... won't Australia be proud to own such men."[230] Simcock was also reported killed "while leading his company in a charge ... after all the officers had been shot down."[231] Howe heard Pink Top was killed rescuing wounded near the beach,[232] and the battalion history stated that, nearly two weeks after the Landing, he bobbed "up once too often" from a trench, "trying to get a look at what was going on."[233] Simcock's official date of death is 2 May 1915.

Mason's is the only account by a witness. Mason's description of his movements earlier in the day is indecipherable, even to Bean, but he is known to have been on Battleship Hill with Reid, and it is reasonable to believe he fought in the evening where he claimed. It is also reasonable to believe Simcock was with him. Another story has it that it was Pink Top's metal shin guards that enabled identification of his body. During the 24 May armistice, a burial party noticed metal beneath a corpse's tattered puttees. Closer examination revealed the soldier had been wearing home made greaves.[234] The fact that Simcock today lies buried on Baby 700 and is one of the few buried there to have been identified, supports Mason's story and possibly the one about home-made shin guards.

With such parties did 11th Battalion survivors fight on. A.J. Webb,[235] C or D Company, was also "on the left," though this could have been anywhere between the head of Monash Gully and

225 1120 Private (at embarkation) George Dick, B Company, 23 at embarkation, born Dunfermline, Scotland.
226 Australian Red Cross Wounded and Missing Enquiry Bureau files, 1DRL/0428. 931 Private J. North, 15 or 16 Platoon, thought he saw Bonavia "shot through the hip as soon as" he landed.
227 114 Corporal George Wilfred Waldy, A Company, 25 at embarkation, electrician, born Canada. Waldy had served five years with the Royal Engineers (Territorials).
228 Mason, 2DRL 301, Book 31.
229 H. Schmitt, "'Pink Top': WA's barrow boy hero", "Big Weekend", p.4, *West Australian*, Saturday, 14 April 1990.
230 Schmitt, "Pink Top': WA's barrow boy hero", quoting West Australian, 1915.
231 W. Olson, "Private David John Simcock, 11th Battalion Australian Imperial Force, "The bloke with the Pink Top", quoting West Australian, 15 June 1915, Ellam-Innes Collection, n.p.
232 Bush, *Gallipoli*, p.178.
233 Belford, *Legs Eleven*, pp.98–99.
234 I have been aware of this story for so long I cannot recall where I acquired it. Howe's version, quoted Bush, p.178, hints at it.
235 849 Private Albert James Webb, C or D Company, 23 at enlistment, labourer, of Geraldton, born Moonta, South Australia.

Walker's Ridge, and "fighting every minute. There were only about 30 of us … we kept great numbers of Turks back … We had no officers, sergeant or corporal," suggesting Webb was not with Mason or Howe. "We had a wall of Turks to shoot at for 60 hours, and we piled them up in heaps." The men alternately rested and fired, for after:

> [a] quarter of an hour … our barrels were red hot and it was impossible to shoot … If we had all kept going no-one would have been firing after the first quarter of an hour, and we would have all been mince-meat … I was in three small bayonet charges, but never … [stuck] my bayonet through a Turk in a charge. I caught a sniper in a bush later on … put my bayonet through the right side of his neck and out under his arm. These snipers … have done all the damage. They can knock the head off a pin. They are bonzer shots.

Webb would be hit six times, but fought on until the last put him "out of action."[236]

Pittersen could have fought anywhere between 400 Plateau and Baby 700, but coincidentally refers to "about 30 of us" being "cut off" and having "our work cut out to keep them back." Bullets had been "flying everywhere," whistling past and kicking "the dirt in your face … one chap got shot alongside me, and in less than two minutes the chap on the other side of me was shot." At about 2:00 p.m. Pittersen had his "gallop stopped with a bullet through the muscle of the leg … I had my field dressing on and started on my way back to the hospital. When I got there I found several of my mates … it was just as bad there as the Turks were shelling the hospitals."[237] Coincidence is an insufficient foundation for history, but Sergeant F. Coe, 9th Battalion, also described a party of 32 who had "held a trench at 2.30pm", but by 5:30 p.m. had been reduced to two. They had been "under heavy attack by two Battalions."[238]

Stan Williams also appears to have gone to the Russell's Top–Baby 700 area. He found himself alone and joined a man he knew carrying ammunition to the high ground on the left where "things got pretty lively. A fair amount of shooting going on. We could see Turks and our men in the distance but the shrub was pretty thick … there were a number of us more or less in line firing whenever we could see something ahead of us." He was hit in the hand, and "rather stupidly" stood up to check his rifle. Turkish riflemen seized the opportunity and Williams was immediately hit in the "right arm just above the wrist," then "in the left hip and turned round again and I got one in the back of the right thigh and the back of the right knee." Each hit felt like "somebody had whacked me with a big stick … I made a sort of sling out of one of my puttees which had been coming undone all day on account of having been wet."[239] Williams survived but his war was over.

Scott and others "were separated from our Battalion and got into a tight corner on the left flank, and we had to hang onto this, under a major, until they could send us help." As Scott was originally in F Company, he may have accompanied Cooke. Majors were numerous on this flank – Kindon, Grant (killed), Scobie (wounded), Robertson (killed), Elliott (wounded early), Swannell and F. Stuckey (killed); probably others had fought in the area at some stage during the day. "The Turks were trying hard to turn this flank, and though we were a collection from numerous battalions, we managed to hold what we had gained. Our losses were severe, but the Turks went out easily three to one."[240]

There is little to indicate where Roy Thompson fought. He appears to have belonged to Gostelow's platoon, who, after Fisherman's Hut, spent most of the day carrying ammunition to the front lines. On 25 April he wrote nothing about the fighting other than "Our chaps great. Machine gunner gone

236 Webb, letter, *Kalgoorlie Miner*, 7 July 1915.
237 Pittersen, letter, 4 May 1915.
238 Coe, 3 DRL 8042 item 7.
239 Williams, interview, Liddle Collection, pp.5–6.
240 Scott, letter, n.d.

mad, can't stop him, throwing mud."[241] A bullet grazed Thompson's boot, and the battle continued, strain undiminished, in the coming days: "A machine gun all the time, its awful. Bullets whistling round us now like flies … Heavy shrapnel bombardment … something terrible … infantry [strong?] heavy attacks … 3 attacks, once to within 50 yards, stand to arms, prepare to charge, they won't stand the bayonet." Thompson's last entry was on 28 April.[242]

With such groups did the exhausted, scattered survivors of the fighting on the high ground stand and continue the battle through the first night. Most parties were out of touch and could only guess at each others' presence by the crack and flash of rifles in the darkness. The firing swelled ominously into a roar as one party or another defended itself; or as one side or the other spied a real or imagined target in the gloom. Howe's group's withdrawal created a gap in the Anzac line, but various parties, islands in the darkness, stood their ground whenever possible and defended their front and flanks. The exhausted Turks could probe and make minor attacks, but, diminished in numbers and unaware of the situation, did not make a decisive assault into the gap on Russell's Top.

The ANZAC commanders meanwhile had become "increasingly anxious as to how much longer the infantry could endure the almost unbearable strain of the struggle."[243] Bean describes in detail their discussions on the beach during the night. The flow of wounded "had never ceased," stretchers crowded the beach and "stragglers" gathered behind the firing lines.[244] A "most formidable Turkish counter-attack" was expected and it "was doubted even by the most optimistic of the staff"[245] that the exhausted troops could hold it. The men were reported to be "thoroughly demoralised … If … subjected to shellfire again to-morrow morning there is likely to be a fiasco."[246] "The smallest breath of panic" in the firing lines might have decided the issue.[247] The question of urgent evacuation was elevated all the way to Sir Ian Hamilton.[248] By contrast, Bean maintains, the troops in the firing lines "had not the faintest notion that any retirement, much less an evacuation," was being considered. "By no possible extension of their meaning could the term 'thoroughly demoralised' be truthfully applied to the troops at Gaba Tepe that day."[249]

Howe agreed:

The assumption of Bridges, Godley and White was not justified – if there was any demoralisation at Anzac that night it was in their own headquarters … morale in the line had risen to its highest point … Officers and men alike had fought all day … without support from their own artillery. They had stood against all the enemy could bring against them. With the cessation of enemy shellfire at sunset the strain of battle eased tremendously … Every enemy attack was being easily held. A wave of confidence swept through the troops.[250]

He adds a sequel. The following day there was "intense indignation" when the troops in the firing line heard of "the contemplated evacuation … Unit commanders were promptly instructed to deny the story and to threaten 'rumour-mongers' with punishment for spreading it." The troops accepted the denial and discounted the story as one of the night's many "furphies," until publication of the *Official History* in 1921 "aroused almost as much indignation" as on 26 April 1915. "The allegation

241 Thompson, diary, 25 April 1915.
242 Thompson, diary, 26–28 April 1915. Roy Thompson has no known grave.
243 Bean, *Official History*, Volume I (1921 and 1941), p.453.
244 *Ibid*. p.453.
245 *Ibid*., p.455.
246 *Ibid*., p.458.
247 *Ibid*., p.461.
248 *Ibid*., p.460.
249 *Ibid*., p.462.
250 Howe, "Sparks From an Old Controversy", p.20.

of demoralisation was particularly resented."[251] 11th Battalion accounts support Howe's – men spent the night recovering, digging, trying to dry wet uniforms, and fighting.

The full details of the fighting on Baby 700 that day will never be known. A loneliness pervades the men's accounts. Many were, or thought they were, separated from their units. Men they fought beside were killed or disappeared in the charges and withdrawals. Familiar faces were rare. The enemy's strength was unknown, their numbers changing all the time. Men were thrown into this confusion in dribs and drabs. The longer one fought here, the lower were the odds of survival. Ashton believed many who fell behind must have been despatched by the Turks,[252] which would in part explain the great silence from Baby 700. We cannot know of the lonely deaths of many men and boys from Coolgardie, Fremantle, Busselton or Geraldton. Despite Bean's efforts at connecting fragments of evidence, so many pieces of the puzzle are missing that the stories of the survivors appear as islands, both on the battlefield and in our recollections of it, frozen moments in the scrub and a maelstrom of cracking bullets and slashing shrapnel, confusion and movement.

The early Turkish successes on Baby 700 may have been created by 27th Regiment, rather than 57th Regiment. 27th Regiment may have stopped Tulloch and Brockman, and held the Australians on Baby 700 before Kemal arrived. The troops Howe and Margetts saw advancing around the seaward side of Battleship Hill are assumed to be 57th Regiment, but may in fact have been 27th Regiment. There is much contradiction in Bean's chronology and much of the conflicting evidence fits more comfortably with the scenarios proposed in this chapter.

G. Souter summarised 25 April as: "The day was one of desperate but uncoordinated effort, temporary achievement but ultimate failure."[253] This description is particularly appropriate for Baby 700.

---

251 *Ibid.*, p.21.
252 Ashton, manuscript, p.21.
253 G. Souter, *Lion and Kangaroo, Australia: 1901–1919, The Rise of a Nation* (Sydney: Fontana/Collins, 1978), p.220.

10

Baby 700: If the Dead Could Speak

The 11th Battalion features little in secondary source descriptions of the fighting on Baby 700. It is difficult to connect their stories with others like Kindon, Lalor or Robertson, but writers cling to them rather than tackle the confusion beyond the boundaries of the published experiences. Bean devoted much of the first volume of the *Official History* to the Landing, but the battalion tasked with taking the all-important high ground of the Sari Bair range, and whose troops were among the first to reach its crests, is, apart from Tulloch's party, all but invisible.

Obvious 11th Battalion accounts of Baby 700 are in short supply. The confused fighting, lack of named geographical features and limited visibility meant that most did not mention Baby 700 by name. Bean interviewed officers more frequently than private soldiers,[1] meaning that the stories of the enlisted men were less likely to be recorded.[2] Our view is further limited by the disappearance of evidence over the years and the difficulties of reconstructing from the fragments that remain. Eventually, attempts at finding 11th Battalion accounts from Baby 700 led to the realisation that, compared to other parts of the battlefield, relatively few of the battle's 11th Battalion participants survived to tell their story.

The men who left no record because they fell in battle are as much a part of its history as those who lived to describe it. This chapter will examine whatever evidence can be gathered on some of the 11th Battalion men who became casualties on 25 April to attempt to reconstruct their experience, and determine what this source – the dead – can contribute to our knowledge of the battle on Baby 700.

The 11th Battalion men known to have fought in this area were Morgan's and Cooke's platoons, whatever men Tulloch brought back from Battleship Hill, and any number of "stray" men. Chapter 5 noted that the assumed size of Tulloch's party varies greatly, from a "handful"[3] to several platoons[4] and half a company.[5] Despite their achievement in advancing higher and probably further inland than any other known party, despite the many times their story has been re-told and the supposed significance of their clash with the enigmatic Mustafa Kemal, the men who were there have remained largely anonymous. Whether any were left in enemy hands and the number killed on Battleship Hill are also unknown. Any number of this party's survivors may have fought subsequently on Baby 700, and have died there.

Today, the only obvious reminder of the 25 April fighting on Baby 700 is its cemetery. It is by-passed by most tourists. To those who notice it, having had the significance of Anzac Cove, the Nek and Lone Pine explained to them, Baby 700 Cemetery must appear an anachronism, its white walls and monument an island in the scrub beyond the Anzac lines. Yet 493 Commonwealth men are buried or commemorated there,[6] of whom the vast majority, 450, are unidentified.[7] Thirty-three

---

1   K.S. Inglis, Introduction to U.Q.P. Edition, C.E.W. Bean, *Official History of Australia in the War: The Story of ANZAC*, Volume I, University of Queensland Press, St Lucia, Queensland, 1981, p.xxxv.

2   *Ibid*, p.xxxv.

3   Bean, *Official History*, Volume I (1921 and 1941), p.275.

4   Bean, *Gallipoli Mission*, p.84.

5   Bean, *Official History*, Volume I (1921 and 1941), p.270. Carlyon, *Gallipoli*, pp.141, 157 provides recent examples.

6   Commonwealth War Graves Comission, <http://www.cwgc.org>

7   Commonwealth War Graves Comission, <http://www.cwgc.org/find-a-cemetery/cemetery/66603/BABY%20700%20 CEMETERY,%20ANZAC>

of those identified served with the AIF, of whom only 23 have known graves. The others, including Lalor and Swannell, are commemorated by special memorials as they are believed to lie in the cemetery. Remarkably, given the number of units who fought on Baby 700, among the 23 identified Australians lie nine members of the 11th Battalion. As nearly 40 percent of the 23 in a cemetery of nearly 500 belong to 11th Battalion men, they probably represent the tip of an iceberg.

A range of factors make it difficult to establish precise casualty figures for the Landing – the confusion of the fighting, administration of the casualties, the many missing, and that for some men the battle lasted for hours and for others over a week.[8] The 11th Battalion appears to have lost 112 killed between 25 April and 2 May,[9] the latter date being chosen as it is often used to record the deaths of those killed at the Landing when no specific date is available. About 87, or three quarters of the 112, have no known grave.

Looking south south-west from the crest and southern slopes of Baby 700, the white stone of the massive Lone Pine Memorial is clearly visible. Here are listed the names of men known to have died at Anzac or at sea, but who do not have a known grave. Many died on ground afterwards held by the enemy, including the gullies, slopes and ridges surrounding Baby 700 Cemetery. If few of the 11th Battalion survived the fighting on Baby 700, what can be gleaned from the experience of those whose names adorn the distant Lone Pine Memorial? Can any of the story be reconstructed from the experiences of the missing?

Due to his status as an officer and leader,[10] the many witnesses to his wounding, his wife's investigations and the importance of Tulloch's party's achievement in reaching Battleship Hill, Mort Reid's wounding is well documented; thus it can become a valuable reference point as it places any man who witnessed it on Battleship Hill.

The Red Cross Wounded and Missing Enquiry Bureau Files[11] sometimes allow a witness, as well as a casualty, to be located on the battlefield. Unfortunately the brevity of the notes of interview presents problems as often it cannot be assumed that an interviewee actually witnessed the events he describes. Goodlet, a "Corporal Morris" and J.J. Ryan stated that they were in Reid's party or saw him shot, yet Goodlet made no mention of Reid in his manuscript and the identity of "Corporal Morris" is undetermined. T. Hoddell[12] (HQ Company), Private E.T. "Warney," presumed to be E.J. Warren[13] (probably 13 or 14 Platoon), C. Braidwood (probably 7 or 8 Platoon), "Lieutenant McKear," probably G.P. McKenna[14] (probably 1 or 2 Platoon) and Private T. Anderson[15] (11 Platoon) accurately described Reid's wounding, but do not state that they witnessed it. J.D. Orr[16] also accurately describes the event but states that as a stretcher bearer he was not present at the time, and H.A. Axford[17] describes Reid's wounding and knew Reid's wife, but belonged to the 10th Battalion and does not state he was present during the action. Intriguingly, Ashton, who makes no mention in his later accounts of having reached Battleship Hill, was contacted while a prisoner of war by the American Embassy at Constantinople and stated that "he cannot claim to have seen Lieutenant Reid after he was wounded."[18] Does this

8   Hurst, *Game to the Last*, p.53.
9   AWM145 Roll of Honour cards, 1914–1918 War, Army.
10   Bean, *Gallipoli Mission*, p.84.
11   Australian Red Cross Wounded and Missing Enquiry Bureau files, 1DRL/0428.
12   992 Private Thomas Hoddell, HQ Company, 35 at embarkation, labourer, of Manjimup, born Hereford, England.
13   844 Private Edwin John Warren, D Company, 22 at embarkation, salesman, of Geraldton, born Victoria. Warren was one of the intitial party that enlisted in Geraldton and appears on Roy Thompson's roll.
14   1004 Private Gerald Patrick McKenna, A Company, 21 at embarkation, law student, of East Perth, born Geraldton. It is unclear whether McKenna took part in the Landing or was in hospital at the time.
15   627 Private Theodore Anderson, C Company, 19 at embarkation, miner, of Kalgoorlie, born Victoria.
16   700 Private John David Orr, F Company and 27 at embarkation, stretcher bearer at the Landing, mining student, of Kalgoorlie, born Bundaberg, Queensland.
17   1581 Private H.A. Axford, 10th Battalion.
18   Australian Red Cross Wounded and Missing Enquiry Bureau files, 1DRL/0428.

imply that Ashton, who is presumed to have fought somewhere on the high ground on the left flank, was present on Battleship Hill when Reid was wounded? Does this support the idea that he was in fact the prisoner described by Şefik? Or does it mean that Ashton had not seen Reid since earlier that morning? Such is the frailty of primary sources – even if men fought on Battleship Hill, they may have been unaware of it, and even if we have a reliable anchor point, such as Reid's wounding, we cannot tie other men to it solely on the basis of descriptions of the event.

The case of Ivo Brian Joy reveals the difficulties of interpreting primary sources. Assessment of evidence suggests Joy was killed on Baby 700 after withdrawing from Battleship Hill, though many contradictions in accounts confuse the issue considerably. Joy was promoted to corporal and lance sergeant soon after enlisting, but in the re-structure of 1 January 1915 reverted to corporal. His service record states that he was transferred to 16 Section, 16 Platoon at this time, but a range of evidence makes it appear that at the Landing he served with Reid's 15 Platoon. At the instigation of Sir John Forrest, following appeals from Joy's father, the Red Cross sought information on the young man's fate.

Anomalies appear immediately. The first account states that "Sergeant Haslam … said he saw Joy … shot through the stomach" at the Landing, "Reference Sergeant Deasington."[19] Deasington and Haslam[20] were battalion originals, but due to illness, Ivo's friend Haslam missed the Landing. On 23 March 1916 Haslam stated that:

> Joy was out sniping when he was shot in the back by a Turkish sniper. He was kneeling up behind a bush … His chest was almost blown off. This occurred in August. Witness did not see it happen but heard of it immediately.[21]

The following day Haslam reported that he heard:

> when he arrived on the peninsula about 20 May that Sergeant Joy had been shot through the back and killed. He was sniping on the day of the Landing or soon after when he was shot. He was out with the 15th Platoon at the time.[22]

Two other witnesses, H.W. Ellemore,[23] a friend of Ivo's, and H.V. Denis,[24] confirm that Joy's death took place in July or August at Leane's Trench after he rejoined the battalion following an illness, though Denis's information was second-hand, being gained from W.F. O'Meara.[25] There is no evidence that Joy fought or died at Leane's Trench,[26] and his service record shows no activity on his part after the Landing. Joy's sister Jean later passed on to her grandson that at the Landing, Ivo "had been evacuated to a hospital at Gallipoli with severe wounds, but had been blown over a cliff by Turkish artillery and killed."[27] There were no hospitals established ashore at the time and none

19 769 Lance Corporal Joseph William Deasington, D Company, 31 at embarkation, fireman, of Geraldton, born Staffordshire. Deasington was among the first party to enlist in Geraldton. He had previously served in the 1st Kings Dragoon Guards and Manchester Regiment. J.W. Deasington, 51st Battalion, 26 March 1916 Tel-el-Kebir; Australian Red Cross Wounded and Missing Enquiry Bureau files, 1DRL/0428.

20 910 Corporal Hector Albert "Joe" Haslam, corporal and 20 at embarkation, D Company, bank clerk, of Katanning, born Rochester, Victoria.

21 Australian Red Cross Wounded and Missing Enquiry Bureau files, 1DRL/0428.

22 *Ibid.*

23 892 Private (at embarkation) Harry William Ellemore, D Company, 20 at embarkation, mill hand, of Worsley, born North Carlton, Victoria. Often spelt "Ellemor" in official sources.

24 773 Private Herbert Victor Denis, D Company, 22 at embarkation, labourer, of Northam, born Portsmouth, England.

25 1164 Sergeant William Francis O'Meara, 21 at embarkation, of Katanning, born Lambeth London, England. Australian Red Cross Wounded and Missing Enquiry Bureau files, 1DRL/0428.

26 Hurst, *Game to the Last*, photographic section between pp.156 and 157.

27 I thank David James for our many discussions and exchanges of notes many years ago on his relation, Ivo Joy. D. James, family history notes, private collection, Sydney.

is likely to have been positioned on exposed cliffs. Ivo's nephew was later told by a man named Bob Gibson "who claimed to be a tent mate and friend of Ivo," that he had seen him "mortally wounded in the head as he rose to get out of the boat."[28] The problem with this account is that R.B. Gibson[29] served in A Company and therefore landed from *London*, whereas Joy landed from *Usk*. Some accounts have a wounded Joy making it to or being taken to North Beach where he died and was buried, supposedly by a 16th Battalion friend from Katanning, Ted Eames.[30]

Harry Ellemore wrote to his mother from hospital in Malta that:

> Our company, was in the centre, but we got orders to reinforce the right flank. Bob Edwards,[31] our sergeant, and I were further round than the others of our company. We chased the Turks back three-quarters of a mile further than we should, and about 80 of us were cut off, and had to run for our lives … I beard Bob call me, but I was too busy at the time. I moved along five minutes after, but Bob was gone. I heard a chap groaning right behind me. It was our sergeant, Ivo Joy, so I gave him a drink … I was hit … I don't know if they got Joy, but I hope so, he was a fine fellow, and so young.[32]

Ellemore's mother forwarded this letter to Joy's parents; it was the first indication they had received that their son had been wounded.[33] Perhaps the most reliable evidence about Joy's death comes from an anonymous source. Joy's mother wrote on his Roll of Honour circular[34] that he had been "wounded ten hours after the landing – was acting as Senior Sergeant of his platoon, consequent on disappearance of Lieut. Mort Reid."[35] She confirms this in a letter to the Department of Defence in November 1919: when "Reid disappeared, Sergeant G. Mason took his place and my boy acted as senior sergeant." She received this information "in a letter," presumably from a battalion member, in 1915.[36] Given our knowledge of Reid and Mason, this account has a ring of accuracy. A decade later, Mrs Joy was still endeavouring to find out the truth or gain recognition of her son's actions, as she wrote to Defence again in 1929 confirming the statement of 1919 and adding that her son "died of wounds on the afternoon of the Landing … or morning of the next day, we never heard which."[37]

There are clearly a great many contradictions in these accounts. Mistaken identity, flawed memory or note taking, rumour, aggregation of stories from different events or a "drifting" of fact caused by hearsay, perhaps explain the anomalies. It is also possible that family members of those who died a bloody death on distant battlefields were told kinder stories by those who knew the truth.

Joy's mother's version of events is probably the most accurate. That she was aware of the story of Reid and Mason, had heard this at the time, presumably from someone in the unit who knew her son, and was consistent and adamant about the story, confirm her conviction that it was correct. In addition, Haslam confirmed Joy being with 15 (Reid's) Platoon on the day, Joy's rank is listed on the Lone Pine Memorial as "lance sergeant," and official records confirm his death at the Landing. The evidence suggests that he accompanied Reid to fight the losing battle on Battleship Hill, and was

---

28 James, family history notes.
29 47 Private (at embarkation) Robert Bradford Gibson, A Company, 24 at embarkation, drill sharpener, born Gympie, Queensland.
30 James, family history notes. 591 Edward Eames, 16th Battalion, 37 at enlistment, carpenter, born Wales.
31 890 Private Robert Edwards, D Company, 25, mill hand, of Worsley, born Glasgow, Scotland. Edwards enlisted as 'George Edwards', yet was known as 'Bob'.
32 *Great Southern Herald* (Katanning, WA: 1901–1954), Wed 30 Jun 1915 Page 3. Ellemore had been hit in the left thigh. Harry Ellemore described Bob Edwards as "beloved friend … deeply regretted." Letter, *Western Mail*, 25 June 1915, p.23.
33 *The West Australian*, 29 June 1915.
34 Roll of Honour circulars, AWM 131.
35 *Ibid.*
36 James, family history notes, private collection, Sydney.
37 *Ibid.*

later mortally wounded continuing the fight, possibly as he fired from behind a bush at the advancing enemy on Baby 700. His may be one of the many unidentified bodies in the Baby 700 cemetery.[38]

The two 11th Battalion officers Brockman took to Baby 700 were Morgan and Cooke. Cooke crossed "the base of Pope's Hill" and continued "towards Baby 700"[39] with Morgan. He is not mentioned again in the *Official History* until Bean lists some of those who fell during the day,[40] and Belford notes only that "Cooke was never seen again after one" of the charges over Baby 700.[41] A member of Cooke's platoon, Frank Marshall,[42] described him on the day as:

> one of the whitest men I ever met, and … a glorious leader. He led us in all our charges and was always first all through the terrible times we had the first day and showed great bravery. When … ordered to fall back … on the first night we were cut to pieces … we have not heard of him since, so he must have been killed. We all loved him, and any of us would give anything to see him back again; but we'll never see him again.[43]

Cooke has consequently been missing from the history since 25 April 1915. Most of the 11th Battalion men who disappeared at the Landing were officially declared deceased in 1916, when, in the absence of evidence to the contrary, their status was changed from "missing" to "killed in action." A 1916 Court of Enquiry pronounced Cooke "killed in action" between 25 April and 2 May 1915. He has no known grave.

In fact, a single eyewitness account of Cooke's death exists. "A. Pickles,[44] A Company," stated that:

> Mr Cooke was hit about five o'clock on the afternoon of 25 April … witness was about 50 yards away … Seeing Mr Cooke fall, witness went up to him … he had been shot through the chest. Witness and another man remained with Mr Cooke until his death which was in about half an hour. He was conscious, did not seem to be suffering but said very little indeed. Shortly after his death there was a retirement so his body had to be left. Mr Cooke came from Fremantle where witness lives.[45]

Pickles' reference to Fremantle is confusing as the roll shows his address as Barrabupp, while Cooke lived in Wickepin. Perhaps as Pickles' mother lived in Barrabupp and Cooke's wife in Wickepin, these addresses were given as contacts for next of kin. It appears Cooke's platoon fought throughout the afternoon on Baby 700, with its survivors being scattered among other units as the fighting progressed. Pickles spoke "warmly" of the former Lancashire Fusilier "as a very good officer indeed."[46]

It has been possible to trace one member of Cooke's platoon and his story affirms that men could have associations with areas far removed from their addresses in official records. Corporal Leslie Job[47] belonged to 16 Section of Cooke's 12 Platoon. E.J. Turner[48] was not in Job's platoon but the two

---

38 The most difficult contradictory evidence is Ellemore's statement about being on the "right", rather than "left."
39 Bean, *Official History*, Volume I (1921 and 1941), p.286.
40 *Ibid.*, p.310.
41 Belford, *Legs Eleven*, p.78.
42 1077 Private (at embarkation) Frank Keith Marshall, C Company, 21 at embarkation, schoolmaster, of Bejooibring, via Toodyay, and Kalgoorlie, born NSW.
43 Letter, *Wickepin Argus*, Thursday 22 July 1915.
44 1029 Private Alfred Herbert Pickles, A Company, 27 at enlistment, labourer, of Barabupp, born Fitzroy, Victoria.
45 Red Cross Wounded and Missing Files. Pickles was interviewed at Ras-el-Tin Convalescent Hospital, Alexandria on 29 May 1915.
46 Australian Red Cross Wounded and Missing Enquiry Bureau files.
47 674 Corporal Leslie Job, C Company, 19 at enlistment, postal employee, of Boulder, born Fitzroy, Victoria.
48 397 Private Edward John Turner, Army Medical Corps, 23 at enlistment, "machine man" of Boulder, born South Melbourne. Turner served in the 11th Battalion Medical Section as he was half an inch too short to be accepted into the infantry. He is believed to appear "bandaging head of one of troops" in a "moving picture" made in Mena Camp, Egypt, possibly F00129, Australian War Memorial. Turner was wounded at Gallipoli on 12 June 1915.

had been "school mates together and later worked in the Perth General P.O."[49] Turner "heard that Job who had been promoted Sergeant was in charge of a party at the Landing who went off to the right near Fisherman's Hut. Job was never seen again after setting out with the party, none of which returned. Job's body was specially looked for on the day of the armistice, but could not be found."[50]

"Private H.A. Stevens" told the Red Cross that "Job and a mate of his, a man from the goldfields … were out together sniping a day or two after the … Landing. Neither of them were seen again alive. The other man's body was found and buried." There was "no trace" of Job, who was "generally believed" to have been "killed. If not a prisoner he must certainly have been shot. Witness knew him well … They were school mates. Job was a tall man. He came from Boulder City." The witness appears to be "A.J.," not "H.A." Stevens[51], of the original G Company. It might appear that this account is a case of mistaken identity, as G and H Companies were recruited from the Murchison, south-west and other country areas of WA and it would seem unlikely Stevens attended school in the goldfields with Job. It could be assumed Joy, a member of the original H Company, was confused with Job, but Andrew Stevens proved to be a youthful horse driver from Gwalia – a mining town in the West Australian goldfields, 233 km north of Kalgoorlie, where he may well have attended school

The most reliable account of Job's fate, in that the details that can be checked appear accurate, was by "B.B. Alston," actually B.R. Alston,[52] a clerk at the Union Bank, Kalgoorlie. Alston confirms that Job "went out with Lieutenant Cooke on the left flank … on the 1st day and never returned. Witness was told by Job's platoon comrades that he was killed … He knew Job personally and made enquiries about him. He enlisted at Kalgoorlie."[53] This version was confirmed by Private Orr.[54]

There are obvious anomalies in these accounts. Most are unlikely to be significant, as unofficial or unrecorded adoption of rank at this time and mistaken transcription of left and right are not uncommon. Such discrepancies can often be reconciled on the balance of evidence. The specifics of Job's movements during the battle and manner of his death are still unknown, though it appears probable he went to Baby 700 with Cooke and died there. Perhaps he too lies in Baby 700 Cemetery.

There was hope in the battalion that Job had been taken prisoner, but Turner added to his statement that "Sergeant Chamberlain had written lately from Constantinople saying that there are no other men of the 11th Battalion prisoners there. Chamberlain was taken prisoner the first day."[55] This is curious as, officially, no man other than Ashton survived capture on 25 April.

Sergeant John Chamberlain[56] appears to have been platoon sergeant of 8 Platoon, B Company. The belief in the battalion during the campaign was that Chamberlain was a "prisoner in Constantinople. Everyone in the company" believed "this to be the case," with Private H.S. Truran[57] telling the Red Cross in September 1915 that "the information came originally from the American Consul."[58] In September 1915, Private Dan Cocking[59] thought a letter had been "received from Chamberlain from

49   Turner may also have worked at the *Kalgoorlie and Boulder Post and Telegraph*. *Sunday Times*, 25 July 1915; Australian Red Cross Wounded and Missing Enquiry Bureau files, 1DRL/0428.
50   Australian Red Cross Wounded and Missing Enquiry Bureau files, 1DRL/0428. Incidentally, this suggests that during the armistice of 24 May 1915, the 11th Battalion sent men to other sectors looking for their dead, adding weight to Pink Top's "greaves" story.
51   837 Private Andrew James Stevens, D Company, 19 at embarkation, horse driver, of Gwalia, born Ballarat.
52   626 Private Bernard Rourke Alston, C Company, 22 at embarkation, bank clerk, of Kalgoorlie, born Alexandra, Victoria.
53   Australian Red Cross Wounded and Missing Enquiry Bureau files, 1DRL/0428.
54   *Ibid.* Presumed to be 700 Private (at embarkation) John David Orr, 27 at embarkation, mining student, of Kalgoorlie, born Bundaberg.
55   Australian Red Cross Wounded and Missing Enquiry Bureau files, 1DRL/0428.
56   420 Sergeant John Chamberlain, B Company, 32 at embarkation, lumper, of Fremantle, born Croydon, England. Chamberlain had served 12 years with the Royal Navy.
57   488 Private Herbert Spencer Truran, B Company, 24 at embarkation, builder, of East Fremantle, born Melbourne.
58   Australian Red Cross Wounded and Missing Enquiry Bureau files, 1DRL/0428.
59   980 Private Daniel Cocking, D Company, 29 at embarkation, prospector of Cue, born Ballarat.

Constantinople,"[60] and in October Lance Corporal Carl Morris stated that the "news was officially given to B Company ... during August" by its acting CO, Darnell, that Chamberlain "had been a prisoner since April."[61] One can imagine the living, despite their many current trials and battles, eagerly awaiting and receiving information about a missing comrade. Truran believed the sergeant had been reconnoitring ahead "of his men" when he "was lost in a sudden Turkish attack."[62]

On 10 April 1916, Chamberlain was officially recorded as killed on the day of the Landing although the Red Cross did not acknowledge his death until 1919.[63] The matter is further confused by the fact that in 1921 Chamberlain's sister reported that his comrades believed that Chamberlain had "died in Anzac cove," and that his body must have been recovered as she had received "a belt he was wearing at the time of his death." She knew "the belt well."[64]

On this conflicting information, Chamberlain's fate remains a mystery, but the records of other battalion members contain clues. A.L. Devenish,[65] B Company, was reported missing after the Landing. In response to enquiries into the fate of Devenish "and four others," a Sergeant Westbrook[66] stated that "These five men were reported KIA, previously reported missing, in the *Western Mail* 2 June 1916 ... They were all in 8 platoon ... with me. We landed together ... I knew them very well, but have seen and heard nothing of them since."[67]

The other four names are not given, but in response to enquiries about "Devenish and Carrington," Corporal J. Durward[68] recalled: "These men were last seen on the left flank of the line ... about as far as the line penetrated though a good many individuals got a bit further. Of those only a small proportion returned, some of these not till next day." Durward added that the last time he saw Devenish and Carrington, "Chamberlain ... was with them."[69] Devenish, Carrington and Chamberlain therefore appear to have been together and may have shared a similar fate. Durward appears to have been a member of 7 Platoon, as was Truran. A third name appears in this record. Private H.F. Hearle, formerly 12th Battalion, responded "My people knew that both Devenish and my brother," Private Ernest Alfred Hearle,[70] "were killed at the Anzac Landing. Their discs have been handed in by the Turkish authorities. My people wrote to me to this effect ... from Fremantle where they and Devenish's people ... live."[71] As late as March 1916 a report appeared that Devenish had been seen in hospital with a wounded forearm,[72] but as with Chamberlain, in April 1916 he was pronounced killed in action. In 1921 Devenish's grieving father was still trying to determine at least the whereabouts of his son's body, stating that some of his comrades had seen him "aboard the *London* after ... the Landing."[73] This is unlikely.

Searching the files of other 11th Battalion casualties of the Landing, looking for any "cross-over" of evidence, revealed Westbrook's "five men" comment in Hearle's "Wounded and Missing" file, suggesting Hearle also accompanied Chamberlain. Hearle, like Chamberlain and Devenish, has no known grave and was not pronounced killed in action, 25 April 1915, until the following year.

---

60 Australian Red Cross Wounded and Missing Enquiry Bureau files, 1DRL/0428.
61 *Ibid.*
62 *Ibid.*
63 *Ibid.*
64 B2455, Chamberlain.
65 423 Lance Corporal Arthur Lancelot Devenish, B Company, 20 at embarkation, warehouseman and agriculturalist, of Victoria Park, born Northam.
66 493 Private (at Landing) Baxter Westbrook, B Company, 23 at embarkation, labourer, of Fremantle, born Prahran Victoria.
67 Australian Red Cross Wounded and Missing Enquiry Bureau files, 1DRL/0428 and B2455, Devenish.
68 421 James Durward, B Company, 25 at embarkation, labourer, of South Fremantle, born Aberdeen Scotland.
69 Australian Red Cross Wounded and Missing Enquiry Bureau files, 1DRL/0428; B2455, Devenish.
70 444 Private Ernest Alfred Hearle, B Company, 20 at embarkation, french polisher, of Fremantle, born Adelaide.
71 Australian Red Cross Wounded and Missing Enquiry Bureau files, 1DRL/0428; B2455, Devenish.
72 Australian Red Cross Wounded and Missing Enquiry Bureau files, 1DRL/0428.
73 B2455, Devenish.

Chamberlain, Devenish, Carrington and Hearle belonged to 8 Platoon, whose OC, Newman, fought forward of Wire Gully with Peck, towards the right of the line; it is known that Newman had possibly only two of his platoon with him. The evidence in the files of the missing men suggests that they fought somewhere on the left. References to "the left" are unlikely to represent a mistake as they appear repeatedly in these men's records, and are supported by Duncan Sharp,[74] 7 Platoon, who was "on 25 April in front of a position called Quinn's Post when the order to advance was given. Private Carrington was with the informant; half an hour later on leaving to retire he was missed. The ground was lost." Sharp believed Carrington, the storeman who had "worked it" to land with his platoon, had been killed, as he was "the kind of man who would never allow himself to be taken alive." Corporal L.J. Holmes,[75] 7 or 8 Platoon,[76] also stated that "Carrington … was with me right in front of what was later known as Quinn's Post. We received an order … to retire and I did not see Carrington again. All that ground was reoccupied by Turks."[77] At the Landing, references such as "forward" of "Quinn's" or "Pope's", neither of which was named at the time, often included Baby 700 or even Battleship Hill.

Expanding the search for the two remaining men to include all possible members of B Company killed on 25 April, revealed Westbrook's testimony against two more names. The pair were brothers, and the evidence about their whereabouts and fate even more contradictory.[78]

Frank Henry Burton Adcock[79] and his younger brother Frederick Brenchley Adcock[80] belonged to the original D Company. Both were reported "wounded and missing" on 25 April, but later declared "killed in action" by the same board as Chamberlain. A cable noting the boys' wounding was sent in June 1915, but that September their mother was still seeking, without success, information about them.[81] As late as 31 December 1915, W. Shields,[82] B Company, advised that he knew two brothers named Adcock, that both survived the Landing and "were both alright about three weeks later, though one had been wounded in the hand and had lost some of his fingers … (the elder) had been shot through the lungs" and "was in No 15 General Hospital Alexandria with informant May last."[83]

Some of this is confirmed by Sergeant Percy Dunham,[84] who was "emphatic that the two men … were in hospital … in England … both in his platoon … Corporal Kirton[85] … recently returned from England … saw both at Manchester Hospital."[86] Kirton was dead at the time of this interview. He had been a member of 8 Platoon and, after evacuation from Gallipoli in May 1915, had been scheduled for repatriation to Australia, but instead served with the School of Instruction for Officers and NCOs in Egypt. He was considered an NCO of great promise and was promoted to sergeant instructor, "the only Australian engaged in that capacity at that time."[87] He was killed in a bomb accident in Egypt in February 1916.

74   478 Private Duncan Sharp, B Company, 22 at embarkation, carpenter, of Fremantle, born Edinburgh, Scotland. Sharp had served with the Black Watch Territorials.
75   438 Corporal Lewis John Holmes, B Company, 19 at embarkation, dairyman, of Cottesloe, born Nottingham, England.
76   As he had belonged to the original D Company.
77   Board finding, Etaples, 19 July 1916, Australian Red Cross Wounded and Missing Enquiry Bureau files, 1DRL/0428.
78   One page of the Adcock Red Cross file confirms all five names.
79   394 Private Frank Henry Burton Adcock, B Company, 25 at embarkation, labourer, of Fremantle, born Leicestershire.
80   1044 Private Frederick Brenchley Adcock, B Company, 21 at embarkation, sailor, of Fremantle, born Leicestershire.
81   B2455, F.H.B. Adcock.
82   983 Private William Shields, B Company, 26 at enlistment, timber feller/sleeper hewer, of East Kirrup, born Deloraine, Tasmania. Shields had been state log chopping champion and was a D Company original. He was wounded on 25 April and returned to Australia the following year.
83   Australian Red Cross Wounded and Missing Enquiry Bureau files, 1DRL/0428.
84   424 Sergeant Percy Dunham, 8 Platoon, B Company, 32 at embarkation, bootmaker, of Perth, born Bedford, England.
85   450 Alexander Mann Kirton, B Company, 20 at embarkation, bank clerk of Fremantle and Bunbury. Kirton's rank at the Gallipoli Landing is unclear. The embarkation roll records his rank as lance-sergeant on 2 November 1914, but this is not supported by his service record.
86   Australian Red Cross Wounded and Missing Enquiry Bureau files, 1DRL/0428.
87   Unsourced newspaper account, author's collection.

Shields' account confirms Westbrook's in that the Adcock boys participated in and survived the Landing. Their mother learnt that the elder brother, Frank, "was wounded in the landing at Anzac. He wrote a card," dated 1 May 1915, "bearing the Alexandria postmark (21 May 1915) in which he said" the brothers "have been cruising about in an old whaler for the past month. We have had a glorious time. Occasionally we would take a walk over the hills." A wounded soldier elaborated on this by saying that the boys had been detached for special duty running "stores from Lemnos to the transports. He also said that Frank was wounded in the knee."[88] A letter by the Red Cross in Western Australia seeking details from Egypt combines elements of a number of stories: "Both men were reported in Melbourne as wounded at Dardanelles on June 22 … last letter received was dated early June. They were employed on special service in connection with the landing of troops and drafted to the front in June. A returned soldier verbally stated …[they] were immediately wounded, one in the leg, the other in the arm."[89]

Neither "is reported as killed or missing."[90] This seems to suggest that the boys were detached from their battalion to run stores and troops from Lemnos to Gallipoli. In November 1915 the boys' mother still wrote "to them every mail."[91] In August the following year she was still making enquiries and was "almost distracted" with worry and grief.[92]

It is likely that by that time both her sons were long dead, the most conclusive evidence being that Frank lies buried in Baby 700 cemetery, with a date of death of 25 April. An account by B Company's Percy Clark,[93] given to the Red Cross in August 1916, provides a clue as to the fate of her other son, Fred. On Monday 26 April, Clark "saw one of the Adcock brothers being carried on to a hospital ship wounded. I cannot tell which one it was. I was running past the stretcher and called out to him." Clark was later told by Braidwood, who had also been wounded, that the wounded Adcock had died.[94]

With such conflicting evidence it is not possible to establish an irrefutable account of the Adcock brothers' fate. Fred was a sailor before the war, and, living in the port of Fremantle, Frank also may have had experience handling boats. In the busy weeks before the Landing, the 11th Battalion sent work parties ashore at Lemnos to assist with loading and unloading stores, and perhaps the Adcocks had been assigned duty aboard boats in this period, rather than in the early weeks of the Landing; it is also unlikely that detached boat duty would have kept trained infantrymen away from their unit at the Landing. Further examination of the letter quoted above reveals that the "returned soldier" who "verbally stated" that the brothers "were immediately wounded" after arriving at Gallipoli in "June", may have been referring to events in April – the reference to June came from another source and bears no relation to his comment.[95]

The dates of correspondence are extremely confusing. Perhaps the letter of 1 May is incorrectly dated, such errors not being unusual in letters, diaries, and official records of the time, and perhaps 1 April was meant. As for the postmark date, one possibility might be that the card was posted after the man's death by a friend or whoever recovered it from his body or his abandoned kit. Frank's correspondence from Alexandria in May and reports that one of the brothers was in hospital there may suggest a mix-up of the brothers' names, though there is no official record of evacuation or hospitalisation of either of them. All that can be said of the stories that one or both boys had been seen in hospitals in England or elsewhere is that such mistakes at the time are common.

With no official record of either of the brothers being seen after 25 April, and the presence of what is marked as Frank's grave on Baby 700, it would seem the most likely explanation is that the

---

88   Australian Red Cross Wounded and Missing Enquiry Bureau files, 1DRL/0428.
89   *Ibid.*
90   *Ibid.*
91   *Ibid.*
92   *Ibid.*
93   416 Private Percy Clark, B Company, 21 at embarkation, fireman, of Namil, born Broken Hill. KIA 30 October 1917.
94   Australian Red Cross Wounded and Missing Enquiry Bureau files, 1DRL/0428.
95   *Ibid.*

brothers ran stores around Mudros Harbour and went for walks over the hills of Lemnos in the weeks before the Landing, and became casualties on 25 or 26 April. Frank or both probably fought with others of their platoon in the vicinity of Baby 700.

Another member of 8 Platoon to die at the Landing was H.L.I. Finch,[96] who was officially recorded as dying of wounds at Gallipoli on 28 April, though his service record provides no details of admissions to any of the medical facilities ashore, the type of wound or cause of death. His body may lie unidentified in one of the cemeteries near the Anzac beaches, though his family apparently had reason to believe that he died in hospital, possibly in Malta.[97] The only information about Finch's fate appears in a document written after the war by Finch's employer, the Bank of NSW, which states that "Expecting reinforcements, they went too far inland and had to retreat, and as Private Finch turned round to fire he was shot in the body, and died of his wounds a few days later."[98] Where this occurred is not known, though the reference to "retreat" suggests Baby 700 or Third Ridge. It is likely Finch either died or received his fatal wound on his birthday – 25 April.[99]

That references to ground should be taken in context, rather than being accepted literally, is reinforced by the case of another missing man of B Company, Private H.J.V. Priestley. Priestley was, according to letters written by his brother-in-law, serving in 6 Platoon at the time of the Landing. For many years after he was simply recorded as "missing." He was first officially reported missing in June, it being believed that he had disappeared on 25 or 26 April.[100] In September a nurse, apparently Priestley's sister, sent a letter to his brother-in-law, Dr Nelson. The nursing sister "had been on hospital ship duty between Alexandria and the Dardanelles for the last five weeks. It was the 'real thing' up there," with "bullets … whizzing over the decks." She had been making enquiries about Priestley, but without success.[101] Nelson later received a letter from the Australia and New Zealand Base Depot, Weymouth, stating that "Personally, I should say … that when a man is reported as missing and no later news comes to hand, that it is better to give up all hope."[102] Hope was cruelly rekindled in the family when, in December 1915, the Red Cross Society advised that "we have received information unofficially" that Priestley was "a POW in Turkey."[103] The source was apparently a report from the American Ambassador in Constantinople,[104] though later the American Embassy wrote that Turkish correspondence of January 1916 made no reference to Priestley being a prisoner.[105] In Egypt at about the same time, Priestley's sister wrote that she had seen a report noting that her brother was in hospital, though his condition and location were not stated.[106] It was "heartrending" to get such "vague" information that raised hope but presented no leads to follow, and any accurate information "would earn" the family's "undying gratitude." She had heard of "a prisoner of war at Constantinople with a similar name. Could he possibly be in hospital in Constantinople?"[107] In May 1916 Priestley's "Report of POW withdrawn, stated unknown as POW."[108]

This agonising paper-chase continued for years, as Priestley's family waited for months between letters from the authorities, their letters to him were returned and conflicting fragments of

96   428 Private Herbert Lionel Ingle Finch, 30, bank clerk, Perth and Fremantle, born N.S.W.
97   S. Law Smith, niece of H.L.I. Finch, interview by J.P. Hurst, ACT, 22 May 2007.
98   Bank of NSW, *Bank of New South Wales Roll of Honour*, Bank of NSW, Sydney, 1921, p.121.
99   Finch is related to actor Peter Finch and mountaineer Professor G.L. Finch, who, with partner G. Bruce, reached a record altitude attempting to climb Mount Everest in 1922. G.L. Finch is best known for his pioneering work in developing mountaineering oxygen apparatus.
100 B2455, Priestley.
101 Letter to Dr Nelson, 27 September 1915, H.J.V. Priestley papers, private collection.
102 S.M. Wood, letter to Dr Nelson, 8 October 1915, H.J.V. Priestley papers.
103 Letter, 15 December 1915. B2455, Priestley.
104 Australian Red Cross Wounded and Missing Enquiry Bureau files, 1DRL/0428.
105 B2455, Priestley.
106 *Ibid.*
107 *Ibid.*
108 *Ibid.*

information cropped up to torture his mother and others. W.D. LeFort,[109] A Company, told the Red Cross on 28 November 1915 in Malta that "Priestley went away sick in August from Anzac, and returned about 5 September when he was well and unwounded … there was no other Priestley in the Battalion."[110] This appears in fact to refer to Thomas Priestman[111] of the battalion's Medical Section, who was evacuated with influenza in August after the hard fighting at Leane's Trench.[112] By contrast, J.J. Jose[113] was "a personal friend of Priestley's and in the same section." On 12 November 1915 at Atelier Hospital, Heliopolis, he told the Red Cross that "Priestley was lost in the first day … no-one knew anything more, or ever would, unless he is a prisoner."[114]

On 18 October 1917, two and a half years after the Landing, the Red Cross wrote to Priestley's mother that "the poor boy must have been so severely wounded that he died," as he did not appear on a list of prisoners in Turkey. "We have never been able to get into touch with him or anyone knowing anything of him."[115] The previous August the Department of Defence had informed his mother that her son's name was included on a list of POWs "dispatched … on 4/6/17."[116] In June 1918, more than three years after the Landing, Priestley's sister in Tasmania was still unsure whether he was alive, dead or a prisoner, had not heard from Defence for six months and was awaiting confirmation of this and other reports.[117] The previous January she had written that "If you cannot give us anything more definite it would be better for us all, especially mother who it is telling on very much, to give up hoping … the suspense is much harder to bear than anything else."[118] Possibly in response to these letters, a Board of Enquiry held in London on 11 July 1918 pronounced Priestley killed in action on 25 April 1915.[119]

Could Priestley and other missing men have been captured and perished without their names being reported? Priestley's service record contains extracts from a report by "American Consul Nathan stationed in the district of Adana" on the treatment of British prisoners during a forced march, in which they were "driven along by the butt of a gendarme's musket," with "practically no provision for their feeding," "most were robbed," many fell "by the way, and their passage resembled a scene from Dante's Inferno."[120]

The main reason a missing man was deemed to have been killed at the Landing was that there was no evidence that he was alive[121] – in other words, an absence of evidence, rather than proof of death. Priestley had in fact been spared the deprivations of prisoners in Turkey and his family finally received definite information – after the war his body was identified, his identity disc sent home and today he lies in Baby 700 Cemetery. The last recorded sighting of Priestley on 25 April was by Frank Doig,[122] probably of his platoon, who stated that "the last time he saw" Priestley "was at Pope's Hill in the charge on Sunday morning April 25th. The report was that he had been buried by the Turks."[123] This tends to support the idea that terms such as "forward of Quinn's Post," "Popes" and the "left" are general terms often used to describe the fighting on Baby 700 or Battleship Hill.

---

109 69 Private William Douglas LeFort, A Company, 23 at embarkation, painter, born London, England.
110 B2455, Priestley.
111 396 Private Thomas Priestman, locomotive fireman, of Kalgoorlie, born Hull, England.
112 Hurst, *Game to the Last*, p.154.
113 313 Private John Joseph Jose, B Company, 30 at embarkation, wood machinist, of Perth, born Kerang Victoria.
114 Australian Red Cross Wounded and Missing Enquiry Bureau files, 1DRL/0428.
115 *Ibid.*
116 Letter, 23 August 1917, B2455, Priestley.
117 Letter, 28 June 1918, B2455, Priestley.
118 Letter, 1 January 1918, B2455, Priestley.
119 B2455, Priestley.
120 *Ibid.*
121 Such as collecting pay, appearing on a roll or in a POW list.
122 298 Private Frank Ernest Doig, B Company, 28 at embarkation, railway employee, of Midland Junction.
123 Australian Red Cross Wounded and Missing Enquiry Bureau files, 1DRL/0428.

Priestley may not have been the only member of 6 Platoon to fight on Baby 700. Alfred Henry Smith[124] was last seen by D.J. Melville[125] "with a party led by Sergeant Chamberlain advancing on the morning of 25 April. They … were not seen again." Melville also confirms that a letter "from Sergeant Chamberlain" appeared in the Sunday times "saying that he was a POW in Constantinople … possible that Private Smith is a prisoner also. Witness … knew Smith well, he was in No 6 Platoon."[126] Private Charles Brown[127] knew Smith "personally in same platoon. Saw him just above the beach … lay down and took cover together."[128] Brown "Never saw him again," but provides evidence that Chamberlain may have survived the fighting on Baby 700, reporting that "Sergeant Pride"[129] believed "he saw Smith that Sunday night with Sergeant Chamberlain. Chamberlain subsequently wrote from Constantinople … but did not mention Smith."[130] There are several other accounts about Smith which contain the usual contradictions, but Pride, Brown, Smith and Priestley all belonged to the original C Company, from which 5 and 6 Platoons were formed, and they are likely to have known each other. Less weight may be placed on the accounts by members of other platoons or units, especially as Smith was a common name.[131]

A letter[132] to Defence enquiring about Smith's fate includes enquiries about another missing man, Wallie Roach.[133] The letter is written in part on behalf of Roach's mother,[134] and attempts to make sense of the contradictory fragments of information appearing in newspapers, official correspondence and from battalion members. Roach had "not been heard of since they landed. Wounded chaps reckon he is a prisoner in fact one says he saw him taken prisoner."[135] Beyond some evidence that he was a POW in Turkey,[136] no further record was ever found of Roach; perhaps he had been captured but did not survive the day. He too was a member of 6 Platoon and has no known grave.

Today Private William Hobbs[137] also lies in Baby 700 Cemetery, but he was recorded as missing until the 1916 Court of Enquiry. The only documented information at the time was from J.J. Jose, who told the Red Cross that "Hobbs was missing the first day not," as had been reported, "in July. Informant … was in the same section."[138] The facts that Hobbs and Jose served under consecutive regimental numbers, were both members of the original C Company and that Hobbs was the only man by that name in the battalion, reduce the chance of mistaken identity. Identification of his body after the war confirms the presence of another of Strickland's 6 Platoon on Baby 700.[139]

These cases demonstrate the great contradictions between primary sources, and the consequent suffering by the missing men's families. It is only by examining such evidence in a much broader context that enables weight to be given to certain accounts over others and for the evidence to assume value. For Priestley, Hobbs, Simcock and Frank Adcock, the most compelling evidence of where they fought is where they lie. The evidence compiled here also reveals trends: a significant

124 357 Private Alfred Henry Smith, B Company, 21, iron-moulder of Claremont, born South Australia.
125 323 Private Donald Jackson Melville, B company, 22 at embarkation, civil servant, of Maylands, born Brunswick Victoria.
126 Australian Red Cross Wounded and Missing Enquiry Bureau files, 1DRL/0428.
127 278 Private Charles Brown, B Company, 34 at embarkation, lumper, of Bunbury. Brown was wounded on 25 April 1915.
128 Australian Red Cross Wounded and Missing Enquiry Bureau files, 1DRL/0428.
129 342 Corporal William Alfred Pride, B Company, 34 at embarkation, blacksmith's striker, of Maylands, born Surrey, England. Boer War veteran Pride was later awarded a Mention in Despatches for performing "various acts of conspicuous gallantry or valuable service" at the Landing.
130 Australian Red Cross Wounded and Missing Enquiry Bureau files, 1DRL/0428.
131 Smith's brother Leslie would be killed on 24 April 1918. He too would be 21 when he died.
132 C. Nielsen to Defence Base Records, Melbourne, letter, 30 December 1915, B2455, A.H. Smith.
133 348 Private Wallace Passmore Roach, B Company, 22 at embarkation, sawyer, of Guildford, born Kilkenny, South Australia.
134 B2455, A.H. Smith.
135 *Ibid.*
136 In October 1915.
137 312 Private William Hobbs, B Company, 20 at embarkation, farmer, born Devon, England.
138 Interview at Atelier Hospital, Cairo, 12 November 1915. B2455, Hobbs.
139 Hobbs lies in Baby 700 Cemetery.

number of B Company, primarily of Strickland's 6 and Newman's 8 Platoons, fought in the vicinity of Baby 700 on 25 April. As Bean records Strickland taking a party to Fisherman's Hut and Newman moving forward with Peck to support Loutit, their presence on Baby 700 appears as something of a mystery. Fragmentation of the 11th Battalion appears not to be the reason, given the presence of relatively high numbers of men of these platoons on Baby 700.

The only evidence of Strickland's movements after Fisherman's Hut is Gostelow's, which states that the two officers spent the day commanding ammunition carrying parties.[140] Perhaps some of their men, after carrying ammunition to Baby 700, reinforced the battered firing lines there. Siefken's account is the only one from 6 Platoon to have as yet come to light and he does not appear to have been involved in ammunition carrying. He described about "15 of us" joining "the others on top of the ridges" and advancing "about two miles inland ... we got stopped. The Turks had got big reinforcements up, and things were looking pretty crook when the New Zealanders came up and reinforced us and eased things off."[141] He thought that most troops who advanced further "got cut off only a few got back, the others were either killed or captured."[142] Siefken does not appear to have attacked Fisherman's Hut, and Gostelow wrote that after the action Strickland had only a few men with him. It is therefore possible that when Strickland moved left to tackle Fisherman's Hut, Siefken and others climbed to Russell's Top.

Tulloch stated that he had a platoon of B Company with him,[143] though whether this refers to a single platoon or a mixed party the size of a platoon is not stated, nor is it known which platoon this could be. The preceding analysis of varied and confused information of missing men and reconstruction of their stories, grounded on the identified graves on Baby 700, suggests that the "platoon" that accompanied Tulloch up Walker's Ridge consisted largely of men from 8 Platoon. We know Newman had few of his platoon with him near Adana Bair[144] and that Blay, of Newman's platoon, appears to have climbed to Russell's Top from the beach. It is possible that some men from 6 Platoon, two of whom are known to be buried on Baby 700, also joined this party and, by implication, fought with Tulloch on Battleship Hill. Perhaps Priestley, Smith and others, after becoming detached from their platoons, attached themselves to their company 2IC, Tulloch, either on the beach or later. Other members of B Company, such as "stray" members of 5 and 7 Platoons, may also have joined their 2IC – Duncan Sharp, who accompanied Carrington forward of Quinn's Post, appears to have been a member of 7 Platoon.

Another possibility is that B Company men began the move to Second Ridge with Barnes, and somehow became detached and embroiled in the fighting on the left – there is evidence of parties being sent from the right to fight on the left.[145] Of note is the fact that five of the six members of 8 Platoon listed above – Chamberlain, Hearle, Carrington and the Adcocks – lived in Fremantle before the war. Smith, 6 Platoon, who may have joined Chamberlain at some stage, was from a suburb nearby – Claremont. One wonders if the men knew each other before the war, and once separated from their platoons and commanders, gravitated to men they knew.

There is no direct evidence in secondary sources to identify which members of B Company fought on Battleship Hill. This reconstruction shows that many previously unidentified B Company men fought and disappeared in the vicinity of Baby 700. For some, the probable reason for being there is that they fought with Tulloch on Battleship Hill, and withdrew to continue the fight on or around Baby 700. Others of these platoons may have been left crumpled in the scrub, their names now lost to history.

---

140 Gostelow, diary, 25 April 1915.
141 Siefken, letter, 3 September 1915.
142 *Ibid.*
143 Tulloch, 3DRL 606 item 206 – diaries nos. 192–205.
144 Lock, *The Fighting 10th*, pp.213–214.
145 Goodlet, manuscript, p.12; Bean, *Official History*, Volume I (1921 and 1941), p.434.

The stories of a number of other 11th Battalion men known to be buried on Baby 700 have also been investigated.

The fact that Percy Williams[146] is now buried on Baby 700 did not spare his family the anxiety of others as he was initially reported wounded and missing. As an F Company original, Williams may have fought with Cooke. A Captain James, presumably the 11th Battalion's first Signals Officer, Herbert James,[147] wrote in February 1916 that "Personally I am afraid that he went under as many men who were wounded out in front had to be left when our men retired and goodness knows what may have happened if he were among them. Of course you will treat this as confidential because I know nothing for certain." In accordance with James's instruction, this comment was omitted from letters to Williams' family.[148] The family received the usual fragments of worrying misinformation, being informed in July 1915 that Williams had been wounded, though as this was "not reported" serious, his mother was "not to trouble further."[149] She heard nothing officially, but two of his wounded "camp mates" who returned home told her that Williams was with them until death.[150] Percy was her only son, his father having been killed in a mining accident when he was seven, and for the next "eight long years"[151] Percy had been her only companion. She was understandably bereft, but was still almost apologetic about being a "bother" to the military authorities in seeking information.[152]

Hope leapt heartbreakingly from the gloom in February 1916 when Williams' mother saw his name on a list of mentally deranged wounded soldiers, but her enquiries received the reply that no such official list existed.[153] Percy was even identified in a photograph of soldiers in hospital in England,[154] but like many others, in 1916 he was officially reported killed in action. After the war his body was identified and his identity disc sent to his family.[155] Williams' mother did not claim her son's pay until 1920, as she had hoped he would "come … to claim it" himself.[156]

A Company's William Hastie Waugh,[157] 3 or 4 Platoon, appears to have fought in the vicinity of Baby 700 as he saw Lance Corporal C.O. Holcombe,[158] A Company, "lying on the ground wounded in the thigh. I was about twelve yards off … The Turks came over the ground later. On the following day we counter-attacked and went over the same ground, but I myself did not pass over the ground where I saw Holcombe lying."[159] Holcombe is buried on Baby 700 and may have been a member of Morgan's 2 Platoon. The fact that Waugh describes this as happening "when we were retiring in front of Plugge's Plateau" reaffirms the general nature of men's descriptions of location and their use of known reference points. Lowson, 3 or 4 Platoon, recalled landing with Holcombe, who was later "in a party which got detached from the rest and was never seen again … they must have been cut off and made prisoners."[160]

A female friend of Holcombe's in Western Australia reasoned that his situation must be "very serious" as if he could only speak he would have contacted her, "for up until 21st April I had received

146 738 Private Percy Williams, C Company, 22 at death, miner and grocer, of Kalgoorlie, born South Melbourne.
147 Second Lieutenant (at embarkation) Herbert James, 21 at embarkation, telephone engineer, of West Perth.
148 James' comments were made 18 February 1916. He was then Adjutant of the 11th Battalion at the Suez Canal. Australian Red Cross Wounded and Missing Enquiry Bureau files, Australian War Memorial, 1DRL/0428.
149 B2455, P. Williams.
150 *Ibid.*
151 *Ibid.*
152 *Ibid.*
153 *Ibid.*
154 Australian Red Cross Wounded and Missing Enquiry Bureau files, 1DRL/0428.
155 B2455, P. Williams.
156 *Ibid.*
157 118 Private William Hastie Waugh, A Company, 28 at embarkation, clerk, of Mount Lawley, born Fitzroy, Victoria.
158 965 Lance Corporal Cuthbert Oliver Holcombe, A Company, 33 at enlistment, farmer, born London, England. Holcombe had served with the 2nd Life Guards and possibly the South African Constabulary.
159 Australian Red Cross Wounded and Missing Enquiry Bureau files, 1DRL/0428.
160 *Ibid.*

letters every possible chance he had."[161] The only information she had was "rumours from returned soldiers and one was that he was killed on the 25th April" and she beseeched the authorities to "please cable … I will pay for it if necessary."[162] Despite assurances that "the absence of further particulars may be accepted as indicative of satisfactory progress," Holcombe, farmer and "old soldier," was in 1916 declared killed in action on 25 April.[163]

Such was the humility of friends and family seeking news of missing loved ones that it was not uncommon for them to enclose stamps when, in some cases apologetically, requesting information. A "(Miss) F. Durkin" of Subiaco added "(Enclosed please find stamp)" when seeking news of Maurice O'Donohue,[164] D Company, school teacher of Northam and Kalgoorlie. A family friend wrote on behalf of O'Donohue's parents, "an aged couple" who were aware only that their "son was reported missing from the first day," and were "naturally very troubled … I thought a letter from you … would pacify them to some extent … they are in poor circumstances, relying mainly on the pension."[165] No news was forthcoming until the Court of Enquiry in April 1916, though after losing her son Mrs O'Donohue was denied a "death or invalidity" pension as she was neither a dependant nor deemed to be "without adequate means of support."[166] After the war Lance Corporal O'Donohue's body was identified and buried on Baby 700. How he, as a member of 13 or 14 Platoon, D Company, came to be fighting here is, as in many other cases, unknown, further evidences the fragmentation of the 11th Battalion and the flaws in our image of the battle. It will be noted that Ashton also belonged to either 13 or 14 Platoon and found himself on the high ground. It might be expected that members of the wounded Walker's platoon would have accompanied Denton to Second Ridge, but perhaps they instead joined Buttle and Reid.

Although a report stated that Private William John Wilcox, A Company, was buried about 31 July, the 23-year-old labourer lies buried on Baby 700, having been killed on 25 April. Wilcox was originally from Peckham, London, and when his parents in England heard of his death, they requested they be sent his possessions from the battalion stores in Egypt, as was normal practice for the dead of the AIF. They were informed that, as the force had departed for the Western Front, no stores remained in Egypt and nothing was available to be sent. Having lived for a year with the anxiety of not knowing what happened to him, his family was left with neither body, facts of death nor mementoes. Wilcox, originally of B Company, probably belonged to Morgan's platoon.

The sister of "Jack" Thompson,[167] C Company, wrote to the military authorities in September 1915, "begging your help" in finding information about her brother.[168] In April 1916, Thompson's grandfather was still under the impression that he had been "wounded 28 June," the date of the 11th Battalion action on Silt Spur, then "reported missing … can't be found." The grandfather, Thompson's "Guardian, as his mother died when he was two years old," had "reared him and his two sisters." Enquiries at the Drill Hall at Francis Street, Perth, had been unsuccessful. Thompson was officially reported as wounded and missing on 2 May 1915, but in April 1916 this was changed to killed in action on 2 May 1915. After the war the family was notified that Thompson lay buried on Baby 700 and his identity disc was sent to them.[169] Thompson was a first reinforcement but appears to have joined C Company; the most likely explanation for his presence on Baby 700 is that he accompanied Cooke to Baby 700.

161 B2455, Holcombe.
162 *Ibid.*
163 *Ibid.*
164 817 Lance Corporal Maurice O'Donohue, 23, school teacher, originally from Horsham, Victoria.
165 B2455, O'Donohue.
166 *Ibid.*
167 1185 Private John Thompson, 20 at death, sleeper cutter, of Weroona, born Niagara.
168 Letter, Mrs H.S. Birch, 18 September 1915, B2455, J. Thompson.
169 B2455, J. Thompson.

Many suffering families had to be satisfied that a decision based on an absence of evidence, made by a Court of Enquiry in France, represented the true fate of a loved one on a battlefield in Turkey. As shown here, nearly a century after men disappeared in battle on 25 April 1915, it is still possible to find traces of the lost life behind what is otherwise merely a name on a headstone or a memorial to the missing. Connecting missing men to a place, time, event or people can provide a context for their last hours, offering an insight into their movements on 25 April and ascribing to them a possible place of death and last resting place. The names and otherwise invisible experience of those who were there on the day but did not live to tell their stories, can then be included in the written history. Probably some of those examined here were among the anonymous men who fought on Battleship Hill. Others may have fought and fallen on Baby 700, and may lie unidentified in Baby 700 Cemetery. At a broader level, this evidence contributes missing pieces with which to reconstruct the battle, filling gaps and suggesting answers, and providing a more complete picture of the role and experience of this battalion at this battle.

The primary sources used in this reconstruction have been shown to often be extremely unreliable. In some cases, the number of possible fates of a missing man is directly proportional to the number of "witnesses" interviewed. Such evidence should consequently be regarded as virtually useless in isolation – indeed, in 1916, enquiries into the fate of Percy Williams received a response that "previous experience causes us to place practically no reliance upon the stories supplied to the Red Cross Enquirers."[170] Yet, by analysis of such records in the context of broader research, using the reconstructed battalion roll, biographical detail, the course of the battle, letters, diaries and interviews and the geography of the battlefield, such unreliable accounts can be reassessed, information given more or less weight as evidence, and an insight provided into previously invisible parts of the battle and the experience of those who fought it.

The reconstruction in this and previous chapters suggests that, rather than the 11th Battalion's B, D and half of A Company occupying Second Ridge, C being in reserve and too few others being on Baby 700 to be noticeable, as described in nearly every history of the past 90 years, members of nearly every platoon of the 11th Battalion may fought on or near Baby 700. In addition to members of A Company, significant numbers of B Company's 5, 6, 8 and possibly 7 Platoons, and D Company's 15 and 16 Platoons, with probably lower numbers of 13 and 14 Platoons, fought in the vicinity of Baby 700. 8 Platoon, and smaller numbers of 6 and 7 Platoons, may have accompanied Tulloch from the beach to Battleship Hill, with 5 Platoon members more likely to have accompanied Jackson. Anecdotal evidence and the previously examined fragmentation of C Company suggests members of other than Cooke's 12 Platoon may also have fought here. Gaps in the existing history, created largely by casualties on the battlefield and omissions or assumptions by writers since, have created a skewed image. The picture emerging from the work presented above appears to be the opposite of the existing one, in that a great many of the 11th Battalion may have made it to and fought on the high ground of the left flank.

This examination of the fate of the dead and missing has created a picture where before there was none, revealing, for example, significant numbers of men in places where the existing histories state they should not be. As with other reconstructions of events this day, it is an image from which the majority of pieces are still missing and assumption remains fraught. In a few cases, the most definite evidence is a man's burial place. This validates Bean's vision of the "battlefield cemetery", of paying tribute to Gallipoli's dead by, wherever possible, burying them close to where they died. Whether he envisaged the "battlefield cemetery" contributing such value as an instrument of historical research, is another question.

---

170 Letter from Base Records to General Secretary, Red Cross Society, Perth, 4 May 1916, B2455, P. Williams.

11

Conclusion

"A quarrel between the model and actuality ... is the creative quarrel at the heart of cognition. Without this dialectic, intellectual growth cannot take place."[1]

Over the generations there has been a gradual drift from the "reality" of the Gallipoli Landing, as anecdotes and stories have distorted passing from mouth to mouth, memories have faded, documents have disappeared, and the veterans, once no doubt the custodians of "truth," have passed on. Today the public acquire much of their knowledge from generations who were not there. Inaccurate perceptions and beliefs, both on the battlefield and in our collective memory, have become enshrined as the history of the day. This may be true of all historic events over time, but because of the Gallipoli Landing's place in the Australian psyche, and our very attempts to ensure preservation of its memory, it is unique in Australian history. The methodology used here aims to bypass much of the rhetoric of recent decades to reconnect with the "foundation data" of the event – the story of those who were there.

The majority of accounts of the Landing have accompanied those who fought that day to the grave. For every two accounts we have, dozens lie invisibly between them.[2] One aim of this book was to use detail to carve a closer and clearer picture of the participants' experience and rescue the stories of some of those who lived and fought "in unredeemed time."[3] It is hoped that this detailing and contextualising of individual experience reveals the stories of some of those missing from the history. If their names can't be seen in the text, perhaps their lives and experience can be glimpsed alongside or in the background of those whose stories are reconstructed here.

Biographical history may be known for being rich and "personally ... meaningful,"[4] but these attributes can also make it an essential ingredient for reconstructing history. This work takes a new tool to an old topic by reinterpreting such sources, separating the historical "wheat" from the erroneous "chaff". Rather than taking Bean's account as the "actuality" of the battle and using it to assess, ascribe and interpret accounts, it uses other evidence to build the story, and compares it with Bean's. It uses a study of a relatively small group, a battalion, to reassess a battle, rather than the other way around. This tight focus allows research to a depth at which invisible connections begin to reveal themselves, connections that, once united, form a grid on which the battle can be rebuilt. Without these connections, details in veterans' accounts are often little more than anecdotes, flecks of personal experience floating on a background of disconnection, myth and vagueness. The detailed prosopographical approach used here creates a body of evidence where there was none, evidence that can be applied to discussion of some of the larger questions of the battle, and reveals anomalies and gaps that were invisible when examined in isolation or until examined at this level of detail. The greatest single body of work behind this book is largely unseen – the aggregation and analysis of detailed biographical and historical information to connect men to their companies, platoons, times, ground, common events, homes, jobs, and each other.

---

1 E.P. Thompson, "The Peculiarities of the English", p.350.
2 Hurst, *Game to the Last*, p.vi.
3 Thompson, "The Peculiarities of the English", p.358.
4 Halbwachs, *On Collective Memory*. p.29.

Figure 31. The Sphinx, Plugge's Plateau and Ari Burnu from Walker's Ridge, showing the terrain that confronted the covering force and the slopes assaulted by them in the pre-dawn darkness of 25 April. (Photograph by J.P. Hurst, n.d., author's collection)

The use of eyewitness testimony to get "inside" historical episodes is not new. Yet paradoxically this testimony is here revealed to be highly unreliable. In isolation, such accounts often appear of little historical value, contributing more to the mythology and misunderstandings of the Landing, yet they are often used without further examination. This study has endeavoured to establish the reliability and value of eyewitness accounts as historical evidence, to create a framework with which to assess them, and to dig and keep digging to identify the more trustworthy clues and thereby elevate them, when possible, to historical building blocks with which to rebuild the battle. The clues that allow one piece of evidence to be given greater credence than another may lie in details of lives remote from the battlefield, of deaths and disappearances on it, descriptions of ground covered or events witnessed. Accounts were rigorously examined before being presented here, and the extent to which sources can be reliably used varies greatly. In many cases, resolution is impossible; in others, "balance of evidence" assumptions are the closest that can be attained. This approach has been of particular benefit when applied to the confused and fragmented story of the Landing, but could be applied to other battles and historical events involving numbers of people and conflicting eyewitness and secondary accounts.

Examination at this level of detail might be expected to answer only questions of detail, but it also clarifies or resolves some of the greater issues of the day. The 11th Battalion's dispositions were not as they have previously been portrayed and the battalion was far more fragmented than believed. The 27th Regiment reached the battlefield possibly two hours earlier than realised by western historians. The men of 27th Regiment fought the 3rd Brigade from 400 Plateau to Fisherman's Hut, and it is probably they who stopped the drive to Third Ridge and forced adoption of an inferior position on Second Ridge. They may have prevented reinforcement of Tulloch and even to have forced his withdrawal, a part of the struggle that remained invisible until subjected to the approach presented here. If so, this book represents a dramatic change in the way the battle has been read since 1921.

The words "may well," "apparently" and "probably" appear repeatedly in this book. This is both an acknowledgement of the fragility of evidence and the dangers of assumption. I cannot be sure the events on Baby 700, Battleship Hill and elsewhere were as I have portrayed them, but I present them as evidence-based alternative reconstructions which, in many places, match Şefik's account more closely than does the history accepted since 1921. It is difficult to refute or disregard the 'facts' stated in any account, especially one as detailed and thorough as Şefik's, but at times a statement in such an account will even contradict another in the same account. Bridges' after-action report, in the First Division's War Diary, for example, describing the fighting in the late afternoon, claims that "No ground was lost by us on any part of our line."[5] It was during this period that Baby 700 fell. No one account tells the whole story, and it is unwise to assume any are without flaw. I have also questioned my own arguments when evidence demanded it.[6] A key point of this work is that the story of the Landing has been told many times, but much of the existing history is a product of assumption and acceptance of what went before.

The evidence presented here suggests that the failure to take and hold key objectives at Z Beach on 25 April was caused in part by a disintegration of resolve by Allied commanders. This was a consequence of many factors. Pre-landing changes to the 11th Battalion's orders meant an all-out thrust for two objectives evolved until defence of the right flank assumed the greater priority. The time available for MacLagan to push forward was reduced by 27th Regiment's earlier than previously recognised arrival. The Turkish outposts' fighting withdrawal and the Australians' inexperience and misreading of events[7] blurred the line between the battle with the outposts and the arrival of the Turkish counter-attack.

One of the significant findings revealed in this book is the level of fragmentation of the 11th Battalion. This must have reduced MacLagan's ability to manoeuvre and attack, and encouraged caution, defence and consolidation. Whether the rest of the 3rd Brigade was in a similar state is an area that requires more research, but if the other battalions were as fragmented as the 11th,[8] MacLagan may have had little choice but to stop on Second Ridge. For example, an intact brigade could have mitigated risks while still pursuing its principal objectives, by using support weapons and co-ordination of units to cover a co-ordinated advance; a fragmented or disorganised brigade probably denied MacLagan any such options. More will no doubt be revealed and additional work undertaken as Ottoman and other sources become available.

The findings in this book support some of Aspinall-Oglander's conclusions about disintegration of the force and its command. The Australians had all the disadvantages of inexperience and of being thrown ashore as though shipwrecked on unfamiliar ground without their field artillery, and the Turks enjoyed the corresponding advantages.[9] Şefik and Kemal used their advantages to act aggressively and with speed. Şefik's arrival held the 1st Division in place, and Kemal's placed the high ground beyond reach. Şefik's prompt action tipped the scales in Turkey's favour; Kemal's arrival sealed the fate of the Landing.

No criticism of the men who fought the battle is implied or intended. I have not undertaken the first steps in any such assessment, such as examining the men's training. The 3rd Brigade, without

---

5   1st Division War Diary, April 1915, Part 2, report, p.5.

6   A "historian must be able to regard his model with a radical scepticism, and to maintain an openness of response to evidence for which it has no categories." Thompson, "The Peculiarities of the English", p.350.

7   Intelligence has not been assessed in this book, but accurate and reliable intelligence would have compensated for some of these factors and no doubt instilled confidence in commanders.

8   The 12th Battalion was also scattered over much of the battlefield, but as they had landed from seven destroyers, this should have been anticipated.

9   Aspinall-Oglander, *Military Operations, Gallipoli*, Vol. I, pp.199–200.

specialist training or equipment, armed with rifle and bayonet[10] and little reliable intelligence about what to expect, attacked a defended coast in the dark. This was their first action. They were confronted by unexpectedly steep terrain (Figure 31), but launched themselves forward regardless and endured a day of attack and bombardment without effective artillery support. The AIF's abilities in attack, defiance in defence and stoicism throughout are not being questioned.[11] Many were young but are unlikely to have appreciated the tag "kids." Bernie Walther was a dedicated machine gunner, both before the war and during it. He landed at Gallipoli a 19-year-old private and was a captain when killed at Pozieres the following year; he was still a machine gunner. The approach behind this book has been to get as close to these people's experience as possible, so as to pay them the respect of representing it as accurately as possible, and thereby include their story in the history.

For those on the battlefield, hindsight and reflection were for the future. The tired and tattered Australians in the firing lines did not know where most of their friends were, nor whether they were alive or dead. Claremont and Kanowna, Perth and Geraldton, home and loved ones must have seemed a very long way away. Some had lost brothers, probably all had seen many men killed and more wounded. Many must have begun to doubt they would ever see home again. Today we can only wonder how the survivors of this first day of battle felt, peering over their rifles in the gathering gloom, with the dying sun spilling its last bronze rays over the splintered and trampled scrub, and the body-littered ridges and gullies of this bloodiest of Sundays.

---

10   The eight machine guns in the brigade certainly landed with their brigade and faced the same dangers and experiences, but the guns were not brought into action until further inland.

11   *Game to the Last* documents this battalion's experience throughout the Gallipoli campaign. Hurst, *Game to the Last*.

Appendix I

The Fate of Lieutenant M.L. Reid

With his thigh smashed by an Ottoman bullet, electrical engineer Mort Reid disappeared into the scrub of Sari Bair. The retiring 11th Battalion troops neither saw nor heard him as they made their fighting withdrawal over the ground they and a fit, "inspiring"[1] Reid had crossed earlier. The last reference to Reid in the *Official History* states that one "of his men went to help him crawl to the rear, but Reid was never thereafter seen or heard of by his battalion."[2]

During the withdrawal, Buttle, who had seen Reid "pass over a ridge in our rear," made for the "spot where I last saw him"[3] but could find no sign of him. About two hours later Mason heard from a 12th Battalion man that he had seen Reid "in the gully. He thinks he can get along alright."[4] At "about noon" Buttle heard that Reid was seen on the beach, though this proved incorrect.[5]

Reid's wife, working at the Palace Hospital, Heliopolis, to be near her husband, was to spend the coming months trying to find him or confirm his fate. Some held hopes that he had been taken prisoner and was recuperating in Constantinople. A report in the *Kalgoorlie Sun* stated that Reid was "in hospital at Malta and in a very sad plight indeed. His legs are paralysed, his mind has given way and thus his identity was lost for the time being."[6] Such reports about missing men were common but generally proved groundless, as in this instance.

One branch of the Chatal Dere has particularly steep sides, where it bites into the ridge between Battleship Hill and Baby 700. Even a fit person in this country can find their passage blocked by deceptively steep, sandy slopes or dense scrub. Reid, in great pain, unable to stand to establish his bearings, suffering from loss of blood and dragging a swollen, broken leg, may have slid into this gully, only to discover he could not climb back out. His only option may have been to follow the valley down as he was too weak to do anything else. He may have become disoriented, as others were to do later in the day, and crawled south down the wrong valley believing it led to the beach, or have collapsed and died of loss of blood. If he lived long enough, he would have encountered enemy troops.

Braidwood, apparently one of those to accompany Tulloch, told the Red Cross that Reid "Was seen making his way back … when the Turks made a rush and no more was seen of him,"[7] and Ryan that Reid had "got behind a bush," and the "Turks missed him as they were advancing but found him as they were retreating."[8] This level of detail suggests that Ryan had either seen Reid or had heard from someone who had, though it was not uncommon for the rumour mill to turn conjecture into "fact." Other men were convinced Reid was captured and a prisoner of the Turks.[9]

A number of parties of 27th and 57th Regiment were fighting in this area during the day, and 72nd and 77th in the evening. Any of these could have discovered Reid and either left him to die,

1   Bean, *Gallipoli Mission*, p.84.
2   Bean, *Official History*, Volume I (1921 and 1941), p.290.
3   Buttle, 3DRL 8042 item 7.
4   Mason, 2DRL 301, Book 31.
5   Buttle, 3DRL 8042 item 7.
6   The *Kalgoorlie Sun*, 12 September 1915.
7   Braidwood, Al Hayat Cairo 7 November 15, Red Cross files, 1DRL/0428.
8   Ryan, Red Cross files, 1DRL/0428.
9   Such as F.B. Cox and "Pte Paine."

or killed him – Ashton wrote that "Some hundreds of our brave fellows must have lost their lives in this terrible fashion."[10]

Mort's youngest brother, Lindsay,[11] was also killed at the Landing, fighting with the 7th Battalion. He too would remain missing, until his remains were identified and buried after the war. No trace of Mort has ever been found, or at least, identified. Perhaps his remains lie in Baby 700 cemetery or the Chatal Dere.

Şefik tantalisingly wrote that during the Australian withdrawal from Incebayir Ridge, "Three maps were found on officers who were among the casualties."[12] Whether this refers to Reid, the only officer known to have become a casualty on Incebayir Ridge, cannot be known.

---

10   Ashton, manuscript, p.21.
11   989 Private Cyril Lindsay Reid, 25, electrician, of East Melbourne, born NSW, is buried at Lone Pine.
12   Şefik, para. 104, footnote 2.

Appendix II
Joe Adlam's Sword

By the morning of 26 April, Howe was in a battle outpost "20 or 30 yards in front of the main line ... subsequently known as Steele's Post ... Joe was there with his sword." The trench was only "about a foot deep ... scraped out to a width of about 5 feet" and crowded with about 30 men. "There was barely room to move" and the men crammed even closer "to let the wounded lie more comfortably. Everyone was tired, bad-tempered and fed up to the teeth with Joe and his sword." Men continued to be hit and eventually someone "told Joe he would throw him and his sword out of the trench unless he got rid of it." One man suggested sending "it out by the next wounded man as a gift to the Colonel ... turned down flat ... we didn't know where he was and didn't care." Another suggested sending it to that "red-haired kid," the midshipman from their boat the previous morning:

> Carried unanimously. The cardboard cover was torn off a message pad and addressed in pencil to "the red-headed midshipman from HMS *London* who landed 1 and 2 platoons of A Company 11th Battalion" and tied to the sword hilt. Shortly after a fellow named Wilcox was pretty badly hit through the shoulder.

Private W.J. Wilcox,[1] A Company, is in fact buried on Baby 700. Perhaps A Company's E. Wilkerson[2] is meant. "We bandaged him up, gave him the sword and told him to give it to the first naval officer he saw on the beach." After the war Howe met this man, "a very good type of chap," who assured Howe he had "carried out his instructions," but decades later, Howe discovered the sword hadn't reached its destination. It had probably been souvenired by someone in the Navy, or stolen "by one of our fellows on the beach." Howe was "only sorry to learn that" the sword had not reached the young man who had carried 1 and 2 Platoons, 11th Battalion, "into trouble ... some 47 years ago."[3]

---

1   245 Private William John Wilcox, A Company, 23 at enlistment, labourer, born London, England.
2   250 Private Ernest Wilkerson, A Company, 32 at enlistment, farmer, of East Guildford, born Toodyay.
3   Howe to Churchill, 30 November 1962.

Key Geographical Features of the Anzac Area

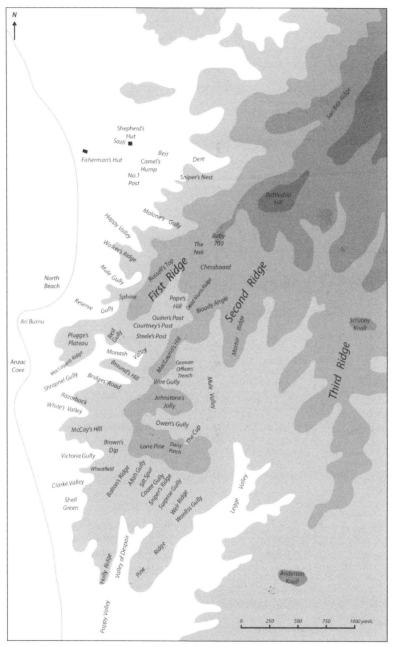

Map 12. Key geographical features of the Anzac area. Most of these features were not named at the time of the Landing, but for the sake of clarity their later names, as shown here, are used throughout this book. (Bean, Map 12, *Official History*, Volume I (1921 and 1941), following p.268)

11th Battalion Structure

11th Battalion structure at the time of the Landing, as determined in this book:

Headquarters (HQ)

Lieutenant-Colonel J.L. Johnston	Officer Commanding (OC)
Major S.R.H. Roberts[1]	Second-in-Command (2IC)
Captain J.H. Peck	Adjutant
Captain E.T. Brennan	Medical Officer
Lieutenant J. Peat[2]	Machine Gun Officer

A Company

Major E.A.D. Brockman	Officer Commanding
Captain R.W. Everett[3]	Second-in-Command
Lieutenant A.R. Selby[4]	1 Platoon
Lieutenant J.H. Morgan[5]	2 Platoon
Second Lieutenant A.H. MacFarlane[6]	3 Platoon
Lieutenant W.H. Rockliff[7]	4 Platoon

B Company

Captain C.A. Barnes	Officer Commanding
Captain R.R. Reilly[8]	Second-in-Command
Second Lieutenant S.H. Jackson[9]	5 Platoon
Second Lieutenant F.P.D. Strickland[10]	6 Platoon
Lieutenant A.H. Darnell[11]	7 Platoon
Lieutenant J. Newman	8 Platoon

C Company

Captain R.L. Leane	Officer Commanding

---

1 Stephen Richard Harricks Roberts, 40 at embarkation, civil servant, of Subiaco, born Ararat, Victoria.
2 Lieutenant James Peat, 27 at embarkation, surveyor, of Boulder.
3 Captain Reginald William Everett, 42 at embarkation, business manager of Subiaco, born Goulburn, New South Wales.
4 Lieutenant Arthur Roland Selby, 21, soldier, of Perth, born New South Wales. Selby attended Scotch College, Perth, Adelaide University and graduated from the Royal Military College, Duntroon.
5 Lieutenant James Harold Morgan, 22, civil servant, of West Leederville, born Victoria.
6 Second Lieutenant (Lieutenant by 25 April 1915) Archibald Henry MacFarlane, 27, metallurgist and analytical chemist, of Perth and Subiaco, born Victoria.
7 Lieutenant William Hudson Rockliff, 29 at embarkation, schoolteacher, of West Perth, born New South Wales.
8 Lieutenant Reginald Ronald Reilly, 36 at embarkation, civil servant, of Perth. Assumed command of the battalion signallers shortly before the Landing.
9 Second Lieutenant (Lieutenant by 25 April 1915) Samuel Henry Jackson, 24 at embarkation, civil servant, of Mount Lawley, born Bundaberg, Queensland.
10 Second Lieutenant (Lieutenant by 25 April 1915) Frederick Phillip David Strickland, 39 at embarkation, civil servant, of South Perth, born Melbourne. Strickland had served with the West Australian forces in the Boer War.
11 Second Lieutenant (Lieutenant by 25 April 1915) Aubrey Hugh Darnell, 28, civil servant, of Claremont, born Ireland.

Captain W.R. Annear	Second-in-Command
Lieutenant D.H. MacDonald	9 Platoon
Lieutenant A.P.H. Corley	10 Platoon
Lieutenant C.A. La Nauze[12]	11 Platoon
Second Lieutenant J.H. Cooke[13]	12 Platoon

D Company

Major J.S. Denton[14]	Officer Commanding
Captain A.E.J. Croly	Second-in-Command
Lieutenant J. Williams[15]	13 Platoon
Second Lieutenant H.H. Walker[16]	14 Platoon
Lieutenant M.L. Reid	15 Platoon
Second Lieutenant C.F. Buttle[17]	16 Platoon

12   Lieutenant Charles Andrew La Nauze, 32 at embarkation, bank officer/accountant, of Boulder, born Mauritius.

13   Second Lieutenant Joseph Henry Cooke, 32 at enlistment, accountant, of Wickepin, born India. Cooke had served 12 years with the 1st Battalion, Lancashire Fusiliers, finishing as colour sergeant.

14   Major James Samuel Denton, 38 at embarkation, civil servant, of Pazely, Great Southern Railway, born Port Adelaide.

15   Lieutenant John Williams, 41 at embarkation, clerk, c/o Military HQ Perth.

16   Second Lieutenant Harold Holmes Walker, D Company at Landing, 23 at enlistment, clerk, of East Perth, born South Melbourne. Walker was promoted lieutenant on 25 April 1915.

17   Second Lieutenant Clement Francis Buttle, 20 at enlistment, engineering cadet/mechanical engineer, of Perth. Buttle was promoted to lieutenant in February 1915.

Appendix V
Orders of Battle

Turkish Fifth Army

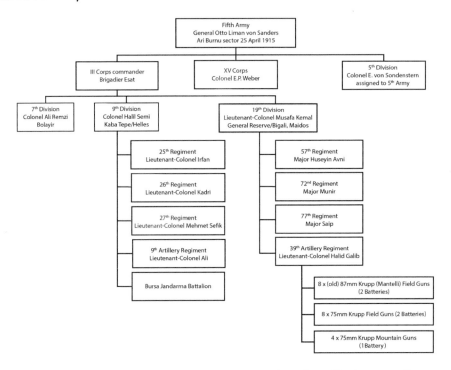

Compiled from a range of sources, primarily Uyar, Broadbent, Ericksson; spelling and ranks from Uyar. For simplicity some non-fighting elements not included.

Turkish 57th Regiment

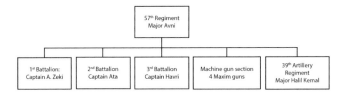

Turkish 27th Regiment

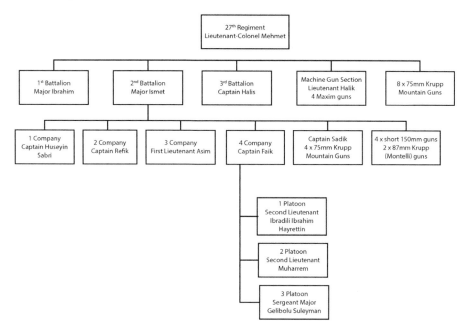

In most sources, 1, 2, 3, 4 Companies, 2nd Battalion, 27th Regiment are referred to as 5, 6, 7, 8 Companies. In this text Şefik's convention of 1, 2, 3, 4 is used.

Overleaf: Australian and New Zealand Army Corps

ANZAC Orbat, 25 April 1915

This list of units fighting with the Australian and New Zealand Army Corps was compiled from a range of sources. It is incomplete as many units were not of relevance to the scope of this work. For example, no light horse units landed on 25 April, nor, due to illness, did Colonel F.E. Johnston of the New Zealand Infantry Brigade.[1] Nor does it imply that all these units fought on 25 April 1915 – some may have landed that evening, others in the following days.[2] This list is included to provide a context for the many units mentioned in the text.[3]

---

1   Bean, *Official History*, Volume 1 (1921 and 1941), pp.300, 301.
2   For example, the 3rd Field Company, Engineers, were replaced by the 1st Field Company for the pre-dawn landing.
3   Bean includes a table of units who landed between 25 April and 1 May. Bean, Volume 1, preceding p.282.

Australian and New Zealand Army Corps

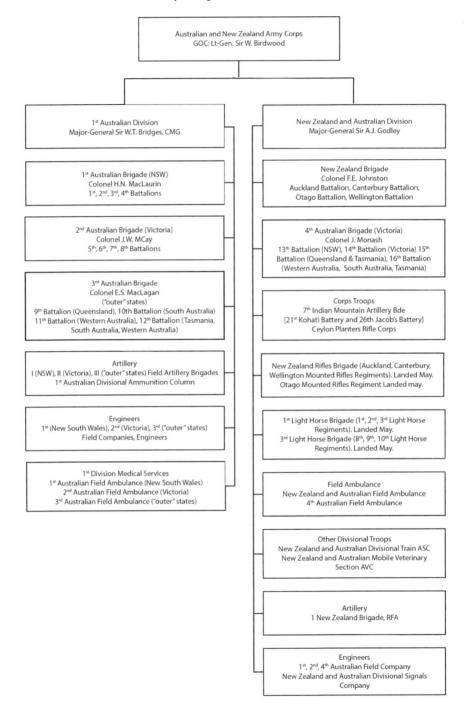

Australian and New Zealand Army Corps
GOC: Lt-Gen. Sir W. Birdwood

1st Australian Division
Major-General Sir W.T. Bridges, CMG

1st Australian Brigade (NSW)
Colonel H.N. MacLaurin
1st, 2nd, 3rd, 4th Battalions

2nd Australian Brigade (Victoria)
Colonel J.W. MCay
5th, 6th, 7th, 8th Battalions

3rd Australian Brigade
Colonel E.S. MacLagan
("outer" states)
9th Battalion (Queensland), 10th Battalion (South Australia)
11th Battalion (Western Australia), 12th Battalion (Tasmania, South Australia, Western Australia)

Artillery
I (NSW), II (Victoria), III ("outer" states) Field Artillery Brigades
1st Australian Divisional Ammunition Column

Engineers
1st (New South Wales), 2nd (Victoria), 3rd ("outer" states)
Field Companies, Engineers

1st Division Medical Services
1st Australian Field Ambulance (New South Wales)
2nd Australian Field Ambulance (Victoria)
3rd Australian Field Ambulance ("outer" states)

New Zealand and Australian Division
Major-General Sir A.J. Godley

New Zealand Brigade
Colonel F.E. Johnston
Auckland Battalion, Canterbury Battalion,
Otago Battalion, Wellington Battalion

4th Australian Brigade (Victoria)
Colonel J. Monash
13th Battalion (NSW), 14th Battalion (Victoria) 15th Battalion (Queensland & Tasmania), 16th Battalion (Western Australia, South Australia, Tasmania)

Corps Troops
7th Indian Mountain Artillery Bde
[21st Kohat) Battery and 26th Jacob's Battery]
Ceylon Planters Rifle Corps

New Zealand Rifles Brigade (Auckland, Canterbury, Wellington Mounted Rifles Regiments). Landed May.
Otago Mounted Rifles Regiment Landed may.

1st Light Horse Brigade (1st, 2nd, 3rd Light Horse Regiments). Landed May.
3rd Light Horse Brigade (8th, 9th, 10th Light Horse Regiments). Landed May.

Field Ambulance
New Zealand and Australian Field Ambulance
4th Australian Field Ambulance

Other Divisional Troops
New Zealand and Australian Divisional Train ASC
New Zealand and Australian Mobile Veterinary Section AVC

Artillery
1 New Zealand Brigade, RFA

Engineers
1st, 2nd, 4th Australian Field Company
New Zealand and Australian Divisional Signals Company

Bibliography

Primary Sources

Australian War Memorial, Canberra, ACT

AWM4, Sub-class 1/42: 1st Division War Diary, Australian Imperial Force Unit War Diaries, 1914–18 War.

AWM4, Sub-class 1/42/3 Part 2: 1st Division War Diary, Australian Imperial Force Unit War Diaries, 1914–18 War.

AWM4, Sub-class 23/3: 3rd Brigade War Diary, Australian Imperial Force Unit War Diaries, 1914–18 War.

AWM4, Sub-class 23/26: 9th Battalion War Diary, Australian Imperial Force Unit War Diaries, 1914–18 War.

AWM4, Sub-class 23/27: 10th Battalion War Diary, Australian Imperial Force Unit War Diaries, 1914–18 War.

AWM4, Sub-class 23/28: 11th Battalion War Diary, Australian Imperial Force Unit War Diaries, 1914–18 War.

AWM4, Sub-class 23/29: 12th Battalion War Diary, Australian Imperial Force Unit War Diaries, 1914–18 War.

AWM8, Nominal Roll, 11th Infantry Battalion, Sub-class 23/28. First World War Embarkation Roll.

AWM9, Unit roll books, 1914–1918 War.

AWM131, Roll of Honour circulars, 1914–18 War.

Aitken, J.M., diary/letter to mother, 1DRL item 13, Folder 1.

1DRL/0428: Australian Red Cross Wounded and Missing Enquiry Bureau files.

Barnes, C.A., diary, 1DRL/0091.

Brand, C.H., interview, AWM38 3DRL 606 item 28a.

Brockman, E.A.D., interview, AWM38 3DRL 606 item 27.

Buttle, C.F., letters to C.E.W. Bean (1 June 1920 and n.d.), AWM38 3DRL 8042 item 7.

Churchill, C.F.H., letter to E.W. Bush (n.d.), written Ponterwyd, Cardiganshire, 3DRL 6673/477.

Darnell, A.H., letter to F.A. Darnell (27 May 1915), 1 DRL 233.

Darnell, A.H., letter to Henley Darnell (12 June 1915), PR82/175.

Denton, J.S., letter to C.E.W. Bean (16 June 1920), 3DRL 8042 item 7.

Forrest, C.F., letter to mother (n.d.) 3DRL 7247.

Forrest, letter to father of G.H.H. Smith (n.d.), 3DRL 7247

Fortescue, D., letter to C.E.W. Bean (2 October 1919), 3DRL 8042 item 7.

Harrison, P.W., diagram, AWM38 3DRL 8042 item 7.

Hearder, D., manuscript, Private Records, 3DRL/3959.

Howe, H.V., interview, AWM38 3DRL 8042 item 7. AWM38, 3DRL 606 198 [2] contains a transcript of this interview, with slight variations in wording.

Howe, H.V., letter to C.F.H. Churchill (30 November 1962), 3DRL 6673/477.

Johnston, J. Lyon., Operation Order No 1. 1915, AWM4, Battalion orders (21 April 1915), 3rd Brigade War Diary, Appendix 3, Sub-class 23/3, Australian Imperial Force Unit War Diaries, 1914–18 War.

Johnston, J.L., Report on Landing of 11th Battalion, AWM4, 3rd Brigade War Diary, Sub-class 23/3, Australian Imperial Force Unit War Diaries, 1914–18 War, 1915.

Leane, R.L., interview, AWM38 3DRL 606 item 28(2).

Louch, T.S., interview, AWM38 3DRL 606 item 27 – 206–215.

Loutit, N.M., interview, AWM38 3DRL 606 Item 227 [2] – diaries nos. 206–215.

Loutit, N.M., letter to father (22 May 1915), quoted in letter from T.L. Loutit to C.E.W. Bean (23 May 1919), 3DRL 6673/110.

Loutit, N.M., letters to C.E.W. Bean (5 April 1920 and 4 June 1920), AWM38, 3DRL 8042 item 7.

Loutit, T.L., letter to C.E.W. Bean (20 September 1919), quoting a letter from 948 R.A. Rayney, A Company, 10th Battalion. 3DRL 6673/110.

MacLagan, E.G. Sinclair, J.H. Peck, A.M. Ross, interviews, AWM38 3 DRL 606 Item 25.

MacLagan, E.G. Sinclair, Operation Order No. 1. 1915 (21 April 1915), AWM 4, 3rd Brigade War Diary, Sub-class 23/3, Australian Imperial Force Unit War Diaries, 1914–18 War.

Margetts, I.S., letter to parents (23 May 1915), 1DRL 0478/2.

Margetts, I.S., interview, 3DRL 606 Book 31.

Mason, G.F., interview, 2 DRL 301 Book 31.

Morris, G.L., interview, Australian Red Cross Wounded and Missing Enquiry Bureau files, 1DRL/0428.

Peck, J.H., interview, AWM38 3DRL 606 Item 25.

Peck, J.H., J. Lyon Johnston, interview, AWM38 3DRL 606 item 25.

Richards, E.J., manuscript, 2 DRL 301.

Selby, A.R., interview, AWM38 3DRL 8042 item 7.

Smith, G.H.H., letter to father (n.d.), 3DRL 7247.

Tulloch, E.W., correspondence with C.E.W. Bean, AWM38 3DRL 8042 item 7.

Tulloch, E.W., interview, AWM38 3 DRL 606 item 206 – diaries nos. 192–205.

Unidentified interviewee, possibly J.L. Haig, 9th Battalion, AWM38 3DRL 606 item 25.

Imperial War Museum, London

8684, Typed anonymous account of the Anzac Landing, 11th Battalion.

72/113/3: Aeroplane Report, Folio 41.

69/61: Aker, Lieutenant-Colonel (Ret.) Şefik, 'The Dardanelles: The Ari Burnu Battles and 27 Regiment', manuscript (1935), Rayfield papers, Box 8.

314/16 K354B, Ataturk, manuscript.

08/100/1, Austin, J.B., papers.

75/65/5, Bush, E.W., papers.

6440, Dix, C.C., private papers.

CHD/1, Drage, C.H., diary (January 1914–27 October 1916), Vol. I.

76/43/1, England, H.T., papers.

4771, Evans, E.J., Private Papers.

86/8/1, Hearder, D., manuscript.

76/75/1, Igdemir, Ulug, Ataturk, 'Ataturk's Memoirs of the Anafarta Battles' (1955).

4155, Kirk, Andrew, interview, Sound Reference.

84/56/1, Longley-Cook, E.W., diary.

P271, Louch, T.S., manuscript.

10360, Macleod, M., letter.

72/113/1, Samson, C.R., Flying Log, Samson Collection, Part 33.

4240, Stagles, W., interview, Sound Reference.

Liddle Collection, Brotherton Library, University of Leeds

Bachtold, W., letter, photographs, typed transcript of interview recorded with Peter Liddle (1974), 244 and 250, ANZAC (Aust) Recollections (Australian Imperial Force).

Bradshaw, W.A., typed transcript of interview with Peter Liddle (May 1974), Tape 244, ANZAC (Aust) Recollections (Australian Imperial Force).

Clark, W.M., diary, ANZAC (Aust) Recollections (Australian Imperial Force).

Dilman, S., typed transcript of interview with Peter Liddle (July 1972), Tape 46, TU01 item 4.

Hitch, H.V., typed transcript of interview with Peter Liddle (May 1974), Tapes 235 and 252, ANZAC (Aust) Recollections (Australian Imperial Force).

Howe, H.V., interview, ABC Historical Library Record – WRP15 (3 July 1967), Tape 584, Transcripts of Recorded Interviews (and Tapes), G–J.

Jones, A.E., typed transcript of interview with Peter Liddle (n.d.), Tape 1635B, ANZAC (Aust) Recollections (Australian Imperial Force).

Jones, R.L., typed transcript of interview with Peter Liddle (May 1974), Tape 238, ANZAC (Aust) Recollections (Australian Imperial Force).

Joyce, A.E., diary, typed transcript of interview with Peter Liddle (June 1974), Tape 238, ANZAC (Aust) Recollections (Australian Imperial Force).

Keast, J.R.T., diary, ANZAC (Aust) Recollections (Australian Imperial Force).

Ozgen, A., typed transcript of interview with Peter Liddle (July 1972), Tape 69, TU01.

Paterson, W.W., letter, ANZAC (Aust) Recollections (Australian Imperial Force).

Ross, W.G., manuscript, ANZAC (Aust) Recollections (Australian Imperial Force).

Stagles, W., manuscript (January 1972), ANZAC (Aust) Recollections (Australian Imperial Force).

Stagles, W., typed transcript of interview with Peter Liddle (April 1972), Tape 102, ANZAC (Aust) Recollections (Australian Imperial Force).

Williams, S.M., typed transcript of interview with Peter Liddle (May 1974), Tape 235, ANZAC (Aust) Recollections (Australian Imperial Force).

Historic Collections, Senate House Library, University of London

ICS 84 A/11/1–4 and ICS84/D: Ashmead-Bartlett, E., diary and photographs, Ashmead-Bartlett Papers.

National Archives of Australia

Ashton, F., statement (10 December 1918), Statement made by Repatriated Prisoner of War, First Australian Imperial Force Personnel Dossiers, 1914–1920, 1 Jan 1914–31 Dec 1920, B2455.

First Australian Imperial Force Personnel Dossiers, 1914–1920, 1 Jan 1914–31 Dec 1920, B2455.

Nielsen, C., to Defence Base Records, Melbourne, letter (30 December 1915), B2455.

Journals and Newspapers

Anonymous, letter (15 May 1915), account of the Landing by an unidentified scout, *Sunday Times* (11 July 1915).

Ayling, A.W., letter to wife (n.d.), *Sunday Times* (1 August 1915).

Bradley, C.J., letter (n.d.), *Sunday Times* (n.d.).

Brennan, E.T., letter (n.d.), unidentified newspaper (1915), Army Museum of Western Australia.

Brockman, E.A.D., letter (n.d.), *The Swan* (August 1915).

Brockman, E.A.D., letter to wife (25 May 1915), West Australian (28 July 1915).

Brodribb, R.H., interview, *Kalgoorlie Miner* (24 August 1915).

Brodribb, R.H., letter to Mr T.J. Callery (17 July 1915), *Kalgoorlie Miner* (23 August 1915).

Browne, A.J., letter to Geraldton Sub-Branch, RSL (n.d.), *Geraldton Guardian* (Tuesday 4 May, year not visible).

Davis, T., letter (24 April 1915), *Sunday Times* (25 July 1915).

Everett, R.W., interview, *Sunday Times* (12 September 1915).

Ewen, M., "The Gallipoli Maxims," *The Gallipolian* (Autumn 2014), pp.17–28.

Fahey, J., letter to the Archbishop of Perth (n.d.), *Advocate* (31 July and 7 August 1915).

Forbes, S.T., letter (29 May 1915), *Sunday Times* (11 July 1915).

Gallaher, D.W., letter to wife (n.d.), *Kalgoorlie Miner* (illegible day, June 1915).

Hallahan, W.R., letter to father (n.d.), *Kalgoorlie Miner* (16 August 1915).

Hastings, W.G., letter (10 June 1915), unidentified newspaper, private collection.

Hilliard, J.C., letter (n.d.), *Kalgoorlie Miner* (21 June 1915).

Higham, E., letter to father (n.d.), *West Australian* (3 June 1915).

Kalgoorlie Sun newspaper (12 September 1915).

La Nauze, C.A., letter to wife (n.d.), *Kalgoorlie Miner* (June 1915).

Leane, R.L., letter to M. Crisp (n.d.), *Kalgoorlie Miner* (17 August 1915).

Loud, F., diary, quoted *Journal of the Australian War Memorial* (April 1990), pp.66–70.

Luttrell, W.P., letter to father (16 May 1915), *Kalgoorlie Miner* (7 July 1915).

Marshall, A.F., letter (9 and 15 May 1915), *Sunday Times* (25 July 1915).

McCleery, J.M., letter (n.d.), *Kalgoorlie Miner* (1915).

Murphy, F.U., letter to father (n.d.), *Sunday Times* (6 June 1915).

Ozachin, Adil, Big Weekend, *West Australian* (4 April 1990).

Peck, J.H., letter to wife (n.d.), unidentified newspaper (13 July 1915), Army Museum of Western Australia.

Pittersen, N., letter to mother (4 May 1915), *Swan Express* (4 June 1915).

Retchford, A.R., letter to mother and brother (14 and 15 May 1915), *Kalgoorlie Miner* (7 July 1915).

Salter, J., letter to parents (14 May 1915), *Kalgoorlie Miner* (July 1915).

Scott, W.W., letter to unidentified friend (n.d.), *Kalgoorlie Miner* (6 September 1915).

Taylor, L.B., letter to mother (15 May 1915), *Kalgoorlie Miner* (7 July 1915).

Taylor, L.B., letters to Mr G. Stack and Mrs R. Sharpen, *Kalgoorlie Miner* (7 July 1915).

Walther, B.H., diary extract *Sunday Times* (19 April 1998).

Webb, A.J., letter to mother (n.d.), *Kalgoorlie Miner* (7 July 1915).

Private Collections
Cockburn, R.C., diary, family collection, Perth.

De Mole, C.M., letter to mother (21 May 1915), family collection, copy in author's collection.

Fahey, J., letter, inherited from 258 Signaller J.J. Ryan, 11th Battalion, private collection.

Gostelow, C., diary, family collection, Western Australia.

Hurst, J.P., 'The earliest photograph of the ANZAC Landing?', unpublished at time of writing.

James, D., untitled – Family history notes on I.B. Joy by D. James, private collection, Sydney.

Loutit, N.M., interviews by D.A. Wilson (13 March, 28 June 1979), private collection, Courtesy D.A. Wilson.

Lumsden, W.D., letter to father (7 May 1915), private collection.

Morris, E.W., diary, copy in author's possession, courtesy Mrs P. Beck.

Newham, Sydney, 'Recollections of a Returned Soldier', manuscript (n.d.), private collection, Perth.

Parsons, L.A., letter to Mr Williams (4 August 1915), private collection.

Priestley, H.J.V., letters, private collection.

Riekie, N., correspondence with J.P. Hurst (2012–2013).

Siefkin, O.J., letter to mother (3 September 1915), private collection.

Thompson, R., papers (1914–1915), private collection.

Walther, B.H., diary, private collection, Perth.

White, D., telephone interview, David White, son of John Joseph White, with James Hurst, Canberra (1999).

Whiting, L., "Blood Will Tell!'", unidentified newspaper, family collection.

Whiting, L., manuscript, family collection.

Wood, S.M., letter to J.S. Seddon (3 May 1915), collection of Enid Rose, Toodyay, Western Australia, courtesy Wes Olson.

Ellam-Innes Collection, Perth
Anonymous manuscript by Leane's observer, an unidentified member of C Company, 11th Battalion.

Blay, G.H., diary.

Clifton, A.R.C., letter.

Clohessy, J., diary.

Combs, G.F.S., manuscript.

Eastcott, H.J., manuscript.

Everett, R.W., interview, probably by C.E.W. Bean.

Fox, J.F., 'I Was There', manuscript.

Goodlet, W.W., manuscript.

Hardy, E.A., letter to Mrs C.A. LaNauze (5 September 1915).

Jackson, S.H., interview.

Leane, R.L., letter to Mrs C.A. La Nauze (4 July 1915).

Louch, T.S., manuscript.

Lowson, R.J., 'Under Fire, My Impressions', manuscript (1 July 1915).

Murray, W.B., letter to parents (16 May 1915).

Palmer, J., letter (n.d.), unidentified newspaper, n.p.

Turner, B., letter to parents (28 May 1915).

Turner, J.W.G., letter to father (14 May 1915).

Turner, J.W.G., letter to mother (25 June 1915).

Other

Anonymous. Document on the history of the 11th Battalion. Author unidentified. Defence Library, Perth.

Ashton, F., Interview by S. Welborn (14 September 1976), Reid Library, University of Western Australia.

ACC 973A: Ashton, F., manuscript, J.S. Battye Library, Perth.

940.481MYL: Beevor, M.F., manuscript, 'My Landing at Gallipoli', Defence Regional Library, Adelaide.

Forsyth, M., interview by J.P. Hurst, Perth (n.d.)

MsC 254: Guy, W.A.C., letter to A.A. Tanner (10 May 1915), Library, University of Calgary.

Hurst, J.P., 'Ottoman Machine Guns at the ANZAC Landing, 25 April 1915', unpublished.

Inman, E.S., diary, Army Museum of Western Australia, Fremantle.

Law Smith, S., niece of H.L.I. Finch, interview by J.P. Hurst, Canberra (22 May 2007).

McCleery, J.M., taped interview by S. Welborn (1976), Reid Library, University of Western Australia.

3868A: Medcalf, F.G., letter (11 June 1915), J.S. Battye Library, Perth.

MN 1265: Medcalf, F.G., manuscript, J.S. Battye Library, Perth.

Mofflin, E.W., letter to Nesta and Family (20 October 1915), Army Museum of Western Australia, Fremantle.

Spicer, M., letter to 'Mr Duckworth' (14 August 1915), quoted in I. Gill, Fremantle to France, 11th Battalion AIF 1914–1919, Perth (2003), p.409.

Telford, W.A., letter to wife (21 May 1915), quoted in I. Gill, Fremantle to France, 11th Battalion AIF 1914–1919, Perth (2003), pp.419–421.

Secondary Sources

Books

1st Battalion A.I.F. History Committee, *First Battalion A.I.F., 1914–1919* (Sydney: 1931).

Adam-Smith, P, *The Anzacs* (West Melbourne: Nelson, 1978).

Akcelik, Rahmi (ed.), *Before and After Gallipoli: A Collection of Australian and Turkish Writings* (Melbourne: Australian-Turkish Friendly Society Publications, 1986).

An Officer's Manual of the Western Front 1914–1918 (London: Army Printing and Stationery Service); (London: Conway, 2008).

The Anzac Book, written and illustrated in Gallipoli by the men of Anzac (London, New York, Toronto, Melbourne: Cassell, 1916).

Ashmead-Bartlett, E, *The Uncensored Dardanelles* (London: Hutchinson and Co., 1928).

Aspinall-Oglander, C.F, *Military Operations, Gallipoli. Vol. I, Inception of the Campaign to May 1915* (London: Imperial War Museum, Department of Printed Books, 1929).

Aspinall-Oglander, C.F., *Military Operations, Gallipoli*. Volume I, *Inception of the Campaign to May 1915* and *Gallipoli Maps and Appendices VI*, Appendix 15, Maps and sketches by A.F. Becke (London: Imperial War Museum, Department of Printed Books, 1929).

Austin, R.J., *As Rough as Bags: The History of the 6th Battalion, 1st AIF, 1914–1919* (Victoria: McCrae, 1992).

Austin, R.J., *Where Anzacs Sleep: The Gallipoli Photos of Capt Jack Duffy, 8th Battalion* (Victoria: Slouch Hat Publications, 2006).

Bank of New South Wales Roll of Honour, Bank of NSW (Sydney: 1921).

Bay, A., *Ataturk: Lessons in Leadership from the Greatest General of the Ottoman Empire* (New York: Palgrave Macmillan, 2011).

Bean, C.E.W., *Anzac to Amiens* (Canberra: Australian War Memorial, 1946).

Bean, C.E.W., *Gallipoli Mission* (Canberra: ABC Enterprises and the Australian War Memorial, 1990).

Bean, C.E.W., *Official History of Australia in the War: The Story of ANZAC*, Volume I (Sydney: Angus and Robertson, 1921 and 1941).

Bean, C.E.W., *Official History of Australia in the War: The Story of ANZAC*, Volume I (St. Lucia, Queensland: University of Queensland Press, 1981).

Bean, C.E.W., *Official History of Australia in the War: The Story of ANZAC*, Volume II (Sydney: Angus and Robertson, 1939).

Bean, C.E.W., et al., *Official History of Australia in the War*, Volume XII, *Photographic Record of the War* (Sydney: Angus and Robertson, 1939).

Belford, W.C., *Legs Eleven, Being the Story of the 11th Battalion (AIF) in the Great War of 1914–1918* (Perth: Imperial Printing Coy Ltd, 1940).

Black, J., *The Battle of Waterloo, A New History* (London: Icon Books Ltd, 2010).

Brenchley, F. and E., *Myth Maker: Ellis Ashmead-Bartlett, The Englishman Who Sparked Australia's Gallipoli Legend* (Milton, Queensland: John Wiley & Sons Australia, 2005).

Broadbent, H., *Defending Gallipoli: The Turkish Story* (Carlton: Melbourne University Press, 2015).

Broadbent, H., *The Boys Who Came Home, Recollections of Gallipoli* (Crows Nest: ABC Enterprises, 1990).

Broadbent, H., *Gallipoli – The Fatal Shore* (Camberwell, Victoria: Viking, Penguin Books, 2005).

Broadbent, H., *Gallipoli – The Turkish Defence, The Story From The Turkish Documents* (Carlton: The Megunyah Press, 2015).

Bush, E.W., *Gallipoli* (London: Allen & Unwin, 1975).

Cameron, D.W., *25 April 1915: The Day the Anzac Legend was Born* (Crows Nest: Allen & Unwin, 2007).

Carlyon, L., *Gallipoli* (Sydney: Pan Macmillan Australia, 2001).

Carne, W.A., *In Good Company: An Account of the 6th Machine Gun Company A.I.F. in Search of Peace 1915–19* (1937) (Reprinted Swanbourne: W.A. Burridge, n.d.)

Clausewitz, C. von, *The Essential Clausewitz: Selections from On War* (New York: Dover Publications, 2003).

Corbett, Sir Julian S., *Naval Operations*, Vol. II, *History of the Great War* (London: Longmans, Green, 1921).

Crowley, F.K., *Australia's Western Third, A History of Western Australia from the first settlements to modern times* (Melbourne: William Heinemann Australia, 1960).

Curran, T., *Across the Bar: the Story of "Simpson", The man with the donkey: Australia and Tyneside's great military hero* (Yeronga, Queensland: Ogmios Publications, 1994).

Denton, K., *Gallipoli: One Long Grave* (North Sydney: Time-Life Books (Australia), 1987).

Doyle, P., *Gallipoli 1915* (Gloucestershire: Spellmount, 2011).

English, J.A. and B.I. Gudmundsson, *On Infantry* (London: Praeger, 1994).

Erickson, E.J., *Gallipoli: The Ottoman Campaign* (Barnsley, South Yorkshire: Pen and Sword Books, 2010).

Erickson, E.J., *Ordered to Die: A History of the Ottoman Army in the First Word War* (Greenwood Press, 2001).

Erickson, E.J., *Ottoman Army effectiveness in World War I: A Comparative Study* (London and New York: Routledge, 2007).

Facey, A.B., *A Fortunate Life* (Ringwood, Victoria: Penguin Books, 1985).

Fewster, K. (ed.), *Gallipoli Correspondent, The Frontline Diary of CEW Bean* (Sydney: Allen and Unwin, 1983).

Fewster, K., Basarin, V. and Basarin, H.H., *Gallipoli: The Turkish Story* (Crows Nest, NSW: Allen and Unwin, 2003; first published 1985).

Frame, T.R., *The Shores of Gallipoli: Naval Aspects of the ANZAC Campaign* (Sydney: Hale & Iremonger, 2000).

Gammage, W., *The Broken Years* (Ringwood: Penguin Books, 1990).

Gardner, B., *German East: The Story of the First World War in East Africa* (London: Cassell, 1963).

General Staff, War Office, *Field Service Pocket Book 1914* (London: His Majesty's Stationery Office, 1914).

Gill, I., *Fremantle to France* (Perth: Ian Gill, 2003).

Glen, F., *Bowler of Gallipoli: Witness to the Anzac Legend* (Canberra, ACT: Australian Military History Publications, 2004).

Goodchild, John C., *Where the Australians Rest: A Description of Many of the Cemeteries Overseas in which Australians, Including Those Whose Names Can Never Now be Known, are Buried* (Melbourne: Government Printer, 1920).

Grant, I., *Jacka VC, Australia's Finest Fighting Soldier* (South Melbourne: Macmillan, 1990).

Griffith, Paddy, *Battle Tactics on the Western Front; The British Army's Art of Attack, 1916–1918* (New Haven and London: Yale University Press, 1994).

Halbwachs, M., *On Collective Memory*, edited and translated by L.A. Coser (Chicago: University of Chicago Press, 1992).

Halis Bey, *Canakkale Raporu* (Istanbul: Arma Publications, 1975).

Hanman, E.F., *Twelve Months with the ANZACs* (Brisbane: Watson, Ferguson, 1916).

Harvey, N.K., *From Anzac to the Hindenburg Line: The History of the 9th Battalion, A.I.F.* (Brisbane: 9th Battalion A.I.F. Association, 1941).

Hobsbawm, E.J. and T.O. Ranger (eds.), *The Invention of Tradition* (Cambridge: Cambridge University Press, 1992).

Horner, D.M., *The Gunners* (St. Leonards, NSW: Allen and Unwin, 1995).

Hurst, J.P., *Game to the Last: The 11th Australian Infantry Battalion at Gallipoli* (South Melbourne: Oxford University Press, 2005).

James, R.R., *Gallipoli* (London, Sydney: Pan Books, 1984; first published Batsford, 1965).

Kinross, Lord, *Ataturk* (New York: William Morrow and Company, 1965; first published Great Britain 1964).

Kuring, I., *Redcoats to Cams: A History of Australian Infantry, 1788–2001* (Australian Military History Publications, 2004).

Lee, J.E., *The Chronicle of the 15th Battalion, A.I.F.* (Sydney: Mortons, 1927).

Limb, A., *History of the 10th Battalion AIF* (Cassell, 1919).

Liddle, P., *Men of Gallipoli: The Dardanelles and Gallipoli Experience, August 1914 to January 1916* (Wiltshire: David & Charles, 1988).

Lock, C.B.L., *The Fighting 10th: Souvenir of the 10th Battalion AIF* (Adelaide: Webb, imprint, 1936).

Longmore, C., *The Old Sixteenth: being a record of the 16th Battalion, A.I.F., during the Great War, 1914–1918* (Perth: 1929).

Mango, A., *Ataturk* (London: John Murray, 2002).

Masefield, J., *Gallipoli* (London: William Heinemann, 1916).

McKernan, M., *Padre: Australian Chaplains in Gallipoli and France* (Sydney: Allen and Unwin, 1986).

McNicoll, R.R., *The Royal Australian Engineers, 1902–1919: Making and Breaking* (Canberra: 1977).

Moorehead, A., *Gallipoli* (London: Four Square, 1956).

Murray, P.L. (ed.), *Official Records of the Australian Military Contingents to the War in South Africa* (Melbourne, Government Printer, 1911).

Newton, L.M., *The Story of the Twelfth: A Record of the 12th Battalion, A.I.F. during the Great War of 1914–1918* (Hobart: J. Walch & Sons, 1925).

Nora, P., *Realms of Memory: The Construction of the French Past*, Volume II, *Tradition* (New York; Columbia University Press, 1997).

Olson, W., *Gallipoli, The Western Australian Story* (Crawley, WA: University of Western Australia Press, 2006).

O'Riley, I., *Giant in the Sun* (Perth: Ivan O'Riley, 1968).

Örnek, T. and F. A, *Gallipoli: the Front Line Experience*, Second Edition (Strawberry Hills: Currency Press, 2006).

Pedersen, P., *The ANZACs: Gallipoli to the Western Front* (Melbourne: Viking, Penguin, 2007).

Prior, R., *Gallipoli: The End of the Myth* (Sydney: University of New South Wales Press, 2009).

Pugsley, C., *Gallipoli: The New Zealand Story* (Auckland: Hodder and Stoughton, 1990).

Reid, R., *Gallipoli* (Canberra: Department of Veterans' Affairs, 2010).

Reynaud, D., *Celluloid Anzacs: The Great War through Australian Cinema* (North Melbourne: Australian Scholarly Publishing, 2007).

Roberts, C., *The Landing at Anzac: 1915* (Newport, NSW: Big Sky Publishing, 2013).

Roberts, C., *The Landing at Anzac: 1915*, Second Edition (Sydney: Big Sky Publishing, 2015).

Robertson, J., *ANZAC and Empire* (Melbourne: Hamlyn Australia, 1990).

Robson, L.L., *The First AIF* (Melbourne: Melbourne University Press, 1970).

Rule, E.J., *Jacka's Mob: A Narrative of the Great War* (Prahran: Military Melbourne, 1999).

The Silver Jubilee Book, The Story of 25 Eventful Years in Pictures (London: Odhams Press, 1935).

Sandes, J., *ANZAC Day: Landing in the Dawn* (Sydney: W.C. Penfold, 1916).

Souter, G., *Lion and Kangaroo, Australia: 1901–1919, The Rise of a Nation* (Sydney: Fontana/Collins, 1978).

Steel, N. and Hart, P., *Defeat at Gallipoli* (London: Papermac, 1995).

Steel, N., *The Battlefields of Gallipoli: Then and Now* (London: Octopus Publishing, 1990).

Strachan, H., *The First World War: A New Illustrated History* (London: Simon and Schuster, 2003).

Swifte, T., *Gallipoli: The Incredible Campaign* (Sydney: Magazine Promotions Australia, 1985).

Taylor, F.W. and T.A. Cusack, compilers, *Nulli Secundus: A History of the Second Battalion, A.I.F., 1914–1919* (Sydney: New Century Press, 1942).

Tuncoku, A., *Anzaklarin Kaleminden Mehmetcik, Canakkale 1915* (Ankara: Basimevi, 2000).

Tuncoku, A. (ed.), *The Turkish Yearbook of Gallipoli Studies*, Issue 3 (March 2005).

Travers, T., *Gallipoli 1915* (Stroud: Tempus Publishing, 2001).

Treloar, J.L., *An ANZAC Diary* (Armidale: Alan Treloar, 1993).

The Turkish General Staff, Ankara, *A Brief History of the Canakkale Campaign in the First World War (June 1914–January 1916)* (Ankara: Turkish General Staff Printing House, 2004).

Uyar, M., *The Ottoman Defence Against the ANZAC Landing, 25 April 1915* (Sydney: Big Sky Publishing, 2015).

Wahlert, G., *Exploring Gallipoli: An Australian Army Battlefield Guide* (Canberra: Army History Unit, 2011).

Wallis, M., *Billy the Kid: The Endless Ride* (New York: W.W. Norton and Company Inc., 2008).

Wanliss, N., *The History of the Fourteenth Battalion, A.I.F.: being the story of the vicissitudes of an Australian unit during the Great War* (Melbourne: The Arrow Printery, 1929).

Welborn, S., *Lords of Death, A People, A Place, A Legend* (Fremantle: Fremantle Arts Centre Press, 1982).

Williams, J.F., *German ANZACs and the First World War* (Sydney: UNSW Press, 2003).

Williams, P.D., *The Battle of Anzac Ridge, 25 April 1915* (Loftus, NSW: Australian Military History Publications, 2007).

Williamson, J., *Soccer Anzacs, The Story of the Caledonian Soccer Club* (Perth: John Williamson, 1998).

Winter, D., *25 April 1915: The Inevitable Tragedy* (St. Lucia, Qld: University of Queensland Press, 1994).

The World War I Collection, Gallipoli and the Early Battles, 1914–1915. Includes *The Dardanelles Commission, 1914–16. 1917*; and *British Battles of World War I, 1914–1915, originally Naval and Military despatches, 1914, 1915, 1916*, HMSO (London: The Stationary Office, 2001).

Wren, E., *Randwick to Hargicourt, The History of the 3rd Battalion A.I.F.* (Sydney: Ronald G. McDonald, Australia, 1935).

Wrench, C.M., *Campaigning with the fighting 9th: In and Out of the Line with the 9BN A.I.F., 1914–1919* (Brisbane: Boolarong Publications, for 9th Battalion's Association, 1985).

Journals, Newspapers and Articles

Anonymous, 'Major Arthur Croly: A Tribute', *Reveille* (31 July 1931), n.p.

Ashmead-Bartlett, E., 'Cabled report of Mr Ashmead-Bartlett's account of the Landing … Published in the daily papers on 8 May 1915', Quoted Department of Public Instruction, New South Wales (18 May 1915).

Bean, C.E.W. "How the Heights Were Stormed." Correspondent's report, 13 May 1915. *Commonwealth of Australia Gazette*, No. 39 (27 May 1915).

Brand, C.H., 'Memories of ANZAC Day – 20 years Ago', *Reveille* (1 April 1935), pp.4, 64.

Bush, E.W., 'Anzac Remembered', *The Gallipolean, the Journal of the Gallipoli Association*, Number 7 (Christmas, 1971), pp.26–33.

Coulthard-Clark, C., 'From Eureka to Gallipoli', *Defence Force Journal*, No. 44 (January/February 1984), pp.44–48.

Davies, M.J., "Military Intelligence at Gallipoli – 'A Leap in the Dark?'", *Australian Defence Force Journal*, No. 92 (January/February 1992), pp.37–43.

'Dent-Young Family', *Reveille* (August 1931), n.p.

Dent-Young, Mrs, 'In Memory: 11th Bn. Officers', *Reveille* (31 December 1931), p.11.

Everett, R.W., Account of Landing, probably late 1915, St. George's House, Perth, copy in author's possession.

Faulkiner, J.A., *Legs Eleven Minor* (April 1961), p.8.

Graco, W., 'Some Reasons for the Failure at Gallipoli', *Defence Force Journal, Journal of the Australian Profession of Arms*, No. 64 (May/June 1987), pp.40–42.

Howe, H.V., 'The Senior Private of the AIF', Celebrities of the AIF, No. 42, *Reveille* (1 February 1934), pp.7, 30–31.

Howe, H.V., 'Sparks From an Old Controversy', *Australian Army Journal*, Number 191 (April 1965), pp.4–21.

Hurst, J.P., 'A Mother's Pain', *Wartime*, Issue 30 (2005), pp.30–33.

Hurst, J.P., 'Damn little to Laugh At', *Wartime*, Issue 26 (April 2004), pp.8–11.

Hurst, J.P., 'Gallipoli, The First Photo?', *Wartime*, Issue 58 (Autumn 2012), pp.32–35.

Hurst, J.P., 'The Bloke with the Pink Top, Denny Neave (ed.), *Soldiers' Tales Number 2, A Collection of True Stories From Aussie Soldiers*, Big Sky Publishing, Newport (nd), pp.45–50.

Hurst, J.P., 'The fruit seller at war', *Weekend Extra, West Australian* (21 April 2006).

Hurst, J.P., 'The Mists of Time and the Fog of War, *A Fortunate Life* and A.B. Facey's Gallipoli Experience', *Melbourne Historical Journal*, Volume 38 (2010), pp.77–92.

Hurst, J.P., 'Tough But Fair, The 11th Infantry Battalion, Australian Imperial Force, and their enemy, Gallipoli 1915', *Gallipoli in Retrospect – 90 Years On*, Conference papers of the International Symposium (21–22 April 2005), Atatürk and Gallipoli Campaign Research Center (AÇASAM), Canakkale, Turkey.

Isaacs, K., 'Wings Over Gallipoli', *Defence Force Journal* (March/April 1990), pp.5–18.

Loutit, N.M., 'The Tragedy of Anzac', *Reveille* (1 April 1934), p.8.

Pugsley, C., 'Stories of Anzac' in MacLeod, J., *Gallipoli, Making History* (London: Frank Cass, 2004), pp.44–52.

Roberts, C.A.M., 'The Landing at Anzac: A Reassessment', *Journal of the Australian War Memorial*, No. 22 (April 1993), pp.25–34.

Roberts, C.A.M., 'The Landing at ANZAC: an Australian Defensive Action', Australian War Memorial History Conference, paper (9–13 July 1990).

Roberts, C.A.M., 'Turkish Machine-guns at the Landing', *Wartime*, Issue 50 (2010), pp.14–19.

Rosenzweig, P.A., 'The Chase, Anzacs on the Third Ridge', *Australian Army Journal* (Autumn 2005), Volume 2, Number 2, pp.227–235.

Schmitt, H., "'Pink Top': WA's Barrow-boy Hero", *Big Weekend*, p.4, *West Australian* (Saturday 14 April, 1990).

Sinclair-MacLagan, E.G., 'Armada Moves: Egypt to Gallipoli', *Reveille* (31 March 1932), pp.10, 58, 59.

Thompson, E.P., 'The Peculiarities of the English', *The Socialist Register*, Volume 2, 1965, pp.311–362.

Thomson, A.S., 'Anzac stories: using personal testimony in war history', *War & Society*, Volume 25, issue 2, School of Humanities and Social Sciences, University of New South Wales, Canberra, ACT, Australia , pp.1–21.

Wilson, D.A., 'Morphettville to ANZAC', *Australian Infantry* magazine, Part 1 (Jul–Dec 1980), pp.25–29; Part 2 (Jan–June 1981), pp.20–27.

Films, Documentaries, Television Productions

A Fortunate Life, PBL Productions (1985).

Gallipoli/Gelibolu, Tolga Örnek (2005).

Gallipoli's Deep Secrets, Prospero Productions (2010).

King, J., interview by T.J. Grimshaw, Anzac Day Dawn Service television coverage, Anzac, Gallipoli (25 April 2005).

Revealing Gallipoli, Looking Beyond the Myth, Wain Fimeri (2005).

Ten days of glory: the Gallipoli pilgrimage 1990, Harvey Broadbent, ABC Television Features (1990).

The Anzacs, Burrowes-Dixon Company (1985).

Other

Olson, W., (ed.), 'Private David John Simcock, 11th Battalion Australian Imperial Force, 'The bloke with the Pink Top'', Ellam-Innes Collection (n.d.)

Electronic Sources

Bardwell, B.E., diary, State Library of Western Australia, <purl.slwa.wa.gov.au/slaw_b3967614_35.pdf> (20 January 2016).

Broken Rites Australia website.
<http://brokenrites.alphalink.com.au/nletter/page205-elmer.html> (accessed 10 January 2013).

The Çanakkale (Gallipoli) Report of Major Halis. Major Halis, *Çanakkale Raparu*, Arma Yayinlari, Istanbul, 1975. the Gallipoli Centenary Turkish Archives Research Project, MacQuarie University
<http://www.mq.edu.au/about us/faculties and departments/faculty of arts/mhpir/research/research by staff/ gallipoli centenary research project/project outcomes/translated turkish works on gallipoli/#halis> (accessed 16 November 2015).

The Collected Works of Ataturk, Volume 1 (1903–1915), Translated excerpts by Banu Şenay, Kaynak Publishing, 1998. the Gallipoli Centenary Turkish Archives Research Project, MacQuarie University
<https://drive.google.com/file/d/0B5l4v9YR6fd3aWRaRHdJQV9aeWM/view?pli=1> (accessed 13 December 2015).

Ibdradili Ibrahim Hayrettiin. Letter to Feridun Fazıl Tülbentçi (1945), Great War Forum
<http://1914-1918.invisionzone.com/forums/index.php?showtopic=40505&page=7> (accessed 18 Aug 2015).

Izzettin (Çalışlar), "Battle of Gallipoli Memoir," April 12 1331/April 25 1915, Askeri Mecmua 1920, Military Journal. The Gallipoli Centenary Turkish Archives Research Project (Macquarie University, Australian War Memorial)
<https://www.mq.edu.au/about/about-the-university/faculties-and-departments/faculty-of-arts/departments-and-centres/department-of-modern-history,-politics-and-international-relations/research/gallipoli-centenary-research-project/project-outcomes/translated-turkish-works-on-gallipoli#izzettin> (accessed 18 November 2015).

National Collection of War Art, Department of Internal Affairs, New Zealand
<http://warart.archives.govt.nz/files/images/NCWA_Q00388.jpeg> (no access date).

Parliament of Victoria website, Child Abuse Inquiry papers, Appendix 10
<http://www.parliament.vic.gov.au/images/stories/committees/fcdc/inquiries/57th/Child_Abuse_Inquiry/
    Submissions/Anthony__Chrissie_Foster_Appendix_10.pdf> (accessed 10 January 2013).

Website of the Commonwealth War Graves Commission
<http://www.cwgc.org/find-a-cemetery/cemetery/66603/BABY%20700%20CEMETERY,%20ANZAC>
    (accessed 2007).

Unpublished Secondary Sources
'Completing the Story – Researching Gallipoli in the Turkish Military Archives', Gallipoli Centenary Research
    Project, Macquarie University, The Australian War Memorial and Turkey's Middle East Technical
    University.
Losinger, I.D., "Officer–man Relations in the Canadian Expeditionary Force, 1914–1919" (Master of Arts,
    Carleton University, Ottawa, Ontario, 1990).
Williams, P.D., 'Z Beach, the Landing of the ANZAC Corps, April 25, 1915', Master of Arts, Northern
    Territory University, 2000.

Index

INDEX OF PEOPLE

INDEX OF PLACES – BATTLEFIELD

INDEX OF PLACES – OTHER

INDEX OF MILITARY UNITS – ANZAC

INDEX OF MILITARY UNITS – TURKISH